Communications in Computer and Information Science   1496

More information about this series at https://link.springer.com/bookseries/7899

Xiangke Liao · Wei Zhao · Enhong Chen ·
Nong Xiao · Li Wang · Yang Gao · Yinghuan Shi ·
Changdong Wang · Dan Huang (Eds.)

Big Data

9th CCF Conference, BigData 2021
Guangzhou, China, January 8–10, 2022
Revised Selected Papers

 Springer

Editors
Xiangke Liao
National University of Defense Technology
Changsha, China

Enhong Chen
University of Science and Technology
of China
Hefei, China

Li Wang
Taiyuan University of Technology
Taiyuan, China

Yinghuan Shi
Nanjing University
Nanjing, China

Dan Huang
Sun Yat-sen University
Guangzhou, China

Wei Zhao
Shenzhen University of Technology, Chinese
Academy of Sciences
Shenzhen, China

Nong Xiao
Sun Yat-sen University
Guangzhou, China

Yang Gao
Nanjing University
Nanjing, China

Changdong Wang ⓘ
Sun Yat-sen University
Guangzhou, China

ISSN 1865-0929   ISSN 1865-0937 (electronic)
Communications in Computer and Information Science
ISBN 978-981-16-9708-1   ISBN 978-981-16-9709-8 (eBook)
https://doi.org/10.1007/978-981-16-9709-8

This Springer imprint is published by the registered company Springer Nature Singapore Pte Ltd.
The registered company address is: 152 Beach Road, #21-01/04 Gateway East, Singapore 189721, Singapore

Preface

This book constitutes the proceedings of the 9th CCF Conference on Big Data, CCF BigData 2021, held in Guangzhou Guangdong, China, in January 2022.

CCF BigData 2021 achieved great success in further exploring the theory, techniques, and applications of big data. The submitted papers covered a broad range of research topics on big data, including big data analysis and applications, image and natural language big data, big data intelligent algorithms, network data and network science, big data and deep learning, big data privacy and security, big data clustering retrieval, and big data systems. CCF BigData 2021 served as a prominent forum for researchers and practitioners from academia, industry, and government to share their ideas, research results, and experiences, and to promote their research and technical innovations in the field.

This volume consists of 21 accepted English papers from CCF BigData 2021 and covers most research topics on big data. The papers come from both academia and industry, reflecting current research progress and future development trends in big data. All the accepted papers were peer reviewed by at least three qualified and experienced reviewers selected from the Program Committee. Review forms were designed to help reviewers determine the contributions made by the papers.

CCF BigData 2021 would like to express sincere thanks to CCF, the CCF Task Force on Big Data, Sun Yat-sen University, and our many other sponsors, for their support and sponsorship. We thank all members of our Steering Committee, Program Committee, and Organization Committee for their advice and contributions. Also, we thank all the reviewers for reviewing papers in such a short time during the reviewing period.

We are especially grateful to Springer for publishing the proceedings. Moreover, we really appreciate all the keynote speakers, session chairs, authors, conference attendees, and student volunteers, for their participation and contribution.

November 2021

Enhong Chen
Nong Xiao
Dan Huang

Organization

CCF BigData 2021 was organized by the China Computer Federation and co-organized by the China Computer Federation Task Force on Big Data and Sun Yat-sen University, China.

Honorary Chairs

Guojie Li	Institute of Computing Technology, Chinese Academy of Sciences, and Chinese Academy of Engineering, China
Hong Mei	Academician of Chinese Academy of Sciences, China

Conference Chairs

Xiangke Liao	Chinese Academy of Engineering and National University of Defense Technology, China
Wei Zhao	International Academy of Eurasian Sciences, Shenzhen University of Technology, and Chinese Academy of Sciences, China

Program Committee Chairs

Nong Xiao	Sun Yat-sen University, China
Enhong Chen	University of Science and Technology of China, China

Organizing Committee Chairs

Weishi Zheng	Sun Yat-sen University, China
Zhiguang Chen	Sun Yat-sen University and National Supercomputer Center in Guangzhou, China

Essay Solicitation and Publication Chairs

Li Wang	Taiyuan University of Technology, China
Yang Gao	Nanjing University, China
Dan Huang	Sun Yat-sen University, China
Yinghuan Shi	Nanjing University, China

Forum Chairs

Weigang Wu	Sun Yat-sen University, China
Rui Mao	Shenzhen University, China

Publicity Chairs

Changdong Wang	Sun Yat-sen University, China
Shaoliang Peng	Hunan University, China
Tong Xu	University of Science and Technology of China, China

Finance and Sponsorship Chairs

Zhi Zhou	Sun Yat-sen University, China
Feifei Li	Alibaba Group, China
Rui Mao	Shenzhen University, China
Yuting Guo	Institute of Computing Technology, Chinese Academy of Sciences, China

Conference Reward Chairs

Jiwu Shu	Tsinghua University and Xiamen University, China
Jian Yin	Sun Yat-sen University, China

Program Committee

Alfred Liu	SAS, China
Jiyao An	Hunan University, China
Andy J. Ma	Sun Yat-sen University, China
Benjamin Wah	Chinese University of Hong Kong, China
Bin Guo	Northwestern Polytechnical University, China
Bin Jiang	Hunan University, China
Bin Zhou	National University of Defense Technology, China
Can Wang	Zhejiang University, China
Changdong Wang	Sun Yat-sen University, China
Chao Gao	Southwest University, China
Chao Shen	Xi'an Jiaotong University, China
Chao Yu	Sun Yat-sen University, China
Chen Xuebin	North China University of Science and Technology, China
Cheng Deng	Xidian University, China
Chi Harold Liu	Beijing Institute of Technology, China
Chongjun Wang	Nanjing University, China
Chuan Chen	Sun Yat-sen University, China
Chunxiao Xing	Tsinghua University, China

Cuiping Li	Renmin University of China, China
Dan Huang	Sun Yat-sen University, China
Dong Zhang	Inspur, China
Dongyan Zhao	Peking University, China
Dongyu Zhang	Sun Yat-sen University, China
Fei Teng	Southwest Jiaotong University, China
Fengfeng Zhou	Jilin University, China
Gang Chen	Sun Yat-sen University, China
Gang Xiong	CASIA, China
Gansen Zhao	South China Normal University, China
Gong Cheng	Nanjing University, China
Guanlin Chen	Zhejiang University City College, China
Guoliang He	Wuhan University, China
Guoxian Yu	Shandong University, China
Guoyong Cai	Guilin University of Electronic Technology, China
Hai Wan	Sun Yat-sen University, China
Haitao Zhang	Beijing University of Posts and Telecommunications, China
Hanhua Chen	Huazhong University of Science and Technology, China
Hanjiang Lai	Sun Yat-sen University, China
Hengshu Zhu	Baidu Inc., China
Hong Chen	Renmin University, China
Hongmin Cai	South China University of Technology, China
Hongzhi Wang	Harbin Institute of Technology, China
Huawei Shen	Institute of Computing Technology, Chinese Academy of Sciences, China
Jiadong Ren	Yanshan University, China
Jiahai Wang	Sun Yat-sen University, China
Jiajie Xu	Soochow University, China
Jian Yin	Sun Yat-sen University, China
Jian-Fang Hu	Sun Yat-sen University, China
Jianfeng Zhan	Institute of Computing Technology, Chinese Academy of Sciences, and University of Chinese Academy of Sciences, China
Jiangtao Cui	Xidian University, China
Jianmin Wang	Tsinghua University, China
Jianquan Ouyang	Xiangtan University, China
Jianxin Li	Beihang University, China
Jianxing Yu	Sun Yat-sen University, China
Jianye Yu	Beijing Wuzi University, China
Jianyong Sun	Xi'an Jiaotong University, China
Jianzhou Feng	Yanshan University, China
Jianzong Wang	Ping An Technology (Shenzhen) Co., Ltd, China
Jie Liu	Nankai University, China
Jie Wang	University of Science and Technology of China, China
Jieyue He	Southeast University, China
Jin Tang	Anhui University, China

Jingyuan Li	Tencent, China
Jinhu Lu	Beihang University, China
Jinpeng Chen	Beijing University of Posts and Telecommunications, China
Jiwu Shu	Tsinghua University and Xiamen University, China
Jiye Liang	Shanxi University, China
Jiyi Wu	Hangzhou Normal University, China
Joshua Zhexue Huang	Shenzhen University, China
Ju Fan	Renmin University of China, China
Jun He	Renmin University of China, China
Jun Long	Central South University, China
Jun Ma	Shandong University, China
Junming Shao	University of Electronic Science and Technology of China, China
Junping Du	Beijing University of Posts and Telecommunications, China
Junqing Yu	Huazhong University of Science and Technology, China
Kai Huang	Sun Yat-sen University, China
Kai Li	University of Science and Technology of China, China
Ke Li	Beijing Union University, China
Ke Xu	Tsinghua University, China
Keqiu Li	Tianjin University, China
Kui Ren	Zhejiang University, China
Kun Guo	Fuzhou University, China
Laizhong Cui	Shenzhen University, China
Lan Huang	Jilin University, China
Lei Wang	Institute of Computing Technology, Chinese Academy of Sciences, China
Lei Zou	Peking University, China
Li Wang	Taiyuan University of Technology, China
Liang Bai	Shanxi University, China
Liang Chen	Sun Yat-sen University, China
Liang Wang	NLPR, China
Limin Xiao	Beihang University, China
Lin Shang	Nanjing University, China
Ling Qian	China Mobile Cloud Computing Center, China
Liqiang Nie	Shandong University, China
Lizhen Cui	Shandong University, China
long chen	Sun Yat-sen University, China
Lu Qin	University of Technology Sydney, Australia
Ma XueBin	Inner Mongolia University, China
MaoQiang Xie	Nankai University, China
Miao Hu	Sun Yat-sen University, China
Min Yu	Institute of Information Engineering, Chinese Academy of Sciences, China
Min-Ling Zhang	Southeast University, China
Ning Gu	Fudan University, China
Peiquan Jin	University of Science and Technology of China, China

Peng Cui	Tsinghua University, China
Pengfei Chen	Sun Yat-sen University, China
Pengpeng Zhao	Soochow University, China
Qi Liu	University of Science and Technology of China, China
Qi Wang	Northwestern Polytechnical University, China
Qing Wang	Sun Yat-sen University, China
Qinghua Zhang	Chongqing University of Posts and Telecommunications, China
Qingshan Liu	Nanjing University of Information Science and Technology, China
Ru Li	Inner Mongolia University, China
Rui Mao	Shenzhen University, China
Ruichu Cai	Guangdong University of Technology, China
Ruixuan Li	Huazhong University of Science and Technology, China
Shaojing Fu	National University of Defense Technology, China
Shifei Ding	China University of Mining and Technology, China
Shijun Liu	Shandong University, China
Shuai Ma	Beihang University, China
Tao Xie	Peking University, China
Tao Zhou	Alibaba Group, China
Tianrui Li	Southwest Jiaotong University, China
Tong Ruan	East China University of Science and Technology, China
Tuergen Yibulayin	Xinjiang University, China
Tun Lu	Fudan University, China
Wangqun Lin	Beijing Institute of System Engineering, China
Wei Chen	Microsoft, China
Wei Lu	Sun Yat-sen University, China
Wei Wei	Xi'an University of Technology, China
Weidi Dai	Tianjin University, China
Weigang Wu	Sun Yat-sen University, China
Wei-Shi Zheng	Sun Yat-sen University, China
Wendong Xiao	University of Science and Technology Beijing, China
Wenji Mao	Institute of Automation, Chinese Academy of Sciences, China
Wenwu Zhu	Tsinghua University, China
Wenyuan Cai	Shanghai Hypers Data Technology Inc., China
Wu-Jun Li	Nanjing University, China
X. Sean Wang	Fudan University, China
Xiang Zhao	National University of Defence Technology, China
Xianghua Xu	Hangzhou Dianzi University, China
Xiangnan He	University of Science and Technology of China, China
Xianwei Zhang	Sun Yat-sen University, China
Xiaofang Zhou	Hong Kong University of Science and Technology, China
Xiaofei Zhu	Chongqing University of Technology, China
Xiaohua Xie	Sun Yat-sen University
Xiaohui Yu	York University, China

Xiaojie Yuan	Nankai University, China
Xiaojun Chen	Shenzhen University, China
Xiaojun Quan	Sun Yat-sen University, China
Xiaolong Jin	Institute of Computing Technology, Chinese Academy of Sciences, China
Xiaolong Zheng	Institute of Automation, Chinese Academy of Sciences, China
Xiaoru Yuan	Peking University, China
Xiaotong Yuan	Nanjing University of Information Science and Technology, China
Xin Wang	Tianjin University, China
Xinran Liu	Institute of Computing Technology, Chinese Academy of Sciences, China
Xiuzhen Cheng	Shandong University, China
Xu Chen	Sun Yat-sen University, China
Xuanhua Shi	Huazhong University of Science and Technology, China
Xuemei Liu	North China University of Water Resources and Electric Power, China
Yadong Zhu	Mobvista, China
Yan Yang	Southwest Jiaotong University, China
Yanfeng Zhang	Northeastern University, China
Yang Gao	Nanjing University, China
Yang Xiang	Tongji University, China
Yangfan Zhou	Fudan University, China
Yangyong Zhu	Fudan University, China
Yantao Jia	Huawei Technologies Co., Ltd., China
Ye Yuan	Beijing Institute of Technology, China
Yi Chang	Jilin University, China
Yi Du	Computer Network Information Center, Chinese Academy of Sciences, China
Yidong Li	Beijing Jiaotong University, China
Yimin Wen	Guilin University of Electronic Technology, China
Yong Li	Tsinghua University, China
Youfang Lin	Beijing Jiaotong University, China
Yu Su	iFLYTEK Research, China
Yuanchun Zhou	Computer Network Information Center, Chinese Academy of Sciences, China
Yuanqing Xia	Beijing Institute of Technology, China
Yubao Liu	Sun Yat-sen University, China
Yuedong Yang	Sun Yat-sen University, China
Yu-Feng Li	Nanjing University, China
Yulun Song	China Unicom, China
Yun Xiong	Fudan University, China
Zhang Le	Sichuan University, China
Zhanyu Ma	Beijing University of Posts and Telecommunications, China
Zhaohui Peng	Shandong University, China

Zhen Liu	Beijing Jiaotong University, China
Zheng Qin	Hunan University, China
Zhenying He	Fudan University, China
Zhibo Wang	Zhejiang University, China
Zhicheng Dou	Renmin University of China, China
Zhiguang Cheng	Sun Yat-sen university, China
Zhi-Jie Wang	Chongqing University, China
Zhiming Ding	ISCAS, China
Zhiyong Peng	Wuhan University, China
Zhongbao Zhang	Beijing University of Posts and Telecommunications, China
Zhonghai Wu	Peking University, China
Zhonghong Ou	Beijing University of Posts and Telecommunications, China
Zhuo Su	Sun Yat-sen University, China
Zili Zhang	Southwest University, China
Zizhen Zhang	Sun Yat-sen University, China

Sponsor

China Computer Federation (CCF)

Contents

Big Data Analysis and Applications

In-Depth Integration and Exploration Practice of "Rain Classroom" in the Teaching of Big Data Courses for Medical Colleges and Universities

Mingyou Liu[✉], Yingxue Zhu, and Li Li

Institution of Biology and Engineering, Guizhou Medical University, The New Area
Between Guiyang and Anshun, Guiyang 550025, Guizhou, China
{liumingyou,zyx,lilia6701}@gmc.edu.cn

Abstract. Purpose: Proposed a big data course teaching reform plan to improve the teaching effect, strengthen the interaction between students and teacher, So as to build a Multidimensional teaching atmosphere, through the implementation of a new type of big data course experiment plan, ultimately strengthen students' hands-on practice ability, and cultivate a group of cross-integrated big data talents who can understand the professional terminology of doctors and medical experts. Method: Taking medical information engineering and data science and big data majors in medical schools as examples, It introduced "Rain Classroom" technology into the teaching environment, and carrying out online and offline integrated teaching innovation, It can pushing teaching content to students before class, so students can be preview it in advance; This reform could carry out better interactive teaching atmosphere during class, and increase student participation, teacher could respond to students doubts and difficulties in real time; After class, teacher could summarize students learning, and then distinguish students at different levels, conduct differentiated guidance; It could manage all students through diversified assessment schemes; The learning process truly and objectively reflects the student's learning situation. Conclusion: The teaching reform plan is applied to actual teaching work. Through questionnaire surveys, interviews and other evaluation methods, it is found that the teaching reform plan can significantly improve the teaching effect; it also improved students' independent learning ability, and promoted the cultivation of interdisciplinary professional talents. It is conducive to promoting the education and teaching reform of big data subjects in medical schools.

Keywords: Inter disciplinary · Big data course teaching · Online and offline teaching integration · "Rain Classroom" technology · Virtual laboratory · Medical big data

---

Y. Zhu and L. Li—These authors contributed equally to this work.

X. Liao et al. (Eds.): BigData 2021, CCIS 1496, pp. 3–17, 2022.
https://doi.org/10.1007/978-981-16-9709-8_1

1   Introduction

The advent of the era of big data marks an increase in the demand for big data talents. To educate a new generation of big data talents, it is necessary to innovate the current teaching methods, and use the current mature teaching methods such as "Rain Classroom" to integrate these teaching methods. Integrate into the teaching process to form a good interactive teaching atmosphere, thereby it can enhance teaching effects and training qualified for big data talents.

As a carrier of cultivating and promoting innovation, colleges and universities undertake the important tasks of serving society, developing science, and cultivating talents. Facing the medical information engineering professionals of social market background urgently needed, the medical schools need to optimize their subject positioning, and build a big data curriculum teaching system, its need to pay attention to the frontiers of the subject, and grasp the characteristics of subject teaching, so as to improve the comprehensive professional skills of big data employed talents, and the competitiveness of the healthcare big data industry. On the basis of adapting to the needs of talent training, the school has set up two big data majors: medical information engineering and data science and big data technology, and successively set up big data courses as compulsory courses to meet the needs of training information talents. The teaching of big data courses is a new teaching subject. The big data courses offered in medical schools focus on the processing and analysis of big data for health care. Students will not only be able to perform general big data analysis in the future, but more importantly, they will enter the health care industry deals with big data in health care and provides counseling support for doctors. Therefore, the teaching process must be combined with professional characteristics, especially during the epidemic. How to solve the problem of online and offline teaching integration of big data courses is the research and development of this topic.

Facing the challenges of the new technological revolution and the requirements for cultivating high-quality talents, countries around the world have carried out large-scale curriculum changes. After many curriculum reforms in China, curriculum teaching has gradually become integrated, balanced, and selectivity, however, the previous curriculum teaching reforms mainly focused on traditional basic teaching, and teaching reforms were needed for the special professional characteristics of colleges and universities. At this stage that the teaching of big data courses in colleges and universities, too much emphasis is placed on the integrity and theoretical nature of the course system, but lack of interconnection between big data and professional courses, the practical applications is unable to train students' ability to comprehensively apply big data knowledge. In addition, classroom teaching is mainly concentrated in the teaching system, and the teaching method is relatively traditional, which leads to poor learning effects for students [1]. In order to solve the problems existing in the current stage of course teaching, the innovation of online and offline teaching methods is carried out, the latest teaching methods are introduced, and the emphasis is on improving students learning enthusiasm, conducting personalized teaching, and using multiple methods. This assessment method evaluates and analyzes the reformed big data curriculum teaching system, so as to ensure that the curriculum reform method can play a better teaching effect.

The "Rain Classroom" introduced in the teaching process was jointly developed by "Xue tang" Online and the Online Education Office of Tsinghua University. The intelligent terminal based on PowerPoint and WeChat can establish a bridge of communication between students independent learning and teachers classroom teaching, realizing learning before class. The organic combination of preview-classroom and teaching-after-class review, "Rain Classroom" is a tool that can organically integrate the above-mentioned network resources with classroom teaching, it is to achieve student-centered, individualized students Effective means of training talents [2].

The introduction of "Rain Classroom" technology provides convenient conditions for the development of big data courses; especially the in-depth integration of online and offline gives students and teachers an opportunity. Teaching not only comes from the classroom, but can also be extended to before and after class. The knowledge system of the big data course involves a wide range of topics and contains a lot of content. Students need to be fully prepared before the class and strengthen their learning after class, so that they can be integrated into the teaching process. At the same time, through the active interaction of the "Rain Classroom", the teaching will be more enhanced. Interesting, they can master the essentials of knowledge in a relaxed learning atmosphere.

2   Design of Teaching Reform Program

Because big data teaching research is an activity process that uses scientific theoretical methods to explore teaching rules purposefully, consciously, and in a planned way. The reform of big data teaching is inseparable from an effective theoretical basis of teaching as support. Therefore, it is necessary to analyze the relevant theories of teaching reform before perfecting the teaching reform plan. Use advanced teaching methods such as "Rain Classroom" to guide the teaching reform of big data courses in medical schools. By mobilizing students subjective initiative, teaching students learning methods, to cultivate students' learning ability. On the basis of the above-mentioned related theories of teaching reform, the application goals of big data and the current big data technology are used as the realistic basis to determine the plan of big data course teaching reform and carry out teaching practice.

2.1   Clarify the Curriculum Goals

The future employment goal of big data majors in medical colleges and universities is to enter medical-related institutions to process medical data. Due to the various types and forms of medical and health big data, students are required to have certain data processing and analysis capabilities, and have the ability to process medical data; Therefore, this course sets up a corresponding teaching curriculum system, it could satisfy the students professional needs, professional characteristics, and core competences required for employment goals. From the perspective of the inverted triangle talent job requirements, the training of big data application, operation, maintenance talents should be the key goal of discipline talent training, and relying on school-enterprise cooperation, leading students to participate in the deployment of big data operation platforms to strengthening the big data technology Analysis and processing capabilities, and preliminary understanding the current state-of-the-art technology. As the application of big data technology in the medical industry becomes more and more extensive, a clear development trend has formed, various medical institutions have increased the construction of big data, the collection, sorting, analysis, processing and transmission of related data will face big data. This has led to an increase in the demand for medical big data talents. Based on the above analysis, it is suggested that the big data professional courses of medical colleges and universities should construct a curriculum reform plan from multiple directions, highlight the curriculum reform goals of big data professional application, and form the characteristics of big data teaching courses, incorporating the training of medical data processing capabilities.

2.2   Adjust the Teaching Plan

According to the characteristics of big data courses in medical schools, the teaching plan of big data courses should be adjusted. Based on the existing big data curriculum system, highlighting the teaching concept of medical data processing practical ability training, colleges and universities contact relevant companies in the medical industry, determine the current talent demand standards in the industry, and comprehensively use big data-related technology to innovate curriculum teaching models to adapt to demand for talents in hospitals and medical institutions. The teaching mode of the big data course, as a specific form of subject teaching, is dynamically adjusted according to the actual situation to meet the learning needs of students. In order to adapt to the times and the development trend of the big data industry, especially during the special epidemic period, the teaching mode should be appropriately adjusted, and the teaching mode should be adjusted to a targeted online learning program; the teaching mode adopted in this project is the integration of online and offline, online Classroom teaching tools are mainly used in class teaching. Students use WeChat programs commonly used by students to allow students to change their mobile devices from entertainment tools to learning tools. During class, teachers and students can interact in real time, answer questions online, count students learning status, and check performance. Some better students offer praise, and those who poor performance need encourage them in time. The course is divided into pre-class preparation, in-class learning, and after-class review. After the course is over, the courseware for class includes electronic courseware and video courseware, and students can listen and learn repeatedly. Even during the epidemic, students can complete their learning goals at home even if classes can be suspended without suspension.

2.3 Repositioning the Teaching Content

The professional courses of medical colleges and universities include introduction to big data, high-level programming language design and computer networks, data mining, introduction to clinical medicine, cell and molecular biology, etc., with more teaching content and diverse teaching methods. According to the knowledge curriculum system of big data, then adjust the teaching content. The basic knowledge system of big data is shown in Fig. 1, including the data source layer. There are many sources of medical big data, and most of the data comes from medical institutions; the data is based on the structure Different, stored in different databases, such as relational databases, distributed databases, data warehouses, etc.; then use data mining, BI analysis and other tools to extract useful knowledge from the data and use it in medical decision-making.

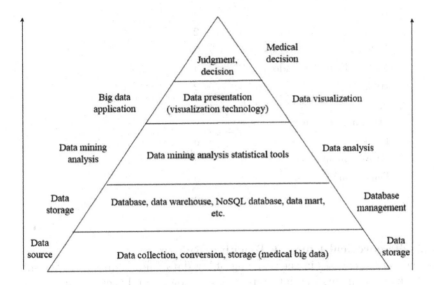

Fig. 1. Big data knowledge architecture

The data knowledge structure shown in Fig. 1, the degree of difficulty of relevant knowledge, starting from the two aspects of theory and practice, it will face the different target levels of big data talent training, and have the professional characteristics of medical information engineering, it need reasonable Teaching content.

2.3.1 Curriculum Setting and Class Hours Arrangement

The hierarchical teaching model conforms to the teaching principles of modern education theory, unifies the knowledge structure of the big data course and the cognitive structure of the students, based on the original course teaching method, re-formulates the teaching plan, and adjusts the course arrangement. The traditional theoretical teaching mode is transformed into a "theory + practice" teaching mode, in which the practical environment is deployed in the network cloud, and students can network experiments at any time or anywhere, obtain design and experimental results, submit experimental reports. After re-selecting the content of the big data course, different class schedules were obtained, some of the big data course teaching arrangements are shown in Table 1.

Table 1. Big data course content setting and class time distribution

Contents	Theory	Experiment	Teaching hours
Basic concepts	6	0	6
Processing architecture	3	2	5
HDFS	4	2	6
HBase	6	2	8
NoSQL	6	0	6
MapReduce and Hadoop	7	4	11
Hive	3	2	5
Spark	6	2	8
Stream computing	4	2	6
Flink	2	0	2
Graph calculation	4	2	6
Data visualization	3	0	3
Total	54	18	72

2.3.2   Theoretical Content Teaching Reform

The theoretical courses in the teaching of big data courses are one of the important tasks for realizing big data-related technologies, and they are also the basis for students' technical mastery and ability training. It can be seen from Fig. 2 that the theoretical content of the big data course is what the big data basic course needs to master. Therefore, in the course content reform process, use the latest teaching methods, use the WeChat program that students are all using, and add the latest "Rain Classroom" teaching methods, so that students can use their mobile phones to view courseware during the course, certainly teachers can check the learning of students at any time. Teacher-student interaction can be carried out at any time. If students have any ideas or dont understand something, they can send a bullet screen to contact the teacher at any time. The teacher can also know the student's learning status through questions, tests and other means at any time, So as to achieve a seamless connection outside the classroom and in the classroom.

Pre-class teachers can use "Rain Classroom" technology to push preview content, conduct pre-class tutoring, conduct face-to-face teaching with students during class, it integrate students into the classroom through an interactive teaching atmosphere, teachers could view teaching summary after class, according to the performance of different students FAQ teachers achieved individualization.

In the field of education, advanced computer technology is gradually becoming an effective teaching medium and teaching management method. Among them, the multimedia method of teaching is a teaching method that integrates text, images, animation, video and audio and other media. This teaching method has the advantages of high storage, fast transfer and copy speed. The relevant technical means in the big data teaching process can enhance the interactivity of classroom teaching, increase students memory points in the classroom, and improve the logic of teaching, so as to achieve the integrity and unity of the teaching links of big data courses. "Rain Classroom" technology has more Multidimensional teaching methods in the aspects of scenario evolution and simulation classrooms, which can be directly applied to actual big data classroom teaching.

2.3.3   Experimental Content Teaching

Experiments are a way of obtaining specific abilities that can be accomplished by applying certain theoretical knowledge and experience through repeated practice. In the teaching of big data courses, the tasks and requirements proposed in the syllabus, in order to meet the problems of students doing experiments anytime and anywhere, the reform of this course focuses on the big data cloud virtual experiment platform. Through cooperation with related enterprises, a simple an easy-to-use, purely distributed big data experiment platform. Students complete experiments at home. The experiment platform is deployed on a campus server cluster, which can dynamically allocate resources to meet all the big data experiment needs of big data courses.

2.3.4   Professional Integration Teaching

In the teaching process, selected the latest big data technology as the teaching content, through the addition of the actual project content, allows students to understand the operation process of big data technology in practical applications, especially the integration of the medical big data training system, which can enable students after graduation, its easier to quickly master the latest medical big data skills; at the same time, because the major belongs to a medical school, the focus is on integrating medical knowledge in the construction of professional characteristics, offering comprehensive medical and biomedical courses, and training a group of students who know doctors and understand the language of life science experts.

2.4   Optimize Teaching Plan

Generally speaking, the course teaching conditions of colleges and universities include textbooks, teachers, laboratories, etc. Due to the reform of the big data course teaching, some teaching methods have been optimized on the basis of the original teaching conditions; online teaching platforms and practical education have been introduced. New teaching conditions such as resources. Among them, the teaching laboratory uses a virtual big data experimental platform to optimize the computer system in the laboratory, it upgrades the network environment in the laboratory, allowing students to fully simulate the purely distributed characteristics during the experiment process, and achieve comparisons. Next experiment a more complete experimental program. Offline experiments can only be performed in a pseudo-distributed manner, especially in labs or student computers, which are unevenly configured, which cannot meet the needs of data analysis; while online, each experiment will start 3 to 4 virtual machines. The master server has multiple slave hosts, and development hosts according to different experiments. These configurations can complete the whole process of professional big data experiments.

2.4.1   Complete Teaching Curriculum Resources

In the teaching process of big data courses, it is necessary to fully reflect the foundation of big data theoretical knowledge and the service nature of professional courses. At the same time, the professional courses of big data technology should be closely integrated and reflected in specific project cases. Since the teachers in the class mainly explain the theoretical content, not all knowledge can be explained, and not all students can take care of it. Therefore, in the process of teaching big data courses for students, the "Rain Classroom" platform provides rich course teaching resources, Upload teaching materials to the "Rain Classroom" system, including video learning materials, document learning materials, audio learning materials, teacher's course recordings, etc., to centrally summarize the learning difficulties of students, and provide solutions for students to learn at any time, the big data textbooks selected for this course are equipped with comprehensive teaching resources on the Internet. In addition to experimental guidance, theoretical courses are also equipped with special online teaching videos, so that students can study and consolidate in a targeted manner after class.

2.4.2   Integration of Teaching Platforms

This course integrates the online teaching platform equipped by the school to solve a series of problems of student work submission, correction, feedback, etc. Through the application of the big data course online teaching platform, it can break through the time and space limitations of school teaching, and it can also be used in practical teaching. Through the platform to consolidate theoretical knowledge, you can also get accurate answers when you encounter professional problems. The most important role of the online teaching platform can be as a platform for teachers and students to interact with courses. Students can find learning resources on the platform, discuss learning content, and teachers can post learning notices, correct homework, and answer questions for students.

2.5   Strengthen the Experimental and Practical Teaching

In the process of big data teaching, it is necessary to strengthen the importance of big data course teaching practice teaching. The reason for constructing the big data virtual experiment platform is that in addition to the experiments that students need to complete in teaching, there are a lot of experiment cases arranged on the platform. Students can complete more experiments according to their learning progress and interests to improve their professional level. Teaching through experimental practice of big data courses can not only improve students application ability in professional technology, but also help students understand the latest big data technology. Complete the big data experiment through the big data integrated platform. The experiment platform is rich in resources. Starting from the Hadoop basic experiment, it covers a series of experiment contents such as Map Reduce, HBase, spark, storm, etc., from the experimental practice to the internship stage. It is a practice for students. Exercise provides platform support.

2.6   Multidimensional Assessment Method

Because the big data course belongs to a kind of practical and application course, it is diversified in the form of assessment. "Rain Classroom" can provide statistics on the learning data of the entire semester, and the comprehensive performance of students in class can also be classified and counted. For example, students preview and review or not during class, interact with teachers or not, the quality of experiment completion, the experiment process, the experiment report, the class attendance circumstances, the usual test situation and other dimensions. To get the assessment results of the big data course teaching. The final student assessment will comprehensively evaluate the theoretical end-of-term assessment and normal class conditions to obtain the final grades of the students. The final evaluation of the students is a comprehensive performance of the entire semester, It reflects that through the aggregation of multi-platform information, it can more objectively reflect the learning status of students.

3   Teaching Practice and Effect Evaluation

In order to explore the teaching effect of the big data course teaching reform results of the big data major of medical colleges and universities in actual teaching work, follow the principles of essential, comprehensive, scientific, orientation, effectiveness and feasibility, so selected the class that is in class as a research object, it dynamically feedbacks students learning effects. The teaching feedback process runs through the entire teaching process, and constantly adjusts unreasonable places through feedback, especially the intervention of "Rain Classroom" technology. Teachers can see the students preview before class. Learn about the students receiving status through the answers to the questions. After class, there is a special teaching summary, which introduces each students learning in detail, so as to provide a reference for the next teaching.

3.1   Teaching Practice

In the process of Big Data teaching theoretical courses, it was introduced and integrated the "Rain Classroom" technology into the class of teaching, include before, during and after. After several semesters of tests for the medical information engineering major of medical schools, it was found that the "Rain Classroom" technology is a good auxiliary teaching work to improve teaching effects; at the same time, an online virtual platform is introduced in the experimental course teaching, which can simulate a distributed cluster environment and meet the unique practical needs of big data courses. The feedback of experimental results is introduced into the online teaching platform. Students can submit experiment reports and give feedback on experiment results. Teachers can use it to grasp the process and status of students' experiments. The practice teaching link is a three-dimensional comprehensive teaching process, and the result feedback is so slow. After multiple semesters of teaching practice and result collection, ultimately formed a teaching result data set that meets the analysis needs. As shown in Fig. 2, the specific theory teaching practice include preview before class, teachers teaching in class, students study after class, The whole teaching process is integrated.

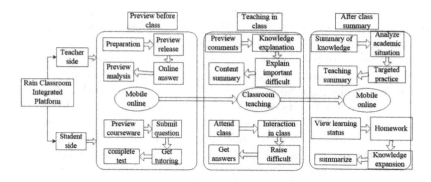

Fig. 2. "Rain Classroom" teaching flow chart

After class, statistics show that when the "Rain Classroom" integrated into the teaching process, students actively interact with teachers, and more participate in the teachers teaching process. In the course of theoretical lessons, students can dynamically communicate with teachers online through barrage. Figure 3 reflects the active interaction between students and teachers in class. Through the intervention of the "Rain Classroom", college students are reluctant to answer the teachers questions. Due to this reason, the "Rain Classroom" dilemma turns into an anonymous way for students to express their opinions, and express their true thoughts, the students will be open, daring to express, and willing to express, teachers can also understand the students learning status by viewing the students bullet screen, and communicate with the student in real time. And every one could online communication activities.

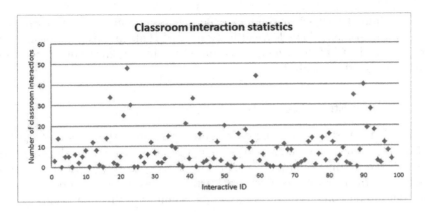

Fig. 3. Big data experiment platform

For the development of the course, a virtual experiment platform was constructed, as shown Fig. 4, the platform for students to complete the experiment, through which students can complete all the experimental content needed for the semester.

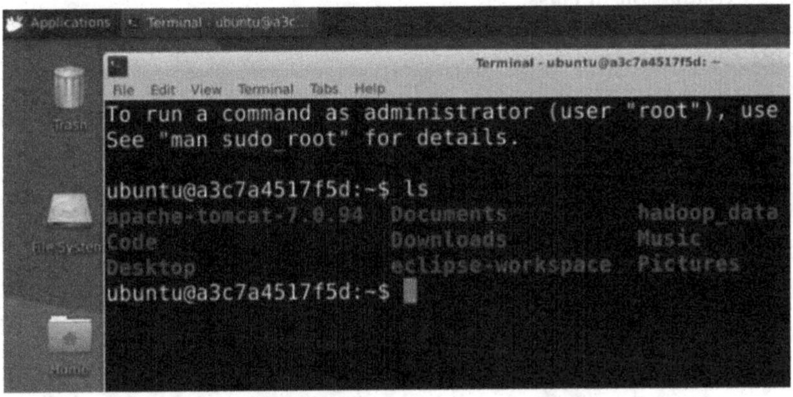

Fig. 4. "Rain Classroom" teaching flow chart

In the teaching of the experimental part of the big data course teaching, the big data experiment environment is mainly configured according to the tasks and requirements stipulated in the syllabus. During the experiment, students actively participate in the experiment, and the number of experiments reaches more than 23 times. In addition to completing the teacher assignment experiment content, you can also choose other experiments to complete and your selected Those experiments you interests. In order to meet the purpose of flexible learning for students, teachers will open multiple experiments at the same time, with flexible deadlines, and students can conduct experiments anytime and anywhere. On the platform, students have learned knowledge of Hadoop, HBase, storm, hive, spark, etc., and 90% of the students have mastered the core knowledge framework required for big data analysis.

3.2 Teaching Effect Feedback

The teaching statistics of the big data course come from the class that opened the big data course. The number of students is more than 90. In the course of the class, the "Rain Classroom" technology is used to collect all the student classroom data, including courseware learning statistics, test score statistics, classroom interaction data, etc. Analyze and summarize the final results.

3.2.1 Theoretical Teaching Feedback

Through the statistical results of the summary data, it is found that the students' pre-class and after-school learning can be completed through the "Rain Classroom" technology, and the online test results of the students are counted through the "Rain Classroom" platform. Figure 5 shows the student's learning enthusiasm and test results Positive correlation, the more active students are, the better their grades will be, and they will be more able to understand the teacher's explanation in class.

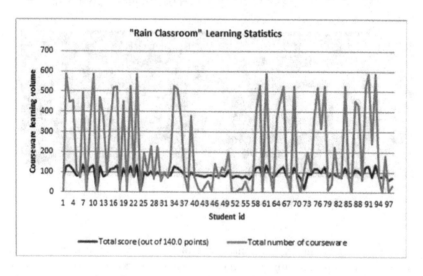

Fig. 5. Student learning statistics

3.2.2   Assessment

In this part of the evaluation, the final comprehensive assessment results of the students are mainly combined. The final assessment results of the students truly reflect the learning situation of the students throughout the semester. After the final assessment, and through comparison, it is found that the scores of the students who have used the "Rain Classroom" are 9% higher than those who have not used the "Rain Classroom" between 90–100, and 38% higher than the scores of the students who have not used the "Rain Classroom", as shown in Fig. 6 below.

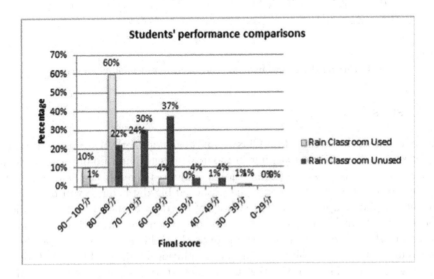

Fig. 6. Students performance comparisons

For the final test scores of who used the "Rain Classroom", we conducted a final statistical analysis. The student numb is 94, Full score is 100. The student score standard deviation is 9.6, the reliability is 0.76, and the discrimination is 0.22, Full range Pass is 98%, Average score is 81.8, the Excellent rate is 32%, Full range is 60.0, Difficulty is 0.76. Through the actual test; the final assessment results of the students meet the reform requirements.

At the same time, as shown in Fig. 7 that students enthusiasm for interaction on the online teaching platform is very high. It can be seen from the figure that the longer the study time, most of them the final test scores better than other students, which reflects the advantages of the learning platform. The platform provides an online communication center for teachers and students.

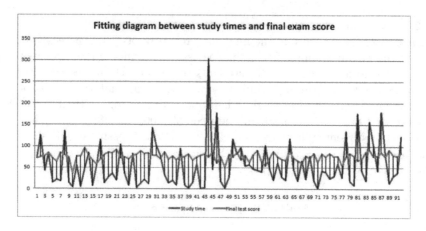

Fig. 7. Fitting diagram between study times and final exam score

4   Discussion

The article uses the latest "Rain Classroom" teaching methods to integrate into the latest big data course teaching in medical colleges, and finally uses various data analysis tools in a Multidimensional manner to verify the reform effect. Through research and comparison, the proposed big data course will be taught. The reform plan is applied to the teaching of big data courses in actual medical colleges, and it has been improved in terms of curriculum effect, theory, practice and so on. It can be proved that the proposed teaching curriculum plan has a good reform effect. The solution is a better solution to the problem of students studying at home. Through the WeChat applet, students can achieve a seamless connection between online and offline courses, which provides very convenient conditions for students to learn anytime, anywhere.

5   Conclusion

The advent of the era of big data is driving the wave of information development, which will definitely change the current status of education. Medical colleges and universities have also set up relevant majors to take advantage of the trend, actively adapt to the educational needs of the big data era and the application needs of big data courses in medicine, when integrated "Rain Classroom" technology to big data courses, the goal of interdisciplinary theory teaching, the goal of students' active integration into teaching and learning has been realized. After evaluating the reform effect, it is found that applying the reform plan to actual teaching work can effectively improve the teaching quality and effect. The plan can be applied to the teaching reform of other courses, and provide big data courses teaching sample for other medical colleges and universities. In the future teaching process, big data courses will increase the time for students to explain knowledge points on stage, let students consciously prepare the content of the explanation in advance, increase students' enthusiasm for learning before class, and add more discussion times after class, allow students exchange their learning experiences each other, Answer each other's questions, consolidate what you have learned.

Acknowledgments. I would like to thank the Guizhou Provincial Department of Education for the project funding: Guizhou Provincial Department of Education undergraduate teaching and curriculum system reform project, and also thank the members of the project team for their efforts in the development of the project.

Declarations. Funded Project: Guizhou Provincial Department of Education undergraduate teaching and curriculum system reform project: Cultivating practical and innovative medical information engineering professionals "Big Data" course content and system structure research (Number: 2018520059).

References

1. Li, X., et al.: Curriculum reform in big data education at applied technical colleges and universities in China. IEEE Access **7**, 125511–125521 (2019)
2. Wang, S.: Rain classroom: smart teaching tools under the background of mobile internet and big data. Mod. Educ. Technol. **27**, 26–32 (2017)
3. Zheng, Z.: Design of mixed teaching activities in rainy classrooms in a smart education environment. China Educ. Inf. **16**, 55–59 (2019)
4. Chen, H., Qiuying, H., Peng, Z., Wei, S.: Research on the teaching reform of computer specialty database courses under the background of big data. Microcomput, Appl. **35**(08), 15–16 (2019)
5. Zhou, L., Fan, H., Pan, J.: Research on the big data knowledge service framework based on the process of knowledge fusion. Libr. Sci. Res. **000**(021), 53–59 (2017)
6. Yizhan, X.: Research and analysis report on the demand for internet finance professionals. Chin. Bus. **9**, 3–4 (2017)
7. Bez, M.J.P.: Big data and learning analytics in health and medical education applications. Investigacin en Educacin Mdica **7**(25), 61–66 (2018)
8. Bajpai, S., Mani, S.: Big data in education and learning analytics. TechnoLearn Int. J. Educ. Technol. **7**(12), 45 (2017)
9. Maciel-Monteon, M., et al.: Measuring critical success factors for six sigma in higher education institutions: development and validation of a surveying instrument. IEEE Access **8**, 1813–1823 (2019)
10. Wang, Y., Ji, S., Zhai, W.: Research on the new teaching model of computer basic education based on big data analysis. Wirel. Internet Technol. (2019)
11. Shi, Q., Wang, L., Jianying, L.I., et al.: Study on the mixed teaching of modern education technology based on rain classroom. Off. Inf. (2019)
12. Zq, H.: Exploration and practice of autonomous learning teaching mode for accounting professional courses based on "Rain Classroom". Univ. J. Educ. Res. **6**, 1692–1696 (2018)
13. Gao, H.: Analysis of network classroom environment on the learning ability of college students. Technol. Knowl. Learn. **26**(1), 1–12 (2021)
14. Li, L., Hu, X.: Reforming the key teaching links of "C Language Programming" with rain classroom for the engineering education accreditation. Comput. Era (2019)

Research on Hadoop Task Scheduling Problem Based on Hybrid Whale Optimization-Genetic Algorithm

Jun Xu and JunFeng Peng[✉]

College of Computer,
Guangdong University of Education, Guangzhou 510303, Guangdong, China
{xujun,pengjunfeng}@gdei.edu.cn

Abstract. In the complex grid environment, how Hadoop's scheduling tasks effectively use the shared available resources to complete the assigned tasks in the shortest time, which is a NP hard problem. In this paper, a Hybrid Whale Optimization-Genetic Algorithm (HWO-GA) algorithm is proposed to solve the task scheduling problem. The new HWO-GA algorithm introduces the mutation and crossover operator of Genetic Algorithm (GA) to overcome the defect that the traditional Whale Optimization Algorithm (WOA) is easy to fall into local optimal solution, so as to increase the global optimization ability of the algorithm. Experiments show that the HWO-GA algorithm has better convergence and optimization ability than the traditional WOA and GA algorithms, and can make more full use of shared resources.

Keywords: Hadoop · Genetic algorithm · Whale optimization algorithm

1 Introduction

Apache Hadoop framework is a software library that allows the use of a simple programming model to process a large number of data sets distributed in a computer cluster. In this framework, MapReduce applications can be executed [1, 2]. MapReduce [3, 4] programming model is used to process large-scale data sets, which means the minimum correlation between tasks. The two types of tasks in MapReduce model are map and reduce. However, MapReduce applications are difficult to schedule. They not only need the location of data, but also need to consider the dependencies between tasks. Therefore, scheduling is a hot issue in distributed computing. Task scheduling problems are of paramount importance which relate to the efficiency of whole cloud computing facilities. In this paper, for the goals of maximizing their utilization while minimizing the total task execution time, we propose an Hybrid Whale Optimization-Genetic Algorithm (HWO-GA) for task level scheduling in Hadoop's MapReduce.

X. Liao et al. (Eds.): BigData 2021, CCIS 1496, pp. 18–24, 2022.
https://doi.org/10.1007/978-981-16-9709-8_2

2 Task Scheduling Optimization Problem of Hadoop

Because Hadoop's MapReduce mainly includes two user defined functions: Map functions and Reduce functions, this is a complex combination optimization problem, we do mathematical modeling of the task scheduling. First, given M new tasks and N processing nodes, the required computing power of task J is T_i, the computing resource capacity of processing node i per unit time is K_i, and the maximum number of parallel processing tasks is Max_i. How to allocate M tasks to N processing nodes to minimize the total task completion time? The objective function is as follows:

$$\min \sum_{i=1}^{M} \sum_{j=1}^{N} \frac{U_{i,j} T_i}{K_j} \tag{1}$$

In the above formula $U_{i,j}$: task i occupies the computing resources of processing node j, the value of this symbol is 1; Otherwise, the value is 0.

The constraint condition: the number of the processing node j tasks cannot exceed the maximum number of the node processing tasks, i.e.:

$$s.t. \sum_{i=1}^{M} K_{i,j} \leq Max_i \tag{2}$$

3 Description of Hybrid Whale Optimization-Genetic Algorithm

Whale Optimization Algorithm (WOA) [5, 6] is an algorithm based on the behavior of the whale hunting prey. Whale is a kind of social mammal. They also cooperate with each other to drive and round up their prey during hunting. Whale algorithm has not been proposed for a long time. It is also a new optimization algorithm, and there are few research and application cases. In the whale algorithm, the position of each whale represents a feasible solution. In the process of whale hunting, each whale has two behaviors: one is to surround the prey, and all the whales are moving towards other whales; The other is a drum net, in which whales swim in circles and blow out bubbles to drive away their prey. In each generation of swimming, whales will randomly choose these two behaviors to hunt. In the process of encircling the prey, the Whale will randomly choose whether to swim to the best position or choose a whale as its target and approach it.

Whale Optimization Algorithm includes two core operators, as follow:

(1) Surround predation: the whales first observe the location of prey and then surround it. In the whale algorithm, it is assumed that the optimal problem solution and problem variables are also the location of the leading whale. After defining the best whale's position, other whales will swim towards the whale's position to update their position. This process is represented by the following equation:

$$D = \left| CX^*(t) - X(t) \right| \tag{3}$$

$$X(t+1) = \left| X^*(t) - A \cdot D \right| \tag{4}$$

Here, t represents the current number of iterations, A and C represent the correlation coefficient, X^* represents the existing optimal solution, and X represents the current position vector. The optimal solution of each generation is likely to change. The determination of correlation coefficient depends on the actual situation, which will be discussed later.

(2) Bubble predation: the whale first calculates the distance between itself and its prey (the best position so far), and then the whale swims upward in a spiral posture and spits bubbles of different sizes to prey on fish and shrimp. The mathematical model of this behavior is as follows:

$$D' = |X^*(t) - X(t)| \tag{5}$$

$$X'(t+1) = D' \cdot e^{bl} \cdot \cos(2\pi l) + X^*(t) \tag{6}$$

Where: $D' = |X^*(t) - X(t)|$ is the distance from the i whale to food, l is $[-1,1]$ random value, b is the helix constant.

(3) Random predation: When $A > 1$, whales will randomly search for prey and conduct global search to avoid falling into local optimization. The mathematical expression of this stage is as follows:

$$D = C \cdot X_{rand} - X \tag{7}$$

$$X(t+1) = |X_{rand} - A \cdot D| \tag{8}$$

Where X_{rand} is the position of a random whale (or prey) in the current population.

In the process of predation, whales have two mechanisms: swing surrounding predation and spiral swimming bubble spitting predation. Therefore, it is assumed that the probability of whales performing the two predation behaviors is 50% respectively, that is, the probability of whales updating their position with formula (4) or formula (6) is 50% respectively. The mathematical model is as follows:

$$X(t+1) = \begin{cases} X^*(t) - A \cdot D & \text{if } p < 0.5 \\ D' \cdot e^{bl} \cdot \cos(2\pi l) + X^*(t) & \text{if } p \geq 0.5 \end{cases} \tag{9}$$

Where p is $[0,1]$ random value.

The main advantages of WOA algorithm is its simplicity and speed. However WOA algorithm lacks a solid mathematical foundation and easily converge local optima. To overcome these problems, HWO-GA algorithm integrates the respective advantages of WOA and GA. In this paper, we attempt to introduce GA mutation and crossover operators to quickly find the best solution in the WOA algorithm.

The key operator of Genetic Algorithm (GA) [7, 8] is mutation in a successful search for the optimal solution. Algorithms mutation operator is to find a better solution in maintaining the basic features of its parent. Crossover retains beneficial characteristics of candidate solutions and eliminates the bad parts.

Mutation: according to the following expression, for each individual t-th iteration, each x_j^t does mutation operation, to give the corresponding individual variation y_j^{t+1}:

$$y_j^{t+1} = x_a^t + R(x_b^t - x_c^t) \tag{10}$$

Where: $a, b, c \in \{1, ..., N_P\}$ and $a \neq b \neq c \neq j$; x_j^t as the base vector generation; scaling factor R is random control parameter between [0, 2].

Cross: according to the following formula, the individual vector x_j^t and variation individual y_j^{t+1} do vector cross operates, to give individual v_j^{i+1}:

$$v_j^{t+1} = \begin{cases} y_j^{t+1}, if\,(rand \leq C_R) \\ x_j^t\ otherwise \end{cases} \tag{11}$$

Where: $rand$ is a random number in the range [0, 1] uniformly distributed; C_R usually choose crossover probability [0, 1] helps algorithm escape from the local minim.

HWO-GA algorithm combines WOA and GA in this paper. The mutation and crossover operators of GA algorithm are applied to whale motion. The following are the specific steps of the whole HWO-GA algorithm:

1) Determine whale population size, randomly generated population;
2) Calculate the fitness value of each whale and compare it to determine the optimal whale individual with the current fitness value, according to the formula (1);
3) Enter the main loop of the algorithm. If $p < 5.0$ and $|A| < 1$, each individual Whale will update the current position according to formula (3), otherwise update the individual whale position according to formula (8). If $5.0 \geq P$, each individual whale updates its position according to formula (6);
4) Mutating: do mutation and crossover operation according to the formula (10) and (11);
5) Selecting: select the next generation's individual according to the Eq. (5);
6) Ordering: the whole whale population is evaluated to find the globally optimal whale individual and its location, and update the optimal solution;
7) If the termination condition (maximum number of iterations) of the algorithm is satisfied, it ends and output the optimal solution; Otherwise, go to step 2 and continue the algorithm iteration.

4   Simulation Experiment and Data Analysis

In Hadoop framework, HWO-GA algorithm is implemented by MapReduce programming. The experimental test platform is tested on a group composed of five machines. The configuration of each machine is as follows: operating system: is Windows 7; CPU is Intel Core i5-4590; Memory is 4 GB; On the Hadoop 2.0 cluster, all nodes have the same configuration, that is, one CPU and 50 GB hard disk..

4.1 HWO-GA's Convergence Speed

Suppose there are 50 tasks and 5 processors. Figure 1 shows the performance of Hybrid-Whale Optimization-GeneticAlgorithm (HWO-GA). Compared with WOA and GA algorithms, it can obtain better objective function value by completing the same task allocation in the same time range, which shows that HWO-GA algorithm has faster convergence speed.

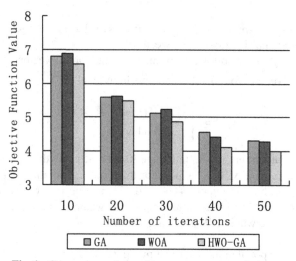

Fig. 1. Comparison of algorithm convergence performance

4.2 HWO-GA's Resource Utilization

Figure 2 shows that HWO-GA has higher resource utilization because the algorithm fully considers the processing capacity of resources. The figure shows that under the comparison of maxmips with the maximum processing capacity of each processor, the resource utilization of HWO-GA algorithm on most processors is higher than that of WOA and GA algorithm.

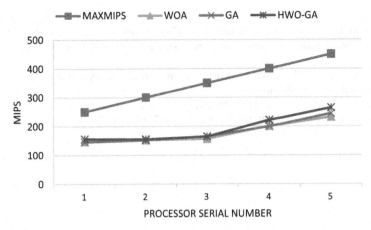

Fig. 2. Comparison of resource utilization

5   Conclusions

Through the above experimental simulation analysis, it can be verified that the proposed HWO-GA algorithm can better jump out of the local optimal solution and find the better global optimal solution than the traditional WOA and GA algorithm. This is because when WOA particles fall into the local optimal solution, the mutation and crossover of GA will diversify the positions of particles, so as to jump out of the local optimal solution. The stochastic nature of HWO-GA makes it more robust and expansible. In the search process, it avoids the premature phenomenon of falling into local optimization, and can make better exploration in the search space. This paper gives a detailed description of the flow and advantages of HWO-GA algorithm. The experimental results show that HWO-GA has better performance than WOA and GA, provides better resource utilization and optimization ability, and fully explains the scalability and reliability of the algorithm.

Acknowledgments. This work has been supported by projects of colleges and universities in Guang dong Province (No.2021ZDZX3016). Scientific research platforms and Young innovative talents project of colleges and universities in Guangdong Scientific research platforms and projects of colleges and universities in Guang Province (N2021KQNCX061)

References

1. Qin, X.P., Wang, H.-J.: Big Data analysis-competition and symbiosis of RDBMS and MapReduce. J. Softw. **23**(1), 32–45 (2012)
2. Lin, J.-C., Leu, F.-Y., Chen, Y.-P.: Impact of MapReduce policies on job completion reliability and job energy consumption. IEEE Trans. Parallel Distrib. Syst. **26**(5), 1364–1378 (2015)
3. Dean, J., Ghemawat, S.: MapReduce: simplified data processing on large clusters. Commun. ACM **51**(1), 107–113 (2008)
4. Wang, G., et al.: Behavioral simulations in MapReduce. Proc. VLDB Endowm. **3**(1–2), 952–963 (2010)

5. Mirjalili, S., Lewis, A.: The whale optimization algorithm. Adv. Eng. Softw. **95**, 51–67 (2016)
6. El Aziz, M.A., Ewees, A.A., Hassanien, A.E.: Whale optimization algorithm and moth-flame optimization for multilevel thresholding image segmentation. Exp. Syst. Appl. **83**, 242–256 (2017)
7. Muñoz, A., Rubio, F.: Evaluating genetic algorithms through the approximability hierarchy. J. Comput. Sci. **53**, 101388 (2021)
8. Ongcunaruk, W., Ongkunaruk, P., Janssens, G.K.: Genetic algorithm for a delivery problem with mixed time windows. Comput. Industr. Eng. **159**, 107478 (2021)

Towards Indonesian Phrase Extraction:
Framework and Corpus

Xiaotian Lin[1], Nankai Lin[1], Lixian Xiao[2,3], Shengyi Jiang[1,2(✉)],
and Xinying Qiu[1,2(✉)]

[1] School of Information Science and Technology, Guangdong University of Foreign Studies,
Guangzhou, Guangdong, China
[2] Guangzhou Key Laboratory of Multilingual Intelligent Processing, Guangdong University
of Foreign Studies, Guangzhou, Guangdong, China
[3] Asian Languages and Cultures, Guangdong University of Foreign Studies, Guangzhou,
Guangdong, China

Abstract. Mining quality phrases is one of the basic tasks of natural language
processing. Current research mainly focuses on universal languages but is rarely
conducted for low-resource languages such as Indonesian. To the best of our
knowledge, there is no evaluation dataset available for phrase extraction task in
Indonesian. Phrase extraction is a challenging task for Indonesian due to the lack
of language analyzing tools and large data set. Therefore, we propose a framework
to construct Indonesian phrase extraction corpus using Wikipedia as high-quality
resource and match extracted phrases with our POS-tagged corpus. Our linguistic
experts manually classified the extracted POS patterns. With the annotated patterns, we re-extract phrases and construct a corpus with 8379 Indonesian phrases
in total. In addition, we experiment with three deep learning models achieved superior performances for phrase extraction and finalize the baselines for Indonesian
phrase extraction task.

Keywords: Indonesian · Phrase extraction · Corpus construction

1 Introduction

As one of the fundamental tasks in text analysis, mining quality phrases refers to automatically extracting salient phrases from a given corpus. It is important in various tasks such
as information extraction, taxonomy construction, and topic. In these tasks, researches
are often interested in phrases of various lengths and of various categories such as scientific concepts, events, organizations, products, slogans and so on. Phrase extraction can
be applied to support many NLP tasks such as keyword retrieval, dependency parsing,
and machine translation.

Current researches on phrase extraction can be divided into three categories: rule-
based methods, machine learning-based methods and deep learning-based methods. In

---

X. Lin and N. Lin—The co-first authors. They have worked together and contributed equally to
the paper

© Springer Nature Singapore Pte Ltd. 2022
X. Liao et al. (Eds.): BigData 2021, CCIS 1496, pp. 25–37, 2022.
https://doi.org/10.1007/978-981-16-9709-8_3

light of rule-based methods, the conventional approach is to utilize pre-defined Part-of-Speech (POS) rules to identify phrases in POS-marked documents as phrase candidate sets. As regards the machine learning-based methods, Uxoa Inurrieta et al. [1] proposed to classify candidate words extracted from the Spanish corpus. Their research uses a variety of machine learning methods including logistic regression models, random forest algorithms, and naive Bayes algorithms. As for deep learning-based methods, Taslimipoor et al. [2] proposed a language-independent neural network model which consists of a convolutional neural network layer, a recurrent neural network layer and a CRF layer to solve the phrase extraction problem.

Many of the state-of-the-art methods require a lot of human effort at certain levels and rely on complex linguistic analyzers (e.g., dependency parsers) to locate phrase mentions. For example, the domain-independent method SegPhrase proposed by Liu et al. [3] outperforms many other approaches, but still needs domain experts to first carefully select hundreds of varying-quality phrases from millions of candidates, and then annotate them with binary labels [4]. During this process, how to reasonably select candidate phrases is also a problem needing to be addressed to. In addition, without extra but expensive adaption, these methods may achieve unsatisfactory performances on text corpora of new domains and genres.

Expert annotation of large-scale phrase corpus is time-consuming and laborious. The Indonesian is a typical adhesion language with rich and complex morphological variations, To the best of our knowledge, there has been very limited research on methods for corpus construction of large-scale, high-quality Indonesian phrases. To address these research gaps, we propose in this study a framework that adopts POS tagging system and Wikipedia as high-quality resources for candidate phrase extraction. We identify phrase patterns and invite a number of linguistic experts in Indonesian to manually classify these phrase pattern with two labels (not a phrase pattern and maybe a phrase pattern). Based on the classification results, we re-extract phrases from the corpus to finalize an Indonesian phrases corpus. In addition, in order to estimate the quality of the corpus, we further applied three deep learning models to the corpus, achieving superior performances and establishing phrase extraction baseline.

The main contributions of this paper are as follows:

(1) We propose an efficient framework for large-scale Indonesian phrase corpus construction.
(2) We provide a phrase extraction corpus for Indonesian language to support other related NLP tasks for Indonesian.
(3) The ideas in our phrase corpus construction are feasible and applicable to many other languages.
(4) We further use three deep learning models to experiment on this corpus to finalize a benchmark and the baseline.

2 Related Work

2.1 Quality Phrase Mining

With the development of the big data era, automatic extraction of quality phrases (i.e., multiword semantic units) from massive, dynamically growing corpora gains increasing attention [3]. Altenbek and Sun [5] proposed to use the statistical information and linguistics rules to predict the base noun phrase boundary with mutual information and correct the boundary with base noun phrase constitution rules. With predefined POS rules, Ahmad et al. [6] proposed to generate noun phrases from each document. However, such rule-based methods usually suffer from domain adaptation. Ulteriorly, Rohanian et al. [7] built a neural network model combining Graph Convolutional Network (GCN) and Multi-head self-attention to achieve phrase extraction. In automatic recognition of Indonesian compound noun phrases, Qiu et. al. [8] proposes a method with Self-Attention mechanism, n-gram convolution kernel neural network, and CRF. Their methodology improves over SHOMA method but the data set was limited. Taslimipoor et al. [2] proposed a language-independent neural network model to solve the phrase extraction problem. The neural network model consists of a convolutional neural network layer, a recurrent neural network layer and a CRF layer. Nevertheless, such deep learning methods rely on a large-scale corpus while existing phrase corpus cannot meet the requirements of deep learning technology in terms of scale and quality.

2.2 Phrase Extraction Corpus Construction

In order to reduce the workload of manual labeling, sun et al. [5] studied the str4ucture of basic noun phrases in Kazakh language according to the characteristics, and summarized the basic noun phrase structure rules of Kazakh language. Based on these rules, they programmatically annotate the basic noun phrases in the 300,000-word level Hark corpus. Birke et al. [9] automatically constructed a corpus of English idiomatic expressions (words that can be used non-literally). They targeted 50 expressions and collected about 6,600 examples. Hashimoto et al. [10] further expands the phrase corpus. They have constructed an idiom corpus for Japanese. The corpus targets 146 ambiguous idioms, and consists of 102,846 sentences, each of which is annotated with a literal/idiom label.

3 Framework

As shown in Fig. 1, the model proposed in this paper mainly consists of three modules: (1) phrase matching with POS corpus (2) candidate phrase pattern extraction and classification (3) reverse search to extract candidate phrases.

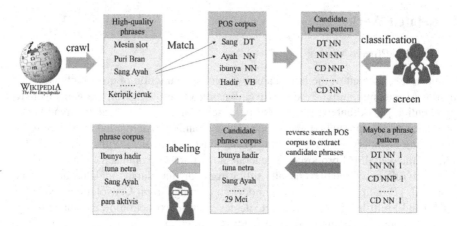

Fig. 1. Flowchart of our framework.

3.1 Phrase Matching Based on POS Corpus

According to Shang et al. [4], public knowledge bases such as Wikipedia[1] usually include high-quality phrases in their titles, keywords and anchors text links. Although it seems rare to find standardized grammar system that could be automatically applied to analyze Indonesian, a number of high-quality POS corpora are available for Indonesian.

We choose 1614242 phrases crawled in Wikipedia as high-quality phrases to filter out the phrase patterns based on POS corpus by Fu et al. [11]. The data set contains 355000 tokens and 29 POS tags shown in Table 1. For each Wikipedia phrase, if it exists in the POS corpus, we match and extract the corresponding POS tags for it to construct a pair <pattern, phrases> as shown in Table 2. For example, given a Wikipedia phrase 'Sang Ayah' which we can get the tags as 'DT' and 'NN' in the POS corpus for each of the two words, we construct a pattern pair <DT NN, Sang Ayah>.

Table 1. Indonesian POS tagset.

Tag	Description	Tag	Description
CC	Coordinating conjunction	PRF	Reflexive pronoun
CD	Cardinal number	PRI	Indefinite pronoun
DT	Determiner	PRL	Relative pronoun
FW	Foreign word	PRP	Personal pronoun
ID	Indefinite number	RB	Adverb
IN	Preposition	SC	Subordinating conjunction
JJ	Adjective	SP	Subject-predicate structure

(continued)

---

[1] https://id.wikipedia.org/.

Table 1. (*continued*)

Tag	Description	Tag	Description
JJS	Adjective, superlative degree	SYM	Symbol
MD	Auxiliary verb	UH	Interjection
NN	Common noun	VB	Verb
NNP	Proper noun	VO	Verb-object structure
OD	Ordinal number	WH	Question
P	Particle	X	Unknown
PO	Preposition-object structure	Z	Punctuation
PRD	Demonstrative pronoun		

Table 2. The example of pattern pair < pattern, phrases >

Pattern	Phrases
NN NN	adanya keterlibatkan, keterlibatkan kepolisisan, pintu belakang
CD NN	suatu took, dua tahun, empat orang
RB JJ	sudah lama, sudah penuh, paling benar

3.2 Candidate Phrase Pattern Extraction and Classification

After matching the high-quality phrases based on POS corpus, for all of the pattern pairs, we further count the quantity and frequency of the phrases contained in each pattern. In order to improve the quality of phrase patterns, we only keep the patterns with frequency higher than the pattern frequency threshold k as candidate phrase patterns. The value of this threshold is set to 5 and will be verified in the subsequent experiment. After screening, a total of 43 candidate phrase patterns were preserved. We then invited a number of experts with Indonesian background to manually annotate these candidate phrase patterns with two labels (i.e. "not a phrase pattern" and "maybe a phrase pattern").

3.3 Reverse Search to Extract Candidate Phrases

Aiming to meet the corpus needs of existing phrase extraction researches in terms of quality and scale, we further reversely search the phrases in POS corpus to extract candidate phrases. Specially, according to the classification results of the phrase patterns in Sect. 3.2, we select the patterns which are labeled as "maybe a phrase pattern", and match them on the POS corpus reversely to extract the phrases corresponding to some pattern. After that, for each pattern, we also randomly screen μ phrases respectively for manual labeling in order to construct the large-scale corpus for phrase extraction.

4 Experiment

4.1 Part-Of-Speech Pattern

We choose the patterns with frequencies higher than 5 for labeling via threshold experiment described in Section 4.3 among the 179 candidate phrase patterns. At the annotating process, we stipulate that each pattern is labeled by two persons with two single-labels (1: Maybe a phrase pattern; 0: Not a phrase pattern). Then patterns with the same labeling results are added to the corpus. Instead, patterns with different annotation results will be annotated again by a third expert. If the annotation results are the same as one of the first two persons, the pattern result will also be added to the corpus. The annotated results which contained 43 patterns marked with 1 and 7 patterns marked with 0 are shown in Table 3. Most of the patterns marked with 0 have a similar structure to ones marked

Table 3. The results of patterns classification

Pattern	Label	Pattern	Label
NNP NNP	1	NNP NNP NNP CD	1
NN NN	1	NN NNP NNP NNP	1
NNP NNP NNP	1	NNP IN NNP	1
NN JJ	1	NN VB	1
NN NNP	1	FW FW	1
CD NNP	1	JJ NN	1
NNP NNP NNP NNP	1	NNP NNP CC NNP	1
NN NN NN	1	NNP NNP CD	1
VB NN	1	NNP NN	1
VB VB	1	DT NN	1
CD NN	1	DT NNP	1
NN NNP NNP	1	NN VB NN	1
NN NN JJ	1	VB JJ	1
NN NN NNP	1	NN FW	1
NN OD	1	NN NN CD	1
NNP NNP NNP NNP NNP	1	NN IN NN	1
IN NN	1	NN JJ NN	1
RB VB	1	NNP NNP NNP CC NNP	1
NN IN NNP	1	NNP CD NNP	1
NN NN NNP NNP	1	NN VB VB	1
RB JJ	1	JJ VB	1
JJ JJ	1	NNP CD	0
CD NNP CD	0	NN CD	0
NN CC NN	0	NNP SYM	0
FW FW FW	0	NN IN	0

with 1 such as "NN CD" and "CD NN", "NN IN" and "IN NN", which seems that such patterns marked as 0 are caused by correct patterns under the influence of grammatical errors.

4.2 Phrase Extraction Corpus

Based on the self-constructed phrases corpus, for each pattern, we randomly screened 200 candidate phrases which include 50 phrases in our high-quality corpus crawled by Wikipedia and extract all the phrases if the number of phrases is lower than the threshold of 200. There is a total of 8379 candidate phrases that contain 1015 items from Wikipedia being constructed in this paper. Besides, there are 983 items be marked as label 1 among these 1015 phrases from Wikipedia which is ratio of 0.968. Through this result, it is obvious to see that the Wikipedia corpus is of relatively high quality, which further demonstrated the effectiveness of the Phrase matching method we proposed in Sect. 3.1. The number of phrases in each pattern and the phrase ratio are shown in Table 4. Among them, the five patterns with the highest quality are "RB JJ", "NN OD", "CD NN", "NN NN NNP NNP" and "RB VB" while the ones with lowest quality are "DT NNP", "NN VB VB", "NN VB NN", "NNP NN" and "NNP NNP CD".

Table 4. The number and ratio of the phrase of each pattern.

Pattern	Num. of phrases	Ratio of phrases	Pattern	Num. of phrases	Ratio of phrases
CD NN	192	0.96	NNP NNP CD	87	0.435
CD NNP	146	0.73	NNP NNP NNP CC NNP	109	0.736
DT NN	145	0.725	NNP NNP NNP CD	65	0.699
DT NNP	46	0.23	NNP NNP NNP NNP NNP	162	0.81
FW FW	124	0.62	NNP NNP NNP NNP	156	0.78
IN NN	168	0.84	NNP NNP NNP	151	0.755
JJ JJ	152	0.76	NNP NNP	144	0.72
JJ NN	135	0.675	RB JJ	196	0.98
JJ VB	91	0.455	RB VB	189	0.945

(*continued*)

Table 4. (*continued*)

Pattern	Num. of phrases	Ratio of phrases	Pattern	Num. of phrases	Ratio of phrases
NN FW	144	0.72	VB JJ	144	0.72
NN IN NN	142	0.71	VB NN	187	0.935
NN IN NNP	159	0.795	VB VB	168	0.84
NN JJ NN	139	0.695	NN NNP NNP	180	0.9
NN JJ	184	0.92	NN NNP	181	0.905
NN NN CD	145	0.725	NN OD	146	0.973
NN NN JJ	172	0.86	NN VB NN	56	0.28
NN NN NN	176	0.88	NN VB VB	21	0.105
NN NN NNP NNP	189	0.945	NN VB	129	0.645
NN NN NNP	185	0.925	NNP CD NNP	143	0.761
NN NN	188	0.94	NNP IN NNP	154	0.77
NN NNP NNP NNP	188	0.94	NNP NN	73	0.365
NNP NNP CD NNP	182	0.91			

4.3 Patterns Frequency Threshold Screening

In order to further verify the validity of the pattern frequency threshold, we proposed in Sect. 3.2, a threshold screening experiment is conducted. Specially, we proposed the Modify Pattern Frequency (MPF) feature and Cumulative Phrase Ratio (CPR) feature where MPF feature refers to the changing of the pattern frequency and CPR feature represents the quality of phrase patterns.

Since there are phrase patterns with the same frequency in the corpus, we merge the phrase patterns with the same frequency and sort them in descending order by pattern frequency shown in Table 5.

Table 5. Pattern frequency

Pattern	NNP NNP	NN NN	...	JJ JJ	NNP NNP NNP CD	NN NNP NNP NNP	NN VB VB	JJ VB
Frequency	2115	1411	...	5	5	5	5	5
Order	1	2	...	28				

Suppose the proportion of phrases corresponding to all patterns is expressed as $f = (f_1, f_2, f_3, \ldots, f_n)$, $q = (q_1, q_2, q_3, \ldots, q_n)$ where f_i, q_i is defined as the frequency of the phrase patterns and the ratio of the phrases corresponding to the i-th order and n refers to the number of orders. Hence, given a pattern frequency k, the Modify Pattern Frequency (MPF) feature and Cumulative Phrase Ratio (CPR) feature are calculated as follow.

$$MPF_k = \frac{1}{\frac{1}{i} \log_{10}\left(\sum_{c=1}^{i} (f_i)\right)}$$

$$CPR_k = \frac{1}{i} \sum_{m=1}^{i} q_i$$

Where i refers to the order of the phrase pattern.

We have fitted and drawn the relation curves of Modify Pattern Frequency (MPF) feature and Cumulative Phrase Ratio (CPR) feature. The results are shown in Fig. 2. Through this figure, it is obvious to see that the results are dropped sharply when the MPF is 1.4307 corresponding to the pattern frequency of 5. Therefore, we choose candidate phrase patterns whose pattern frequency threshold is higher than 5 as pattern.

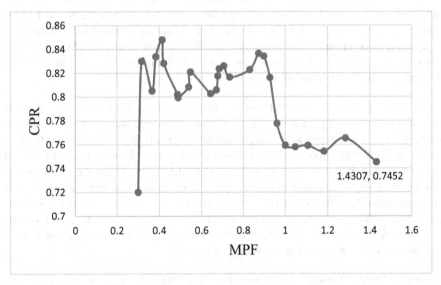

Fig. 2. Patterns frequency threshold screening

4.4 Evaluation

To further evaluate the quality of our corpus, we used three deep learning models to experiment on the self-constructed corpus and built a benchmark for Indonesian phrase extraction task. We divide the corpus into training set, validation set and test set according to the ratio of 6:2:2 and estimated the performance of the self-constructed corpus with three commonly used models (Bi-LSTM [12, 13], CNN [14] and BERT [15]) and the state-of-the-art phrases extraction method proposed by Shang et al. [4]. As for BERT, we employed its own word piece separator, while utilized BPE [16] and Char embedding to encoder the text for CNN model and LSTM model. The F1 score and accuracy result are shown in Table 6.

Bi-LSTM. Recurrent neural networks (RNN) [17] are among the most popular architectures used in NLP problems because their recurrent structure is very suitable to capture all the available future information. However, it does not deal well with long-term dependency problems that may cause gradient vanishing and gradient exploding. In order to solve these problems, a special form of RNN: Long Short-Term Memory (LSTM) [18] is proposed. LSTM allows the model to selectively save the context information through a specially designed gate structure. To make up for one-way LSTM's inability to obtain information in multiple ways, a Bidirectional Long Short-Term Memory (Bi-LSTM) model is used in this paper. Bi-LSTM neural network can model the sentence in both forward and backward directions, which can not only save the previous context information, but also take future context information of the sentence into account.

CNN. CNN has achieved remarkable successful for image field and most of the NLP tasks. Compared with other classical deep learning models such as RNN and LSTM, the advantages of CNN are as follows. (1) It can well capture various local features by a sliding window composed of several words. (2) Similar to N-gram convolutional neural network, it can automatically combine and screen N-gram features to obtain semantic information at different levels of abstraction.

BERT. BERT is a language model based on bidirectional encoder characterization. Its network structure is composed of attention mechanism, which makes the model address well the long-distance dependence and parallelism problems. Besides, at the pre-training stage, BERT is comprised of two unsupervised subtasks, namely Mask Language Model (MLM) and Next Sentence Prediction (NSP): (1) MLM refers to masking some words from the input sequence and then predicting the masked word through the context; (2) NSP is designed to enhance the relationship between a sentence pair. Its objective is to predict whether the sentence pair are continuous. After pre-trained, BERT can be fine-tuned for a variety of downstream tasks such as text classification, named entity recognition (NER) and question answering (QA) tasks.

Automated Phrase Mining. Automated phrase mining [4] develop a POS-guided phrasal segmentation model, which incorporates the shallow syntactic information in part-of-speech (POS) tags to further enhance the performance. Aiming at the problem that the existing phrase extraction methods need a certain level of expert marking and rely on a complex, well-trained language analyzer, this method uses the existing knowledge bases (such as Wikipedia) for remote supervision training and uses part-of-speech information to increase the accuracy of extraction. Besides, this method can support any language as long as a general knowledge base (e.g., Wikipedia) in that language is available. However, since we do not have a corresponding part-of-speech tagging corpus, semantic segmentation is omitted in this paper.

Table 6. Results on the self-constructed dataset.

Model	F1-score		Accuracy	
	Dev	Test	Dev	Test
BERT	0.908	0.902	0.860	0.852
Bi-LSTM(Char)	0.859	0.862	0.769	0.774
Bi-LSTM(BPE)	0.867	0.868	0.777	0.778
CNN(Char)	0.862	0.861	0.768	0.765
CNN(BPE)	0.848	0.855	0.756	0.767
Automated Phrase Mining	0.851	0.852	0.741	0.743

We can see that the model with BPE outperforms the one with Char embedding, which indicates that sub-word level features can better help the model to capture the phrase features. BERT, as the existing pre-trained model with the best performance on many classification tasks, also achieves excellent results in phrase extraction, outperforming the CNN and Bi-LSTM. Therefore, we regard BERT model as the benchmark for Indonesian phrase extraction task.

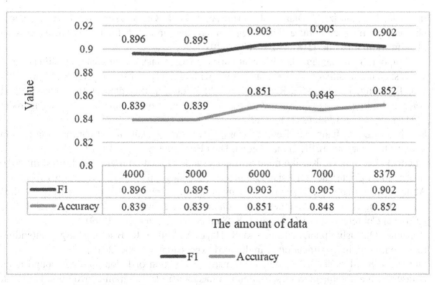

Fig. 3. Experimental results under different amounts of data.

We further explore the effect of the BERT model under different data scale. Specially, we randomly selected 4000, 5000, 6000, 7000 pieces of data from the corpus according to the label ratio to construct the model. For each scale of data, we randomly selected three times, with the average acc and average f1 as the final evaluation indicator. As shown in Fig. 3, it is obviously to see that when the amounts of data reaches 6000, the performance of the model is basically stable, which indicates that the scale of the corpus we built meets the requirements.

5 Conclusion

In this paper, we propose a framework for constructing Indonesian phrase extraction corpus. The framework is easily adaptable and applicable to other languages. We use this framework to construct an Indonesian phrase corpus containing 8379 phrases in total. We further applied three deep learning models to experiment on this corpus and achieve satisfactory performances. With the models, we to finalize the Indonesian phrase extraction baselines, and further validate the quality of our corpus. In the future, we will study how to design algorithms to improve model performance on the Indonesian phrase extraction task.

Acknowledgements. This work was supported by the Key Field Project for Universities of Guangdong Province (No. 2019KZDZX1016), the National Natural Science Foundation of China (No. 61572145) and the National Social Science Foundation of China (No. 17CTQ045).

References

1. Inurrieta, U., Aduriz, I., Díaz de Ilarraza, A., Labaka, G., Sarasola, K.: Learning about phraseology from corpora: a linguistically motivated approach for multiword expression identification. Plos one **15**(8), e0237767 (2020)
2. Taslimipoor, S., Rohanian, O.: Shoma at parseme shared task on automatic identification of vmwes: Neural multiword expression tagging with high generalisation. CORR (2018)
3. Liu, J., Shang, J., Wang, C., Ren, X., Han, J.: Mining quality phrases from massive text corpora. In: Proceedings of 2015 ACM SIGMOD International Conference on Management of Data, pp. 1729–1744. (2015)
4. Shang, J., Liu, J., Jiang, M., Ren, X., Voss, C.R., Han, J.: Automated phrase mining from massive text corpora. IEEE Trans. Knowl. Data Eng. **30**(10), 1825–1837 (2018)
5. Altenbek, G., Sun, R.: Kazakh noun phrase extraction based on n-gram and rules. In: 2010 International Conference on Asian Language Processing, pp. 305–308. IEEE (2010)
6. Ahmad, K., Gillam, L., Tostevin, L.: University of surrey participation in trec8: Weirdness indexing for logical document extrapolation and retrieval (wilder). In: The Eighth Text REtrieval Conference (TREC-8), pp. 1–8. Gaithersburg, Maryland (1999)
7. Rohanian, O., Taslimipoor, S., Kouchaki, S., Ha, L. A., Mitkov, R.: Bridging the gap: attending to discontinuity in identification of multiword expressions. CORR (2019)
8. Qiu, X., Chen, H., Chen, Y., et al.: Automatic recognition of Indonesian compound noun phrases with a combination of self-attention mechanism and n-gram convolution kernel. J. Hunan Univ. Technol. **34**(3), 1–9 (2020)
9. Birke, J., and Sarkar, A.: A clustering approach for nearly unsupervised recognition of nonliteral language. In: 11th Conference of the European Chapter of the Association for Computational Linguistics, pp. 329–336 (2006)
10. Hashimoto, C., Kawahara, D.: Construction of an idiom corpus and its application to idiom identification based on WSD incorporating idiom-specific features. In: Proceedings of the 2008 Conference on Empirical Methods in Natural Language Processing, pp. 992–1001 (2008)

11. Fu, S., Lin, N., Zhu, G., Jiang, S.: Towards indonesian part-of-speech tagging: corpus and models. In: Proceedings of the Eleventh International Conference on Language Resources and Evaluation (LREC 2018), European Language Resources Association (ELRA), France (2018)

12. Schuster, M., Paliwal, K.K.: Bidirectional recurrent neural networks. IEEE Trans. Signal Proc. **45**, 2673–2681 (1997)

13. Yao, Y., Huang, Z.: Bi-directional LSTM recurrent neural network for Chinese word segmentation. In: Hirose, A., Ozawa, S., Doya, K., Ikeda, K., Lee, M., Liu, D. (eds.) ICONIP 2016. LNCS, vol. 9950, pp. 345–353. Springer, Cham (2016). https://doi.org/10.1007/978-3-319-46681-1_42

14. Kim, Y.: Convolutional Neural Networks for Sentence Classification. In: Proceedings of the 2014 Conference on Empirical Methods in Natural Language Processing, pp. 174–1751 (2014)

15. Devlin, J., Chang, M. W., Lee K., Toutanova K.: BERT: Pre-training of deep bidirectional transformers for language understanding, In: Proceedings of NAACLHLT 2019, pp. 4171–4186 (2019)

16. Heinzerling, B. and Strube M. BPEmb: Tokenization-free pre-trained subword embeddings in 275 languages. In: Proceedings of the Eleventh International Conference on Language Resources and Evaluation, European Language Resources Association (ELRA) (2018)

17. Chung, J., Gulcehre, C., Cho, K., Bengio, Y.: Empirical evaluation of gated recurrent neural networks on sequence modeling. CORR (2014)

18. Sepp, H., Jürgen, S.: Long short term memory. Neural Comput. **9**(8), 1735–1780 (1997)

A Review of Data Fusion Techniques for Government Big Data

Bo Zhang, Yunxiang Yang, Jing Guo, Chenshen Liu, Junjie Liu, Siyuan Chen[✉], and Xiaobin Ning

China Academic of Electronics and Information Technology, Shuangyuan Street, Beijing 100041, China
liuchenshen@yeah.net

Abstract. Nowadays, the development of e-government has ushered in the era of big data. Data is playing an increasingly important role in the government's social management and public services. Government big data refers to various information resources such as documents, forms, or charts generated or obtained by government departments in the process of performing their duties. Government data is large in scale, various sourced, and diverse, so there are some difficulties in how to effectively fuse and analyze the complex government data to gain accurate decisions under the premise of ensuring key information will be preserved and key features will be taken seriously. Starting from the definition of government data, this paper firstly analyzed the meaning and the characteristics of government data, and problems in dealing with government data. Then discussed data fusion framework and techniques for government data in three directions: data level, feature level, and decision level. Finally, summarized existing technology and put forward problems that needed to be studied in the future.

Keywords: Government big data · Data fusion · Data level · Feature level · Decision level

1 Introduction

In the era of big data, data penetrates all works of life and becomes an important factor of production. The same goes for government departments. When government departments perform duties and process business, a large amount of data is generated, which plays a key role in improving government service levels and decision-making capabilities. Government data include information resources that are collected by government affairs departments or third parties, authorized and managed according to law, and produced through information systems to perform duties. At present, the amount of government cross-departmental

---

Y. Yang, J. Guo, C. Liu, J. Liu, S. Chen, X. Ning—These authors contributed equally to this work.

X. Liao et al. (Eds.): BigData 2021, CCIS 1496, pp. 38–55, 2022.
https://doi.org/10.1007/978-981-16-9709-8_4

business data is increasing, coupled with the deepening of government information construction in recent years, the content of government big data is being
enriched. It aggregates generous business data of government departments at
all levels, and the data are of various kinds and related to almost all aspects of
life. To effectively use the value of data and facilitate the government to make
more scientific decisions, it is necessary to discover valuable information from
multi-source government data.

Data fusion is a technology that analyzes and merges data to obtain more
consistent, informative, and accurate information. Data fusion started earlier in
foreign countries. In 1973, the United States firstly applied data fusion technology to the military field, mainly in the solar understanding system, which
can fuse multiple independent continuous signals. In 1991, Joint Directions of
Laboratories (JDL) firstly established a terminology retrieval dictionary and a
basic system model on data fusion systems [1]. This model is currently the most
widely used and improved one in the field of data fusion. In 1997, Hall put forward a definition of data fusion, that is 'Data fusion techniques combine data
from multiple sensors, and related information from associated databases, to
achieve improved accuracies and more specific inferences than could be achieved
by the use of a single sensor alone'. This definition was accepted in academic
circles. Hall also divided data fusion into three levels, namely data level, feature
level, and decision level [2].

Data fusion technology was originally only used in the military field. As time
goes by, the application field of data fusion has become wider and wider, and the
demand for data fusion in the government affairs field is also increasing. Before
the 21st century, government data was collected by people, and the amount
of data was small. In the early time of the 21st century, government data has
begun to take shape, but they were stored in the database of many different
departments. From 2016, data penetrated all fields, processes, and parts of government management. Make decisions and manage according to data has become
the norm. In recent years, government data fusion technology are applicated in
many areas. For instance, the Pudong New Area data fusion service platform
mainly realizes the exchange and fusion of government data, and the interconnection between various business systems. The platform mainly focuses on address
information fusion, it uses NLP technology and ETL tools to standardize data,
and introduces multi-dimensional data model design methods and intelligent
algorithms to improve the processing capabilities of mufti-source data fusion
[3]. In Singapore, Smart Nation Project has been proposed, which can enhance
the digitization of the nation. One of the most important sub-projects of Smart
Nation Project is a Integrated Data Management Framework, which provides
the ability to fuse government data, and maximize the value of them [4]. Now,
government data can sufficiently reflect the overall situation of a city, so it is
comprehensive. Government data are collected and stored under standards and
specifications, so it is authentic. Government data can reflect the content of government work, so it is internal. Therefore, the current government systems store
a great amount of government data. Data also became the key to government

daily management. These have brought huge difficulties about data management and analytics, which are mainly reflected in the following four aspects:

(1) Broad coverage. The scale of government data is huge and covers the work of every government department. Thus, this requires the ability to handle a good deal of data in data management and analysis.
(2) Extensive comprehensiveness. The content of government data includes arrangements, requirements, issues, etc., and the format of government data includes text, images, charts, etc. Thus, this requires the ability of data fusion in data management and analysis.
(3) Uncertain value. The sources of government data are different, which may contain many duplications, or the content of the same data from different data sources are different, resulting in different value densities of data. Thus, this requires the ability of quality control in data management and analysis.
(4) Strict timeliness. There are strict time limits for government data in both collection, edition, and submission, and the data itself is dynamically updated. Thus, this requires the ability to extend new data and respond to data changes in data management and analysis.

According to the above analysis, government data is facing the following issues. (1) Government data contains every aspect of the work of government departments, so each piece of data cannot be ignored easily, otherwise, it may cause information loss during data fusion. (2) Government data has a large scale and multiple modalities, and the features are redundant, which leads to a large amount of computing in data processing and poor real-time performance. Also, it is difficult to learn the characteristics of cross-modal data. It causes the effect of data fusion to be not satisfying. (3) The value density of government data is inconsistent, resulting in low accuracy of the decision made based on government data. We can solve the above issues effectively through data fusion, and make better use of government data, also provide more help for situation analysis, forecast, and decision.

At first, this paper describes the definition of government data and data fusion and leads to the topic of government data fusion. The second chapter comes up with a data fusion framework according to the characteristics of data fusion. And discusses data fusion techniques from data level, feature level, and decision level. The third chapter looks forward to the problems existing in the fusion government data and directions worth studying in the future. Finally, sum up the paper. The main contribution of this paper is as follows:

(1) Summarize characteristics of government big data, Review the developed history of data fusion technology, and put forward the difficulties in manage and analyze government data in a combination of their characteristics.
(2) Come up with a framework of government data fusion application to provide a reference for government data fusion applications.
(3) Summarize current data fusion research status, and explain the concepts and characteristics of the method of the data level, feature level, and decision level.

(4) Discuss difficulties and problems worth studying of data fusion technology for government big data.

2   Research on Government Data Fusion

In recent years, with the development of data fusion technology, its application field has been rapidly expanded, from a tool for data analysis and processing to a systematic way of thinking. In this section, from the perspective of systematic thinking, a government data fusion application framework is proposed to provide reference for the application of government data fusion.

According to the operation object of government data fusion technology, and the level and scope of dealing with problems, the government data fusion method is analyzed from the perspective of data level fusion, feature level fusion and decision level fusion. In the following chapters, this paper introduces the concept, connotation and method of government data fusion method from the above-mentioned levels, and summarizes the applicability of government data fusion scene.

2.1   Government Data Fusion Application Framework

In terms of government data fusion, scholars have constructed a government data fusion framework from different perspectives. Li Gang [5] studied emergency information fusion and proposed an information fusion framework based on emergency information and serving emergency decision-making purposes. Zhang Yi [6] proposed the theoretical framework of multi-mode data fusion, including service information description model, metadata model and data interconnection model, and proposed a data sharing and fusion framework. Ma Jie et al. [7] proposed a semantic-oriented metadata model, combined with user demand classification, to build a smart city data fusion framework based on multi-source data. The technical level of the government data fusion framework can be roughly divided into three aspects. One is that there are many applications of the government data fusion framework based on Web API, but the disadvantage is that the open interfaces are inconsistent. Specific APIs only allow access to specific data or services, and cannot realize the inter-data; the second is that the metadata-based government data fusion framework uses a unified metadata standard to aggregate government data, but there may be cases where different data sets represent the same entity, ignoring the semantic relationship and corresponding matching between entities Relationship; Third, the government data fusion framework based on semantic aggregation uses domain-specific ontology to collect government data, aggregates data with intrinsic semantic connections, and integrates it into a unified, semantically interoperable model based on multi-domain ontology.

Aiming at the application requirements of government data, an application framework of government data fusion is proposed. Government data acquisition module obtains multi-source heterogeneous government data through government information system business data, front-end sensors, and other equipment.

The data level fusion module preprocesses the format of collected multi-source government data, and then conducts data cleaning and data association, which are mostly used for the construction of government data fusion library.

Feature level fusion module for government data performs feature extraction, feature representation and feature fusion, and is mostly used in scenarios such as prediction, early warning, and problem discovery. The decision level fusion module obtains the local decision-making results through analysis and discrimination, and then integrates the local decision-making results. Finally, a multi-source government data fusion database is formed and managed. The application layer of government data fusion can be used for big data analysis of multi-source government data fusion database Fig. 1.

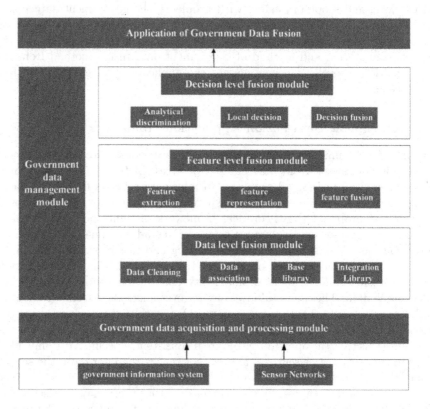

Fig. 1. Government data fusion application framework

2.2   Data Level Fusion of Government Data

2.2.1   Conception and Connotation

The data level fusion of government data mainly deals with the basic government information at the front end. The main task of data level fusion is to clean the original data in the base library, eliminate redundant and abnormal information in the data, unify the data structure, and then directly process the data association Fig. 2.

M. Lenzerini [8] believes that the data level fusion is to integrate data from different sources in certain form and provide users with a unified view. Wang Ping et al. [9] believes that data level fusion is not a simple superposition of data, but associate the original data after format conversion, structure reorganization, ontology matching, and scale conversion cleaning. It can be concluded from the research of scholars that data level fusion refers to the logical and physical cleansing of data from multiple information sources according to certain rules, and the fusion of data with different characteristics into new data. The new data should contain the meaning expressed by the previous data, and even excavate some potential rules and knowledge.

The advantage of government data level fusion is that it can maximally retain the content of the original government data, but the disadvantage is that the calculation burden is heavy. Government data often comes from multi-sectoral databases and multi-source heterogeneous data collected by multi-front-end sensing devices. The fusion of government data with the same departments, areas or objects generally uses data layer fusion. Compared with the feature level and decision level data fusion, the fusion information loss of data level fusion of government data is less, and it can retain more details of the original information.

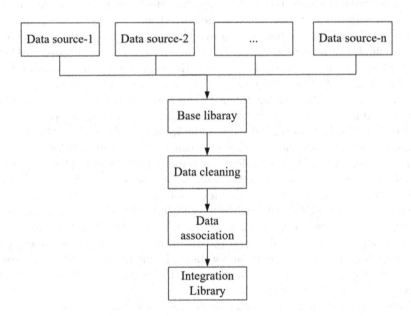

Fig. 2. Data level fusion of government data

2.2.2   Related Research

The original government data collected through the government information system and the front-end perception network are called irregular government data. Such data cannot be directly processed effectively. They need to be cleaned first, and then conduct data fusion through data association technology. The key supporting technologies needed for data level fusion of government data are data cleaning and data association.

(1) Data cleaning

Data cleaning is the technology of data repair and quality cleaning for the problems existing in the original data. It is the core part of data level fusion of government data to realize the correction, supplement, and unified specification of data. The original government data is stored in the base library after data collection. Each entity data in the base library has several attributes, and the main targets of attribute cleaning include error data, duplicate data, inconsistent data, etc. Generally speaking, data level oriented data cleaning technology mainly solves three kinds of problems: attribute error, structural error and repetitive error [10].

Attribute error is a value in a database that obviously violates the attribute definition. For example, in the population database, the age of someone is 10 years old, and the marital status is married, which is an abnormal value obviously inconsistent with the facts. General methods to detect attribute errors are mainly based on statistical methods and distance-based methods. Statistical methods use a certain distribution function to model the data, and then detect values that are significantly deviate from the normal value. Distance-based methods measure the distance between data values, the value that is too far away from most data is identified as outliers.

Structural error refers to the integrity constraint that data do not meet the semantic requirements of specific fields. The most direct way to detect structural errors is to input domain-related constraints from outside, such as the working organization determines the city. However, this method is often time-consuming and labor-intensive, and it is difficult to achieve universality. Thus, the main solution is to find the potential constraints from the data, such as conditional function dependence, rejection constraint rules and so on [11]. In recent years, some scholars have considered using external generic knowledge maps and publicly available crowdsourcing services on the Internet [12]. The basic idea is to induce structural errors by discovering parts of the data that are contrary to knowledge maps or crowdsourcing annotations. In the field of database research, Li G et al. [13] and others use crowdsourcing to improve the efficiency of data cleaning.

Record duplication is very common in real data. There are many reasons for data duplication, such as data may be provided by different institutions, or internal and external channels of data integration and self-organization. Record repetition has a great impact on data fusion. At present, entity recognition technology is generally adopted to solve the problem of record repetition.

(2) Data association

Data association is a technology that associates the cleaned and standardized government data according to the correlation of events, and finally stores the associated data in the fusion library. Association data mainly includes three types: relational association, homogeneous association, and lexical association. The data association of government big data can be divided into internal association and external association. The internal correlation of government data is mainly concentrated on homogeneous correlation, that is, to find descriptions of different aspects of the same entity between different government data sets, and to use one of the data sets as a supplement to the other. For external association, current research mainly focusses on similarity matching based on geometric attributes and association computation based on spatial relations [14].

Similarity calculation in similarity matching based on geometric attributes is to establish association by comparing and analyzing the attributes of object instances in data sets, which is mainly based on homogeneous association. Common similarity matching algorithms are mainly based on characters, morphemes, numbers, graphs and so on. The above similarity algorithms can be used alone or aggregated. Common aggregation methods include averaging, weighted averaging, maximum and minimum.

For spatial relation-based objects, it contains not only general non-spatial attributes, but also spatial information expressed by geometric coordinates or geographical names. If only non-spatial attribute comparison is considered in attribute-based similarity calculation, there may be synonymy and synonymy. Calculating the similarity based only on the "name" attribute and the text attribute will often get wrong association results. Therefore, in the attribute-based similarity calculation, the calculation of spatial geometric similarity can be considered, and the similarity can be calculated by combining spatial attributes with other non-spatial attributes to improve the matching accuracy.

2.2.3   Summary

Data level fusion of government data is the direct integration of the original government data, which belongs to the low-level fusion. For government data, the data layer fusion is mainly oriented to data processing of a single object or the same business scope. The data level fusion can retain the value of the data itself to the maximum extent, but for the data generated by cross-sectoral collaborative business, it is difficult to meet the actual needs, and it is more and more necessary to excavate the intrinsic value of the data itself to facilitate decision-making. Therefore, it is necessary to investigate the feature and decision level of government data fusion.

2.3   Feature Level Fusion of Government Data

2.3.1   Conception and Connotation

Feature level fusion is the fusion of government data in the middle layer, and the operation object is the characteristics of government information system business data and front-end sensor data. Firstly, the features of multi-source, multi-mode and heterogeneous government data are extracted, and then the data are analyzed and processed to form a joint feature matrix or vector of multi-source, multi-mode, and heterogeneous data. Finally, the decision is made by processing the joint features. Compared with the data level fusion, its advantage is lies in the completion of a large number of data compression, which greatly reduce the communication traffic, and is conducive to real-time data processing. Different modes of government data contain different information. Each mode has its own unique characteristics. Feature level fusion can conduct cross-modal feature representation learning, enrich feature information, and improve the performance of government data fusion Fig. 3.

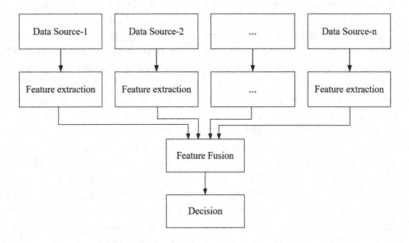

Fig. 3. Feature level fusion of government data

2.3.2 Related Research

The scale of government data is large. When cross-sectoral data fusion is needed, if the original government data is fused directly, it often requires a large amount of calculation. The fusion of feature level can effectively reduce the amount of calculation on the basis of characterizing the original data, and can enrich the feature information of multimodal government data. Feature level fusion mainly includes feature vector direct splicing method, sparse representation matrix method and feature fusion method based on deep neural network.

(1) Feature vector splicing

The early feature level fusion method directly fuses the features of all multi-source, multi-mode and heterogeneous data in series, and then completes data mining tasks such as clustering and classification based on the features after series [15]. This method does not consider the weight or correlation between vectors, and using all vector data to generate a higher dimensional vector directly. However, the difference in the same feature of different samples is small, and the difference in different features is large. Therefore, the feature fusion of multi-modality cannot be simply added, subtracted, or spliced, which will lead to the situation that the features that may be fused will be dominated by a certain feature.

(2) Sparse representation matrix

Simple splicing of feature vectors into high-dimensional feature vectors will increase the complexity of data analysis, and ignore the correlation between modes, resulting in data redundancy and dependence. The feature fusion algorithm based on sparse representation theory is to establish a joint sparse representation matrix of features after extracting features from samples, which is the fusion result of multiple features.

Image fusion method based on sparse representation uses the "select-max" rule to fuse sparse coefficients [16]. Only the features with the largest activity level are transferred to the fused image, which often leads to the fused image is too sharp and not smooth. The "weighted average" principle is used to weighted average the common features and innovative features of the fused image. The weight ratio between each innovation and common feature in the fused image is reduced, resulting in less obvious innovative features in the fused image than in the source image. Yu [17] used the joint sparsity of all source images to extract the common features and innovative features of source images simultaneously through joint sparse representation. The fusion of common features and innovation features has better fusion performance.

Based on sparse or low rank representation of multimodal data, the most advanced results are obtained in various multimodal recognition problems. Zhang [18] proposed a joint dynamic sparse representation method to identify targets from multiple observations. Yan et al. [19] introduced the idea of sparse and combined with the feature fusion method, improved the original rank reduction regression model, and proposed a sparse kernel rank reduction regression model, which fuses the speech features and facial expression features when people speak to realize the dual-mode expression recognition. Reference [20] proposed a multi-modal feature level fusion method, which simultaneously performs low-rank and joint sparse constraints in the representation corresponding to multiple modes, and simultaneously couples information under different modes.

(3) Deep neural network

The application of deep neural network in the field of government data fusion is still relatively new. Deep neural network has excellent feature representation ability, which makes it widely used in the field of data fusion. The deep neural network has multiple hidden layers and a large number of parameters, which is suitable for describing uncertain complex systems. The feature representation of traditional data fusion methods mainly relies on manual work. When it comes to specific simple tasks, manual feature extraction will be simple and effective, but it lacks generality. Compared with the multi-layer structure of deep neural network in traditional methods, it has more advantages in feature extraction of massive data [21], and the extracted feature quality is much better than that obtained by manual annotation and other methods [22]. But deep neural networks also have the problem of data dependence and low interpretability.

Deep neural network can learn multi-layer representation and abstraction of data, and then convert data into high-level abstract features of deep network [23]. This new feature is more expressive. In recent studies, more methods use deep neural network to learn the unified feature representation of different modal data, and the learned feature vectors are connected to a unified feature vector representation by a specific method. The vector contains multiple different modal information and can capture the correlation between different modal data. Zhang X et al. [24] introduced feature fusion into deep learning model and proposed a deep fusion learning architecture for learning high-level semantic feature representation in multimedia video.

Deep neural network learns hierarchical features of data through unsupervised training and monitoring of test set parameters. Scholars has achieved remarkable results in feature learning and extraction, and has also made preliminary research in feature fusion of multimodal data. Ngiam et al. [25] proposed a dual-mode depth autoencoder, which can simultaneously learn joint feature representation from audio and video, and apply the model to cross-modal learning and dual-mode fusion. Srivastava and Salakhutdinov [26] proposed a multi-modal constrained Boltzmann machine model. Firstly, the two branches of the network are pre-trained in a completely unsupervised manner, and an additional layer is added at the top of the two branches of the pre-trained network. Then, a multi-modal restricted Boltzmann machine model is constructed, and all layers are fine-tuned by backward propagation. This method can learn the joint representation of images and texts.

Different from the fusion network [25] and [26], Reference [27] did not set any fusion layer at the top of the whole network, but trained a unique sub-network for each feature group. All these sub-networks share the same optimization objective in the back-propagation period of the fine-tuning stage. These sub-networks are combined to form a multi-modal neural network, which consists of a top-level objective function layer and several sub-networks at the bottom. In this way, heterogeneous feature groups are converted into a unified representation, eliminating the heterogeneity between feature groups.

Multimodal feature fusion based on deep neural network first learns the representation of specific modes, and then learns the shared representation across multiple modes at the top of deep neural network. In Reference [28], deep network is used to learn the representation of specific modes, and learn the representation of one mode from another. Based on the correlation characteristics of multimodal data, a new multi-level pre-training and fine-tuning method is proposed to learn the weights in the network.

2.3.3 Summary

The data level fusion is no longer suitable for the real-time change of massive government data, while the feature level fusion fuses the original government data after extracting features, which reduces the amount of data, facilitates real-time data processing, enriches the feature information of government data, and realizes the cross-modal feature representation learning.

The government data are massive. The fusion of feature level enables the government to shorten the response time and deal with events in time when dealing with business or emergencies. The multi-source, multi-mode and heterogeneous characteristics of government data can realize the cross-sectoral association of government data through feature level fusion, and solve the problem of data island and improve the efficiency of government business.

2.4 Decision Level Fusion of Government Data

2.4.1 Conception and Connotation

Decision level fusion is a high-level government data fusion for decision application, which refers to the fusion of local decision results to obtain the global optimal decision results. The fusion process is mainly divided into two steps. Firstly, the original data are analyzed and discriminated with the help of certain rules or algorithms to obtain the preliminary decision results. Then, all local decision results are combined under certain rules to obtain the final joint decision result Fig. 4.

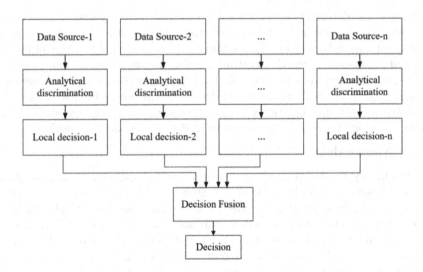

Fig. 4. Feature level fusion of government data

Decision level fusion has high requirements for data preprocessing. It only carries out early analysis and discrimination processing for decision objectives, which has relatively strong purpose and anti-interference, and the execution fusion time is usually short. The local decision results before decision level fusion are often different, complementary or even contradictory. Therefore, multi-source decision fusion can improve the fault tolerance of decision results, but the problem of data conflict still needs to be solved. The final result of decision level fusion is based on a variety of local decision results, which often has good interpretability and can provide support for upper-level applications.

2.4.2 Related Research

Based on the characteristics of multi-source, inconsistent information value and fast update speed of government big data, we can make full use of the advantages of decision level fusion to explore information association in multi-source information, solve data conflict, improve the accuracy and reliability of decision fusion results, and obtain the optimal scheme for decision application. The methods of decision level fusion mainly include Bayesian theory, D-S evidence theory and fusion method based on artificial neural network.

(1) Bayesian theory

Bayesian theory is a probabilistic reasoning method commonly used to deal with uncertain knowledge. The credibility of information is measured by a priori probability, then the information is inferred to obtain the local discrimination results, and finally the global decision results are obtained by fusion. In recent years, scholars have studied the correlation and causality between variables, which improves the reliability of reasoning results.

Wang et al. [29] Studied the Bayesian risk and its membership function in the fusion process, and gave the optimal fusion rules in the case of fuzzy prior distribution, but did not study the relationship between variables. Xiao et al. [30] Proposed a Bayesian network structure learning algorithm which can integrate association rules and knowledge to effectively improve the accuracy of Bayesian reasoning algorithm. S kharya et al. [31] Proposed the method of calculating the confidence and lift of association rules and combining with Bayesian network for prediction, which improved the reliability of Bayesian reasoning results.

(2) D-S evidence theory

Bayesian theory is often difficult to obtain a priori probability. As a generalization of Bayesian theory, D-S (Dempster Shafer) evidence theory method does not need to obtain a priori probability, and is often used to solve the problem of data conflict. D-S theory expresses the uncertainty of data by introducing confidence and uncertainty, obtains the trust function of different observation results, and then judges the trust function according to Dempster evidence combination rules, then finally realize fusion and decision-making. In recent years, the research on D-S theory mainly improves the following two aspects to make the fusion result more reliable.

a) For the accuracy of the original evidence, Liu et al. [32] used the average evidence to the original evidence, but did not consider the importance of each evidence. Chen zhe et al. [33] obtained the weight of evidence from the importance of each piece of evidence and made weighted correction, and obtained new evidence of the same importance, which is effective in dealing with high conflict situations. Wang Xuan [34] and others comprehensively considered the reliability and uncertainty of evidence to measure the discount coefficient of final fusion of evidence, and corrected the original evidence through the discount coefficient.

b) Improvement of Dempster evidence combination rule, Sun et al. [35] introduced the concept of credibility, but he believed that the credibility of all evidence was the same, and modified the synthesis rule by weighted summation. Han et al. [36] Divided the evidence into credible evidence and unreliable evidence by calculating the evidence distance, and introduced reliability entropy to measure the uncertainty of evidence. Guo Xinglin et al. [37] proposed an evidence conflict measurement method based on Pignistic probability transformation and singular value decomposition, which has wide adaptability and high accuracy in a variety of evidence conflict scenarios such as full conflict scenarios and variable reliability scenarios.

(3) Artificial neural network

The decision fusion method based on artificial neural network is suitable for multi-modal data fusion [25], and is suitable for government data which containing multiple modal data (such as video, voice, image and text). Compared with the feature level neural network method, the decision level fusion is further to fuse the semantics expressed by data features. Firstly, the data features of different modes are studied and trained, and the different training results are semantically described as multiple local decision results, and then the local decision results are fused as the input of decision fusion. In recent years, scholars improve the accuracy of local decision-making results by retaining information value, studying the correlation between modes, and discovering hidden information, to improve the reliability of the final decision-making fusion results.

Microsoft researcher He Xiaodong [38] and others proposed deep structured semantic model (DSSM) in 2013. By using deep neural network (DNN), two different modal data are expressed as low-dimensional semantic vectors, and the semantic similarity of the two modes can be calculated, which helps to retain the unique semantic description of each mode. The normalized discounted cumulative gain (ndcg) index is significantly better than the traditional late semantic analysis (LSA) and other methods, but the interaction between modes is not considered. Amir Zadeh et al. [39] proposed a memory fusion network (MFN) model to process the sequence of multiple views, establish the association relationship between different views in the time series, and compare it with the multi view learning method on multiple public benchmark data sets. The robustness and accuracy of the fusion results are optimal, but it has not been applied in practice. H Le et al. [40] proposed the multi-modal transformer network (MTN) to encode video frame sequences to obtain audio, image, and text semantic information that depends on the time sequence and then fuse them, and retains as much information value as possible. It has good performance in Visual Dialogue tasks. Holzinger A et al. [41] used graph neural network to fuse multimodal causal associations, and gave the measurable degree of causal understanding among images, texts and genomic data. Zhang et al. [42] proposed multi graph reasoning and fusion (MGRF) model to infer the spatial and semantic association of visual objects, explore the implicit relationship in multimodality, and designed interpretation generation module to demonstrate decision motivation, which has good interpretability.

2.4.3 Summary

The fusion of decision level is the fusion of the results of local decision-making, and its fusion results directly affect the practical application. Due to the high efficiency and fault tolerance of decision level fusion, it is suitable for multi-source cross media, cross language and other government scenes. Bayesian theory, D-S evidence theory and fusion method based on artificial neural network consider the richness and accuracy of information. Through the correlation, analysis and discrimination between data, the problems of low information value and unreliable decision-making results of government data are solved. However, due to the characteristics of cross departmental and real-time update of government data, the existing decision level fusion methods lack the research on real-time data processing. Also, the problem of cross departmental data security and privacy also brings challenges to data fusion.

3   Problems and Prospects

Government data fusion is an interdisciplinary problem. Combining existing research achievements, future research can proceed from the following questions:

(1) Security issues of data fusion

Nowadays, most research on data fusion focuses on how to improve the performance of algorithms and pays little attention to the security of data fusion. Government data is always applied to related fields such as public security and social management, so the data is sensitive and has high requirements for data security. Government data fusion makes the correlation between datasets closer and clearer, and the risk of data leakage also increases. Therefore, it is necessary to study the strategy of lowering data leakage risk and risk assessment model.

(2) Knowledge implicitness of data fusion

According to the above analysis, existing data fusion methods mainly focus on the integration and fusion of multi-source heterogeneous data itself, and lack of revealing and analyzing the deep knowledge behind the data. There is a wide range of government big data, which implies deep values such as social development and industry changes. For instance, in the field of public security, to achieve early warning, it is necessary to understand and summarize the rules behind the data. Therefore, it is necessary to study the implication of knowledge and analyze them.

(3) Evaluation system of data fusion

The evaluation system for data fusion should be comprehensive and supported by sufficient evidence. Currently, most data fusion methods are evaluated based on simulation or idealized assumptions. This made it difficult to make precise evaluations on the actual application effect of the modal. After research on the research paper of data fusion in the past 5 years, there is no universally accepted evaluation system for data fusion, especially data fusion methods for government data. Therefore, it is necessary to study how to build a sound evaluation system to effectively estimate the effect and value of data fusion.

4   Conclusions

This paper refines the difficulties and challenges of government data fusion from the characteristics of government data and the concept and development of data fusion. In response to the urgent need for government data fusion, an application framework for government data fusion is proposed. The technical development of the data level, feature level, and decision level fusion module is explained separately, and the fusion application scenarios at each level are further clarified. Further research directions are put forward, which provides a concise and comprehensive reference for researchers in the field of government data fusion.

References

1. White, F.E.: Data fusion lexicon (1991)
2. Hall, D.L., Llinas, J.: An introduction to multi-sensor data fusion (2016)
3. Shen, W.: Exploration for pudong new district government data integration service platform. Inf. Technol. Stand. 13–18 (2021)
4. Lau, B.P.L., et al.: A survey of data fusion in smart city applications. Inf. Fusion **52**, 357–374 (2019)
5. Yujie, C., Gang, L., Jin, M., Xiao, W.: Emergency information fusion oriented to the whole process of decision making in big data environment. Doc. Inf. Knowl. (5), 95–104 (2018)
6. Yi, Z., Yujun, C., Bowen, D., Juhua, P., Zhang, X.: Multimodal data fusion model for smart city (2016)
7. Jie, M., Yan, G., Hongyu, P., Yunkai, Z.: Intelligent city data fusion framework based on multi-source data. Libr. Inf. Serv. **63**(15), 6 (2019)
8. Lenzerini, M.: Tutorial-data integration: a theoretical perspective. In: Symposium on Principles of Database Systems, pp. 233–246 (2003)
9. Ping, W., Huang, F., Li, G., Liu, X.: Framework for multi-sources spatial data integration analysis. In: IEEE International Conference on Geoscience and Remote Sensing Symposium (2006)
10. Dong, W.X., Dong, B.B., Zheng, D.X., Yang, W.: Data governance technology. J. Softw. **9**(30), 2830–2856 (2019)
11. Zhou, J., Hong, X., Jin, P.: Information fusion for multi-source material data: progress and challenges. Appl. Sci. **9**(17), 3473 (2019)

12. Bohannon, P., Fan, W., Geerts, F., Jia, X., Kementsietsidis, A.: Conditional functional dependencies for data cleaning. In: IEEE 23rd International Conference on Data Engineering, ICDE 2007 (2007)
13. Chu, X., Ilyas, I.F., Papotti, P.: Holistic data cleaning: put violations into context (2013)
14. Xu, C., Jiang, L., Yue, P., Wu, Z., Liang, Z.: Study on government data sharing and spatial association based on linked data technology. J. Geomat. **45**(210(06)), 149–153 (2020)
15. Wang, Z., Zhang, D., Zhou, X., Yang, D., Yu, Z., Yu, Z.: Discovering and profiling overlapping communities in location-based social networks. IEEE Trans. Syst. Man Cybern. Syst. **44**(4), 499–509 (2013)
16. Yang, B., Li, S.: Multifocus image fusion and restoration with sparse representation. IEEE Trans. Instrum. Meas. **59**(4), 884–892 (2010)
17. Yu, N., Qiu, T., Bi, F., Wang, A.: Image features extraction and fusion based on joint sparse representation. IEEE J. Sel. Top. Signal Process. **5**(5), 1074–1082 (2011)
18. Zhang, H., Nasrabadi, N.M., Zhang, Y., Huang, T.S.: Multi-observation visual recognition via joint dynamic sparse representation. In: IEEE International Conference on Computer Vision, ICCV 2011, Barcelona, Spain, 6–13 November 2011 (2011)
19. Yan, J., Zheng, W., Xu, Q., Lu, G., Li, H., Bei, W.: Sparse kernel reduced-rank regression for bimodal emotion recognition from facial expression and speech. IEEE Trans. Multimedia **18**(7), 1319–1329 (2016)
20. Zhang, H., Patel, V.M., Chellappa, R.: Low-rank and joint sparse representations for multi-modal recognition. IEEE Trans. Image Process. **26**(10), 4741–4752 (2017)
21. Xin, Z.: Research on image feature representations based on deep neural network. Ph.D. thesis, National University of Defense Technology (2018)
22. Wenkai, W.: Text feature representation and sentiment analysis based on deep neural network (2018)
23. Krizhevsky, A., Sutskever, I., Hinton, G.E.: Imagenet classification with deep convolutional neural networks. Adv. Neural. Inf. Process. Syst. **25**, 1097–1105 (2012)
24. Zhang, X., et al.: Deep fusion of multiple semantic cues for complex event recognition. IEEE Trans. Image Process. **25**(3), 1033–1046 (2015)
25. Ngiam, J., Khosla, A., Kim, M., Nam, J., Lee, H., Ng, A.Y.: Multimodal deep learning. In: ICML (2011)
26. Srivastava, N., Salakhutdinov, R., et al.: Multimodal learning with deep Boltzmann machines. In: NIPS, vol. 1, p. 2. Citeseer (2012)
27. Zhao, L., Hu, Q., Wang, W.: Heterogeneous feature selection with multi-modal deep neural networks and sparse group lasso. IEEE Trans. Multimedia **17**(11), 1936–1948 (2015)
28. Rastegar, S., Soleymani, M., Rabiee, H.R., Shojaee, S.M.: MDL-CW: a multimodal deep learning framework with cross weights. In: Proceedings of the IEEE Conference on Computer Vision and Pattern Recognition, pp. 2601–2609 (2016)
29. Wang, G.-H., Mao, S.-Y., He, Y., Che, Z.-Y.: Optimal decision fusion when priori probabilities and risk functions are fuzzy. Inf. Fusion **5**(1), 5–14 (2004)
30. Xiao, H.H., Kui, Y.U., Wang, H.: The method of learning Bayesian networks combining association rules with knowledge. Microelectron. Comput. **25**(12), 7072 (2008)
31. Kharya, S., Soni, S., Swarnkar, T.: Weighted Bayesian association rule mining algorithm to construct Bayesian belief network. In: 2019 International Conference on Applied Machine Learning (ICAML), pp. 27–33. IEEE (2019)

32. Liu, X., Deng, J.: Improved DS method based on conflict evidence correction. J. Electron. Meas. Instrum. **31**(9), 1499–1506 (2017)
33. Chen, Z., Wang, J.-Y.: The research on evidence combination method based on conflict relation network. Acta Electonica Sinica **49**(1), 125 (2021)
34. Wang, X., Di, P., Yin, D.: Conflict evidence fusion method based on lance distance and credibility entropy. Syst. Eng. Electron. **9**(5), 1–14 (2021)
35. Sun, Q., Ye, X., Gu, W.: A new combination rules of evidence theory. Acta Electron. Sin. **28**(8), 117–119 (2000)
36. Han, D.-Q., Deng, Y., Han, C.-Z., Hou, Z.: Weighted evidence combination based on distance of evidence and uncertainty measure. J. Infrared Millim. Waves **30**(5), 396–400 (2011)
37. Guo, X., Sun, Z., Zhou, Y., Qi, L., Zhang, Y.: Evidence conflict measurement method based on pignistic probability transformation and singular value decomposition. J. Commun. **42**(4), 150–157 (2021)
38. Huang, P.-S., He, X., Gao, J., Deng, L., Acero, A., Heck, L.: Learning deep structured semantic models for web search using clickthrough data. In: Proceedings of the 22nd ACM International Conference on Information and Knowledge Management, pp. 2333–2338 (2013)
39. Zadeh, A., Liang, P.P., Mazumder, N., Poria, S., Morency, L.P.: Memory fusion network for multi-view sequential learning (2018)
40. Le, H., Sahoo, D., Chen, N.F., Hoi, S.: Multimodal transformer networks for end-to-end video-grounded dialogue systems. In: Meeting of the Association for Computational Linguistics (2019)
41. Holzinger, A., Malle, B., Saranti, A., Pfeifer, B.: Towards multi-modal causability with graph neural networks enabling information fusion for explainable AI. Inf. Fusion **71**(7639), 28–37 (2021)
42. Zhang, W., Yu, J., Zhao, W., Ran, C.: DMRFNet: deep multimodal reasoning and fusion for visual question answering and explanation generation. Inf. Fusion **72**(3), 70–79 (2021)

Data Exploration and Mining on Traditional Chinese Medicine

Xueyan Li[1], Chuitian Rong[2(✉)], Zhengyi Chai[1], and Huabo Sun[3]

[1] School of Computer Science and Technology, Tiangong University, Tianjin, China
1930081303@tiangong.edu.cn
[2] Tianjin Key Laboratory of Autonomous Intelligence Technology and Systems,
School of Computer Science and Technology, Tiangong University, Tianjin, China
chuitian@tiangong.edu.cn
[3] Institute of Aviation Safety, China Academy of Civil Aviation Science and
Technology, Beijing, China

Abstract. The theory of traditional Chinese medicine (TCM) has been developed for a long history and accumulated plenty of knowledge about combating diseases, which is a part of Chinese culture. There have been some related works to analyze TCM data but lack comprehensive insights. With the development of big data analysis technology, it brings new ways to get deep insights from TCM data. In this work, we applied big data techniques to explore the latent knowledge and information of TCM data. The data comes from *Chinese Pharmacopoeia* and famous ancient classics. We extracted the important attributes of herbs and prescriptions then conducted comprehensive analysis. Specifically, the extracted data are explored and mined by applying the following techniques: statistical analysis, clustering, association rules mining, topic model analysis and so on. By doing above analysis, we have drawn many important unknown conclusions from TCM data and explored the latent patterns and knowledge of it. The results of this paper is helpful to verify the TCM theory and provide assistance and reference to the clinical process. In order to increase the practicability of our discoveries, we developed a system to provide data exploration and visualization.

Keywords: TCM · Data mining · Data exploration

Mathematics Subject Classification (2020): CR H.2.8

1 Introduction

TCM is a part of traditional Chinese culture and has been developed for thousands of years. In this process, it accumulated some achievements of fighting against diseases. Meanwhile, it plays an important role in health care and cures patients by prescriptions, acupuncture, diet therapy and so on. Prescription is the most common therapy method in clinical practice and composed of multiple

X. Liao et al. (Eds.): BigData 2021, CCIS 1496, pp. 56–70, 2022.
https://doi.org/10.1007/978-981-16-9709-8_5

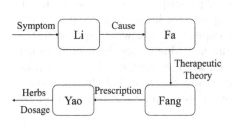

Fig. 1. *Li-Fa-Fang-Yao* in TCM

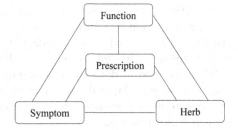

Fig. 2. Data connection in TCM

herbs. It is of great values to explore and there have been some researches to discover the knowledge of TCM data. However, a large proportion of them just focused on the prescriptions with some specific functions. Due to the lack of data diversity, they cannot do representative and thorough analysis, such as analyzing the common characteristics of prescriptions and herbs. In addition, there are a few researches to explore the traditional and classic therapeutic prescriptions.

With the rapid development of data mining, there are many technologies providing strong support for data analysis. Meanwhile, more and more authentic TCM data can be collected conveniently. In order to understand the inherent principles of TCM data more deeply, we explored and mined TCM data, including the herbs and prescriptions. We applied the following techniques in the experiment, such as statistical analysis, clustering, association rules mining, topic model analysis, and so on. Furthermore, for the convenience of utilizing our experimental results, we developed a system to provide data exploration and visualization on the website.

In this study, the details of data will be explored and analyzed by the guidance of the classics of TCM, such as *Sheng Nong's herbal classic* and *Inner Canon of the Yellow Emperor* (the most authoritative text of early medical theory and drug therapy). Herbs, the component of prescriptions, are the ingredients extracted from the plants and have functions of physical therapy. Prescriptions, composed of several herbs with different doses, have functions on specific organs and symptoms. Except that, there are some other basic knowledge, such as *li-fa-fang-yao* and *four diagnostic methods*. For instance, *li-fa-fang-yao* elaborates the process of diagnose and treatment as shown in Fig. 1. It represents the pathogenesis of the disease, the methods of treatment, appropriate prescriptions and the best choice of herbs respectively. Based on this we try to explore the relationships among herbs, symptoms and functions as shown in Fig. 2.

Overall, this work can be divided into two parts: data processing and data analysis. In the first part, we collected the data from *Chinese Pharmacopoeia(Ch.P.)* and famous ancient classics. Specifically, it contains the composition of herbs, functions, symptoms for prescriptions. On the other hand, it contains the natures, flavors, meridian tropisms for herbs. In the second part, the data of herbs and prescriptions will be explored in following aspects: statistical analysis, clustering, association rules mining. Finally, the discovered results will be presented by data visualization techniques. This work is helpful to explore the knowledge of TCM data and verify the traditional classical clinical theory. It also can provide great reference and support to the practical work, especially for the junior practitioners.

2   Related Works

2.1   Data Mining

In recent years, the technology of data mining and many kinds of classical algorithms have been great developed, which have a great impact on data analysis. [1] pointed out most of important data mining algorithms including classification, clustering, prediction and association rules mining, etc.al. Clustering algorithms has been applied in many areas. [2] summarized the most relevant method and provided comparisons of them. Association rules mining is also widely used in data analysis. [3] introduced the characteristics and principles of association rules mining algorithms. Topic model is one of the most commonly used and influential method in the area of data mining for the text analysis. This model can discover the latent relationships among text data or documents. It has been widely used in all kinds of area, such as engineering course and linguistics. [4] summarized different variants of LDA in recent years.

2.2   Analysis of TCM Data

The applications of data mining in TCM have been proposed in some works but lack comprehensiveness. For instance, [5] applied the association rules mining to TCM data. [6] also utilized Aprior to explore the relationships between prescriptions and symptoms of insomnia. There are some other works proposed to apply topic model on TCM data. [7] raised their own model based on LDA to explore the process of prescription generation, including the recommendation of herbs and the suggestion of symptoms.

In addition, the knowledge graph also has been applied in this area. [8] established the knowledge graph by exploring the regulation and features of prescriptions. [9] build a system based on TCM data to the literature retrieval and information queries.

3   Data

The data all we used is collected from *Ch.P.* and famous ancient classics about TCM. *Ch.P.* is the most authentic standard of drugs in China and compiled by *Chinese Pharmacopoeia Commission*. The source of data guarantees the authenticity and accuracy of experiments. By the guidance of the classical theories of

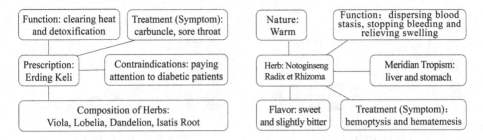

Fig. 3. Attributes of prescription   **Fig. 4.** Attributes of herb

TCM, the data attributes of prescriptions selected and used in this work are components, functions and symptoms. For herbs, data of functions, natures, flavors and meridian tropisms are selected.

3.1   Data Processing

As for one prescription, the original data includes the following contents: id, name, composition of herbs, processing method, function, symptoms, contraindication and so on. These contents were collected by *web crawler*, then we selected what we need through *the regular match expressions*, including id, composition of herbs, function and symptom. In this processing, considering existing the different names of same herbs or functions, these contents were replaced by the one standard. Meanwhile, we also utilized *pandas* to remove the default value. Finally, these words would be segmented.

As for one herb, the original data includes id, name, identification, function, symptom, nature, flavor, meridian tropism, contraindication and so on. The data processing of herb is similar to prescription and we select its function, symptom, nature, flavor and meridian tropism.

3.2   The Characteristics of Data

Through unified processing, we got more than 50,000 prescriptions and more than 600 herbs. Take the prescription *Erding Keli* as an example, its representative attributes are shown in Fig. 3, including component of *Viola, Lobelia, Dandelion, Isatis Root* and so on. The herb *Notoginseng Radix et Rhizoma* is shown in Fig. 4, including the warm nature and so on. Except that, relationships among these data were shown in Fig. 2, which is connected by the straight line. The straight line represents there is a connection between the two items, such as the symptom and function.

4   The Statistical Analysis of Herbs and Prescriptions

In this part, we will analyze the data of prescriptions and herbs by token frequency. The most commonly emerged content of data frequency will be computed.

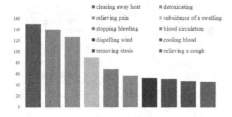

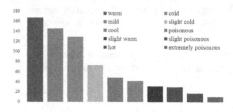

Fig. 5. Herb functions

Fig. 6. Herb natures

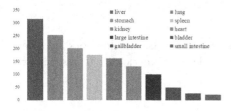

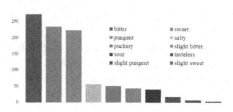

Fig. 7. Herb meridian tropisms

Fig. 8. Herb flavors

4.1   Analysis of Herbs

Herbs are the basic component of prescriptions. It contain the attributes of functions, natures, flavors and meridian tropisms. The results of token frequency are shown in the following figures. Figure 5 shows the top10 functions of herbs, including *clearing away heat*, *detoxicating* and *relieving pain*, etc. al. In this result, the number of herb can *clear away heat* is 150 and there are 127 kinds herbs can *relieve pain*. It is obvious we can see that most herbs have the functions of *clearing away heat* and *detoxicating*. Figure 6 shows the rank of herb natures and they mainly perform *warm*, *cold* or *mild*, which are aroused 167, 145 and 129 times. Figure 7 shows the meridian tropism of herbs, from it we can see the emerged times of the top are 315, 253 and 202. It means the targeted organs of herbs are mostly liver, lung or stomach. Figure 8 shows the results of flavors and it is obvious that most of herbs taste bitter and even appeared 272 times.

4.2   Analysis of Prescriptions

The prescription is one of the most common method used to recover health. It is composed of many herbs and has some specific functions. In this part, the number of herbs, functions and symptoms emerged in prescriptions are computed and results are shown in following figures. From Fig. 9 we can see in the all prescriptions, *Glycyrrhizae Radix Et Rhizoma* are used 14,329 times and the number of *Angelicae Sinensis Radix* used is 9,257. So, we draw the conclusion that the most commonly used herbs include *Glycyrrhizae Radix Et Rhizoma*, *Angelicae Sinensis Radix* and *Poria*. Figure 10 and Fig. 11 show the rank of their functions

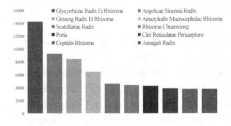

Fig. 9. Herbs in prescriptions

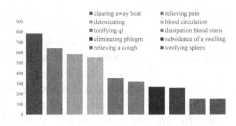

Fig. 10. Prescription functions

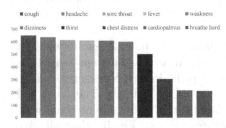

Fig. 11. Prescription symptoms

Fig. 12. Homepage of TCM system

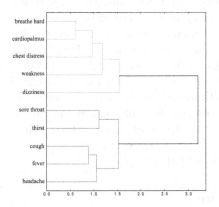

Fig. 13. Cluster of symptoms in prescription

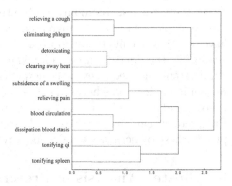

Fig. 14. Cluster of functions in prescription

and treatments respectively. It can be seen 784 prescriptions have the function of *clearing away heat*, 644 prescriptions have the functions of *relieving pain* and 587 prescriptions can *detoxicate*. Meanwhile, 651 prescriptions can relieve cough, 637 prescriptions have effects on headache and 615 prescriptions can treat the symptom of sore throat. In a word, these two results are corresponding in some aspects and consistent in general. For instance, to treat the symptom of a cough, the prescriptions usually need to have the function of clearing away heat.

4.3 Overall Analysis

The data diversities of herbs and prescriptions can reflect in many aspects, such as symptoms, functions and so on. Take herbs as example, one herb can play many roles of functions and the same function can be played by different herbs. For instance, the herb *Glycyrrhizae Radix Et Rhizoma* can not only *clear away heat*, but also can *detoxicate*. On the other hand, in addition to *Glycyrrhizae Radix Et Rhizoma*, the herb *Isatidis Radix* also has the function of *clearing away heat*. As for prescriptions, the prescription with one specific function can have multiple choices of its composition, each of which can be composed of many different herbs. On the other hand, it can be found that the statistical results of herbs and prescriptions have some cross and consistence from the results of above. For instance, most herbs can *clear away heat* and the most functions of prescriptions are the same.

In these experiments we analyzed the attributes of herbs and prescriptions and found it is consistent with the theory of TCM. For instance, they represented the theory of *li-fa-fang-yao*, *tropism* and many *herb pairs*. In the process of the clinic, firstly, doctors observe and ask about symptoms of the patients. Then they will analyze these symptoms belong to which classification and combine them with relevant knowledge to find best method to process disease. Finally, they will give the corresponding prescriptions composed of different types and dosage herbs. For example, some herbs with the functions of *clearing away the heat* usually used to treatment of the *cough* and *fever*. On the other hand, we found there are some herbs not usually used in the treatment of some symptoms. For instance, *Cicadae Periostracum* is not commonly used to treat cold but still have some effects on it. We can explore what active ingredient consists in it. Furthermore, different herbs have functions to different symptoms, if some new herbs all have functions on one syndrome, the doctors can explore what are the common active ingredients and study latent knowledge, even the new effects. Finally, according to the experiment we can infer that some herbs also have effects on specific symptoms and maybe it is not found by people, such as those extremely low frequency herbs in the results. Practitioners can analyze these rarely appeared herbs, and explore what roles they play in these prescriptions and wonder what effects they have.

5 Cluster Analysis of Prescriptions

The algorithm of cluster is the method based on the computation of similarities among different items. Using this method can not only find the latent regulation of complex data, but also provides valuable knowledge and information. It can also generate the tree of cluster, in which the nodes represent different items and the lines represent relationships between them.

Prescriptions are practical results in the clinical, which contains a variety of information. In this part, hierarchical cluster analysis method was used to explore the prescriptions data. On the one hand, it has the simpler algorithm and faster speed of computation, and can get the results more accurately and quickly. On the other hand, it has the more intuitive experimental results to help

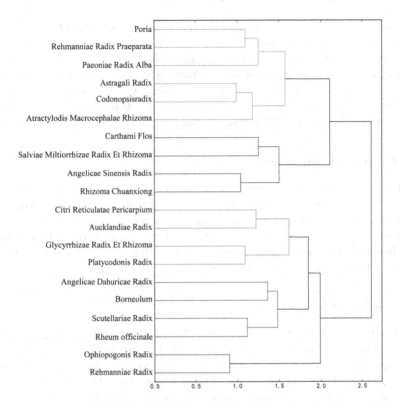

Fig. 15. Cluster of herbs in prescriptions

us analyze. For instance, the relationships of the attributes of prescriptions can be observed conveniently, such as connections of the different herbs, even their classifications. Take the functions as examples, the herbs having some specific effects will be put together. Similar to the herbs, the combination of herbs and symptoms also can be represented. As multiple clusters formed, similar classes are marked in same colors. For instance, the relationships among herbs used in prescriptions can be summarized and explained by the picture clearly. The results of hierarchical cluster also can provide the reference information to the generation of prescriptions. In addition, it can get the results of syndromes, which are the similar symptoms. The functions of prescriptions also can be explored in the same way. Finally, the most important thing is that we can choose the low frequency words of herbs or other contents to do this experiment. It can help us to find the potential value of these rarely used herbs, and even can find some new collocations or functions of them.

5.1   Cluster of Herbs

We select top20 high frequency herbs to analyze the connection among them and the results are shown in Fig. 15. Take the content in yellow as examples, the herb *Poria* and *Rehmanniae Radix Praeparata* have close connection, and both of them are related to the herb *Paeoniae Radix Alba*. Referring to the *Ch.P.*, it can be obviously found that they all have similar functions and effects on same organs. For instance, *Poria* and *Rehmanniae Radix Praeparata* both have effects on curing the *cardiopalmus* and *insomnia*. On the other hand, *Poria*, *Rehmanniae Radix Praeparata* and *Paeoniae Radix Alba* all can treat headache and dizziness. So, three of them can be classified as the same kind of drugs.

5.2　Cluster of Functions

The top10 functions are selected to be analyzed and the result is shown in Fig. 14. Take part of them as examples, *relieving a cough* is always along with *eliminating phlegm* and *clearing away heat* is usually along with *detoxicating*. This result is consistent with the practical clinical experience. When patients suffer from *excessive internal heat*, practitioners often make a diagnosis and give treatment having the functions of *clearing away heat* and *detoxicating*.

5.3　Cluster of Symptoms

We select the top10 results to analyze the cluster of symptoms shown in Fig. 13. This analysis also can be combined with our life experience. For instance, it can be seen sore throat and thirst always appear together frequently. The fever always occurs with cough and both of them follow with the headache. Finally, all of them belong to one class, which is consistent with the symptoms when catching the cold.

5.4　Cluster of Prescriptions Based on Topic Model

Topic model is a statistical model to cluster and analyze the content of text. It can analyze the words in the text through unsupervised learning and determine what topic words included in. Compared with the traditional topic models, LinkLDA [7] has the better performance on consistency and coherence of topic semantics, and rarely generates unexplained topics. So we utilized LinkLDA to the cluster of the prescriptions.

In this part, all content of prescriptions is contained in training data, including composition of herbs, functions and symptoms. From that, the latent semantic structure and information can be found and the results are shown in Table 1. For example, the first topic is the symptoms about *clearing away heat* and *detoxicating*, including their corresponding herbs. It is obvious that this topic is along with cough, sore throat and other symptoms, which is consistent with our life experience. On the other hand, *Glycyrrhizae Radix Et Rhizoma* and *Angelicae Sinensis Radix* have the function of *clearing away heat*, *Scutellariae Radix* and *Platycodonis Radix* can detoxicate, but *Poria* seems not mainly work on this. Except that, it can find herbs rarely appeared in prescriptions also have effects on some symptoms. According to these results, the new application of herb in different prescriptions can be found. For example, in the third result *Houttuyniae Herba* is clustered with the functions of *relieving cough* and *eliminating phlegm*. This usage is not usually seen in the common treatment. In fact, *Houttuyniae Herba* really has the functions of *clearing away the heat, detoxicating* and so on. From this perspective, the corresponding ingredients in this herb can be explored. On the other hand, it can infer some attentions in the clinical. For example, we found that *Gardeniae Fructus* is usually along with *menorrhagia*. One of its functions is *blood circulation* and will cause the *increasing of bleeding*. So, we inferred it is not suitable for the patient during menstruation.

Table 1. Cluster of prescriptions using LinkLDA

No.	Topic	Symptoms	Herbs
1	Clearing away heat, detoxicating, tonifying spleen, relieving a cough	Cough, sore throat, fever, headache, dizziness	Glycyrrhizae Radix Et Rhizoma, Scutellariae Radix, Poria, Angelicae Sinensis Radix, Platycodonis Radix Alba, Citri Reticulatae Pericarpium, Atractylodis Macrocephalae Rhizoma
2	Blood circulation, relaxing the bowels, regulating qi, helping digestion	Pain, menorrhagia, fullness of chest and abdomen	Citri Reticulatae Pericarpium, Rheum officinale, Gardeniae Fructus, Chuanxiong Rhizoma, Aucklandiae Radix
2	Relieving cough, eliminating phlegm, diminish inflammation, relieving asthma	Asthmatic cough, bronchitis, pharyngitis	Adenophorae Radix, Andrographis Herba, Papaveris Pericarpium, Stemonae Radix, Pseudostellariae Radix, Descurainiae Semen Lepidii Semen, Cynanchi Stauntonii Rhizoma Et Radix, Houttuyniae Herba

6 Association Rules Mining of Prescriptions

The algorithm of Eclat and FP-growth are widely used in data analysis to find frequent itemsets and association rules. We select them to explore the regulation and relationships among the attributes of TCM data by setting the value of support and confidence. Eclat is one of the depth-first algorithms. It utilizes the vertical data representation to find itemsets and has a high efficiency. FP-growth is put forward to analyze the association rules. The data of itemsets will be put into a FP-tree and the association information of itemsets is also remained.

In this section, the frequent itemsets of data were firstly generated, including 2-itemsets and 3-itemsets. Based on frequent itemsets, the associations rules were generated, including herbs to symptoms, functions to symptoms and so on. By doing this, the latent information and knowledge of TCM data can be discovered and verified, such as herb pairs and others regulations.

6.1 Frequent Itemsets

In this part, we applied Eclat to find frequent itemsets, including 2-itemsets and 3-itemsets. This data is analyzed in five aspects, such as herb pairs and so on.

Table 2. Herb pairs

2-itemsets	3-itemsets
Platycodonis Radix, Glycyrrhizae Radix Et Rhizoma	Platycodonis Radix, Forsythiae Fructus, Glycyrrhizae Radix Et Rhizoma
Glycyrrhizae Radix Et Rhizoma, Scutellariae Radix	Platycodonis Radix, Scutellariae Radix, Glycyrrhizae Radix Et Rhizoma
Glycyrrhizae Radix Et Rhizoma, Poria	Glycyrrhizae Radix Et Rhizoma, Poria, Citri Reticulatae Pericarpium

Table 3. Functions

2-itemsets	3-itemsets
Clearing away heat, detoxicating	Clearing away heat, relieving pain, detoxicating
Clearing away heat, relieving pain	Subsidence of a swelling, clearing away heat, detoxicating
Relieving pain, dissipation blood stasis	Relieving pain, blood circulation, subsidence of a swelling

Table 4. Functions and herbs

2-itemsets	3-itemsets
Rhizoma Chuanxiong, *blood circulation*	Rhizoma Chuanxiong, *blood circulation, subsidence of a swelling*
Scutellariae Radix, *clearing away heat*	Scutellariae Radix, *clearing away heat, detoxicating*
Forsythiae Fructus, *detoxicating*	Angelicae Sinensis Radix, *relieving pain, blood circulation*

Table 5. Symptoms and herbs

2-itemsets	3-itemsets
cough, Platycodonis Radix	*cough*, Platycodonis Radix, Glycyrrhizae Radix Et Rhizoma
sore throat, Scutellariae Radix	*sore throat*, Forsythiae Fructus, Scutellariae Radix
fever, Lonicerae Japonicae Flos	*headache*, Menthae Haplocalycis Herba, Glycyrrhizae Radix Et Rhizoma

Table 6. Targeted organs of herbs

2-itemsets	3-itemsets
clearing away heat, lung	*clearing away heat, detoxicating*, liver
relieving pain, liver	*relieving pain*, liver, stomach
eliminating phlegm, lung	*clearing away heat*, lung, stomach

For instance, Table 2 shows herb pairs, referring to the mostly used collocations of herbs, such as *Platycodonis Radix* and *Glycyrrhizae Radix Et Rhizoma*, *Glycyrrhizae Radix Et Rhizoma*, *Poria* and *Citri Reticulatae Pericarpium*. Table 3 shows the common collocations of prescriptions functions. For example, one prescription has the function of *clearing away heat* also can *detoxicate*. According to Table 4, we find the most common collocations of functions and herbs. For example, *Scutellariae Radix* can *clear away heat* and *detoxicate*, but it is more frequently used to *clear away heat*. Table 5 shows the relationships between herbs and symptoms, which mean common collocations of symptoms and herbs. These results are also consistent with the TCM theory of prescribing a medicine special for the disease. For instance, *Glycyrrhizae Radix Et Rhizoma* is commonly used to cure sore throat. Table 6 shows the relationship between targeted organ and herbs, the functions of *clearing away heat* and *relieving a cough* always work on lung.

Table 7. Prescription herbs

Association rules	Confidence
{Scutellariae Radix, Coptidis Rhizoma} → Glycyrrhizae Radix Et Rhizoma	0.94
{Perillae Folium, Citri Reticulatae Pericarpium} → Platycodonis Radix	0.75
{Glycyrrhizae Radix Et Rhizoma, Poria} → Angelicae Sinensis Radix	0.64

Table 8. Functions

Association rules	Confidence
{dissipation blood stasis, subsidence of a swelling} → relieving pain	0.95
{blood circulation, subsidence of a swelling} → relieving pain	0.85
{relieving pain, detoxicating} → clearing away heat	0.84

Table 9. Symptoms and herbs

Association rules	Confidence
{*sore throat, cold*, Glycyrrhizae Radix Et Rhizoma} → Platycodonis Radix	0.94
{*fever*, Schizonepetae Herba} → Platycodonis Radix	0.93
sore throat → {Lonicerae Japonicae Flos, Forsythiae Fructus}	0.91

Table 10. Herbs and functions

Association rules	Confidence
{Forsythiae Fructus, Chrysanthemi Flos} → *clearing away heat*	0.94
{Gardeniae Fructus, Platycodonis Radix, Menthae Haplocalycis Herba} → *clearing away heat*	0.94
Menthae Haplocalycis Herba → *clearing away heat*	0.93

6.2 Association Rules

On the basis of frequent itemsets, we utilize FP-growth to explore associations rules by setting the values of confidence. It can get the associations among attributes of data and the results are shown in following tables. For example, Table 7 shows the value of confidence among *Scutellariae Radix, Coptidis Rhizoma* and *Glycyrrhizae Radix Et Rhizoma* is 0.94. This value reflects the association in items. The higher values, the higher associations. So, we conclude that the herb *Scutellariae Radix, Coptidis Rhizoma* and *Glycyrrhizae Radix Et Rhizoma* are highly associated and usually used together. In Table 8, the confidence of *relieving pain, detoxicating* and *clearing away heat* is 0.84. It shows common collocations of prescription functions, which means *relieving pain* and *detoxicating* always along with *clearing away heat*. The common collocations of symptoms and herbs are shown in Table 9. For example, the confidence of sore throat, *Lonicerae Japonicae Flos* and *Forsythiae Fructus* is 0.91. It means when sore throat is treated, the herbs *Lonicerae Japonicae Flos* and *Forsythiae Fructus* are usually used in the prescription. Same with Table 9, Table 10 shows the associations of herbs and functions. For instance, the confidence of *Menthae Haplocalycis Herba* and *clearing away heat* is 0.93. It means when someone use the herb *Menthae Haplocalycis Herba*, he usually needs to *clear away heat*. Table 11 explains the targeted organ of herbs. For example, the confidence of *helping to digest* and stomach is 0.89. It means the doctors should concentrate on the stomach if patients are with the symptom of indigestion.

Table 11. Targeted organs of herbs

Association rules	Confidence
{*relieve uneasiness of mind and body tranquilization*} → heart	0.90
{*helping to digest*} → stomach	0.89
{*eliminating phlegm*} → lung	0.89

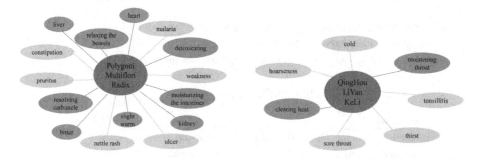

Fig. 16. Searching result of herb   **Fig. 17.** Searching result of function

7 System of TCM Information

This system is designed for the visualization and search for TCM data on the basis of knowledge graph. The results of data analysis are also shown in this system. It is convenient for people to look through the different information and knowledge about TCM. As shown in Fig. 12, people can choose something they want to know and click the related button to view the corresponding data, such as the content of herb and prescriptions, also including the association rules of them. Figure 16 shows the search result of herb, take *Polygoni Multiflori Radix* as an example, its attributes will be shown. It has the function of *detoxicating* and can treat constipation. Figure 17 shows the functions and symptoms of one prescription, take *QingHouLiYanKeLi* as an example, it can treat sore throat and cold.

8 Conclusion

In this paper, the data of TCM was collected and analyzed by many methods. The source of data guaranteed the accuracy of the experiment and the important attributes of data were collected, such as functions and symptoms of prescriptions. Then these data were analyzed by algorithm of cluster, association rules mining and other methods. Meanwhile, the results were also shown in the system. This work not only explored the latent information and knowledge of TCM data, but also inherited the traditional Chinese culture to let other people know. Besides, it also provides precious reference to the clinical practitioners. In future work, we will apply more theory of TCM to this work, for example, the role of herbs playing in prescriptions can be explored with the theory of *jun-chen-zuo-shi*, and the dosage of the herbs also can be analyzed.

Acknowledgment. This work was supported by the project of Natural Science Foundation of China (No. 61972456) and the Natural Science Foundation of Tianjin (No. 19JCYBJC15400, No. 21YDTPJC00440).

References

1. Wu, X., et al.: Top 10 algorithms in data mining. Knowl. Inf. Syst. **14**(1), 1–37 (2008)
2. Mahdi, M.A., Hosny, K.M., El-Henawy, I.M.: Scalable clustering algorithms for big data: a review. IEEE Access **9**, 80015–80027 (2021)
3. Kishore, S., Bhushan, V., Suneetha, K.R.: Applications of association rule mining algorithms in deep learning. In: Smys, S., Palanisamy, R., Rocha, Á., Beligiannis, G.N. (eds.) Computer Networks and Inventive Communication Technologies. LNDECT, vol. 58, pp. 351–362. Springer, Singapore (2021). https://doi.org/10.1007/978-981-15-9647-6_27
4. Jelodar, H., et al.: Latent Dirichlet allocation (LDA) and topic modeling: models, applications, a survey. Multimed. Tools Appl. **78**(11), 15169–15211 (2018). https://doi.org/10.1007/s11042-018-6894-4

5. Chen, W., He, S.: Application of data mining technology in TCM diagnosis and treatment. In: IEEE International Conference on Bioinformatics and Biomedicine, Proceedings - 2017 IEEE International Conference on Bioinformatics and Biomedicine, BIBM 2017, pp. 1350–1353, January 2017

6. Ye, Y., Xu, B., Ma, L., Zhu, J., Shi, H., Cai, X.: Research on treatment and medication rule of insomnia treated by TCM based on data mining. In: 2019 IEEE International Conference on Bioinformatics and Biomedicine (BIBM), pp. 2503–2508 (2019)

7. Yao, L., Zhang, Y., Wei, B., Zhang, W., Jin, Z.: A topic modeling approach for traditional Chinese medicine prescriptions. IEEE Trans. Knowl. Data Eng. **30**(6), 1007–1021 (2018)

8. Xiao, R., Hu, F., Pei, W., Bie, M.: Research on traditional Chinese medicine data mining model based on traditional Chinese medicine basic theories and knowledge graphs. In: ACM International Conference Proceeding Series, pp. 102–106 (2020)

9. Zhou, Y., Qi, X., Huang, Y., Ju, F.: Research on construction and application of TCM knowledge graph based on ancient Chinese texts. In: Proceedings - 2019 IEEE/WIC/ACM International Conference on Web Intelligence Workshops, WI 2019 Companion, pp. 144–147. ACM (2019)

Comparative Analysis of Hadoop MapReduce and Spark Based on People's Livelihood Appeal Data

Lixin Liang, Heng Zhao[✉], and Yongan Shen

College of Big data and Internet, Shenzhen technology university,
3002 Road Lantian, ShenZhen 518118, China
lianglixin@sztu.edu.cn, 15186958102@163.com,
shenyongan2019@email.szu.edu.cn

Abstract. In data research area, one of the most challenging issues is how to extract the key information from massive data with high efficiency. Hadoop and Spark are two widely studied and utilized frameworks for distributed data processing. Hadoop is a disk-based storage and processing system which could break down large dataset into smaller pieces and carry out data processing parallelly. However, especially for the programming framework of MapReduce, it encounters the problem of low speed and high cost in both data reading and writing. Hadoop reads the data sequentially from the beginning and reads the entire data set from the disk instead of the portion needed. Spark, because of its in-memory based processing, effectively avoids many problems in Hadoop. Following the set of vertices and edges called Directed Acyclic Graph (DAG), Spark does not need to repeatedly read and write data from the disk, and reveals much higher efficiency in data processing. In this paper, we will conduct comparative analysis of Hadoop MapReduce and Spark based on people's Livelihood appeal data which is obtained from Pingshan district, Shenzhen, China.

Keywords: Big data · Distributed data processing · MapReduce · Hadoop · Spark

1 Introduction

With the rapid development of society and living standard, the amount of people's livelihood appeal data has increased sharply in recent years. Under such a challenging background, relevant government departments must process these data through emerging and foremost big data technologies, instead of inefficient traditional methods. However, there are already a large number of successful cases about the application of big data technologies, such as health care [1,2],

H. Zhao and Y. Shen—Contributed equally to this work.

intelligent energy management [3,4], smart transportation [5,6], infections prediction [7], as well as smart cities [8,9]. Based on these successful cases, big data technologies have helped the government to solve many social issues [10–13].

Hadoop [14] and Spark [15] are two mainstream frameworks in the field of big data, which is applied to academia and industry. Hadoop is a distributed large data processing framework, primely including Hadoop Distributed File System (HDFS) [16] and MapReduce [17]. Hadoop has extensive applications in source camera identification [18], security and privacy [19], stock market prediction [20] and sports performance prediction [21]. Furthermore, its file storage [22] and performance optimization [23] are researched broadly. Spark is another superior framework that avoids many drawbacks of Hadoop such as time cost, algorithm complexity and storage [24]. Spark is suitable for real-time analysis such as trending hashtags on Twitter [25,26], recommendation system [27,28], traffic analysis [29,30] and computing Heart Rate Variability (HRV) [31].

They are studied and compared in numerous research fields, like performance analysis [32,33], image classification [34], real-time data analysis [35], machine learning algorithms [36–38]. and genetic algorithms [39]. However, the speed of reading data and writing data between them is not paid sufficient attention.

In this paper, both Hadoop and Spark are evaluated and compared. Specifically, we will conduct some studies based on people's livelihood appeal data which is obtained from Pingshan district, Shenzhen, China, including the time of retrieving data from different parts of the dataset, fetching out various numbers of data from the largest type of data in the dataset, fetching out the data from different part of the sorted dataset, as well as writing out and inserting various numbers of data in different parts of the original dataset. Ultimately, these researches conclude that spark has many advantages over Hadoop.

This article is organized as follows. Section 2 introduces the distinct characteristics between Hadoop MapReduce and Spark, and illustrates related study methods. Section 3 compares the results of corresponding research methods. Section 4 makes the comprehensive conclusions of comparative analysis.

2   Materials and Methods

In recent years, Hadoop MapReduce is criticized in three ways: lack of sufficient support for the expression of existing business logic, huge cost of disk input and output, and higher latency for the large dataset in data processing.

Specifically, the cost of disk input and output is due to the fact that in Hadoop's MapReduce, the Map function constantly writes data to the disk and the Reduce function obtains data from the disk. Especially for iterative calculation, Map outputs the temporary result to the disk and Reduce gains it from the disk in each iteration. Thus, the time cost increases dramatically with the number of iterations. However, in Spark framework, the intermediate results can be artificially cached in random access memory (RAM), which save the time of each input and output of the disk. For instance, during an iterative calculation with 100 times of epoch, the MapReduce of Hadoop would have to repeat the same process of input and output 100 times. In contrast. Spark only reads the data from the disk one time and then store it in the RAM. By eliminating the process of disk input and output, the speed of the same calculation could increase significantly.

The testing dataset of people's livelihood appeal data (7941968 items) is obtained from Pingshan district, Shenzhen, China. Due to the hardware and other factors, there are some abnormal values in the experimental data, so we need to pre-process all experimental data. The pre-processing is as follows: after fetching the average of the data, the data with a value between 0.9 and 1.1 times of the average is deemed valid, and the rest of the data is deemed invalid. After removing the invalid data, the rest is the final data for experiment.

2.1 Fetching One Data

For data processing, one of the most common operations is to fetch data, such as fetching one data from different location of the dataset, and fetching various size of data cluster from the dataset. In this section, we will focus on fetching one data from different location of the dataset, and the location includes the top, middle and end. Apparently, the result would be the time cost, besides each process could be studied in different repeating times.

For MapReduce, The Map task would store data in the disk and then Reduce task will obtain it. The method of time recording uses the system time as the starting time, gives it to the global counter when obtaining the target data, then gets the time at the Driver side. Therefore, the duration of the process is the mission starting time - the value of global counter. The entire process is shown in Fig. 1.

For Spark, all the data obtained are stored in the resilient distributed dataset (RDDs) [40]. When Spark finds out the target data, it gets the system time and counts the running times. Both the target data and the running time would be written out from RDDs. MapReduce does not support global variables. Due to its distributed operation characteristics, the counter values in the map and reduce phases exist in the corresponding Map Task or Reduce Task. Only when all tasks are executed and summarized to the Driver will the counters be summarized separately, which means that the correct counter value can only be obtained at the final Driver side. Spark fetches one data as shown in Fig. 2. Spark reads data directly into memory for processing, while MapReduce needs to read data from the hard disk every time.

In a group of data, there are 3 typical locations: the top, the middle and the end. By fetching the data from these 3 locations in the people's livelihood appeal dataset, both MapReduce and Spark would have different operation steps with repeating times, which means that the time cost could be influenced.

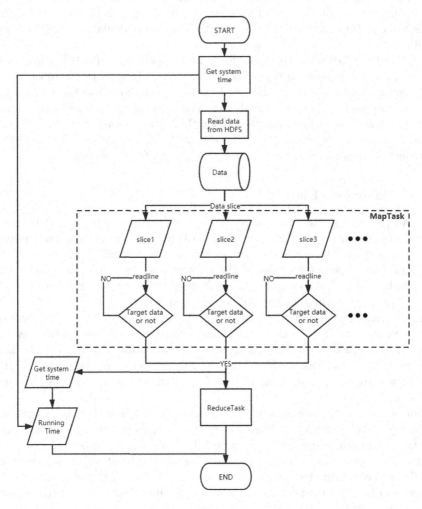

Fig. 1. Fetching one data (MapReduce)

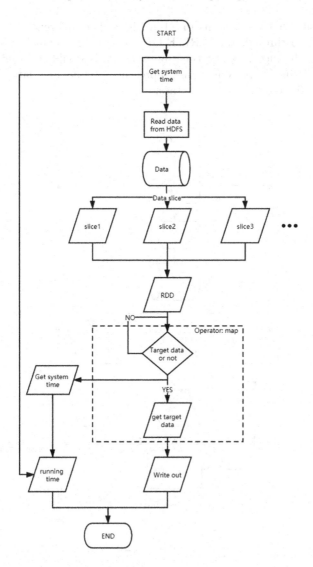

Fig. 2. Fetching one data (Spark)

2.2   Fetching Different Size of Dataset

Besides the location of target data, the size of dataset is also a typical variable that could have impact on the data processing efficiency. The different size of dataset includes one data, the whole dataset and half of the dataset. Specifically, we filter out the type of data with the largest amount of data, then fetching different size of the most dataset.

Fetching one data and the whole dataset could be regarded as one situation, since it does not need to consider the condition of ending. The process detail of these two situations is demonstrated in Fig. 3. The difference is whether the process would go through the WRITE_OUT_RECORDS, which is set to fetch one data to the Reduce task and then jump out, or it would constantly read the data. The black line in the reduce task represents fetching one data, and the red line represents fetching the whole dataset.

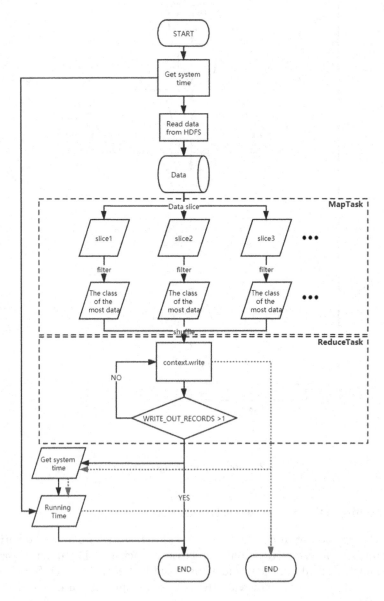

Fig. 3. Fetching one data or the whole dataset (MapReduce)

Based on the characteristics of MapReduce, the second typical situation of fetching half of the dataset could be divided into three methods:

1. A MapReduce program;
2. Map-Map-Reduce chain;
3. The concatenation of two MapReduce programs.

The first two methods aim at saving process time, but the result accuracy would be affected. Only method 3 can achieve the same output results as spark, while the cost is time.

Before introducing these three methods in detail, we need to pay attention to certain details. Since there are no global variables in MapReduce, and the global counters are not interoperable between map and reduce, they are only summarized after the task is executed. Therefore, there are no built-in variables in the framework to propagate parameters between map and reduce. In the cache method, when the parameters to be passed are completed at the end of the map phase, that is, when the run method is finished and before the cleanup method runs, an HDFS IO stream is created, and the result that needs to be passed to the reducer is written to the file. For the Read in the reduce phase, because the map runs in a distributed manner, multiple maps will write to the file at the same time. Therefore, there are multiple values in the cache file. When the reduce is read in, these multiple values must be read after reading. The summary is the sum of the parameters of the map phase. This method is used in all experiments that require map and reduce parameters to interact. In addition, there is one point worth noting: when the map writes to HDFS, HDFS does not support multiple processes to write files and only one process which is holding the object of FS can write at that time. (There are multiple map programs executed in parallel). Therefore, append-file-fail exception will be reported, and if the write is not successful, it will wait and then write serially. This does slightly affect the time complexity and make the running time longer.

Method 1: A MapReduce Program. Specific process is shown in Fig. 4. In this way, Map Task firstly filters out the data of the required category, customizes the counter to obtain the output number, and writes it out to the cache file. Then, Reduce Task reads the cache file, aggregates the output of the file, records the number of outputs, and ends the program after judging that the written value reaches the target value. However, this method has a prime drawback. The target data are aggregated before output, which makes MapReduce faster. But the obtained data is not the same batch as Spark. It only takes half of the data after aggregation, which means that the obtained data at the end would exceed a little bit than the expected result.

Method 2: Map-Map-Reduce Chain. Specific process is shown in Fig. 5. In order to save time, the Map Task could set up many Map work at the same time. By this, the first Map filters out the data of the required category, and customizes the counter to obtain the output number. The second Map gains the counter value to judge if the output data reach the half amount of counter value. Finally, the Reduce task aggregates and outputs the data from the Map Task.

In the Map-Map-Reduce chain structure, the first map filters out the required data, then the second map gets half of the required data, and reduce aggregates the data and writes it out. The two maps are actually controlled by the same map task, running one after another on each machine node in a distributed operation. Therefore, in each node, the counter of the first map can be accurately passed to the next map. However, the counter of each node (with the same name) is relatively independent of the counters of the rest of the nodes, and it is not summarized by the drivers until the distributed tasks of all nodes are executed. Now that the value of the previous map counter can be obtained, half of the data output by the first map can be accurately obtained. In the final result, the obtained data exceeds the exact half a little bit. This is because the writing judgment condition used in the second map is less than or equal to, so each map task actually writes one more round. However, after the map is sliced, the amount of data in each slice may be an odd number, and the "/2" operation in java is divisible and rounded down, so letting map write one more round will ensure that the written data is more than a half.

Due to the characteristics of MapReduce distributed computing, it cannot obtain the first half of the data accurately like Spark. Even though Spark is also distributed, its data has logic order. In MapReduce, the map would logically slice the data into block sizes, and distribute to the different Map Task. Each block is to filter out the required data and take the first half, and then transmit the data to Reduce Task.

Method 3: The Concatenation of Two MapReduce Programs. Specifical process is shown in Fig. 6. Considering the accuracy of the result, two MapReduce could be concatenated. The first MapReduce does not include the Reduce Task. For the Map Task, it filters out the type of data with the largest number, and then gains the output, which is the total numbers of filtered data. In the second MapReduce, Map gains first half of the data, and Reduce aggregates and outputs the data. Moreover, the counter is used as the judgement in run function, and stops at obtaining half of the data. However, this method is not working. The second MapReduce reads the total number in the cache, but because map slices the file and divides it into different tasks for processing, the data in each task is only a small part of the total, and it is impossible to know the actual amount of data being processed in each task. It is definitely much smaller than the total, so the judgment condition rewritten in the run method will be judged to be true anyway, and all of the final data is output, instead of half of the data in each Map task. In addition, the intermediate output of the two jobs will generate additional disk redundancy and IO overtop, so it will reduce the running speed.

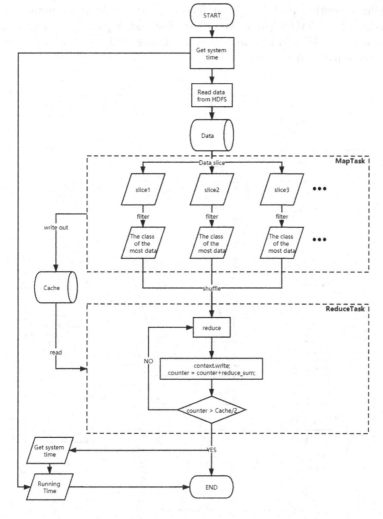

Fig. 4. A MapReduce program (Method 1)

Based on the question above mentioned, we have more superior solution. In the first MapReduce, Map Task filters the highest-amount data, and writes the count of output data to the cache. The Reduce Task compares the amount of data written from the cache by Reduce with the amount of data in the cache, and outputs the first half of the data accurately. In the second MapReduce, Map eliminates the operation, and the Reduce Task aggregates and outputs the data.

As for Spark, it only reads the data and puts it into the RDDs. Specifically, spark uses filter to filter out the data type with the largest amount of data firstly, then adds an index to the most data and acquires the total number. The specific process is shown in Fig. 7.

Specific execution process is that fetching half of the most data does not pass the red line, fetching one data (the first data) passes the red line and judges "index == 1", and fetching the whole dataset (the most data) passes the red line but skips "index == 1".

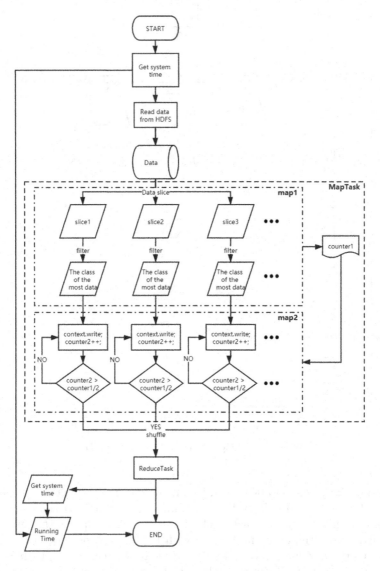

Fig. 5. Map-Map-Reduce chain (Method 2)

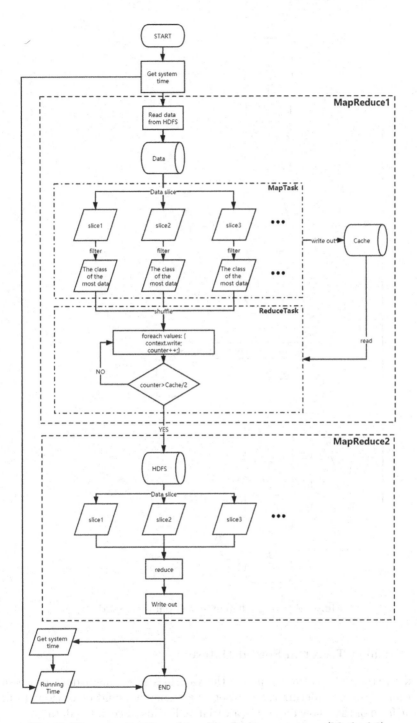

Fig. 6. The concatenation of two MapReduce programs (Method 3)

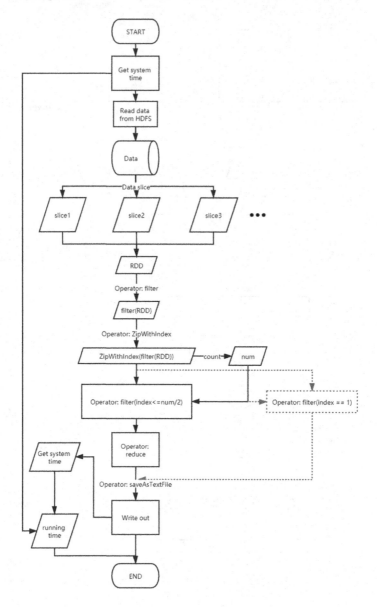

Fig. 7. Fetching different size of dataset (Spark)

2.3   Fetching Target in Sorted Dataset

The data size and location could be the variables in common data processing operation. Also, considering the dataset as a whole, it would be obvious to find out the form of the whole dataset is a variable. For instance, if the data is already ordered, the data filter and counting processing could be different in speed.

In the data preparation stage, three types of data with similar data volumes are arranged at the top, middle, and end of the source dataset to form a sorted dataset. In sorted dataset, the total amount of data is 7792033, including 406,944 pieces of suggested data at the top of sorted dataset, 398304 pieces of consulting data at the middle of sorted dataset and 385440 pieces of other types of data at the end of sorted dataset. Our task is to filter out the corresponding data at the different location of the sorted dataset.

As for MapReduce, the Map Task filters and gets the target class of data, and the Reduce Task writes out the data after aggregation. This is the whole process, which would set the time counter before reading data from the HDFS and stop counting time when the Reduce Task is finished.

As for Spark, it filters out the data at the end of the library separately, then outputs after aggregation. The way to count time is the same as the MapReduce, which is also stop time counting after Reduce Task is finished. The difference is the way the data are stored or taken.

2.4   Inserting Different Size of Dataset

The data writing process is different from the data reading process. For data writing, both the amount of input data and the location could change. To be specific, in people's livelihood appeal data, there are various amount of data (1 million, 2 million, 3 million, 4 million and 5 million. In the following, they are represented by 1m, 2m, 3m, 4m and 5m) and distinct location (top, middle and end) in the dataset.

Because of the characteristic of MapReduce, inserting a large amount of data in a specific location in an existing dataset can only be implemented in the reduce phase (There is only one Reduce Task by default, and there will be multiple Map Tasks due to the characteristics of distributed operation).

The Map Task outputs data, and the Reduce Task acquires the system counter REDUCE_OUTPUT_RECORDS, gets the amount of output data, and judges whether the output value is the target location. If yes, it reads the additional data and write it out. Otherwise, it continues the reduce loop to append data to any location in the dataset (target location).

In addition, from the map phase to the reduce phase, the framework will automatically shuffle the data, so the final result is to append data to the sorted dataset, not the original one.

In contrast, Spark uses ZipWithIndex to add labels to the data. According to the location of the data, Spark uses the filter operator to divide the data into two parts, reads the data that needs to be added into a new RDDs, and uses the union operator to merge the three RDDs. Then the data would be written out. Since no shuffling operation is involved, the running speed is faster. The logical order of the original data exists in each Executor of Spark, so the final result is the same as the original order, as opposed to MapReduce.

3   Results

In this section, we will give comparative analysis results between MapReduce and Spark. The results correspond to the research methods in Sect. 2.

3.1   Fetching One Data

Average running time of fetching one data from different location is displayed in Table 1.

Table 1. Fetching one data from different location

Location	Framework	Average running time (s) of repeating times		
		1 time	10 times	100 times
Top	Spark	7.71	7.56	7.47
	MapReduce	10.64	14.12	14.08
Middle	Spark	8.61	8.75	8.62
	MapReduce	14.22	15.41	15.60
End	Spark	7.84	8.07	8.00
	MapReduce	12.42	14.58	14.70

The result obviously reveals that Spark needs 7 s to 9 s to fetch one data in three typical locations. Fetching the data from the top is the fastest, which spends about 7 s in various repeating times from 1 to 100. Moreover, fetching the data from the middle takes the longest time, which is more than 8.6 s. However, this result is much less than MapReduce. In the operation of MapReduce, due to the fact that the data would repeat the process of input and output through the hard disk after each Map task is finished and before each Reduce task begin, it would take 1.8 to 2 times of time cost than Spark. Most time is wasted at the disk input and output.

3.2   Fetching Different Size of Dataset

The results of fetching different size of dataset are displayed in Table 2. For MapReduce, fetching the whole dataset is not much higher than fetching one data. But for Spark, the time cost increases nearly 2 times by changing one data to the whole dataset.

As mentioned above, MapReduce could be reformed in order to save time or maintain accuracy. Same as the previous analysis, using Map-Map-Reduce chain (Method 2) structure is the most efficient way of MapReduce. On the contrary, concatenating two MapReduce programs (Method 3) remains the same accuracy of output data as Spark, but it is the most time-consuming way. Spark is 4.9 times faster than it.

Table 2. Fetching different size of dataset

Size	Framework	Average running time (s) of repeating times		
		1 time	10 times	100 times
One	Spark	11.52	9.93	9.80
	MapReduce	28.29	30.82	32.01
Whole	Spark	29.16	29.08	28.67
	MapReduce	34.19	26.65	36.24
Half	Spark	15.95	14.78	14.67
	Method 1	35.39	40.33	40.55
	Method 2	29.25	30.40	30.67
	Method 3	81.52	70.59	72.45

Apparently, Spark has obvious difference in time cost for fetching one, half, and the whole dataset. From the flowchart, it can be seen that the time for writing different amounts of data is also different. Spark performs a reduce operation, which involves shuffling, so the time complexity is high. MapReduce takes the same time to fetch one data and the whole dataset, but the time of fetching the whole dataset is 4 s longer than average. The main reason is that shuffling operation in MapReduce is between map and reduce and it is a time-consuming step. For the three methods of MapReduce, method 3 (The concatenation of two MapReduce programs) has the longest time and the most accurate result, method 2 (Map-Map-Reduce chain) results in second-accurate (see the algorithm implementation part for details) and the shortest time. The first two maps actually exist in the same Map Task, so there is no disk I/O transmission consumption. In addition, the data transmitted to reduce is also the most streamlined, and the amount of shuffling data is the most concise, so the time is the shortest. Method 1 (a MapReduce program) uses the first aggregation, then outputs on demand. The order of the aggregated data has been changed, so thus the output result is also not the same as Spark.

3.3   Fetching Target in Sorted Dataset

As shown in Table 3, when the data class is at the top of sorted dataset, the time cost of MapReduce increases as the repeating times increase, on the contrary, the time cost of Spark decreases during the repeating times of adding from 1 to 100.

The middle class of data remains the analogous tendency, but not so obvious as fetching from the top. Compared to fetching target dataset from the top, the time cost of MapReduce decreases at average 0.1 s and increases at average 0.2 s in Spark.

When the data class is at the end of the sorted dataset, the average time cost of MapReduce is longer than the top data class, but retains the same tendency when repeating times change. Spark performs faster than fetching the data from the middle and performs the same tendency as the other two operations. Consequently, MapReduce takes 3 times longer than Spark.

Generally speaking, Hadoop and Spark perform the close result in term of time cost by changing the data cluster location. The reason why MapReduce takes 3 times of longer time than Spark is because Spark is using its RDDs storage.

Table 3. Fetching target in sorted dataset

Size	Framework	Average running time (s) of repeating times		
		1 time	10 times	100 times
Top	Spark	8.54	7.07	6.92
	MapReduce	20.15	22.71	23.10
Middle	Spark	8.70	7.11	7.04
	MapReduce	22.12	22.79	23.00
End	Spark	8.51	6.76	6.66
	MapReduce	23.13	22.58	23.29

3.4 Inserting Different Size of Dataset

For MapReduce, the results are shown in Table 4.

Table 4. Inserting different size of dataset (MapReduce)

Location	Size of insertion	Average running time (s) of repeating times		
		1 time	10 times	100 times
Top	1m	46.70	48.36	48.34
	2m	46.14	48.17	47.95
	3m	47.55	49.02	49.10
	4m	50.02	53.71	53.35
	5m	55.76	55.22	55.39
Middle	1m	47.64	47.97	46.54
	2m	46.88	47.74	47.69
	3m	49.63	49.10	49.06
	4m	50.76	53.06	53.90
	5m	58.91	53.63	55.15
End	1m	43.80	46.04	46.16
	2m	45.69	48.49	47.55
	3m	47.72	49.32	51.97
	4m	49.36	54.08	53.45
	5m	56.81	55.85	55.74

When inserting data to the top, average running time of inserting 1m and 2m data are close. Furthermore, the time cost increases with the increasing of data amount except for inserting 1m and 2m data. Compared to inserting 4m data to the top, inserting 5m data is much more stable. By changing the inserting location to the middle, the tendency of inserting 1m, 2m and 3m data to the middle retains similar and steady. Besides, only at the repeating times of 100, inserting 2m data requires more time than inserting 1m data. When inserting data to the end, the average running time of 1m and 3m data increases steadily with the increasing of the repeating times. On the contrary, inserting 5m data reveals a downward tendency. However, inserting 2m and 4m data keep the same trend of change.

As for Spark, the results of inserting different size of dataset are shown in Table 5. When inserting data to the top, especially for the 3m data, it takes the longest time as 26.07 s at 1 repeating times, but the shortest time is inserting 2m data at 100 repeating times. When inserting data to the middle. In 10 and 100 repeating times, the time cost order is that the 5m and 4m takes the longest time, 1m and 3m are in the middle and inserting 2m data takes the shortest times. In 1 repeating time, inserting 1m data spends more time than inserting 4m data. What is worth mentioning is when the inserting location changes to the end, the time cost of different repeating time is almost the same as inserting to the middle. Specifically, no matter how big the data is inserting at the end, it reveals a downward tendency with the increasing of the repeating times.

Table 5. Inserting different size of dataset (Spark)

Location	Size of insertion	Average running time (s) of repeating times		
		1 time	10 times	100 times
Top	1m	25.26	22.31	22.39
	2m	21.74	21.33	20.58
	3m	26.07	22.02	21.69
	4m	24.70	23.93	23.18
	5m	22.84	24.66	24.62
Middle	1m	25.40	22.78	22.59
	2m	22.36	20.53	20.55
	3m	23.74	21.93	21.96
	4m	24.00	23.27	23.32
	5m	26.39	24.89	24.69
End	1m	25.22	22.67	22.61
	2m	22.58	20.39	20.36
	3m	23.41	22.50	21.85
	4m	24.67	23.19	22.88
	5m	25.94	24.81	24.52

In general, the overall running time of MapReduce is twice of spark. It is mainly related to the framework mechanism. Spark uses memory-based operation, while MapReduce involves a large amount of disk Input/Output. It is also related to the way of writing data. Spark writes data in a distributed manner, so you can see that spark's writing result include multiple parts and each part represents an executor, therefore the writing speed is relatively fast. In contrast, MapReduce only executes one reduce, and only writes out one file, so the writing speed is slow.

4   Conclusion

In this paper, we use Hadoop and Spark to do the same data processing work in order to find out the difference and the reason for the difference between two frameworks. Many cases of basic data processing operation of reading and writing are considered, including the location of the data in the dataset, the size of data cluster, the iteration times of operation and the kinds of data cluster.

For people's livelihood appeal data, when reading one data from the 3 locations of the dataset, Spark performs 1.8 to 2 times better than MapReduce. The reason is that MapReduce has to put the data into the disk after Map Task and then obtains data by Reduce Task. In contrast, Spark puts the data into RDDs, and processes the data without repeating of data input and output. In this way, it reflects the disadvantages that MapReduce has been criticized in these years.

Besides, by changing the amount of data, Spark also performs at least 1.3 times better than MapReduce of Hadoop. What is more, the accuracy of operation result is different. With the changing of MapReduce Task, MapReduce concatenation offers high accuracy as Spark does. But in this way, 2 MapReduce tasks spend much time, which causes the time cost higher than other MapReduce combinations. Using Map-Map-Reduce chain structure, only one MapReduce could be faster but the time cost is still longer than Spark. The reason is because that the Map Task and the Reduce Task change their aggregation order and cannot avoid the disk input and output cost.

In addition, when data in the dataset is sorted in order, the result varies, but Spark still performs faster than Hadoop. Based on the analysis, it illustrates that the reason why Spark performs better in speed is mostly because Spark is using RDDs to store data instead of the hard disk. After finishing the data reading experiment, data writing process is also tested using the same situation such as the location, size of data and so on. When the data size and the target location change, Spark is still faster than MapReduce of Hadoop.

Due to the framework difference, Hadoop and Spark could have distinct efficiency, but what influences the time cost most is still whether using the hard disk or not. In terms of speed, Spark is more suitable for big data processing.

Acknowledgments. The authors thank the researchers who contributed to this paper and the reviewers for their valuable advice.

References

1. Murdoch, T.B., Detsky, A.S.: The inevitable application of big data to health care. JAMA **309**, 1351–1352 (2013)
2. Wang, Y., Kung, L.A., Byrd, T.A.: Big data analytics: understanding its capabilities and potential benefits for healthcare organizations. Technol. Forecast. Soc. Change **126**, 3–13 (2018)
3. Marinakis, V., Doukas, H., Tsapelas, J., et al.: From big data to smart energy services: an application for intelligent energy management. Futur. Gener. Comput. Syst. **110**, 572–586 (2020)
4. Silva, B., Khan, M., Han, K.: Integration of big data analytics embedded smart city architecture with RESTful web of things for efficient service provision and energy management. Futur. Gener. Comput. Syst. **107**, 975–987 (2020)
5. Jan, B., Farman, H., Khan, M., et al.: Designing a smart transportation system: an internet of things and big data approach. IEEE Wirel. Commun. **26**, 73–79 (2019)
6. Balbin, P., Barker, J., Leung, C.K., et al.: Predictive analytics on open big data for supporting smart transportation services. Procedia Comput. Sci. **176**, 3009–3018 (2020)
7. Zhang, Y., et al.: Using big data to predict pertussis infections in Jinan city, China: a time series analysis. Int. J. Biometeorol. **64**(1), 95–104 (2019). https://doi.org/10.1007/s00484-019-01796-w
8. AtiTaLlah, S.B., Driss, M., Boulila, W., et al.: Leveraging deep learning and IoT big data analytics to support the smart cities development: review and future directions. Comput. Sci. Rev. **38**, 100303 (2020)
9. Jindal, A., Kumar, N., Singh, M.: A unified framework for big data acquisition, storage and analytics for demand response management in smart cities. Futur. Gener. Comput. Syst. **108**, 921–934 (2018)
10. Anshari, M., Almunawar, M., Lim, S.: Big data and open government data in public services. In: Proceedings of the 2018 10th International Conference on Machine Learning and Computing (2018)
11. Qi, C.: Big data management in the mining industry. Int. J. Miner. Metall. Mater. **27**(2), 131–139 (2020). https://doi.org/10.1007/s12613-019-1937-z
12. Ruhlandt, R.: The governance of smart cities: a systematic literature review. Cities **81**, 1–23 (2018)
13. Pencheva, I., Esteve, M., Mikhaylov, S.J.: Big data and AI - a transformational shift for government: so, what next for research? Public Policy Adm. **35**, 24–44 (2020)
14. Apache Hadoop. http://hadoop.apache.org
15. Zaharia, M., Chowdhury, M., Franklin, M.J., et al.: Spark: Cluster Computing with Working Sets. HotCloud (2010)
16. Shvachko, K., Kuang, H., Radia, S., et al.: The Hadoop distributed file system. In: 2010 IEEE 26th Symposium on Mass Storage Systems and Technologies (MSST), pp. 1–10 (2010)
17. Hashem, I.A.T., et al.: MapReduce scheduling algorithms: a review. J. Supercomput. **76**(7), 4915–4945 (2018). https://doi.org/10.1007/s11227-018-2719-5
18. Faiz, M., Anuar, N.B., Wahab, A.W.A., Shamshirband, S., Chronopoulos, A.T.: Source camera identification: a distributed computing approach using Hadoop. J. Cloud Comput. **6**(1), 1–11 (2017). https://doi.org/10.1186/s13677-017-0088-x

19. Abouelmehdi, K., Beni-Hssane, A., Khaloufi, H., et al.: Big data emerging issues: Hadoop security and privacy. In: 2016 5th International Conference on Multimedia Computing and Systems (ICMCS), pp. 731–736 (2016)
20. Akshay, M.M., Pappu, U.R., Rohit, H.P., et al.: Stock market prediction system using Hadoop. Int. J. Eng. Sci. Comput. (IJESC) **8**, 16138–16140 (2018)
21. Zhu, H., Xu, Y.: Sports performance prediction model based on integrated learning algorithm and cloud computing Hadoop platform. Microprocess. Microsyst. **79**, 103322 (2020)
22. Liang, H., Liu, J., Meng, W.: A review of various optimization schemes of small files storage on Hadoop. In: 2018 37th Chinese Control Conference (CCC), pp. 4500–4506 (2018)
23. Feng, D., Zhu, L., Lei, Z.: Review of Hadoop performance optimization. In: 2016 2nd IEEE International Conference on Computer and Communications (ICCC), pp. 65–68 (2016)
24. Nikulchev, E.V., Tatarintsev, A.V., Belov, V.: Choosing a data storage format in the apache Hadoop system based on experimental evaluation using Apache Spark. Symmetry **13**, 195 (2021)
25. Shetty, S.D.: Sentiment analysis, tweet analysis and visualization on big data using Apache Spark and Hadoop. IOP Conf. Ser. Mater. Sci. Eng. **1099**, 012002 (2021)
26. Hakdağli, Ö., Özcan, C., Oğul, İ.Ü.: Stream text data analysis on twitter using Apache Spark streaming. In: 2018 26th Signal Processing and Communications Applications Conference (SIU), pp. 1–4 (2018)
27. Sunny, B.K., Janardhanan, P.S., Francis, A.B., et al.: Implementation of a self-adaptive real time recommendation system using Spark machine learning libraries. In: 2017 IEEE International Conference on Signal Processing, Informatics, Communication and Energy Systems (SPICES), pp. 1–7 (2017)
28. Kavitha, S., Badre, R.: Towards a hybrid recommendation system on Apache Spark. In: IEEE India Council International Subsections Conference (INDISCON), pp. 297–302 (2020)
29. Saraswathi, A., Mummoorthy, A., Anantha Raman, G.R., et al.: Real-time traffic monitoring system using Spark. In: 2019 International Conference on Emerging Trends in Science and Engineering (ICESE), pp. 1:1–1:6 (2019)
30. Sundareswaran, A., Sendhilvel, L.: Real-time vehicle traffic analysis using long short term memory networks in apache spark. In: 2020 International Conference on Emerging Trends in Information Technology and Engineering (IC-ETITE), pp. 1–5 (2020)
31. Qu, X., Wu, Y., Liu, J., et al.: HRV-Spark: computing heart rate variability measures using Apache Spark. In: IEEE International Conference on Bioinformatics and Biomedicine (BIBM), pp. 2235–2241 (2020)
32. Ahmed, N., Barczak, A., Susnjak, T., et al.: A comprehensive performance analysis of Apache Hadoop and Apache Spark for large scale data sets using HiBenc. J. Big Data **7**, 1–18 (2020)
33. Lagwankar, I., Sankaranarayanan, A.N., Kalambur, S.: Impact of map-reduce framework on Hadoop and Spark MR application performance. In: IEEE International Conference on Big Data (Big Data), pp. 2763–2772 (2020)
34. Hedjazi, M.A., Kourbane, I., Genc, Y., et al.: A comparison of Hadoop, Spark and Storm for the task of large scale image classification. In: 2018 26th Signal Processing and Communications Applications Conference (SIU), pp. 1–4 (2018)
35. Aziz, K., Zaidouni, D., Bellafkih, M.: Real-time data analysis using Spark and Hadoop. In: 2018 4th International Conference on Optimization and Applications (ICOA), pp. 1–6 (2018)

36. Mostafaeipour, A., Jahangard Rafsanjani, A., Ahmadi, M., Arockia Dhanraj, J.: Investigating the performance of Hadoop and Spark platforms on machine learning algorithms. J. Supercomput. **77**(2), 1273–1300 (2020). https://doi.org/10.1007/s11227-020-03328-5

37. Mostafaeipour, A., Rafsanjani, A.J., Ahmadi, M., et al.: Investing the performance of Hadoop and Spark platforms on machine learning algorithms. J. Supercomput. **77**, 1–28 (2020)

38. Sassi, I., Ouaftouh, S., Anter, S.: Adaptation of classical machine learning algorithms to big data context: problems and challenges: case study: hidden Markov models under Spark. In: 2019 1st International Conference on Smart Systems and Data Science (ICSSD) (2019)

39. Lu, H.C., Hwang, F.J., Huang, Y.H.: Parallel and distributed architecture of genetic algorithm on Apache Hadoop and Spark. Appl. Soft Comput. **95**, 106497 (2020)

40. Zaharia, M., Chowdhury, M., Das, T., et al.: Resilient distributed datasets: a fault-tolerant abstraction for in-memory cluster computing. In: Proceedings of the 9th USENIX conference on Networked Systems Design and Implementation (NSDI). USENIX Association (2012)

Big Data and Deep Learning

Neural Architecture Search as Self-assessor in Semi-supervised Learning

Zhenhou Hong, Jianzong Wang$^{(\boxtimes)}$, Xiaoyang Qu, Chendong Zhao, Jie Liu, and Jing Xiao

Ping An Technology (Shenzhen) Co., Ltd., Shenzhen, China
{hongzhenhou168,wangjianzong347,quxiaoyang343,zhaochengdong343,
liujie732,xiaojing661}@pingan.com.cn, jzwang@188.com

Abstract. Neural Architecture Search (NAS) forms powerful automatic learning, which has helped achieve remarkable performance in several applications in recent years. Previous research focused on NAS in standard supervised learning to explore its performance, requiring labeled data. In this paper, our goal is to examine the implementation of NAS with large amounts of unlabeled data. We propose the NAS as a self-assessor, called NAS-SA, by adding the consistency method and prior knowledge. We design an adaptive search strategy, a balanced search space, and a multi-object optimization to generate a robust and efficient small model in NAS-SA. The image and text classification tasks proved that our NAS-SA method had achieved the best performance.

Keywords: Neural Architecture Search · Automatic learning · Semi-supervised learning · Unlabeled data · Consistency loss

1 Introduction

The development of deep learning (DL) has generated a profound impact in various fields. DL models can now recognize images [8,23], understand natural language [26], play games [20], and automate system decisions (e.g., device placement and indexing). However, the artificial neural network structure still requires much expertise and sufficient time, so the architecture search and model optimization of neural networks has become a research hotspot in recent years. In addition, researchers explore the area of neural architecture search (NAS) [2,3,17] in semi-supervised learning and self-supervised learning [13,25,31], exploring whether the NAS can still achieve good performance without data annotation [13].

A significant bottleneck in obtaining a satisfactory architecture predictor could be collecting a large annotated training set. Given the expensive cost of annotating a neural architecture with its actual performance, the training set for the performance predictor is often small, which would lead to an undesirable

© Springer Nature Singapore Pte Ltd. 2022
X. Liao et al. (Eds.): BigData 2021, CCIS 1496, pp. 95–107, 2022.
https://doi.org/10.1007/978-981-16-9709-8_7

over-fitting result. Existing methods insist on fully supervised way to train the performance predictor while neglecting the significance of those neural architectures without annotations. In the search space of NAS, we propose the adaptive search space for samples of the neural architectures more effectively. Though the actual performance could be unknown, their architectural similarity with those annotated architectures would convey invaluable information to optimize the performance predictor.

In order to explore the performance of NAS in the case of unlabeled data, the labeled data are replaced with soft logits. The soft logits are generated by pretrained models (such as knowledge distillation (KD) [9]). One is to avoid the heavy work of data labeling, and the other is that soft targets are easier to learn their distribution than hard targets. Many pre-training models can be used, such as BERT [6], XLNet [32], ResNet152 [8], which make it easier to obtain relatively high-quality soft labels. In this way, for a training system, the unlabeled data set can be used directly, and only a pretrained model is needed to assist in training the NAS and improve its ability to learn data distribution. The unlabeled data on the other side remains unchanged, and the data is manipulated by data augmentation and input to the NAS to calculate its consistency loss [34]. Consistency loss is used as a regularization term to help NAS learn data distribution. With soft targets and consistency loss, the NAS can be a self-assessor, train and evaluate the model by itself.

We are using the NAS to optimize the network architecture automatically, instead of handmade design. Furthermore, we design an adaptive search space and balanced search strategy for NAS to search small models more robustly and efficiently. Moreover, a multi-object formula ensures the network searching to be accurate and parameter-efficient.

More specifically, the contributions of this paper include:

- We propose a novel framework called NAS-SA which deals with large amounts of unlabeled data. It consists of the soft labels, and consistency loss helps NAS in the semi-supervised learning.
- NAS-SA combines with the proposed adaptive search space and balanced search strategy. As a result, it helps to generate a more robust and efficient small model.
- The experiments have shown that our NAS-SA framework achieved 2% ∼ 4% higher than other methods and light models. Moreover, it almost reduced 227 times the parameters compared to the pretrained model.

2 Related Works

2.1 Semi-supervised Learning

An actual training environment usually provides a finite number of labeled data and an unlimited number of unlabeled data. Many researches have tried to exploit the potential of unlabeled data since the majority of the real-world samples lack annotations. Generally, there have been two methodologies to cope with these circumstances.

Self-training: Self-training methods train a model using labeled data and then make predictions on unlabeled data. If the top-1 prediction score for the input x_u is greater than a threshold σ, the pseudo label of x_u is set as the class y^- whose score is the maximum. Then x_u can be treated as a labeled data in the form of $(x_u, \overline{y})$ [12]. Repetitively applying this process can boost the model's performance but impedes the whole training speed. In addition, depending on the threshold value σ, the amount of added data varies a lot and this makes the performance unstable. A small number of additional pseudo-labeled samples may not improve the performance enough while too many samples may harm the performance with incorrect labeling.

Consistency Loss: Consistency loss applies perturbations to an input image x to obtain x' and minimizes the difference between the outputs predictions $f(x)$ and $f(x')$ [21,34]. It does not require a label because the loss is determined by the difference between the outputs which is known to help smooth the manifold. As mentioned above, this shows the state-of-the-art performance in semi-supervised classification problems.

2.2   Neural Architecture Search

Current NAS framework for obtaining desired DNNs can be divided into two sub-problems, i.e., search space and search method. A well-defined search space is extremely important for NAS, and there are mainly three kinds of search spaces in the state-of-the-art NAS methods. The first is cell based search space [16,28]. Once a cell structure is searched, it is used in all the layers across the network by stacking multiple cells. Each cell contains several blocks, and each of the block contains two branches, with each branch applying an operation to the output of one of the former blocks. The outputs of the two branches are added to get the final output of the block. The second is Direct Acyclic Graph (DAG) based search space [33]. The difference between cell based and DAG based search space is that the latter does not restrict the number of branches. The input and output number of a node in the cell is not limited. The third is factorized hierarchical search space [24], which allows different layer architectures in different blocks.

Besides search space, most of the NAS research focus on developing efficient search methods, which can be divided into combinatorial optimization methods and continuous optimization methods [14,30]. Combinatorial optimization methods include Evolutionary Algorithm (EA) based methods [14,17,30] and Reinforcement Learning (RL) based methods [28,35]. Continuous optimization methods include DARTS [4,15], which makes the search space continuous by relaxing the categorical choice of a particular operation to a softmax over all possible operations, and several one-shot methods that solve the problem in a one-shot procedure. Recently, architecture datasets with substantial full-trained neural architectures are also proposed to compare different NAS methods conveniently and fairly [33].

3   Proposed Method

3.1   Neural Architecture Search as Self-assesor

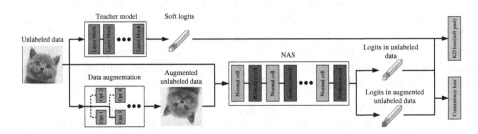

Fig. 1. Illustration of NAS-SA. Opt in the picture means the operation of data augmentation. The dotted line in data augmentation means the operation has not been chosen. Layer block means the layer in the pretrained model.

Our NAS-SA is based on two premises. First, the dataset comprises numerous unlabeled data and a small number of labeled data (labeled with pretrained Model). The second is that the performance of this pretrained network is one of the best networks in the field.

Based on these two prerequisites, our NAS-SA flowchart is shown in Fig. 1. We use the soft target of the pretrained model directly instead of the hard target. In order to make better use of unlabeled data, we sample from it, tag it and then merge it with the labeled data set.

The training is divided into the following steps:

- Use the big models to tag the small amount of unlabeled data.
- Use the data augmentation to the large number of unlabeled data.
- Calculate the soft target: Use the trained big model to calculate the soft target. That is after the large model is "softened", it passes through the output of softmax.
- Using the NAS to search architecture and train, added a soft target loss function and consistency loss function, and adjust the proportion of the two loss functions by lambda.

Given the input feature vector x, we define the loss function:

$$L(\theta) = \sum_i q_i(z/T)log(q_i(g(x;\theta)/T)) + \lambda * JS(g(x;\theta), g(d(x);\theta)) \qquad (1)$$

where L represents the total loss, λ is the weight coefficient, θ represents the NAS-model parameters to be learned. The first term is L^{soft}, same as in the KD [9]. $q_i = \frac{exp(z_i/T)}{\sum_j exp(z_i/T)}$, where T is a temperature parameter which is normally set to 1. $g(x;\theta)$ is the probabilities predicted by NAS, $d(\cdot)$ means the data augmentation, and $JS(\cdot)$ represents the Jensen-Shannon Divergence.

3.2   Adaptive Search Space

We aimed to design a tool for black-box general-purpose model compression. The main idea is to search for a high-quality and light-weight model by mimicking the large-scale model. Moreover, CNN not only supports image classification tasks but also supports text classification and speaker recognition tasks. So our method can be applied to many tasks.

The NAS design includes two parts: search space and search strategy design. The design of the search space is considered by [2,17,35] and others, and the search strategy adopts the evolution algorithm. The specific details will be discussed below.

As shown in Fig. 2, our setting of search space follows NASNet [35] and changes the structure of the cell to support weight sharing.

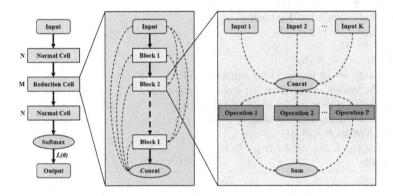

Fig. 2. NAS-SA Search Space. LEFT: the full outer structure (omitting skip inputs for clarity). MIDDLE: the cell structure. The dotted line represents all possible paths RIGHT: the block structure. Abstract operations.

Weight sharing is an effective method for NAS search acceleration. We refer to the super network in [2,3] and make some modifications to the structure to support our NAS-SA. We can train the super network once and then use the weight of the super network to infer the accuracy of the sub-network on the test set multiple times.

Figure 2(left) is the overall structure of NAS-SA. To make the network small enough, we removed some Normal Cell and Reduction Cell. The skip inputs are omitted from the figure. And to achieve weight sharing more effectively, the structure of our Normal Cell and Reduction Cell is the same. Figure 2(middle) is the structure of the cell, and the dashed and solid lines represent all possible paths. There are I blocks of the same type in each cell, and finally, the output of all blocks is concated as the output of the cell. Figure 2(right) is the detailed structure of the block, each block accepts the output of the previous block and concats it as input. Then we choose P operations, we choose different operations for different tasks. Finally, all the output through operations is summed up as the output of this block.

3.3   Balanced Search Strategy

Search strategies fall into two broad categories: reinforcement learning and evolution algorithm. Considering the algorithm's simplicity and the search space is a supernetwork that can infer subnetworks multiple times with one training. Therefore, we choose evolution algorithms as our search strategy. Evolution algorithms include selection, crossover, and mutation. For convenience, we only use mutations to generate new subnetworks.

Algorithm 1. The process of evolution algorithm

Input: *population Set P, model Set M, model Set size N, population Set size C*
Initializing the P and M;
while len(P) < C **do**
    randomly initialize a network *model*;
    eval and calculation **Fitness** of *model*;
    add *model* to P and M;
end while
while len(M) < N **do**
    randomly select K *model* for *candidateSet*;
    highest fitness *model* from *candidateSet* for *parent*;
    generating a new model *child* by mutating *parent*;
    eval and calculation **Fitness** of *child*;
    add *child* to P and M;
    remove the worst *model* from P;
end while

Evolution Algorithm as shown in Algorithm 1. Unlike general evolution algorithms, we first randomly select a candidate set and then choose the best and worst network from the candidate set. The reason for this is to save computing power to a certain extent when the population is large. So first, we select K candidate networks as candidate sets each time and then select a network with the highest fitness and lowest fitness from the candidate set. Then, the highest fitness network acts as a parent and generates a new subnetwork through parental variation. Finally, we remove the lowest fitness network from the population.

The NAS-SA variants are divided into two types, path variations and operation variations. The mutation of the path first selects a block in the cell, then replaces, increases the output of the previous block, or deletes an input condition of the current block to ensure that it has at least one input. The variation of operation is also to select a block first, then conduct replacing, adding or deleting operation, thus ensuring that each block has at least one operations.

To ensure high accuracy and low parameters of the NAS-SA and the balance between them, our fitness includes more than just accuracy. The fitness of our design includes the balance of accuracy and parameter quantities and the limitation of the parameter quantity, as shown below:

$$\Gamma = \begin{cases} P/\log(M), & M \le \theta \\ 0, & M > \theta \end{cases} \tag{2}$$

Where P is accuracy, M is model size, and θ is threshold we set.

4 Experiments

4.1 Experimental Setup

To verify the effect of NAS-SA, we did experiments on two tasks: text classification and image classification. All experiments were trained and tested on a Tesla V100 GPU. The NAS-SA and other models in experiments are implemented by TensorFlow [1] library in Python.

Datasets. We randomly extracted 100 classes from the ImageNet dataset for image classification tasks, and each category has 1300 images. Therefore, the training set has 130000 images. We make the training set as the unlabeled dataset by removing its labels. The test set extracts the categories correspond to the training set, each with 150 images, so the test set has 15000 images. The ratio of test set and training set is 1/9.

Our text classification dataset selects the IMDB movie review dataset. There are 25,000 positive and negative comments for the training set, 25,000 for the test set. With the same process as the image classification task, remove the label of the training set. We randomly choose 2778 samples from the test set. The new test set has 2778 comments. Maintain the ratio of test set and training set to 1/9, same as in the image classification task.

Pretrained Models. In image classification task, we choose the ResNet152 [8] as the pretrained model. The ResNet152 has 82.8% accuracy and 58.16M parameters. In text classification task, we choose the BERT [6] as the pretrained model. The BERT has 93.8% accuracy and $109.5M$ parameters.

Data Augmentation. For image classification, we use the RandAugment [5]. RandAugment used the uniform sample from the same set of augmentation transformations in PIL. For text classification, we use the synonym replacement, random insertion, random swap, random insertion [29] and backtranslation [19]. The backtranslation refers to the procedure of translating an existing example x in language A into another language B and then translating it back into A to obtain an augmented example $\hat{x}$.

Compared Methods. In the text classification task, the NAS-SA compared with the IDCNN [22], TextCNN [27] and the BiLSTM [7] model. In the image classification task, the NAS-SA compared with the MobileNetV1 [11], MobileNetV2 [18] and MobileNetV3 [10]. Using AmoebaNet-A(N,F) [17], DARTS and ENAS [16] for the image classification task and the text classification task. The N is the number of normal cells per stack and the F is the number of output filters of the convolution ops.

If not specified, all the compared models with hard labels represent that they are trained with labeled data. While in our framework, all the compared models are trained with soft logits provided by the pretrained model.

The Choice of Operations. As shown in Table 1. We have designed the choice of operations for image classification and text classification. The operations of the image classification task follow the NASNet [35]. NAS-SA is a word embedding model for text classification tasks. We mimic 1D convolution. For the AmoebaNet-A and DARTS, the choice of operations is also the same as Table 1.

Table 1. Operations for text classification and image classification

	Text classification	Image classification
Operations	Identity	Identity
	1x3 conv	3x3 average pooling
	1x5 conv	1x3 then 3x1 conv
	1x7 conv	3x3 max pooling
	1x3 dilated conv	3x3 separable conv
	1x5 dilated conv	5x5 separable conv
	1x7 dilated conv	3x3 dilated conv
	1x3 max pooling	3x3 conv

4.2 Image Classification Task

Table 2. The result of image dataset. "HL" refers to the hard label, means the labeled datasets. "P" means model parameters.

Model	Acc(%) (with HL)	Acc(%) (ours method)	# P
(pretrained) ResNet152	82.8	——	58.16M
MobileNetV1	68.5	70.4	4.2M
MobileNetV2	69.3	72.9	3.4M
MobileNetV3	71.2	74.9	2.9M
AmoebaNet-A($N=6$, F $=32$)	71.0	74.3	2.9M
AmoebaNet-A($N=6$, F $=36$)	71.6	75.1	3.0M
ENAS	69.5	73.9	3.2M
DARTS	70.0	74.1	3.0M
NAS-SA(ours)	**72.0**	**75.3**	**2.9M**

When training a super network, all paths and operations are opened to obtain their respective weights. Furthermore, to make the accuracy rate of the sub-network using the super-network weight inference positively correlated with the accuracy of the sub-network itself training to convergence, we use the path dropout. Discard some edges randomly during the training process. Inferring the performance of a sub-network using a super-network, we only open some paths and operations, and the remaining paths and operations are disabled or zeroed. Each block of the cell in the sub-network can select the previous output as input and guarantee at least one input, and select one or two operations in each block.

We chose ResNet152 [8] as the pretrained model. The MobileNetV1, MobileNetV2 and MobileNetV3 as the compared models. To compare the NAS, the AmoebaNet-A and DARTS were chosen. Experiments were also performed using both the labeled training set and the unlabeled data set. The specific experimental results are shown in Table 2.

The experimental flow and settings are similar to the text classification task. We limit the size of the NAS-SA to less than 3M. The ResNet152 has 82.8% accuracy and 58.16M parameters. The accuracy is enough in this task as a pre-trained model. In this task, NAS-SA also demonstrates that its results are best in all the small models. Although the accuracy still has a near 5% gap between the pretrained model, the model search by NAS-SA, its parameters are much smaller than ResNet152. It shrinks the size almost 23 times. Compared to the NAS methods, our method outperformance than the AmoebaNet-A, ENAS, and DARTS.

It also can be seen from the experimental results of the image classification task that the NAS of semi-supervised learning can achieve good results. Furthermore, with the adaptive search strategy and the balanced search space, NAS-SA can further improve the model's accuracy under the condition of parameters.

4.3   Text Classification Application

Table 3. The result of NLP dataset. "HL" refers to the hard label, means the labeled datasets. "P" means model parameters.

Model	Acc(%) (with HL)	Acc(%) (ours method)	# P
(pretrained) BERT	93.8	——	109.5M
IDCNN	86.0	90.0	0.57M
TextCNN	86.4	90.2	0.51M
BiLSTM	83.2	89.2	0.53M
AmoebaNet-A($N = 4$, $F = 16$)	87.5	90.6	0.49M
AmoebaNet-A($N = 4$, $F = 20$)	**88.3**	90.7	0.50M
ENAS	86.6	88.4	0.55M
DARTS	86.8	89.7	0.51M
NAS-SA(ours)	87.3	**91.0**	**0.48M**

To ensure high precision, we choose BERT [6] as the pretrained model. The pretrained model has 93.8% accuracy and 109.5M parameters in this task. The accuracy should satisfy the requirement of performance. The more commonly used TextCNN [27], IDCNN [22], and BiLSTM [7] in the text classification task were selected as the baseline model. To compare the evolutional NAS compared, the AmoebaNet-A($N = 4$, $F = 16$) and the AmoebaNet-A($N = 4$, $F = 20$) were chosen. The experimental results are shown in Table 3.

For the pretrained model to predict the unlabeled data more accurately, we use uniform sampling to ensure that each class's number is balanced, eliminating the potentially hard samples. For example, remove samples with prediction probability (less than 0.6) and pick the same amount of data for each class. We separately recorded the accuracy of the two cases except for the pretrained model and the number of parameters for each model. For example, the NAS-SA model was searched in two cases, so there are two parameter quantities. To ensure the model designed by NAS-SA is small enough, we limit the parameter of NAS-SA to less than 0.5M.

The accuracy result of NAS-SA can compare the pretrained model, as shown in Table 3. For the accuracy of using the NAS-SA framework, the average improvement is about 3% ~ 4%, compared with the original method. More importantly, the model size is much smaller. It is almost reduced 227 times. Compared to the NAS methods, our method outperformance than the AmoebaNet-A, ENAS, and DARTS. The experimental results of the text classification task have also proved that NAS-SA can further improve the model's accuracy under the condition of parameters, with the adaptive search strategy and the balanced search space.

5 Conclusions

In this paper, we present a framework called NAS-SA, in which the NAS as a self-assessor searches the model in the unlabeled dataset. It explores the soft labels and consistency loss, can inject prior knowledge with data, especially the unlabeled data, and optimize the NAS more powerfully. We use unlabeled data and NAS to mimic large, high-precision networks in CV task and NLP task in experimental results. We propose the adaptive search strategy and the balanced search space to search the model with high accuracy and maintain the low parameters. By integrating these technologies, we have produced an efficient model generated by NAS-SA. In future work, we will try to use NAS-SA in more different tasks and more datasets.

Acknowledgement. This work is supported by National Key Research and Development Program of China under grant No. 2018YFB0204403, No. 2017YFB1401202 and No. 2018YFB1003500.

References

1. Abadi, M., et al.: Tensorflow: a system for large-scale machine learning. In: 12th {USENIX} Symposium on Operating Systems Design and Implementation ({OSDI} 2016), pp. 265–283 (2016)
2. Bender, G., Kindermans, P.J., Zoph, B., Vasudevan, V., Le, Q.: Understanding and simplifying one-shot architecture search. In: International Conference on Machine Learning, pp. 550–559 (2018)
3. Brock, A., Lim, T., Ritchie, J.M., Weston, N.J.: Smash: one-shot model architecture search through hypernetworks. In: 6th International Conference on Learning Representations (2018)
4. Chen, X., Hsieh, C.J.: Stabilizing differentiable architecture search via perturbation-based regularization. In: International Conference on Machine Learning, pp. 1554–1565. PMLR (2020)
5. Cubuk, E.D., Zoph, B., Shlens, J., Le, Q.V.: Randaugment: practical data augmentation with no separate search. arXiv preprint arXiv:1909.13719 2(3) (2019)
6. Devlin, J., Chang, M.W., Lee, K., Toutanova, K.: Bert: pre-training of deep bidirectional transformers for language understanding. In: Proceedings of the 2019 Conference of the North American Chapter of the Association for Computational Linguistics: Human Language Technologies, vol. 1 (Long and Short Papers), pp. 4171–4186 (2019)
7. Graves, A., Schmidhuber, J.: Framewise phoneme classification with bidirectional LSTM and other neural network architectures. Neural Netw. 18(5–6), 602–610 (2005)
8. He, K., Zhang, X., Ren, S., Sun, J.: Deep residual learning for image recognition. In: Proceedings of the IEEE Conference on Computer Vision and Pattern Recognition, pp. 770–778 (2016)
9. Hinton, G., Vinyals, O., Dean, J.: Distilling the knowledge in a neural network. Statistics 1050, 9 (2015)
10. Howard, A., et al.: Searching for mobilenetv3. In: Proceedings of the IEEE/CVF International Conference on Computer Vision, pp. 1314–1324 (2019)
11. Howard, A.G., et al.: Mobilenets: efficient convolutional neural networks for mobile vision applications. arXiv preprint arXiv:1704.04861 (2017)
12. Kuo, C.-W., Ma, C.-Y., Huang, J.-B., Kira, Z.: FeatMatch: feature-based augmentation for semi-supervised learning. In: Vedaldi, A., Bischof, H., Brox, T., Frahm, J.-M. (eds.) ECCV 2020. LNCS, vol. 12363, pp. 479–495. Springer, Cham (2020). https://doi.org/10.1007/978-3-030-58523-5_28
13. Liu, C., Dollár, P., He, K., Girshick, R., Yuille, A., Xie, S.: Are labels necessary for neural architecture search? In: Vedaldi, A., Bischof, H., Brox, T., Frahm, J.-M. (eds.) ECCV 2020. LNCS, vol. 12349, pp. 798–813. Springer, Cham (2020). https://doi.org/10.1007/978-3-030-58548-8_46
14. Liu, H., Simonyan, K., Vinyals, O., Fernando, C., Kavukcuoglu, K.: Hierarchical representations for efficient architecture search. arXiv preprint arXiv:1711.00436 (2017)
15. Liu, H., Simonyan, K., Yang, Y.: Darts: differentiable architecture search. arXiv preprint arXiv:1806.09055 (2018)
16. Pham, H., Guan, M., Zoph, B., Le, Q., Dean, J.: Efficient neural architecture search via parameters sharing. In: International Conference on Machine Learning, pp. 4095–4104. PMLR (2018)

17. Real, E., Aggarwal, A., Huang, Y., Le, Q.V.: Regularized evolution for image classifier architecture search. In: Proceedings of the AAAI Conference on Artificial Intelligence, vol. 33, pp. 4780–4789 (2019)
18. Sandler, M., Howard, A., Zhu, M., Zhmoginov, A., Chen, L.C.: Mobilenetv 2: inverted residuals and linear bottlenecks. In: Proceedings of the IEEE Conference on Computer Vision and Pattern Recognition, pp. 4510–4520 (2018)
19. Sennrich, R., Haddow, B., Birch, A.: Improving neural machine translation models with monolingual data. In: Proceedings of the 54th Annual Meeting of the Association for Computational Linguistics (vol. 1: Long Papers), pp. 86–96 (2016)
20. Silver, D., et al.: Mastering the game of go without human knowledge. Nature **550**(7676), 354–359 (2017)
21. Sohn, K., et al.: Fixmatch: simplifying semi-supervised learning with consistency and confidence. In: Advances in Neural Information Processing Systems 33 (2020)
22. Strubell, E., Verga, P., Belanger, D., McCallum, A.: Fast and accurate entity recognition with iterated dilated convolutions. In: EMNLP (2017)
23. Szegedy, C., Ioffe, S., Vanhoucke, V., Alemi, A.A.: Inception-v4, inception-resnet and the impact of residual connections on learning. In: Proceedings of the Thirty-First AAAI Conference on Artificial Intelligence, pp. 4278–4284 (2017)
24. Tan, M., et al.: Mnasnet: platform-aware neural architecture search for mobile. In: Proceedings of the IEEE Conference on Computer Vision and Pattern Recognition, pp. 2820–2828 (2019)
25. Tang, Y., et al.: A semi-supervised assessor of neural architectures. In: Proceedings of the IEEE/CVF Conference on Computer Vision and Pattern Recognition, pp. 1810–1819 (2020)
26. Vaswani, A., et al.: Attention is all you need. In: Advances in Neural Information Processing Systems, pp. 5998–6008 (2017)
27. Vieira, J.P.A., Moura, R.S.: An analysis of convolutional neural networks for sentence classification. In: 2017 XLIII Latin American Computer Conference (CLEI), pp. 1–5. IEEE (2017)
28. Wan, A., et al.: FBNetV2: differentiable neural architecture search for spatial and channel dimensions. In: Proceedings of the IEEE/CVF Conference on Computer Vision and Pattern Recognition, pp. 12965–12974 (2020)
29. Wei, J., Zou, K.: EDA: easy data augmentation techniques for boosting performance on text classification tasks. In: Proceedings of the 2019 Conference on Empirical Methods in Natural Language Processing and the 9th International Joint Conference on Natural Language Processing (EMNLP-IJCNLP), pp. 6383–6389 (2019)
30. Xue, C., Yan, J., Yan, R., Chu, S.M., Hu, Y., Lin, Y.: Transferable automl by model sharing over grouped datasets. In: Proceedings of the IEEE/CVF Conference on Computer Vision and Pattern Recognition, pp. 9002–9011 (2019)
31. Yan, S., Zheng, Y., Ao, W., Zeng, X., Zhang, M.: Does unsupervised architecture representation learning help neural architecture search? In: Advances in Neural Information Processing Systems 33 (2020)
32. Yang, Z., Dai, Z., Yang, Y., Carbonell, J., Salakhutdinov, R.R., Le, Q.V.: XLNet: generalized autoregressive pretraining for language understanding. Adv. Neural. Inf. Process. Syst. **32**, 5753–5763 (2019)
33. Ying, C., Klein, A., Christiansen, E., Real, E., Murphy, K., Hutter, F.: NAS-bench-101: towards reproducible neural architecture search. In: International Conference on Machine Learning, pp. 7105–7114. PMLR (2019)

34. Zhou, T., Wang, S., Bilmes, J.: Time-consistent self-supervision for semi-supervised learning. In: International Conference on Machine Learning, pp. 11523–11533. PMLR (2020)
35. Zoph, B., Vasudevan, V., Shlens, J., Le, Q.V.: Learning transferable architectures for scalable image recognition. In: Proceedings of the IEEE Conference on Computer Vision and Pattern Recognition, pp. 8697–8710 (2018)

Automatic Classification of Medicinal Plants of Leaf Images Based on Convolutional Neural Network

Mengisti Berihu, Juan Fang$^{(\boxtimes)}$, and Shuaibing Lu

Faculty of Information Technology, Beijing University of Technology,
No. 100 Pingleyuan Street, Beijing 100124, China
{fangjuan,lushaibing}@bjut.edu.cn

Abstract. Plants are the basis of all living things on earth, supplying us with oxygen, food, shelter, medicine, and preserving the planet from dam-ages that could face climate changes. Concerning their medicinal abilities, limited access to proper medical centers in many rural areas and developing countries made traditional medicine preferable by the community. In addition, their lower side effect and affordability also plays a big role. More than half of the population uses medicinal plants directly and indirectly for animals and personal use in Ethiopia. However, accurate medicinal plant identification has always been a challenge for manual identification and automatic recognition systems mainly because the knowledge transfer between the knowledge holders (traditional physicians, elderly) and modern science have a huge gap. Several studies addressed an automatic plant recognition system using different feature extraction methods and classification algorithms. In this paper, a novel dataset, which was based on Ethiopian medicinal plants, that use the leaf part of the plant, as a medicine was used to automatically classify the plants accordingly using their leaf image. An attempt has been made to collect leaf images of medicinal plants in Ethiopia, to train, test collected dataset images, and classify those images using convolutional neural network models like GoogleNet and AlexNet. The proposed convolutional neural networks were fine-tuned with the adjustment of hyper-parameters like learning rate, the number of epochs, optimizers to the models. Image augmentation is also implemented to enlarge the dataset. The experimental result for the augmented dataset and more training epoch gave better performance and accuracy in the classification of the images. From the two selected convolutional neural network models, the best model is then determined based on the result in accuracy and loss; from an experiment conducted, the best model, which is GoogLeNet with an accuracy of 96.7 % chosen to develop a web-based automatic medicinal plant classification system.

Keywords: Medicinal plants · Leaf images · Convolutional neural network · GoogleNet · AlexNet

S. Lu—Contributed equally to this work.

1   Introduction

Plants are the basis of all living things on earth, serving as oxygen, food, shelter, medicine, and preserving the earth from climate changes and natural disasters. It is therefore becoming increasingly important to identify plants and preserve them [1]. One of the benefits of plants is their medicinal abilities; humans have been using medicinal plants for centuries. Medicinal plants have been used for both curative and preventive medical therapy preparations for human beings and also animals, which also has been used for the extraction of important bioactive compounds [2,3]. It is estimated that nearly 80% of the world's total population, regularly, uses traditional medicine and its products for its healthcare needs especially in third world countries [4]. People from developing countries combine conventional medicine (exercise, meditation, lifestyle) with traditional medicines to treat themselves. Medicinal plants are preferred mostly because of their lower side effect and affordability. Moreover, in rural areas where the accessibility of a proper healthcare system is rare whereby the healthcare facilities are concentrated in cities, People living in these areas tend to get dependent on traditional medicinal plants and traditional physicians, which they think they understand their culture, their symptoms, and environment according to their disease. Ethiopia is one of the countries whereby medicinal plants play an important role in primary health care. About 95% of traditional medicines works in Ethiopia stand to be of plant origin [5]. Scientific investigation of millennia-old community knowledge on plant use is essential to define cultural identities of a particular community and understand links to their history, land and plant use practices, and traditional environmental philosophy. The knowledge on traditional medicinal plants of Ethiopia, which exits for centuries, is now facing extinction the knowledge has mainly been stored in the memories of elderly peoples and handed down verbally for generations [6]. Although medicinal plants play a significant role in supporting primary healthcare in Ethiopia, a few attempts have been done to scientifically identify, document, and promote the widely used medicinal plants and associated knowledge dynamics in the country. Hence, an appropriate investigation, identification, documentation, and usage of the knowledge and linking up with the modern ways on medicinal plants is needed. Moreover, it provides the opportunity for recognition, promotion, management, and protection of indigenous knowledge of a community on medicinal plants as a vital part of a nation's heritage, besides calling policymakers, natural resource managers, stakeholders, and cultural practitioners for conservation actions [6]. This study aims on classifying eight medicinal plants based on their leaf shape, texture, and color. Our contributions are as follow: (1) In this paper, we develop a novel dataset based on Ethiopian medicinal plants. (2) We use fine-tuning techniques for the architecture like changing the output classification layer to optimize such as SGD and Adams and adjust the learning rate. And data pre-processing techniques and data augmentation are used such as image data augmentation, image enhancement, and training epochs as a variable to get better result. (3) We use two models of a convolutional neural network to train and classify the dataset, and we compare both based on their performance on accuracy and chose the best to build a web-based medicinal plant identification system.

2   Related Work

This section defines different techniques used by researchers for identifying and classifying plants using machine methods. Machine learning techniques in classification, recognition, disease detection of plant species have been used for some time. Du et al. (2007) used leaf images of 20 plant species for plant identification based on digital morphological features, in this study K-Nearest neighbor is used for the classification and achieved 93% accuracy [8]. Herdiyeni and Wahyuni (2012) used a fusion of fuzzy local binary pattern and fuzzy color histogram and for classification, a Probabilistic neural network (PNN) is used on a dataset containing 2448 leaf images of medicinal plants from Indonesian forest achieving an accuracy of 74.5% [7]. According to ArunPriya C. and Balasaravanan in their work, 12 features are orthogonalized using Principal component analysis and fed into a classifier called support vector machine (SVM) achieving a result of 96.8% which is far better in performance compared to K-NN which achieved 81.3% [8]. According to Jiachun Liu et al. (2018), a novel classification method based on ten layers convolutional neural network is proposed and used on the Flavia dataset having 4800 images with 32 different kinds of leaf plants, achieving 87.92% accuracy [9]. Sue Han Lee et al. [10] Used deep learning in a bottom-up and top-down manner to classify 44 different plant species, Convolutional neural networks are used to learn the features and classify them. In addition, a Deconvolutional network is used for visualization of learned features, this work attained 99.5% of accuracy in identifying the plant species. Ferreira, Alessandro Dos Santos, et al. [11] used convolutional neural network in order to identify weed plant from soybean crops, More than 15,000 images composed of images of soybean crops, grass weeds, broadleaf is used for training the chosen classification architecture which is CaffeNet architecture of Neural Network. Baizel Kurian Varghese et al. proposed in their work a convolutional neural network that is based on ILSVRC 2012 dataset used for the pre-training process with the final layer, which is fully connected by replacing 1000 neurons with 44 neurons. More than 8800 leaf images were used for testing and 34,672 leaf images were used for training achieving an accuracy of 99.5%. Using a Mobile Net architecture with the same dataset and obtained correct predictions with an accuracy level of 99% [12,13]. This paper aims at comparing two convolutional neural network models named AlexNet and GoogLeNet on a novel image dataset, which is based on Ethiopian medicinal plants; Different variables like such as techniques of image pre-processing like image augmentation and training epoch are put into consideration in choosing the best model from the two.

3   The Proposed System

In this part, we present the system architectures and the deep learning techniques. Figure 1 shows the main architecture of the proposed system. The proposed architecture mainly involves two phases, namely, the training phase and the identification phase. In the training phase, the image acquisition is done by collecting leaf images of medicinal plants; different techniques like image enhancement, image resizing, and image segmentation are used for preprocessing the images. Features extraction is done by selected CNN models, which are AlexNet and GoogLeNet. The Identification phase involves the classification and labeling of medicinal plants based on the trained CNN models. Each model is trained on these models of CNN with the prepared dataset where features are extracted and classified by their names.

3.1   Dataset Preparation

Based on different expertise from the Department of Plant Biology and Biodiversity Management (lecturers, taxonomists) at Addis Ababa University, a list of plants that are used as medicine was prepared with a possible location area for all. From more than 80 medicinal plants, listed, leaf-based medicinal plants are chosen and located. Eight medicinal plants are chosen for the research and the research method used is experimental. More than 2100 leaf images of selected medicinal plants are collected from different parts of Addis Ababa, Ethiopia. To take photos of the leaf's Redmi Mobile phone with 64MP (Mega Pixel) camera is used. The dataset is then divided into two parts, 80% of the dataset is used for training, while the rest 20% is used as a test set and validation set. The total number of medicinal plant leaf images is shown in a table format below (Table 1).

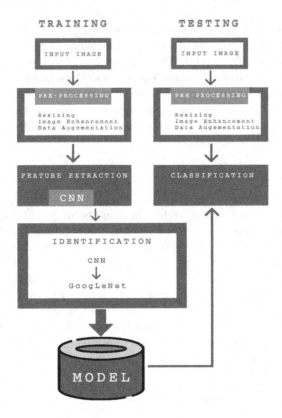

Fig. 1. The main architecture of the proposed system.

3.2 Image Pre-processing

The collected images are first cleaned in a way that does not affect labeled images. Since deep learning performance is improved based on the number of data the algorithm is fed, the total number of images increased using a technique called image augmentation. Image augmentation techniques like horizontal flip, vertical flip and rotate augmentation are used. Likewise, according to the model, different activities that are suitable input for our models are performed including resizing the images. All images are resized to fit the scale represented by AlexNet and GoogLeNet, which are 227 * 227 and 224 * 224 respectively. Below is a table showing the number of images in each class after image augmentation (Table 2).

3.3 Experiment Parameters

Two CNN architectures AlexNet and GoogLeNet were fine-tuned and used. The batch size used was 64 and 16 for both AlexNet and GoogLeNet respectively. For optimization algorithms, Adam and SGD are used which helps to compute the adaptive learning rate for each parameter and improves the accuracy of

Table 1. Total number of images before data augmentation

Local names of medicinal plants	Class id	Training set	Validation set
Gulo	0	176	43
Qetetit	1	220	56
Agam	2	320	40
Birbira	3	250	54
Embis	4	263	69
Endawela	5	200	55
Sama	6	167	40
Shinet	7	178	43
Total		2174	

Table 2. The total number of images after augmentation

Local names of medicinal plants	Class id	Training set	Validation set
Gulo	0	420	167
Qetetit	1	400	148
Agam	2	440	126
Birbira	3	390	119
Embis	4	546	191
Endawela	5	320	156
Sama	6	322	158
Shinet	7	334	158
Total		4395	

the model. For both models, the output classification layers are adjusted to the number of classes, which is eight. Dropout parameter is layer is used with a probability of 40%, to increase the accuracy of the model. After comparing the results of the accuracy of the two models, the one with better performance is chosen to train the dataset with the augmented data. In order to increase the original size of the training dataset and to avoid overfitting data augmentation is used with the following variable horizontal flip, Zoom range and shift range 0.2, rotation range 30°, width, and height shifting. Epochs given for training varied from 50 to 200 for both architectures.

3.4   Training and Classification of the Models

In this study, two architectures of convolutional neural networks are used to train and classify leaf images of medicinal plants collected and preprocessed for identification purposes. AlexNet and GoogLeNet, the two networks, differ in general architecture. Goog-LeNet has Inception Modules, which perform with

Table 3. Classification results of the proposed architectures.

CNNs	Classes			
	AlexNet (A)	AlexNet (A)	Goog-LeNet (A)	Goog-LeNet (P)
Gulo	54	49	54	51
Agam	54	51	54	50
Qetetit	54	46	54	49
Birbira	54	45	54	48
Embis	54	48	54	52
Endawela	54	52	54	51
Sama	54	50	54	49
Shinet	54	49	54	51
Accuracy (%)	90.2%		92.8%	

different convolutions and concatenate the filters for the next layer. AlexNet, on the other hand, has layers input provided by one previous layer instead of a filter concatenation. In this paper, the collected images are trained to classify images on AlexNet and GoogLeNet models to choose which model performs better in terms of accuracy, loss, and validation. After getting better accuracy results in GoogLeNet, this model is chosen to train and classify the medicinal plants and the model to feed for a web-based classification system.

4   Experiment and Results

In our experiment, 1740 leaf images of the original dataset are used for training and 432 leaf images are considered for testing the performance of the system. For AlexNet, 42 samples are misclassified. 5 data is misclassified in class 1. 3 data is misclassified in class 2. 8 data is misclassified in class 3. 9 data is misclassified in class 4. 6 data is misclassified in class 5. 2 data is misclassified in class 6. 4 data misclassified in class 7 and 5 data misclassifies in class 8 as shown in Table 3. Classification accuracy for each class is 90.7%, 89.4%, 85.1%, 83.3%, 88.8%, 96.2%, 96.2%, 92.5%, 90.7% from class1 to class 8 respectively, which gives overall average accuracy of 90.2%. For GoogLeNet in total 30 samples are misclassified. 4 data misclassified in class 1, 4 data misclassified in class 2, 5 data misclassified in class 3, 6 data misclassified in class 4, 2 data misclassified in class 5, 3 data misclassified in class 6, 5 data misclassified in class 7 and 3 data misclassified in class 8 shown in Table 3. Classification accuracy for each class is 94.4%, 92.4%, 90.7%, 88.8%, and 96.2%, 94.2%, 90.0%, 94.4% from class1 to class 8 respectively, which gives overall average accuracy of 92.8%. The classification result for both AlexNet and GoogLeNet before data augmentation is shown in the Fig. 2 table below.

Based on the result, GoogLeNet is chosen as the preferred CNN architecture to train and classify the medicinal plants with the augment-ed dataset and fine-tuned algorithm. The number of epoch given for the training was 100,150 and 200 in which the results were 89.8%, 94.3% and 96.7% respectively.

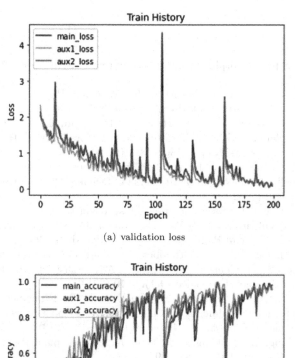

(a) validation loss

(b) accuracy

Fig. 2. The plot for training and testing accuracy and validation loss using GoogLeNet.

5   Conclusion

In this paper, an automatic classification of Ethiopian medicinal plants based on convolutional networks is proposed. We first pre-process images by resizing, enhancement, data augmentation and normalization, and we use fine-tuning technique to improve the accuracy of the model. Two convolutional neural network architectures namely AlexNet and GoogLeNet are used to train and classify the medicinal plants and the results are compared in terms of accuracy and validation loss. Our experimental results showed that the larger the dataset and the number of epochs GoogLeNet showed better achievement in classification the target correctly. GoogLeNet showed 96.7% training accuracy with 200 epochs, which is used for a web-based application to able users to upload a leaf image of a medicinal plant and identify the plant along with a description of their use.

References

1. Cope, J.S., Corney, D., Clark, J.Y., Remagnino, P., Wilkin, P.: Plant species identification using digital morphometrics: a review. Expert Syst. Appl. **39**(8), 7562–7573 (2012)
2. Lambert, J., Srivastava, J., Vietmeyer, N.: Medicinal Plants: Rescuing a Global Heritage, vol. 355. World Bank Publications (1997)
3. Thirumalai, T., Kelumalai, E., Senthilkumar, B., David, E.: Ethnobotanical study of medicinal plants used by the local people in Vellore District, Tamilnadu, India. Ethnobotanical Leaflets **13**(10), 1302–1311 (2009)
4. Musila, W., Kisangau, D., Muema, J.: Conservation status and use of medicinal plants by traditional medical practitioners in Machakos District, Kenya. Nat. Mus. Kenya **22**, 12–18 (2002)
5. Demisew, S., Dagne, E.: Basic and applied research on medicinal plants of Ethiopia. In: Proceedings of the National Workshop on Biodiversity Conservation and Sustainable Use of Medicinl Plants in Ethiopia, Addis Ababa (2001)
6. Giday, M., Teklehaymanot, T.: Ethnobotanical study of plants used in management of livestock health problems by Afar people of Ada'ar District, Afar Regional State, Ethiopia. J. Ethnobiol. Ethnomed. **9**(1), 1–10 (2013)
7. Lulekal, E., Asfaw, Z., Kelbessa, E., Van Damme, P.: Ethnomedicinal study of plants used for human ailments in Ankober District, North Shewa Zone, Amhara region, Ethiopia. J. Ethnobiol. Ethnomed. **9**(1), 1–13 (2013)
8. Du, J.X., Wang, X.F., Zhang, G.J.: Leaf shape based plant species recognition. Appl. Math. Comput. **185**(2), 883–893 (2007)
9. Herdiyeni, Y., Wahyuni, N.K.S.: Mobile application for Indonesian medicinal plants identification using fuzzy local binary pattern and fuzzy color histogram. In: 2012 International Conference on Advanced Computer Science and Information Systems (ICACSIS), pp. 301–306 (2012)
10. Priya, C.A., Balasaravanan, T., Thanamani, A.S.: An efficient leaf recognition algorithm for plant classification using support vector machine. In: International Conference on Pattern Recognition, Informatics and Medical Engineering, pp. 428–432, March 2012
11. Liu, J., Yang, S., Cheng, Y., Song, Z.: Plant leaf classification based on deep learning. In: 2018 Chinese Automation Congress, pp. 3165–3169 (2018)
12. Lee, S.H., Chan, C.S., Wilkin, P., Remagnino, P.: Deep-plant: plant identification with convolutional neural networks. In: 2015 IEEE International Conference on Image Processing, pp. 452–456, September 2015
13. dos Santos Ferreira, A., Freitas, D.M., da Silva, G.G., Pistori, H., Folhes, M.T.: Weed detection in soybean crops using ConvNets. Comput. Electron. Agric. **143**, 314–324 (2014)
14. Varghese, B.K., Augustine, A., Babu, J.M., Sunny, D., Cherian, S.: Plant recognition using convolutional neural networks. In: proceedings of the Fourth International Conference on Computing Methodologies and Communication (2020)

Novelty Detection-Based Automated Anomaly Identification via Optimized Deep Generative Model

Lianye Liu[1], Jinping Liu[2(✉)], Juanjuan Wu[2], Jiaming Zhou[2], and Meiling Cai[2]

[1] Hunan Meteorological Science Institute, Changsha 410007, Hunan, China
[2] Hunan Provincial Key Laboratory of Intelligent Computing and Language Information Processing, Hunan Normal University, Changsha 410081, Hunan, China

Abstract. Novelty detection (ND) is a crucial task in machine learning to identify anomalies in the test data in some respects different from the training data. As an anomaly detection method, novelty detection only uses normal samples for model learning, which can well fit most of the natural scenes that the amount of abnormal samples is in fact strongly insufficient, such as network intrusion detection, industrial fault detection, and so on, due to the rareness of abnormal events or the high cost of abnormal samples collection. This paper proposes a reconstruction-based ND scheme by introducing an optimized deep generative model (ODGM), which combines the concept of Variational Auto-encoder (VAE) and the generative adversarial network (GAN) model jointly to efficiently and stably learn the essential characteristics from normal samples. A novelty index is established by combining signal reconstruction loss and feature loss between the original signal of the reconstructed signal based on the ODGM on normal samples for anomaly point identification in the test data. The effectiveness and superiority of the proposed model is validated and compared with other representative deep learning-based novelty detection models on two public data sets.

Keywords: Novelty detection · Variational autoencoder · Generative adversarial networks · Intrusion detection

1 Introduction

A well-behaved machine learning model depends largely on the assumption that the test data and training data sample from the same distribution [1, 2]. Anomaly detection refers to the problem of finding unexpected patterns or behaviors (also called outliers, discordant observations, exceptions, aberrations, peculiarities, and so on) in data, inherently depending on the data distribution. Hence, anomaly detection plays an important role in machine learning tasks. Specifically, considerable applications require being able to decide whether a new observation (test data point) belongs to the same distribution as existing observations, or should be considered as different (also called anomaly, or outlier).

© Springer Nature Singapore Pte Ltd. 2022
X. Liao et al. (Eds.): BigData 2021, CCIS 1496, pp. 117–134, 2022.
https://doi.org/10.1007/978-981-16-9709-8_9

Anomaly detection has been widely used in diverse scenes, such as credit card fraud detection [3], industrial process fault detection [4], network intrusion detection [5, 6], fault detection of sensor network [7], medical mammography diagnosis [8], and many others, to mention but a few. As summarized in the literature [9], anomaly detection can be mainly categorized into two aspects, i.e., the outlier detection and novelty detection.

The kernel difference between outlier detection and novelty detection is whether the positive samples (outlier samples, or anomaly samples) exist in the training data. The former uses positive samples, whereas the latter only considers the normal samples. Detailedly, novelty detection (ND) [10] is to identify the data samples that are inconsistent with the normal data (also called the target class samples, or negative samples) in the test samples, which are determined as novel data (also called the non-target class samples, or positive samples). In the training phase of ND, only normal samples are used for model learning; in the test phase, the learned novel detector is used to identify the test samples as normal data or anomaly (novel) data. Why only normal data are used for the anomaly detection? Following three reasons can explain it.

a) In some scene, achieving an anomaly sample is intractable or expensive, even nearly impossible, such as the fault diagnosis of High-speed rail, where fault samples is rare and achieving fault samples are too expensive [11].
b) The anomaly samples are quite scarce due to the low frequency of abnormal states in most natural scenes, such as credit card fraud detection, network intrusion detection [6]. Even though some abnormal events can be measured, the abnormal samples is really rare, which cannot fully cover all kinds of potential abnormal events.
c) Oppositely, it can customarily achieve considerable norm samples with low cost. For instance, in industrial production process, most of the conditions are normal in the daily production, and the faulty conditions are scarce or only occur once, and once a serious fault occurs the system may be stopped for maintenance to avoid great loss.

Due to the scarcity of abnormal samples, the anomaly detection model selection and learning are actually nontrivial. Training a detection model based on the idea of novelty detection is an effective solution. Thus, novelty detection-based anomaly identification has received great attention in many application fields involving large datasets acquired from critical systems, such as medical diagnosis [12], fault diagnosis of complex industrial processes [13], credit card or mobile phone fraud detection [14], network intrusion detection [6, 15], and text mining [16], and so on.

ND is conventionally approached by the frame of one-class classification [17], where one class (normal or anomaly data) has to be distinguished from all other possibilities. As summarized in Pimentel's work [10], ND approaches can be categorized into: (1) probabilistic, (2) distance-based, (3) reconstruction-based, (4) domain-based and (4) information-theoretic approaches. Generally, all these methods attempt to assign a proper novelty score $N(x)$ on a test sample x to determine whether x is a novel sample or not based on a learned or predefined novelty threshold k.

Probabilistic approaches [18] learn a probability density function (PDF) using normal samples and then determine the test samples sampled from this distribution model or not. Distance-based approaches rely on well-defined distance metrics [19] to determine whether a test sample is close enough to the normal samples or not. Reconstruction-based approaches evaluate the reconstruction errors of the test sample based on the learned system model [20], such as neural network or state-space model. Domain-based approaches learn a boundary based on the structure of training samples to identify the novelty of a test sample [10]. Information theoretic approaches [21] check the changing of the information content of test samples to determine whether novelty samples exist.

In recent years, as an implicit probability learner, many novelty detection methods based on generative models have emerged with the rapid development of deep generative models. Generally, these methods attempt to learn the essential (distribution) information of normal data using generative models, such as the variational autoencoders (VAEs) [22], adversarial autoencoders (AAEs) model [23], and the generative adversarial network (GANs) [24]. Customarily, these ND approaches can be essentially categorized into the reconstruction-based methods. Since the generative model can well fit the essential distribution of normal samples implicitly, a norm test sample can be well restored by the learned model, and vice versa. Hence, the reconstruction error can be regarded as an effective score to identify whether a sample is a novelty or not. In addition, these deep learning models combine novelty detection and multi-class classifiers into a single model to achieve end-to-end detection results. Thus, they can achieve relatively better performance.

Generally, the explicit or implicit distribution variability of variables between the test samples and training samples is a commonly-used score for the novelty evaluation. However, traditional methods cannot always achieve the essential distribution characteristics of high dimensional data effectively. For instance, in literature [25], a VAE-based novelty detection is addressed. The reconstruction probability based on the learned VAE model is taken into account to measure the distribution variability of variables in test samples. Though VAE can reconstruct the input sample information, the reconstructed information is often not close enough to reality. In addition, GAN can theoretically learn any distribution. However, the training of GAN starts from random noise, which makes the training extremely unstable.

By combining the concept of these two structures [26], it does not only reduce the reconstruction error of VAE, but also improves the stability of GAN training. Thus, it can effectively improve the fitting ability of generative models to the sample characteristics. Taking advantage of the strong feature representation ability of VAE and GAN, this paper proposes an optimized deep generative model (ODGM)-based novelty detection scheme, combining the VAE and GAN model jointly to efficiently and stably learn the essential characteristics from normal samples, for anomaly detection. In the test phase, the reconstruction error from the decoder to the generator and the feature representation loss between the encoder representation and the discriminator feature representation are combined to generate the novelty score. If the novelty score exceeds a threshold, it indicates that the test sample is novel.

The contributions of this article are summarized as follows.

(1) An optimized deep generative model is introduced to generate the novelty detection frame by combining the strong reconstruction ability of VAE and generation ability of GAN model, having strong sensitivity to any novel samples.

(2) A new novelty score combing the reconstruction error and the feature representation loss in the discriminator network feature layer between the original test sample and the generated sample is introduced, which makes a full use of the features of normal sample extracted by the generator and discriminator, effectively improving the novelty detection accuracy.

The rest of the paper is organized as follows. Section 2 briefly addresses the principle of VAE and GAN models. Section 3 details the proposed ODGM-based novelty detection scheme. Section 4 gives the validation and comparative experiment results on multiple public datasets, followed by the conclusions and possible further research directions in Sect. 5.

2 Preliminaries

This section briefly addresses the principles of VAE and GAN models.

2.1 VAE

VAE [27] is a generative model, derived from its predecessor, auto-encoder (AE). VAE makes a projection of a sample x from its original space to a latent space z through an encoding process, $p(z|x)$, assuming that the hidden variable z obeys a multivariate normal (MVN) distribution, i.e., $z \sim N(0, I)$, thus the posterior $p(z|x)$ also obeys a MVN distribution. Based on the assumption, samples are drawn from hidden variables. Thus, the likelihood function can be expressed by using the following mathematical expectation under the distribution of hidden variables,

$$p(x) = \int p(x|z)p(z)dz. \tag{1}$$

The decoding process of generating samples from hidden variables is the generative model that we need. Encoders and decoders can adopt a variety of structures, where Recurrent Neural Networks (RNN) [28], Convolutional neural networks (CNN) [29] are frequently-used network model for the processing of sequence samples and image samples, respectively.

For the purpose of achieving a one-to-one correspondence between the original sample and the reconstructed sample, each sample x should have its own corresponding posterior distribution. Then, it can restore the random hidden variables sampled from the posterior distribution to a corresponding reconstructed sample $\hat{x}$. In each batch of processing, n samples will be fitted by the neural network to get n corresponding parameters to facilitate sample reconstruction by the generator. Under the Gaussian assumption, there are two encoders in a VAE model, which respectively generate the mean $\mu = g_1(x)$ and variance $\log \sigma^2 = g_2(x)$ of the sample in the hidden variable space.

A VAE can be divided into three phases.

(1) Encoding phase. It obtains the mean and variance of the sample by the two neural networks;

(2) Re-parameterization phase. Its purpose is to sample from the posterior distribution and be able to use back propagation algorithm for model training;

(3) Decoding process. It generates artificial samples from the re-parameterized variables through the generative (or decoder) model.

2.2 GAN

GAN [30] has achieved great success in signal translation (especially in image signals) from one domain to another, e.g., style transfer, super resolution, colorization of Gray images, and so on. Generally, it has an absolute advantage in the field of image generation. GAN essentially fits the difficult-to-solve likelihood function by a neural network, letting the model train its own appropriate parameters to fit the likelihood function. This neural network is the discriminator in a GAN.

Detailedly, a GAN involves two game players, i.e., the Generator and the discriminator. The goal of the generator is to generate realistic fake samples so that the discriminator cannot distinguish its authenticity. The goal of the discriminator is to correctly distinguish whether the data is a real sample or a fake sample from the generator.

In the process of game playing, two competitors need to continuously optimize their own generation ability and discriminative ability, and the result of the game is to find the Nash equilibrium between the two players. When the discriminator's recognition ability reaches a certain level but the data source cannot be correctly judged, a generator that learns the true data distribution is achieved.

The generator and discriminator in GAN can be any differentiable function, usually represented by a multi-layer neural network. The generator $G(z; \theta)$ is a network with the model parameter of θ, whose input is random noise and output is the fake sample. The discriminator $D(x; \varphi)$ is a binary classification network, having the model parameter (φ), whose input is real samples or pseudo samples and the output is 0 or 1 (corresponding to pseudo samples or real samples, respectively).

GAN optimizes the parameters of the generator and the discriminator according to the different loss functions of the generator and the discriminator, avoiding the complex computational process of the likelihood function.

3 Proposed Method

This section details the proposed ODGM-based ND scheme.

3.1 Motivation

The proposed ODGM is aimed at optimizing the sample generation performance of VAE [31] and GAN [32]. In other words, ODGM focuses on improving the essential feature learning ability of the original VAE and GAN models. To summarize, VAE and GAN models have the following drawbacks, respectively.

(1) Problems with VAE. Samples generated by a VAE are quite different from the real samples. The first reason is the inherent drawback of the KL divergence used in the

loss function of VAE model, as verified by many works [29]. Another possible reason is that the posterior distribution is too simple, which cannot cover the complex distribution characteristics of various learning scenario.

(2) Problems with GAN. The GAN model is difficult to train well. The model collapse, model non-convergence or training instability are frequent phenomena, due to the problems of gradient disappearance, which makes the model unable to continue training or cause training instability. It is necessary to carefully balance the training level of the generator and the discriminator. The conventionally used alternate training method of updating the discriminator once and then updating the generator k times does not alleviate the training problem very well.

In view of above issues in VAE and GAN, the ODGM is proposed by combining VAE and GAN together for the essential characteristic learning of normal samples, whose architecture is shown in Fig. 1.

The proposed ODGM uses the principle of GAN to optimize the VAE model. It incorporates a discriminator on the basis of the original VAE, and uses the discriminator to judge whether the sample is generated by the generator or not. The closer the result is to the real sample, the higher the score. The addition of the discriminator can effectively improve the similarity between the generator generated samples and the original samples, and simultaneously improve the authenticity of the generated samples.

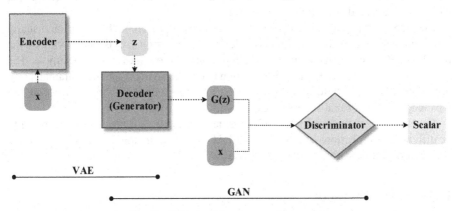

Fig. 1. Optimized deep generative model

From the perspective of GAN, in the traditional training process, the generator starts from random noise to generate samples. It takes a lot of training time from the initial state to the end of the training, and it shows great instability at the same time. The addition of the VAE structure enables the generator to act as a decoder at the same time, generating from the characteristics of real samples, which can effectively improve the stability of training and shorten the training time.

3.2 ODGM-Based Novelty Detection Analysis

As can be seen from Fig. 1, the ODGM involves three network models, i.e., an Encoder, a Generator/Decoder and a Discriminator.

The Encoder and Generator/Decoder can be regarded as a VAE model as the generator part of the GAN model in ODGM. The generator part learns the characteristic information of the input data (normal samples) through the encoder and decoder networks, and uses the encoder and decoder networks to reconstruct the input information. The working flow of this sub-network can be summarized as follows.

The input of the Encoder is any sample point $\mathbf{x} \in R^n$, and its parameter is θ, so the encoder can be expressed as $q_\theta(\mathbf{z}|\mathbf{x})$. The encoder encodes the n-dimensional data x into a latent space $\mathbf{z}$, and the dimension of $\mathbf{z}$ is generally much smaller than n. The encoder effectively compress the data into a low-dimensional space. Under an assumption that $\mathbf{z}$ obeys a Gaussian distribution, the output of $\mathbf{z}$ of the encoder can be actually decomposed into two steps:

(1) The encoder yields the model parameters of the Gaussian distribution (mean, variance), which are different for each data point;
(2) Fuse the noise with the Gaussian distribution and sample from it to obtain $\mathbf{z}$.

The input of Generator/Decoder is the latent variable $\mathbf{z}$, whose output is $\hat{\mathbf{x}} = G(\mathbf{x})$. Given the model parameter ϕ, Generator/Decoder can be expressed as $p_\phi(\hat{\mathbf{x}}|\mathbf{z})$. The network reconstructs the coded information $\mathbf{z}$ into sample information $G(\mathbf{x})$ after dimensionality reduction.

In the VAE sub-network structure, there is a reconstruction error between the original sample $\mathbf{x}$ and its reconstructed sample information $G(\mathbf{x})$, and for sample points from the same category, the reconstruction error can be regarded as a relatively fixed value. When samples from a single type are used for model training, the sub-network can obtain the reconstruction ability for the corresponding sample type. When the input is a novel value, the reconstruction error will shift greatly. Therefore, by checking the reconstruction error, it can determine whether the test sample is novel or note.

By adding an additional discriminator, the decoder/generator and the discriminator can be regarded as a GAN model.

The discriminator is used to judge the authenticity of the generated sample $G(\mathbf{z})$. First, use the real sample $\mathbf{x}$ to train the discriminator network to learn the characteristic information of the real sample. For any input $G(\mathbf{z})$, judge whether it is a real sample or fake sample. In the discriminator network, the loss of $\mathbf{x}$ and $G(\mathbf{z})$ at the feature level for the normal samples should be nearly constant. If an input sample $\mathbf{x}$ is a novel value, the loss at the feature level will theoretically shift greatly. Therefore, based on the changing of the feature loss, the novelty of the sample can be determined.

3.3 Detailed Steps of ODGM-Based Novelty Detection

According to the characteristics of the ODGM, a novelty detection method based on the ODGM is proposed. The novelty score is constructed by combining the reconstruction errors of the encoder and the generator, and compared with a predefined threshold to determine whether the test data is novel or not. The novelty detection model structure is shown in Fig. 2.

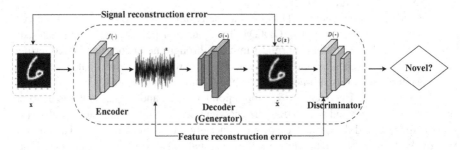

Fig. 2. ODGM-based novelty detection

For each sample **x**, the Encoder converts it into the hidden space feature **z**, and then the Generator/Decoder decodes it into a generated sample $G(\mathbf{z})$. Discriminator makes a classification task to distinguish the real sample **x** from the generated sample $G(\mathbf{z})$. By the parallel game playing of the VAE sub-network and the discriminator, the final ODGM is achieved until the model converges.

After the model training, the Generator/Decoder can restore any latent sample **z** of **x** to the generated sample $\hat{\mathbf{x}}$. Since only the normal samples are used for model training in the training phase, for the normal sample, the signal reconstruction error, $\mathcal{L}_G$ between the generated sample and the original sample tends to be stable and can be used as a novelty scores.

$$\mathcal{L}_G = \left\| \mathbf{x} - \hat{\mathbf{x}} \right\|_2^2 \tag{2}$$

For the sample **x** and its generated sample $G(\mathbf{z})$, if **x** is a normal sample, the loss of **x** and $G(\mathbf{z})$ at the feature layer of the Discriminator network should nearly be a fixed value. Therefore, it can be judged whether the test sample is novelty or not according to the feature loss of **x** and $G(\mathbf{z})$ at the feature level, where $D(\hat{\mathbf{x}})$ stands for the last feature representation of Discriminator.

$$\mathcal{L}_D = \left\| f(\mathbf{x}) - D(\hat{\mathbf{x}}) \right\|_2^2 \tag{3}$$

Combining (2) and (3), a hybrid novelty score is defined as follows,

$$N(\mathbf{x}) = \lambda \mathcal{L}_G + (1 - \lambda)\mathcal{L}_D \tag{4}$$

where λ is a weighting parameter.

To summarize, detailed steps of the ODGM-based novelty detection method are shown as follows.

Algorithm 1: ODGM-based Novelty Detection

Input $\mathbf{x}$, E , G , D , f , Threshold α

Output $N(\mathbf{x})$

1: **Train ODGM based on normal samples**

2: $\tilde{\mathbf{z}} \leftarrow E(\mathbf{x})$

3: $\hat{\mathbf{x}} \leftarrow G(\tilde{\mathbf{z}})$

4: $\mathcal{L}_G = \left\| \mathbf{x} - \hat{\mathbf{x}} \right\|_2^2$

5: $\mathcal{L}_D = \left\| f(\mathbf{x}) - D(\hat{\mathbf{x}}) \right\|_2^2$

6: return $N(\mathbf{x}) = \lambda \mathcal{L}_G + (1 - \lambda) \mathcal{L}_D$

7: if $N(\mathbf{x}) > \alpha$, return 1

    else return 0

8: **end procedure**

---

4   Experimental Validation

To verify the effectiveness of the proposed ODGM-based novelty detection model, this section details the confirmatory and comparative experiments on two public data sets. The related comparative methods involved are: novelty detection method based on GAN (NDGAN) [24]; novelty detection method based on conditional GAN (AnoGAN) [33]; novelty detection method based on traditional ADAE, which directly uses the autoencoder in ADAE to reconstruct samples.

4.1   Performance Evaluation Criteria

Three commonly used criteria are used to evaluate the model performance, i.e., precision, recall and AUC (Area Under Curve).

The following table shows the confusion matrix of true positive (TP), true negative (TN), false positive (FP), and false negative (FN). TP and TN indicate that the positive and negative cases are classified accurately; FP and FN indicate that the positive and negative cases are classified incorrectly (Table 1).

Table 1. Confusion matrix

Confusion matrix		Actual value	
		Positive	Negative
Prediction	Positive	TP	FP
	Negative	FN	TN

The ratio of correctly classified positive samples to all samples classified as positive is Precision. The calculation method is as follows:

$$\text{Precision} = \frac{\text{TP}}{\text{TP} + \text{FP}} \tag{5}$$

The ratio of correctly classified positive samples to actual positive samples is the recall rate (Recall), given by

$$\text{Recall} = \frac{TP}{\text{TP} + \text{FN}}. \tag{6}$$

There is also a common performance evaluation criterion, Receiver Operating Characteristic (ROC) curve. The ROC curve is independent of the class distribution of the data set, and has good robustness to the imbalance of the data set. The vertical axis of the ROC graph is TP rate, and the horizontal axis is FP rate. Each threshold corresponds to a point, change the threshold, and connect all the points obtained is the curve of the classifier on the data set. The closer the curve is to the upper left corner, the better the classifier performance. However, the curve cannot quantitatively evaluate the performance of the classifier, so the area under the curve AUC is often used to replace the ROC curve as an evaluation method. The larger the value, the better the performance of the classifier.

4.2 Experimental Configuration

In this paper, two public datasets, i.e., the MNIST[1] handwritten digits data set and the NSL-KDD[2] intrusion detection data set, are used for the performance validation and comparison.

The MNIST data set comes from the National Institute of Standards and Technology, and the National Institute of Standards and Technology (NIST) training set consists of handwritten numbers from 250 different people. Among them, 50% are high school students and 50% are from the Census Bureau staff. In the experiment, MNIST pixels are compressed to the range of $[-1,1]$.

The NSL-KDD data set contains 41 variables, of which 34 variables are continuous and the remaining 7 are categorical. For classification features, the one-hot representation is used to encode these categorical variables and finally a total of 121 features. In the experiment, the minimum and maximum scaling approach is adopted to normalize the features.

The experimental environment is listed in Table 2. The hyperparameters of the training network are set in Table 3.

---

[1] http://yann.lecun.com/exdb/mnist/.
[2] https://www.unb.ca/cic/datasets/nsl.html.

Table 2. Experimental environment configuration

Project	Configuration
Processor model	Inter(R)I5-8300HCPU@2.30GHz
Running memory	16GB
operating system	Linux(Ubuntu18.04)
GPU model	NVIDIA Geforce GTX 1050Ti

Table 3. Hyperparameter settings

Components	kernel_size	Featuremaps	Activation
Encoder	3 × 2	64	ReLU
	3 × 2	128	ReLU
	3 × 2	192	ReLU
	4 × 1	64	ReLU
	1 × 1	128	ReLU
Generator	4 × 1	64	ReLU
	3 × 2	64	ReLU
	3 × 2	64	ReLU
	3 × 2	32	ReLU
	4 × 1	16	ReLU
Discriminator	3 × 2	16	ReLU
	3 × 2	16	ReLU

4.3 Experimental Results and Analysis

4.3.1 Experiments on MNIST

In this experiment, a randomly-chosen 60,000 samples from the MNIST are used as the training set to train the ODGM in advance. After model training, the model has the ability to reconstruct MNIST samples effectively. The training process is shown in Fig. 3.

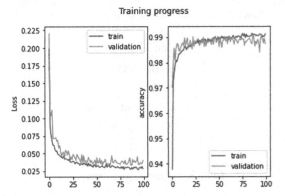

Fig. 3. Training loss function and accuracy rate change graph

The test set consists of 10,000 MNIST samples and 10% notMNI-ST data set. NotM-NIST is similar to MNIST, and the image size is 28 × 28. But compared to MNIST, notMNIST contains 10 types of artistic printed characters from A to J. The shapes of the characters are different, they are noisier, and are more difficult to handle. NotMNIST is selected as a novelty to test the performance of the proposed method, and ROC curve and AUC are selected as evaluation criteria. Experimental results are listed in Table 4.

It can be seen from Table 4 that in MNIST data set, the ODGM-based novelty detection approach has higher detection accuracy and recall rate, which proves that the proposed method can well distinguish novel samples from ordinary sample points.

Table 4. MNIST experiment

Method	Precision	Recall	AUC
AnoGAN	0.7952	0.7865	0.821
NDGAN	0.8213	0.8331	0.762
ADAE	0.8361	0.8032	0.791
ODGM	**0.8503**	**0.8231**	**0.837**

Figure 4 shows the comparative ROC results on MNIST dataset. In Fig. 4, the abscissa of the plane is false positive rate (FPR), and the ordinate is true positive rate (TPR). For a certain classifier, we can achieve a TPR and FPR point pair based on its performance on the test sample. In this way, this classifier can be mapped to a point on the ROC plane. Adjusting the threshold used in the classification of this classifier, we can get a curve that passes through (0, 0), (1, 1), which is the ROC curve of this classifier. In general, this curve should be above the line connecting (0,0) and (1,1). The better the classification performance, the closer the ROC curve to the upper left corner, the greater the AUC value can be achieved.

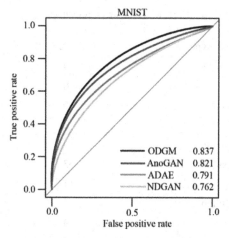

Fig. 4. ROC results of MNIST novelty detection results

As can be seen from Fig. 4 the proposed ODGM-based novelty detection scheme has a higher AUC value, which indicates that the proposed method has better identification capabilities of novel samples.

4.3.2   Experiments on NSL-KDD:

KDD99 [34] is a network connection data set simulated and collected by the US Department of Defense Advanced Planning Agency at MIT Lincoln Laboratory. It contains approximately 5 million network connection data, divided into training set and test set, including 4 categories and 39 sub-categories. Abnormal intrusion type and normal connection. Its identification type is shown in Table 5.

Table 5. Identification type of intrusion detection experiment data

Logo type	Meaning
Normal	Normal record
Dos	Denial of service attack
Probe	Surveillance and other detection activities
R2L	Illegal access from remote machine
U2R	Illegal access by ordinary users to local super user privileges

In intrusion detection, the 10% subset of the entire data set is customarily used. This subset greatly reduces the amount of calculation while extracting valid data. It contains 494,021 training records and 311,029 test records. Its detailed composition is shown in Table 6.

Table 6. Data set composition

Type	Attack type	Training	Test
U2R	loadmodule	9	2
	Butter_overflow	30	20
	rootkit	10	13
	perl	3	2
R2L	ftp_write	8	3
	guess_password	53	1231
	imap	11	1
	multihop	7	18
	phf	4	2
	spy	2	0
	warezclient	890	0
	warezmaster	20	944
Probe	ipsweep	3599	141
	nmap	1493	73
	portsweep	2931	157
	satan	3633	735
DoS	back	956	359
	land	18	7
	neptune	41214	4657
	pod	201	41
	smurf	2646	665
	teardrop	892	12
Normal		67343	9711
Total		125973	18794

NSL-KDD[3] is modified from KDD99. The training set of NSL-KDD removes redundant data, so that the classification results are not biased towards frequent records; in the test set, NSL-KDD also deletes a large amount of duplicate data. The number of records in the NSL-KDD test and training is set reasonably and can be run in the entire experimental group.

Analyzing the data set, it shows that the first 41 items are features, and the 42nd item is a marker. Several typical features among the 41 features are listed as follows.

(1) Protocol_type is the protocol type, which is discrete type variable. There are 3 types in total, i.e., TCP, UDP, ICMP.

---

[3] https://www.unb.ca/cic/datasets/nsl.html.

(2) The service is the network service type of the target host, there are 70 discrete types.
(3) The flag is the normal or error state of the connection. There are 11 types: OTH, REJ, RSTO, RSTO-S0, RSTR, S0, S1, S2, S3, SF, SH. It represents whether the connection is started or completed according to the requirements of the protocol. SF represents the normal state, and the remaining 10 types represent different error states.
(4) Hot is the number of times of accessing system sensitive files and directories, continuous type, and the range is [0, 101].
(5) Num_file_creations is the number of file creation operations, continuous type, and the range is [0, 100].
(6) The is_hot_login feature in the data set is removed, because it represents the status of whether the login belongs to the hot list or not. In most cases, the value of this feature is 0, which has no effect on the classification results of intrusion detection.

By the one-hot representation of categorical variables of the NSL-KDD data set, the input data in all possible feature vectors contains a total of 121-dimensional features, which are expressed as a two-dimensional 11*11 data vector.

The experiment builds a model by calling the pytorch framework, and divides the data set into a training set and a test set according to a ratio of 8:2. The training set samples are all normal (non-intrusion behavior). In the test phase, four types of intrusion (U2R, R2L, Probe, Dos) are used to generate the novel samples. Experimental results are shown in Fig. 5 and Table 7.

As can be seen From Fig. 5, the ROC curve has nothing to do with the category distribution of the data set, and has good robustness to the imbalance of the novelty detection data set.

Table 7. NSL-KDD intrusion detection experiment

Method	Precision	Recall	AUC
AnoGAN	0.7851	0.7745	0.78
ND-GAN	0.7721	0.7923	0.773
ADAE	0.8051	0.7921	0.802
ODGM	**0.8465**	**0.8346**	**0.845**

Compared with these comparative methods, it can be seen from Fig. 5 that the ROC curve of the proposed method is closer to the upper left corner, indicating that the model has an excellent ability to identify novel samples.

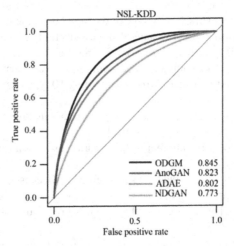

Fig. 5. Comparative ROC results on NSL-KDD data set.

5   Conclusions

Novelty detection, a method that only uses normal samples for model training to identify the difference between the training data and the test data, is a promising solution to remedy the scarcity of the anomaly samples. This paper proposes a novelty detection method based on an optimized depth generation model by integrating the VAE and GAN model. It conducts two sets of adversarial learning through two generative models, which cannot only enable the VAE to achieve better reconstruction ability, but also avoid the mode collapse that is easy to occur in traditional GAN to a certain extent. By combining the sample reconstruction error and feature loss to form a hybrid novelty score, the novel samples can be determined simply by a thresholding method. Extensive experimental results on two public datasets show that the proposed novelty detection method can effectively distinguish novelty samples from normal samples, which poses apparently better classification performance than other deep learning-based ND approaches.

Acknowledgements. This work was supported by the national natural science foundation of China under grant No.61971188 and 61771492, in part by the Scientific Research Project of Hunan Education Department under grant No.19B364.

References

1. Ming, Z.A., Tong, L., Rui, Z., et al.: Conditional Wasserstein generative adversarial network-gradient penalty-based approach to alleviating imbalanced data classification. Inf. Sci. **512**, 1009–1023 (2020)
2. Su, C.T., Hsiao, Y.H.: An evaluation of the robustness of MTS for imbalanced data. IEEE Trans. Knowl. Data Eng. **19**(10), 1321–1332 (2007)
3. Zhu, H., Liu, G., Zhou, M., et al.: Optimizing weighted extreme learning machines for imbalanced classification and application to credit card fraud detection. Neurocomputing **407**, 50–62 (2020)

4. Liu, J., Wang, J., Liu, X., et al.: Mwrspca: online fault monitoring based on moving window recursive sparse principal component analysis. J. Intell. Manufact. (2021). Early Access: https://doi.org/10.1007/S10845-10020-01721-10848

5. Liu, J., Zhang, W., Ma, T., et al.: Toward security monitoring of industrial cyber-physical systems via hierarchically distributed intrusion detection. Exp. Syst. Appl., 158, 113578(113571–113523) (2020)

6. Liu, J., Zhang, W., Tang, Z., et al.: Adaptive intrusion detection via GA-GOGMM-based pattern learning with fuzzy rough set-based attribute selection. Exp. Syst. Appl. **139**(1), 112845(112841–112817) (2020)

7. Domingues, R., Michiardi, P., Barlet, J., et al.: A comparative evaluation of novelty detection algorithms for discrete sequences. Artif. Intell. Rev. **53**(2), 3787–3812 (2020)

8. Liu, J., Liu, H., Gong, S., et al.: Automated cardiac segmentation of cross-modal medical images using unsupervised multi-domain adaptation and spatial neural attention structure. Med. Image Anal. **72**(August), 102135 (2021)

9. Hodge, V.J., Austin, J.: A survey of outlier detection methodologies. Artif. Intell. Rev. **22**(2), 85–126 (2004)

10. Pimentel, M., Clifton, D.A., Lei, C., et al.: A review of novelty detection. Signal Process. **99**(6), 215–249 (2014)

11. Ke, Y., Yao, C., Song, E., et al.: An early fault diagnosis method of common-rail injector based on improved CYCBD and hierarchical fluctuation dispersion entropy. Dig. Signal Proc. **114**(4), 103049 (2021)

12. Lei, A.C., Clifton. D.A., Watkinson, P., et al.: Identification of patient deterioration in vital-sign data using one-class support vector machines; In: Proceedings of The Federated Conference on Computer Science and Information Systems - Fedcsis 2011, Szczecin, Poland, 18–21 September 2011, Proceedings, F (2011)

13. Beghi, A., Cecchinato, L., Corazzol, C., Rampazzo, M., Simmini, F., Susto, G.A.: A one-class SVM based tool for machine learning novelty detection in HVAC chiller systems. IFAC Proceedings Volumes **47**(3), 1953–1958 (2014). https://doi.org/10.3182/20140824-6-ZA-1003.02382

14. Jyothsna, V., Tirupati, A.R., Prasad, V.V.R., et al.: A review of anomaly based intrusion detection systems. Int. J. Comput. Appl. **28**(7), 26–35 (2013)

15. Liu, J., He, J., Zhang, W., et al.: Anid-seokelm: adaptive network intrusion detection based on selective ensemble of kernel ELMS with random features. Knowl.-Based Syst. **177**(1), 104–116 (2019)

16. Hassani, A., Iranmanesh, A., Mansouri, N.: Text mining using nonnegative matrix factorization and latent semantic analysis. Neural Comput. Appl. **154**, 107121 (2021)

17. Dieter, O., Benoit, D.F., Phlippe, B.: From one-class to two-class classification by incorporating expert knowledge: novelty detection in human behaviour - Sciencedirect. European J. Operat. Res. **282**(3), 1011–1024 (2020)

18. Clifton, L., Clifton, D.A., Zhang, Y., et al.: Probabilistic novelty detection with support vector machines. IEEE Trans. Reliab. **63**(2), 455–467 (2014)

19. Silva, S.R., Vieira, T., Martínez, D., Paiva, A.: On novelty detection for multi-class classification using non-linear metric learning. Exp. Syst. Appl. **167**, 114193 (2021)

20. Górski, J., Jaboński, A., Heesch, M., Dziendzikowski, M., Dworakowski, Z.: Comparison of novelty detection methods for detection of various rotary machinery faults Sensors **21**(10), 3536 (2021)

21. Sun, K.: Information-theoretic data injection attacks on the smart grid. IEEE Trans. Smart Grid **11**(2), 1276–1285 (2020)

22. Vasilev, A., et al.: Q-space novelty detection with variational autoencoders. In: Bonet-Carne, E., Hutter, J., Palombo, M., Pizzolato, M., Sepehrband, F., Zhang, F. (eds.) Computational Diffusion MRI. MV, pp. 113–124. Springer, Cham (2020). https://doi.org/10.1007/978-3-030-52893-5_10

23. Han, M., Ozdenizci, O., Wang, Y., et al.: Disentangled adversarial autoencoder for subject-invariant physiological feature extraction. IEEE Signal Process. Lett. 27, 1565–1569 (2020)

24. Simão, M., Neto, P., Gibaru, O.: Improving novelty detection with generative adversarial networks on hand gesture data. Neurocomputing 358, 437–445 (2019)

25. Cho. J.A.A.S.: Variational Autoencoder Based Anomaly Detection Using Reconstruction Probability. SNU Data Mining Center (2015)

26. Larsen, A.B.L., Snderby S.K.H.L.: Autoencoding Beyond Pixels Using A Learned Similarity Mmetric. ICML. (2016)

27. Xie, R., Jan, N.M., Hao, K., et al.: Supervised variational autoencoders for soft sensor modelling with missing data. IEEE Trans. Industr. Inf. 16(4), 2820–2828 (2020)

28. Kim, Y., Alnujaim, I., Daegun, O.: Human activity classification based on point clouds measured by millimeter wave MIMO radar with deep recurrent neural networks. IEEE Sens. J. 21(12), 13522–13529 (2021)

29. Liu, J., He, J., Xie, Y., et al.: Illumination-invariant flotation froth color measuring via Wasserstein distance-based cycleGAN with structure-preserving constraint. IEEE Trans. Cybern. 51(2), 2168–2275 (2021)

30. Goodfellow, I.J., Pouget-Abadie, J., Mirza, M., et al.: Generative adversarial networks. Adv. Neural. Inf. Process. Syst. 3, 2672–2680 (2014)

31. Chen, X., Kingma, D. P., Salimans, T., et al.: Variat. Lossy Autoencoder (2016)

32. Wolterink, J.M., Leiner, T., Viergever, M.A., et al.: Generative adversarial networks for noise reduction in low-dose Ct. IEEE Trans. Med. Imaging 36(12), 2536–2545 (2017)

33. Schlegl, T., Seeböck, P., Waldstein, S.M., Schmidt-Erfurth, U., Langs, G.: Unsupervised anomaly detection with generative adversarial networks to guide marker discovery. In: Niethammer, M., Styner, M., Aylward, S., Zhu, H., Oguz, I., Yap, P.-T., Shen, D. (eds.) Information Processing In Medical Imaging, pp. 146–157. Springer International Publishing, Cham (2017). https://doi.org/10.1007/978-3-319-59050-9_12

34. Tavallaee, M., Bagheri, E., Lu, W., et al.: A detailed analysis of the Kdd Cup 99 data set. In: Proceedings of the 2009 IEEE Symposium on Computational Intelligence for Security and Defense Applications, F, pp. 8–10 July 2009 (2009)

A Deep Learning-Based Herb Pair Discovering Approach

Qi Xue[1], Bo Gao[2], Jing Wen[1], Yan Zhu[2(✉)], and Xiangfu Meng[1(✉)]

[1] College of Electronic and Information Engineering, Liaoning Technical University, Huludao, China
[2] Institute of Information on Traditional Chinese Medicine, China Academy of Chinese Medical Sciences, Beijing, China

Abstract. The use of artificial intelligence methods to assist in the discovery of Traditional Chinese Medicine (TCM) pairs provides practical significance for the inheritance, development, and innovation of TCM. Most of the current herb pair mining methods only consider the attribute information of a single decoction piece and are based on the existing single machine learning model, so the quality of herb pair discovery is not high. This paper uses deep learning methods to solve the problem of TCM herb pair discovering. The properties of nature, taste, and meridian of the decoction composing the herb pair were added to the data set, and the knowledge-enhanced semantic representation (ERNIE) pre-training model was employed based on context and location information. We also compared it with the herb pair discovering effect of CNN, RNN, BERT, ERNIE models and common classification models. The results show that ERNIE can find potential herb pair effectively in the collection of TCM decoction pieces, and has a high effectiveness.

Keywords: Herb pair discovering · Artificial intelligence · TCM · Deep learning · BERT · ERNIE · Decoction piece

1 Introduction

At present, research which combines artificial intelligence (AI) and data analysis is becoming a hot topic in TCM area [1–4]. The combination of artificial intelligence methods and TCM data analysis has played an important role in the field of discovery of herb pairs and analysis of classic famous prescriptions. The herb pairs are the minimum unit of TCM formulae compatibility [5,6], refers to the premise that the corresponding treatment method is adopted for certain syndrome characteristics, combined with the performance and function of the medicinal flavor, to selectively pair the two-flavored Chinese herbal medicine

---

Supported by National Natural Science Foundation of China (82174534) and Fundamental Research Funds for the Central Public Welfare Research Institutes (ZZ13-YQ-126).

X. Liao et al. (Eds.): BigData 2021, CCIS 1496, pp. 135–149, 2022.
https://doi.org/10.1007/978-981-16-9709-8_10

pieces. The herb pairs are the summary and essence of the long-term traditional medical practice of ancient and modern medical scientists, and embodies the basic principles of the application of Chinese medicine [4,5]. The theory of compatibility of TCM contains extremely complex content, but it also has its underlying rules. By studying the minimum compatibility unit pair of medicines, it is helpful to explore the hidden rules in Chinese herbal medicines and provide theoretical support for the scientific and modernization of TCM. However, the existing research on the discovery of herb pairs is not deep and systematic enough. Herb pairs are more of a relatively fixed compatibility composition gradually formed in the process of clinical practice, and herb-related data are mostly scattered in a large number of Chinese medicines, prescriptions and clinical prescriptions of Chinese medicine, making artificial intelligence technology face the great challenges to herb pairs discovering [7,8].

On top of this observation, this paper proposes a herb pairs discovery method based on the Enhanced Language Representation with Informative Entities (ERNIE) model and compares the effects on the current classical artificial intelligence algorithm models, such as CNN, RNN, BERT. Experimental results demonstrated that ERNIE can effectively find potential herb pair in the collection of TCM decoction pieces and achieve high performance.

The rest of this paper is organized as follows. Section 1 reviews some related work for herbs discovering. Section 2 presents the definition of problems and solutions. Section 3 proposes our framework and the herb pairs discovering methods. The experimental evaluation and performance results are presented in Sect. 4. Section 5, the conclusion portion, restates the purpose, significance, method, scope, background and other related information of the research.

2   Related Work

In recent years, the combination of artificial intelligence and machine learning with the medical field has attracted great attention to researchers [4]. Artificial intelligence can automatically find the patterns of a large, complex medical data, resulting in higher prediction accuracy than that of the conventional statistical methods [3,9]. The research on Chinese medicine data analysis and herb pairs discovery can be divided into three categories. The first one is based on association rules, the second is based on deep learning model, and the third is based on the analysis of the characteristics of herb pairs compatibility. The method based on association rules mainly counts the co-occurrence frequency of decoction pieces from TCM data, and then discovers the herb pairs. However, the traditional classical association rule algorithms (such as Apriori algorithm and FP- Growth algorithm, etc.) due to only considering the frequency appear pieces without property. It cannot meet the needs of medical research, so that some researchers have developed the discovering algorithm. Yuan et al. [10] used automatically partitioned the fuzzy sets of medicine dose by means of clustering and proposed an algorithm of discovering dose effect relations of couplet medicines in TCM. Wang et al. [11] started with the herbs in medical records, constructed a joint conditional probability matrix, set the minimum joint conditional probability matrix (minunion) as the herb pairs extraction threshold, and formed the herb community discovery algorithm TCM-HPD, which was combined with the

Apriori algorithm. However, the shortcomings of existing works are all shallow machines learning methods. Most of them focused on counting the frequency of appearance of decoction pieces. The input information lacks the attribute information about decoction pieces and ignores the relationship between attributes of herbs. It is not the best for processing and generalization capabilities for high dimensional data [6].

Nowadays deep learning has made breakthroughs in various application fields [12,13]. The AHMAD et al. [14] used the latest artificial intelligence technology (referred to as deep learning), proposed a classification system for the emotional state of poems and implemented based on the attention to poetry corpus C-BiLSTM model. He et al. [15], proposed a novel reconstruction framework iRadonMAP that uses deep learning (DL) technology for Radon inversion, and constructed an interpretable neural network of three dedicated components. Mohamed et al. [16] proposed a fast and reliable traffic jam detection method based on video dynamic modeling, which effectively takes advantages of motion features and deep texture features to overcome the limitations of existing methods. Tang et al. [17] proposed a new SPAR-RL (Stegographic Pixel Behavior and Reward with Enhanced Learning Function) embedding cost learning framework, which uses the sampling process to simulate the message embedding of the best embedding simulator. It overcomes the use of neural network-based embedded simulators with similar functions and coarse-grained optimization goals. The essence of TCM herb pairs discovery is text analysis and discovering. Therefore, this paper takes advantages of the latest deep neural network models into the herb pairs discovery research and appropriately transforms it in order to make it suitable for the scenario of TCM herb pairs discovering.

3   Problem Definition and Solution

A. Problem Definition. In the clinical prescription of TCM, two herbs are often used together, because there is a good coordination effect or a better restraint effect after such a compatibility. Potential herb pairs are not only beneficial to cure the diseases, but could also have greater coordination capability. In addition, the doctors who work in clinical medicine and herb discovery play a role of enlightening [5]. For example, the herb pair, Pinellia ternate and dried tangerine or orange peel, has the effect of regulating qi, invigorating spleen, drying dampness and removing phlegm to the bark of pinellia, tangerine peel. Pinellia can dry dampness and remove phlegm and reduce anti-sickness. The two can be used together to promote water circulation by regulating qi. In that classic famous "Erchen decoction," which is made of Pinellia ternate and tangerine peel as the main medicine, it has the effect of dry dampness, removing phlegm, regulating qi and stomach, and is used to treat stagnation of phlegm, cough and phlegm, chest distension and stupor, nausea and vomiting. Finding a hidden herb pair is not only beneficial to treating diseases, but also to making fewer pieces play a bigger role. This is instructive for clinical medicine and new herb pairs research. In a Chinese herbal compound, it often contains at least three or four to up to thirty or forty pieces of Chinese herbal medicine with different quantities. Every two are compatible with each other and can form a large number of combinations. Most of these combinations can not be called herb pairs, merely a drugs for different etiologies and pathogenesis happen to co-exist in the same prescription, and only a few are real herb pairs that play a synergistic role. These herb pairs are effective for clinical use and have been recorded, but they have not been summarized and solidified into theory, so they're submerged in a complex and large number of medical herb combinations in pieces. It is a huge and difficult work to find herb pairs from a vast number of ancient medical books only by manual interpretation, so as to explore and summarize the clinical experience of ancient doctors. However, using deep learning model to mine herb pairs, and then manually interpret and summarize experience greatly saves time and energy and reduces the difficulty of work.

The definition of the problem found by the herb pairs is given below.

Given a herb set $D = \{a_1, \ldots, a_n\}$, each herb is described by the attributes $W = \{W_1, \ldots, W_n\}$. The information form of decoction pieces is shown in Table 1. Any combination of decoction pieces is a potential herb pairs. The basic idea of this paper is to quickly and effectively find top-k herb pairs having the highest probability from a large number of pieces and formulas.

Table 1. Decoction pieces information

Name of Pieces	Natures	Tastes	Channel tropisms	Functions
Debark peony root	Slightly cold	Bitter, sour	Liver, spleen	Suppressing hyperactive liver, ease the emergency, healing sore and relieving pain
Liquorice root	Neutral	Sweet	Spleen, stomach, lung	Ease the emergency, moistening lung, detoxication, and harmonizing drugs
Largehead atractylodes rhizome	Warm	Sweet, bitter	Spleen, stomach	Rhizome: invigorating spleen and stomach, removing dampness for regulating stomach
Cinnabar	Cool	Sweet	Heart, kidney, spleen, lung	Clearing heat and removing toxicity, tranquillizing, improving eyesight
Bezoar	Cool	Bitter, sweet	Heart, liver	Clearing heat for resuscitation, heart-clearing, removing toxicity substance

B. Solution. In this paper, CNN, RNN, BERT and ERNIE models are introduced, appropriately transformed, and applied to the herb pairs discovering.

First, the decoction pieces in the decoction piece collection are combined in pairs, $D = \{a_1, a_2\}$. Then, the relevant attributes of each piece can be formed a collection $W = \{W_1, \ldots, W_n\}$. Third, the dataset is sent into the model and then the classification value is outputted from the model, where 0 indicates a nonherb pairs and 1 indicates the herb pairs.

The following is a toy example. A set of the decoction pieces d = {debark peony root, liquorice root, largehead atractylodes rhizome}, By enumerating the combinations of two of them, we can get three potential herb pairs, that are {debark peony root, liquorice root}, {liquorice root, largehead atractylodes rhizome}, {debark peony root, largehead atractylodes rhizome}. For {liquorice root, largehead atractylodes rhizome} using its attributes found in the database, the set was generated: {largehead atractylodes rhizome: bitter, sweet, and warm. Liquorice root: sweet, neutral. largehead atractylodes rhizome: spleen and stomach. channel. Liquorice root: spleen, stomach and lung channel. largehead atractylodes rhizome: invigorating spleen and stomach, removing dampness for regulating stomach. Liquorice root: to ease the emergency, moistening lung, detoxication, and harmonizing drugs}. After this, the pairwise combination of decoction pieces can be treated as a text information representation consisting of several keywords (largehead atractylodes rhizome: bitter, sweet, and warm. Liquorice, ..., and harmonizing drugs) as the input of the model, and then according to the marked the label information of herb pairs is sent to the model for training. The overall construction procedure is showed in Fig. 1.

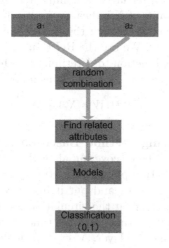

Fig. 1. Overall processing procedure of the solution framework

4   Herb Pairs Discovering Method

A. Herb Pairs Discovering Method Based on Convolutional Neural Network. Convolutional neural network (CNN) is a multi-layered neural network structure, which is showed in Fig. 2. It is divided into three parts: input layer, hidden layer and output layer [18].

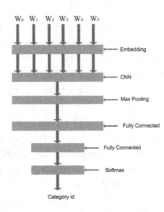

Fig. 2. CNN structure model

Decoction pieces information is first transformed into a text information set $W = \{W_1, \ldots, W_n\}$. It represents a form such as (largehead atractylodes rhizome: bitter, sweet, and warm. Liquorice root: sweet, ..., and harmonizing drugs), which as the input of the model. After word vector mapping, it turns into a shape like (n, 600, 64), and the vector input into the convolutional layers, each layer is composed of a convolution filter layer, a nonlinear layer, and a layer composed of spatial sampling. The value of N indicates the batch_size. The information is extracted from potential herbs through the pooling layer and then we input it into the fully connected layer. We use the ReLU activation function and output 0 or 1 through the softmax function to determine whether it is a herb pairs. The convolution operation function y is computed as follows:

$$y = f((W * X_t) + b) \tag{1}$$

B. Herb Pairs Discovering Method Based on Recurrent Neural Network. In the herb pairs of the discovering algorithm, the text information represents information of decoction pieces $W = \{W_1, \ldots, W_n\}$, that is input to the embedding layer. We get a vector and put it into RNN. It calculates the new state information by a moment on the circulation mechanism of hidden states transferred to the next time. It takes the last time sequence output, and put it into the two-layer fully connected layer. After the calculation of ReLU activation function, it output the predicted category of herbs [18]. This procedure can be described by in Fig. 3. The calculation process of the hidden layer is described as follows:

$$h_{(t)} = \sigma(Ux_{(t)} + Wh_{(t-1)} + b) \tag{2}$$

C. Herb Pairs Discovering Method Based on BERT. BERT (Bidirectional Encoder Representations from Transformers) is a deep pre-training language model based on transformer architecture [19], and its mainly structure showed in Fig. 4 [20].

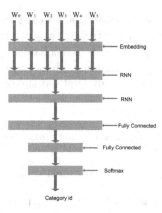

Fig. 3. RNN structure model

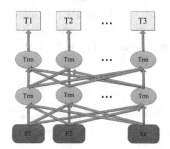

Fig. 4. BERT structure model

This paper divides the information of the decoction pieces into words after pre-processing, and adds [cls] and [sep] symbols before and after the text to distinguish the information of each pair of decoction pieces, such as: W1= { "[cls]", "largehead", "atractylodes", "rhizome", "bitter,", ..., "drugs", "[sep]"} and they are input into the model. BERT input feature mode which is consists of three parts, a flag embedded in the word (Token Embedding), the word fragment embedded (Segment Embedding), and the position of the word embedded (Position Embedding). It adds by their corresponding positions to give the final input vector model. The shape is like [−8.67170e−027, 77080e−02, 9.51530e−02, −7.75340e−02, −2.01572e−01, −3.90500e−02, ... −1.28930e−01], and then we classified it. We do not use traditional left-to-right or right-to-left language models to pretrain BERT. Instead, we pre-train BERT using two unsupervised tasks, Masked LM (the specific process of MASK is shown in Fig. 5) and Next Sentence Prediction [21]. Through the above two pretraining tasks, the model can better learn the attributes of the slices themselves and the semantic information between the attributes of the two slices. Therefore, the Bert model is used to complete the research on herb pairs discovering.

D. Herb Pairs Discovering Method Based on ERNIE. The ERNIE model is a language model based on a multilayer two-way transformer encoder. The transformer encoder uses the full attention mechanism [22]. The attention mechanism is similar to the principle of human understanding of sentences. It is based on the key points in the sentence to understand the overall meaning of the sentence. The principle of that is,

$$attention(Q, K, V) = softmax(\frac{QK^T}{\sqrt{d_k}})V \tag{3}$$

where, Q, K, and V are input term vector matrices, and the input vector dimensions.

The difference from the BERT model is that BERT is based on the basic language unit semantic modeling, and ERNIE is based on the knowledge-enhanced semantic modeling. Therefore, we also attempt to implement the ERNIE algorithm for herb pairs discovering. Unlike BERT masking, ERNIE optimizes in modeling. The difference between BERT and ERNIE is shown in Fig. 5 (The first figure is BERT and the second figure is ERNIE).

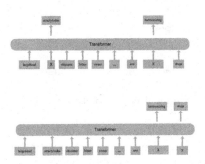

Fig. 5. The difference between ERNIE and BERT

In the experiment, W is preprocessed to W1 = "[cls]", "largehead", "atractylodes", "rhizome", "bitter", ..., "drugs", "[sep]" and input into ERNIE so as to obtain the feature vector of the information of decoction piece. In the training process, a random mask operation is performed on consecutive tokens according to the segmentation boundary. It is shown in Fig. 5. We take the trained vector input into a fully connected layer through the softmax function to obtain its corresponding classification. Then it analyzes the herb pairs to be "yes" or "no". Figure 6 shows the specific process procedure.

The whole model architecture of ERNIE consists of two stacked modules:(1) the underlying textual encoder ($T - Encoder$) responsible to capture basic lexical and syntactic information from the input tokens, and (2) the upper knowledgeable encoder ($K - Encoder$) responsible to integrate extra token-oriented knowledge information into textual information from the underlying layer, so

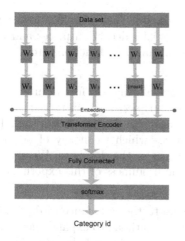

Fig. 6. ERNIE structure model

that we can represent heterogeneous information of tokens and entities into a united feature space.

To be specific, given a token sequence $w = \{w_1, w_2, \ldots, w_n\}$ and its corresponding entity sequence $e = \{e_1, e_2, \ldots, e_n\}$ the textual encoder firstly sums the token embedding, segment embedding, positional embedding for each token to compute its input embedding, and then computes lexical and syntactic features $\mathbf{w} = \{\mathbf{w_1}, \mathbf{w_2}, \ldots, \mathbf{w_n}\}$ as follows:

$$\mathbf{w} = \{\mathbf{w_1}, \mathbf{w_2}, \ldots, \mathbf{w_n}\} = T - Encoder(\{w_1, w_2, \ldots, w_n\}) \tag{4}$$

After computing $\{\mathbf{w_1}, \mathbf{w_2}, \ldots, \mathbf{w_n}\}$, ERNIE adopts a knowledgeable encoder $K - Encoder$ to inject the knowledge information into language representation. To be specific, we represent $\{e_1, e_2, \ldots, e_n\}$ with their entity embeddings $\{\mathbf{e_1}, \ldots, \mathbf{e_n}\}$, which are pre-trained by the effective knowledge embedding model TransE. Then, both $\{\mathbf{w_1}, \mathbf{w_2}, \ldots, \mathbf{w_n}\}$ and $\{\mathbf{e_1}, \ldots, \mathbf{e_n}\}$ are fed into $K - Encoder$ for fusing heterogeneous information and computing final output embeddings.

$$\{w_1^0, \ldots, w_n^0\}, \{e_1^0, \ldots, e_n^0\} = K - Encoder\{w_1, \ldots, w_n\}, \{e_1, \ldots, e_n\} \tag{5}$$

$\{w_1^0, \ldots, w_n^0\}$ and $\{e_1^0, \ldots, e_n^0\}$ will be used as features for specific tasks.

5   Experiments

A. Data Source. All source data used in this article comes from the structured database of TCM formula developed by Institute of Information on Traditional Chinese Medicine, China Academy of Chinese Medical Sciences. The database collected TCM formulas recorded in comprehensive ancient and modern Chinese medicine formula literature. It contains: (1) 33938 well-structured formulas;

(2) 918 established herb pairs and their classification, compatibility mechanism and clinical application; (3) 9207 decoction pieces and their attributes such as natures, tastes, channel tropisms, and functions etc.

B. Data Screening. The information for natures, tastes, channel tropisms and functions of all decoction pieces are extracted, as well as 918 herb pairs. Herb pairs are commonly used together in prescription. Therefore, we randomly selected 150 decoction pieces which frequency of occurrence is higher than 7 from the 459 decoction pieces of the database. We combined in pairs to set of nonherb pairs to ensure the usefulness of this experiment.

C. Experiment Set. Due to the imbalance of data labels, We use text data enhancement EDA technical methods to expand the data to obtain 8699 pieces of data. For example, {largehead atractylodes rhizome: invigorating spleen and stomach, removing dampness for regulating stomach.} through this method can turns to {largehead atractylodes rhizome: Strengthening spleen and stomach, removing dampness and regulating stomach}. Then select the same amount of data which is not on the database. The data are randomly shuffled and divided the training set, validation set, and test set at a ratio of 8:1:1.

All the parameters of the model experiment in this paper are follow, number of training iterations = 5, batch_size = 32, length of each text = 32, learning rate = 5e−5, hidden layer = 768 of BERT and ERNIE models, The number of convolution kernels in CNN = 256 and dropout = 0.5. To reduce the risk of over-fitting model, we follow the training stopped early (Early Stopping) principle to set detect_imp = 1000. That is, if the model continues to 1000 batches, it will not be trained when result not significantly improved.

D. Evaluation Index. For the classification model, for example, assume that only 0 and 1 two classes, the final determination results four cases [23]: True Positive (TP), which means the positive samples predicted true; False Positive (FP), which means the negative samples predicted true; False Negatives (FN), which means the positive model predicted false; True Negative (TN), which means the negative samples predicted false. This study obtained the predicted results and actual results, we could get the number of TP, FP, FN and TN. This paper selects the following four indicators to evaluate the performance of the model [24].

1. Accuracy

$$Accuracy = \frac{TP + TN}{TP + TN + FP + FN} \times 100\% \qquad (6)$$

2. Precision

$$Precision = \frac{TP}{TP + FP} \times 100\% \tag{7}$$

3. Recall

$$Recall = \frac{TP}{TP + FN} \times 100\% \tag{8}$$

4. Measure

$$F - measure = 2 \times \frac{Precision \times Recall}{Precision + Recall} \times 100\% \tag{9}$$

E. Experimental Results and Analysis. Table 2 shows the accuracy, precision, recall and Fl values of CNN, RNN, BERT and ERNIE.

Table 2 shows that BERT and ERNIE enable to obtain complete contextual semantic features and have achieved ideal results for the herb pairs discovering. The accuracy, precision, recall and Fl values are all above 0.7. Compared with BERT, the ERNIE model performs more prominently in the field of herb pairs discovering, where the accuracy rate, recall rate and Fl value are all higher than 0.8. All items are higher than the BERT model. CNN and RNN are relatively inferior. The accuracy, precision and Fl value of CNN were all between 0.59 and 0.75. RNN is good at processing time series data, so the ability of RNN to find potential herb pairs is not effective and the various indicators are between 0.2 and 0.65. BERT spend 3 s and ERNIE spent 2 s about the calculation speed. Therefore, the efficiency of ERNIE is better than BERT. Figure 7 shows indicators of the four models.

Table 2. The indicators of the four models

Prediction model	Accuracy	Precision	Recall	F-measure
CNN	67.03	59.50	74.35	66.11
RNN	39.55	63.55	20.70	31.23
BERT	70.43	82.62	82.51	82.57
ERNIE	72.26	83.02	82.87	82.95

In order to further observe the ability of ERNIE to find potential herb pairs, we analyze the potential herb pairs that are judged to be herb pairs but not in the database. After manual labeling, several potential herb pairs such as medicated leaven, aucklandia root and balloonflower root, lobed kudzuvine root are found. In the combination of medicated leaven and aucklandia root, Aucklandia root has the effect of dredging qi, relieving pain, strengthening spleen and stomach, and promoting food digestion. In addition to the spleen, stomach and large

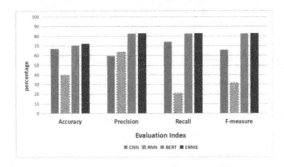

Fig. 7. Model evaluation index comparison

intestine meridians, it also belongs to the triple energizer meridians and the gall-bladder meridians. The liver and gallbladder are the exterior and interior of each other. The drug power of aucklandia root can enter the liver through the meridians to strengthen the power of liver qi drainage. Liver qi drainage can promote the transportation of spleen and stomach and the digestion and absorption of diet; And medicated leaven has the effect of digestion and stomach, returning to the spleen and stomach meridian, can dispel food stagnation. Through the compatibility of the two, the promoting digestion function of medicated leaven was further strengthened by the soothing and ventilating function of aucklandia root, medicated leaven eliminate the tangible evil - Food stagnation, remove obstacles for the smooth flow of qi machine, make qi general without pain, and strengthen aucklandia root qi moving force to relieve pain. Aucklandia root and medicated leaven are often found in some prescriptions for the treatment of stomach cold, qi pain and liver and stomach qi stagnation. The prescription named "aucklandia root and medicated leaven pill" is also included in Puji recipe, which shows that ancient doctors have noticed the increasing effect of the combination of aucklandia root and medicated leaven on the curative effect, but it has not been summarized into a theory, so it is rarely discussed as a drug pair. The discovery of this hidden drug pair provides a new idea for the treatment of clinical gastrodynia.

The accuracy rate of discovering potential herb pairs up 77.27%. Among them, hidden herb pairs such as incised notopterygium, dahurian angelica root, aucklandia root, cassiabarktree branchlet, lobed kudzuvine root, tall gastrodia rhizome and divaricate saposhnikovia root, cassiabarktree branchlet are herb combinations that have common targeting pathogenesis and are often used at the same time in clinic, which opens up new ideas and methods for clinical medication, but they have not been summarized into theory, and there are few relevant exploration and clinical research literatures.

Then, the test set are manually labeled. And it seems the herb pairs, which is the manual label is true, as the real herb pairs shows. Table 3 shows the accuracy of CNN, RNN, BERT and ERNIE. Compare with the two experiments, the accuracy of each model is all increased. The accuracy of ERNIE is increased

13.17 in accuracy, which fully prove that the ERNIE can distinguish the herb pairs well and have the ability to find potential herb pairs. Experimental results show that ERNIE has a better ability to discover potential herb pairs.

Table 3. Comparison of baseline algorithms

Prediction model	Accuracy	Differences between two experiment
CNN	72.23	5.2
RNN	43.65	4.1
BERT	81.72	11.29
ERNIE	85.43	13.17

At the same time, this paper compares the test results of using different decoction piece attributes in the data set, as shown in Table 4 below. Specifically, it is divided into four experiments. The input data set only uses the sexual information of decoction pieces, the sexual and flavor information of decoction pieces, and the sexual and flavor meridian information of decoction pieces, which are compared with the sexual and flavor meridian function information of decoction pieces.

Table 4. Comparison of experimental results of different decoction pieces

Decoction properties	Accuracy	Precision	Recall	F-measure	Training time
Natures	65.264	82.68	75.4	78.82	4:53
Natures, tastes	67.994	84.98	76.34	80.36	4:41
Natures, tastes, channel tropisms	69.53	81.37	78.51	81.8	4:51
Natures, tastes, channel tropisms functions	70.43	82.62	82.51	82.57	5:12

In order to make the test results more convincing, this article puts the same training set, validation set, and test set with attribute information of decoction pieces into the DPCNN, FastText, TextRCNN, and TextRNN_Att algorithms to calculate the accuracy, loss value and running time, and the specific situation See Table 5 below. Many experiments have proved that ERNIE is superior to other commonly used text classification methods in terms of accuracy and speed in judging herb pairs.

Table 5. Comparison of baseline algorithms

Prediction mode	Accuracy	Loss	Time
DPCNN	67.04	1e−02	8 s
FastText	67.10	3.1	2 s
TextRCNN	68.96	0.64	4 s
TextRNN_Att	35.19	0.75	4 s

6   Conclusion and Future Work

Currently, traditional machine learning algorithms are mostly used in herb pairs discovering. In this paper, the current mainstream deep learning models are applied to the herb pairs discovering. And we consider the natures, tastes, channel tropisms, and functions of the herb pairs at the same time. The accuracy, precision, recall and Fl of CNN, RNN, BERT and ERNIE are compared, and it is found that ERNIE uses three levels of masking strategies of word mask, phrase mask and entity mask to dynamically generate the contextual semantic representation capabilities of words. It has a good performance in herb pairs discovering and has the potential ability for discovery herb pairs. This helps clinicians to collect and summarize the compatibility of herbs to a certain extent, and has guiding significance for the use of prescriptions.

In future work, the input text will be expanded. The dose-effect relationship and the number of data sets will be increased. The improved algorithms of BERT and ERNIE will be compared to further improve the efficiency of potential herb pairs discovering.

References

1. Shang, E.X., Li, W.L., Ye, L., Zhou, W., Tang, Y.P., Fan, X.S.: Herb pair research (II) - data mining of herb pair. China J. Chin. Materia Medica **38**(24), 4191–4195 (2013)
2. Shafaf, N., Malek, H.: Applications of machine learning approaches in emergency medicine; a review article. Arch. Acad. Emerg. Med. **7**(1), 34 (2019)
3. Messinger, A.I., Luo, G., Deterding, R.R.: The doctor will see you now: how machine learning and artificial intelligence can extend our understanding and treatment of asthma. J. Allergy Clin. Immunol. **145**(2), 476–478 (2020)
4. Yao, Y.Z., et al.: An ontology-based artificial intelligence model for medicine side-effect prediction: taking TCM as an example. Comput. Math. Meth. Med. **2019**, 8617503:1–8617503:7 (2019)
5. Liu, Z.W., Chen, S.Q., Xu, S., Li, C.X.: Discovery of Chinese medicine pairs based on Association Rule Algorithm. World Latest Med. Inf. **19**(20), 275–276 (2019)
6. Hu, M.M., et al.: A disease prediction model based on dynamic sampling and transfer learning. Chin. J. Comput. **42**(10), 2339–2354 (2019)
7. Tang, Y.Q., et al.: Research on herb pairs (I) - formation and development of herb pairs. China J. Chin. Materia Medica **38**(24), 4185–4190 (2013)

8. Liu, C.H., Geng, G.: Discussion on the prescription of whole scorpion based on herb pair compatibility. J. TCM **60**(18), 1563–1566 (2019)
9. Zhang, D.Z., et al.: Improving distantly-supervised named entity recognition for TCM text via a novel back-labeling approach. IEEE Access **8**, 145413–145421 (2020)
10. Yuan, N., Jin, H., Tian, L., Jiang, Y.G., Yu, Z.H.: Dose effect analysis of couplet medicines in TCM based on clustering and fuzzy association rules. Appl. Res. Comput. **26**(01), 59–61 (2009)
11. Wang, Y.Q., Yang, T., Li, X.X., Xie, J.D., Dong, H.Y., Hu, K.F.: Design and application of medicine pair extraction algorithm based on joint conditional probability matrix. Mod. TCM Materia Medica-World Sci. Technol. **21**(06), 1153–1160 (2019)
12. Lu, P., Qiu, X., Huang, X.: Recurrent neural network for text classification with multi-task learning. In: Proceedings of the 25th International Joint Conference on Artificial Intelligence, pp. 2873–2879 (2016)
13. Heng, Z., Zhong, G.Q.: Improving short text classification by learning vector representations of both words and hidden topics. Knowl.-Based Syst. **102**, 76–86 (2016)
14. Ahmad, S., Asghar, M.Z., Alotaibi, F.M., Khan, S.: Classification of poetry text into the emotional states using deep learning technique. IEEE Access **8**, 73865–73878 (2020)
15. Ji, H., Wang, Y.B., Ma, J.H.: Radon inversion via deep learning. IEEE Trans. Med. Imaging **39**(6), 2076–2087 (2020)
16. Abdelwahab, M.A., Abdel-Nasser, M., Hori, M.: Rapid traffic congestion detection approach based on deep residual learning and motion trajectories. IEEE Access **8**, 182180–182192 (2020)
17. Tang, W.X., Li, B., Barni, M., Li, J., Huang, J.W.: An automatic cost learning framework for image steganography using deep reinforcement learning. IEEE Trans. Inf. Forensics Secur. **16**, 952–967 (2021)
18. Wu, X.U., Xue, G.G.: CNN fast recognition algorithm of traffic signs based on image clustering. CAAI Trans. Intell. Syst. **14**(04), 670–678 (2019)
19. Jacob, D., Chang, M.W., Kenton, L., Toutanova, K.: BERT: pre-training of deep bidirectional transformers for language understanding. In: Proceedings of the: Conference of the North American Chapter of the Association for Computational Linguistics: Human Language Technologies, vol. 2019, pp. 4171–4186. Association for Computational Linguistics, Stroudsburg (2019)
20. Yu, D., Jin, T.H., Xie, W.Y., Zhang, Y., Pu, E.D.: Recognition method based on deep learning for Chinese textual entailment chunks and labels. J. Softw. **31**(12), 3772–3786 (2020)
21. Cai, L.K., Song, Y., Liu, T., Zhang, K.L.: A hybrid BERT model that incorporates label semantics via adjustive attention for multi-label text classification. IEEE Access **2169–3536**, 152183–152192 (2020)
22. Sun, Y., et al.: ERNIE 2. 0: a continual pre-training framework for language understanding. In: Proceedings of the AAAI Conference on Artificial Intelligence, pp. 8968–8975 (2020)
23. Huang, X.F., Chen, M., Liu, P.Z., Du, Y.Z.: Texture feature-based classification on transrectal ultrasound image for prostatic cancer detection. Comput. Math. Meth. Med. **2020**, 7359375:1–7359375:9 (2020)
24. Skrlj, B., Martinc, M.: tax2vec: constructing interpretable features from taxonomies for short text classification. Comput. Speech Lang. **65**, 101104 (2021)

Attention-Based Iterated Dilated Convolutional Neural Networks for Joint Intent Classification and Slot Filling

Junfeng Zhao[✉], Shiqun Yin[✉], and Wenqiang Xu

Faculty of Computer and Information Science, Southwest University, Chongqing 400715, China

Abstract. Intent classification and slot filling are two essential tasks for Spoken Language Understanding (SLU). Considering that Intent classification and slot filling are closely related, the joint model for intent classification and slot filling has been proposed to improve the accuracy of separate modeling. The prevalent joint learning method is mainly to turn the input sequence into a variable length output via a recurrent neural networks model. However, the parallel execution of this model is inefficient. In addition, this method is not very effective in text feature extraction. To solve these problems, this paper proposed an iterated dilated convolutional neural network model combined with multi-head attention mechanism. The method combined convolved features with the features based on multi-head attention mechanism to obtain more word semantic information. Compared to recurrent neural networks model, there are less linear structures, and the parallel efficiency of program execution is higher. Experimental results demonstrate that our joint training model outperforms the accuracy compared to the baseline models on benchmark ATIS and Snips datasets respectively.

Keywords: Spoken Language Understanding · Intent classification · Slot filling · Convolutional neural network · Multi-head attention model

1 Introduction

In a dialogue system, Spoken language understanding (SLU) is very important. Spoken Language Understanding (SLU) aims to find the appropriate answer in the knowledge base through the understanding of the query. SLU typically includes two tasks: intent classification and slot filling [1]. Intent classification can be shown as a classification problem to classify the intent label y^n and slot filling can be a Sequence labeling task that maps input sentence $x = (x_1, x_2, x_3, \ldots)$ to the query $y' = (y'_1, y'_2, y'_3, \ldots)$ that corresponds the slot label. Table 1 shows us an example of joint intent recognition and slot filling.

Intent recognition usually uses classification methods to classify sentences into corresponding intent categories, and popular approaches for intent classification include recurrent neural networks (RNN) [2], long short term memory (LSTM) [3], hierarchical attention networks [4], convolutional neural network (CNN) [5], and other traditional machine learning algorithms, such as support vector machine (SVM) [6].

© Springer Nature Singapore Pte Ltd. 2022
X. Liao et al. (Eds.): BigData 2021, CCIS 1496, pp. 150–162, 2022.
https://doi.org/10.1007/978-981-16-9709-8_11

Table 1. An example from query to semantic frame

Query	Show me flights from Baltimore to Dallas	
Result	Intent	Flight
	Slot	Departure = Baltimore Destination = Dallas

Slot filling can be regarded as a sequence labeling problem, that is, each word in a given sentence is labeled accordingly. It typically involves two tasks: named entity recognition and slot prediction. Some classic methods including deep LSTM [7], Convolutional neural network (CNN) [8], conditional random fields (CRF) [9], recurrent neural networks (RNN) [10] have been explored for Sequence labeling problem.

Intent classification and slot filling are often closely related. Take a flight-related text as an example," show me flights from Baltimore to Dallas", this sentence represents the intent of flight, and We naturally think of the origin and destination of the flight. Finally, we predicted two slots: starting point-Baltimore, ending point-Dallas.

Considering that the internal connection between intent classification and slot filling, the joint models have been proposed to improve the accuracy of individual modeling. Recently, encoder-decoder neural network model [11] has achieved the great performance in many sequence learning problems such as text translation and dialogue management. Encoding uses an encoder to convert the input word sequence into a dense vector of a fixed dimension, and the decode stage generates the target translation from this activation state. Prior works [12] have shown that attention mechanism helps encoder-decoder model integrate the contextual semantic information. Hence, attention-based recurrent neural network Models were proposed for joint intent classification and slot filling, and achieved great performance [13]. However, recurrent neural network has too many linear structures, and makes it easy to produce the vanishing gradient problem and the gradient explosion problem, the parallel execution of this model is inefficient. In addition, this model makes it difficult to obtain more word semantic information.

The main works of this paper are as follows:

1) We propose a dilated convolution network model based on multi-head attention mechanism to improve joint Intent classification and slot filling accuracy.
2) Iterated Dilated Convolution network model is added to obtain more features, and computations over all elements can be fully parallelized.
3) The multi-head attention mechanism allows the model to learn relevant information in different representation subspaces.

2 Related Work

In recent years, neural networks models for joint intent classification and slot filling have achieved great success. Zhang et al. [14] used the RNN model to extract the shared features of the bottom layer. One part of the upper layer is the intention classification, and the other part is the slot filling. The loss function is the weighted sum of the intention loss and the slot loss. Kim et al. [15] proposed that the model uses char-level BLSTM to model the char sequence features of words. Word embedding is taken as the input representation to predict the domain, intent and slot respectively. Experiments have found that pre-training each model is very important. Wen et al. [16] proposed that contextual information and hierarchical information should be considered in the joint model, so that more semantic information can be obtained. Wang et al. [17] proposed that the cross-influence between the two tasks should be considered. They implement it with two related BLSTMs. In fact, the hidden layer output by one LSTM will work together with the other. This model has achieved great results on benchmark ATIS.

In the prior works, the attention-based joint learning methods [18] were proposed and achieved great success. Although this method helps RNN model to deal with long-range dependencies, it is easy to produce the vanishing gradient problem and the gradient explosion problem. Therefore, LSTM network [19] was proposed to solve these problems in order to achieve better prediction and classification of sequence data. The author of the article proposed to concatenate the domain tag and intent tag as the tag of the new token, as a result, the joint model is converted into a standard sequence labeling problem. So far, various methods of sequence labeling can be tried to solve the problem. The attention mechanism is applied to the decoder-encoder structure to learn the semantic information of the text. However, the model only combines the loss functions of the two tasks to optimize, and ignores the connection between the slot and the intent. At this time, a slot-gated mechanism [20] was proposed to solve the above defects and achieves better results.

With the emergence of the BERT model, the relationship between the word vector generated by the pre-training and the specific downstream NLP task has changed. At the same time, the BERT model [21] is used for joint training of sequence labeling tasks and classification tasks, which greatly improves the accuracy of the model.

3   Proposed Method

In this paper, a iterated dilated convolutional neural networks model based on multi-head attention mechanism [22] for joint intent classification and slot filling is proposed. Firstly, we convert the original sentence to word embedding by the pre-trained model word2vec. Then the embedding vector passes through the four-layer convolutional layer and the attention mechanism layer, and the results are spliced into an output vector. The spliced vector passes through a pooling layer to obtain the final classification vector, and passes through CRF layer to get the final sequence labeling vector.

The structure of the model is displayed in Fig. 1. It consists of four parts: word embedding layer, dilated convolution Layer, multi-head attention mechanism layer and CRF layer. The general structure of each layer is described as follows.

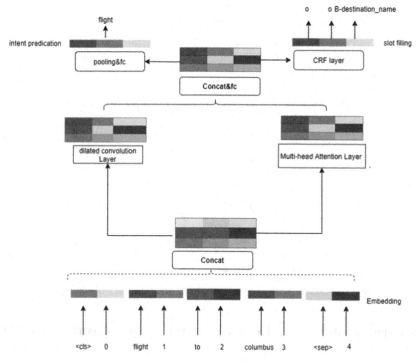

Fig. 1. The structure of the model

3.1 Embedding Layer

Word embedding technology is commonly used for text representation. Generally, a word is mapped to a high-dimensional vector to represent the word. There are various models for word embedding. In this paper, word2vec [23] is used to vectorize the text. This method considers the computability of the semantic similarity between two vocabulary information.

Firstly, we denote the input sentence sequence $x = (x_1, x_2, \ldots, x_n)$ in distributional space, where n represents the input sentence sequence length after padding the sequence and x_n represents a d-dimension vector of the embedding matrix $\delta^{s \times d}$.

In addition, we also consider adding the position information [24] of a word, so that we can get more semantic information. The approximate input structure is shown in Fig. 2.

The positional embedding has the same dimension d as the word embedding, so that the two embeddings can be summed. In our work, we use sine and cosine functions designed in BERT to mark each word.

Each word is converted into a word vector as formula (1).

$$\vec{p_t}(i) = \begin{cases} \sin(w_k.t), & \text{if } i = 2k \\ \cos(w_k.t), & \text{if } i = 2k + 1 \end{cases} \tag{1}$$

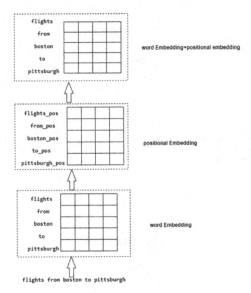

Fig. 2. Combination of word embedding and position embedding

where t represents the position of a word in a sentence x, w_k is shown in formula (2).

$$w_k = \frac{1}{1000^{2k/d}} \tag{2}$$

Among the formula, k refers to the dimension number of the word vector, and d represents the dimension of the word embedding. At time t, the position encoder $\overrightarrow{p_t}$ of the word is a vector containing sine and cosine functions as formula (3).

$$\overrightarrow{p_t} = \left[\sin(w_0.t), \quad \cos(w_0.t), \ldots, \sin\left(w_{\frac{d}{2}-1}.t\right), \cos\left(w_{\frac{d}{2}-1}.t\right)\right]_{d*1} \tag{3}$$

The word embedding $X = (X_1, X_2, \ldots, X_m)^T$ and the positional embedding $\overrightarrow{P} = (\overrightarrow{p_1}, \overrightarrow{p_2}, \ldots, \overrightarrow{p_m})^T$ are combined to obtain the input embedding E_m.

$$E_m = (e_1, e_2, \ldots e_m) = (X_1 + \overrightarrow{p_1}, X_2 + \overrightarrow{p_2}, \ldots, X_m + \overrightarrow{p_m}) \tag{4}$$

3.2 Dilated Convolution Layer

Convolutional neural network was originally proposed for text Classification. The parallel efficiency of program execution is higher compared to the recurrent neural networks model. However, the convolutional neural networks will lose internal data after the convolution operation, so iterated dilated convolutional neural networks [25] is proposed. We incorporate iterated dilated convolutional neural networks into our model to increase the accuracy of the model as Fig. 3.

The model is composed of 4 large Dilated CNN blocks of the same structure, and each block is a three-layer dilated convolutional layer with a dilation width of 1, 2, 4.

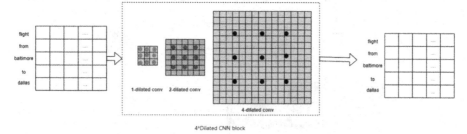

Fig. 3. Iterated dilated convolutional neural networks model

Firstly, the network model inputs a sequence of m vectors E_m, and outputs a sequence of m vectors C_m. We represents sth dilated convolutional layer of dilation width w as $D_w^{(s)}$. The first layer represents D_1^0. Through the layer, the outputs follow as formula (5).

$$i_m = D_1^0 C_m \tag{5}$$

The i_m represents the output through the first dilated convolution layer, and we represent the t layer with L_t. Then i_m needs to pass a RELU layer, and we denotes the layer as R(). Therefore, we define the stack of layers of layers with following formula (6).

$$C_m^s = R\left(D_{2^{im-1}}^{j-1} C_m^{s-1}\right) \tag{6}$$

where $C_m^0 = i_m$. We refer to the stack of the dilated convolution as a block named B(*). Therefore, the output of the first convolutional block follows as formula (7).

$$B(1) = \left[C_m^0, C_m^1, C_m^2\right] \tag{7}$$

where B(1) is the input of the next block. Through four blocks, we finally get the m-dimensional vector $B_m = [B(1), B(2), \ldots, B(m)]$ where m = 4.

3.3 Multi-head Attention Mechanism Layer

Nowadays, attention mechanism is commonly applied to natural language processing tasks. In this paper, multi-head attention mechanism which is shown in Fig. 4 is used to learn the information of the model in different representation subspaces by weighting each character. Firstly, we randomly initialize three m*d dimension matrices w^Q, w^K, w^v, and then multiply them separately with our input $E_m = (e_1, e_2, \ldots, e_m)$ to get matrix Q, K, V. Among them, Q represents the query matrix, K represents the key matrix, and V represents the value matrix.

Then Q is multiplied by K to find the similarity as the weight α, and the weighted sum of all V is performed. The specific calculation process is shown in formula (8) and formula (9).

$$\alpha = \text{softmax}\left(\frac{Q^T \cdot K}{\sqrt{d}}\right) \tag{8}$$

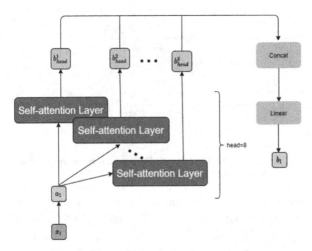

Fig. 4. The multi-head attention mechanism

$$O_m = V \cdot \alpha^T \tag{9}$$

where O_m represents the output owning the same dimension as the input embedding E_m. The multiplication of Q and K makes the result large, therefore the variance becomes d times the original to make the softmax gradient very small.

The multi-head attention mechanism mentioned in this article means that a specific E_m multiples sets of matrices w^Q, w^K, w^v to obtain multiple sets of Q, K and V. Multiple output O_m can be obtained, and then these O_m are spliced. Then the resulting vector passed through a linear layer FC to obtain an output matrix H_m. The embedding vector E_m is transformed into output matrix H_m expressed as formula (10).

$$H_m = FC(O_1, O_2, \ldots, O_m) \tag{10}$$

Multi-head attention mechanism solves the problem that RNN and its variant models cannot be calculated in parallel. Compared with CNN and RNN, it has less complexity and fewer parameters. Remember long-distance information at the same time.

3.4 CRF Layer

Conditional random fields (CRF) uses a neural network method to solve the problem of sequence labeling. Compared with the direct labeling using the argmax output at each time step of the neural network sequence, CRF can learn the constraint relationship between adjacent labels from the training samples. The general structure of the model is shown in Fig. 5.

Firstly, given the input sentence $X = (x_1, x_2, \ldots, x_m)$ and the predicated label sequence $y = (y_1, y_2, \ldots, y_m)$, and we assume that there is a transition matrix M, where $M_{i,j}$ represents the transition probability of y_i to y_j. For the output tag sequence y corresponding to the input sequence X, the score is calculated as formula (11).

$$S(X, y) = \sum_{i=0}^{n} M_{y_i, y_{i+1}} + \sum_{i=1}^{n} P_{i, y_i} \tag{11}$$

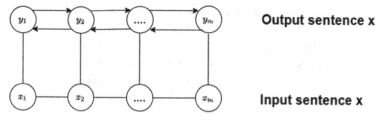

Fig. 5. The CRF model

For input X, the formula $P(y|X)$ to get the correct output y is as follows.

$$P(y|X) = \frac{e^{S(X,y)}}{\sum_{\tilde{y} \in Y_X} e^{S(X,\tilde{y})}} \tag{12}$$

where $\tilde{y}$ represents all possible label sequences. We define the loss function as L_2 as formula (13), and then we can use the gradient descent method to learn the network.

$$L_2 = -\log(P(y|X)) = -S(X,y) + \log\left(\sum_{\tilde{y} \in Y_X} e^{s(X,y)}\right) \tag{13}$$

3.5 Joint Intent Classification and Slot Filling

For the intent classification task, the input sentence is converted to the vector B_m through pooling Layer, then passes through a fully connected layer, and it is transformed into a prediction category. The specific calculation process is shown in formula (14).

$$y^i = \text{FC}(\text{pooling}(W^i B_m + b^i)) \tag{14}$$

For the slot filling task, each word in a sentence is translated into a corresponding label through a language model. The input sentence is converted to the vector y_n^s through the CRF layer, where n represents the length of the sentence.

To obtain both intent classification and slot filling jointly, the specific calculation process is shown in formula (15)

$$p\left(y^i, y^s | X\right) = p\left(y^i | X\right) \prod_{n=1}^{T} p(y_n^s | X) \tag{15}$$

where $X = (x_1, x_2, \ldots, x_T)$ represents the input sentence. The learning model is to maximize the conditional probability $p(y^i, y^s | X)$.

4 Experiment

4.1 Data

The statistical results of the datasets are shown in Table 2. In Table 2, there are two kinds of datasets ATIS and Snips. The respective train set, test set, and verification set

Table 2. Corpora statistics

Datasets	Cn	Sn	Train	Dev	Test
ATIS	21	120	4478	500	893
Snips	7	72	13084	700	700

are divided as follows, where Cn represents the intention contained in the dataset, and Sn refers to the semantic slot of the word.

The ATIS dataset [26] is about the airline Travel information Systems. For this dataset, there are a total of 5871 sentences and 572 words, and these 572 words are divided into 120 classes, that is, each word corresponds to a class label. In order to convert words into operable numbers, the dataset numbers each word and category, that is, the word number is 0, 1, 2, ..., 571, and the category is numbered 0, 1, 2, ..., 119.

In order to verify the performance of our model, we use other dataset Snips [27]. Compared to the ATIS dataset, Snips is more complicated due to the various Intentions and numerous grammatical structures. The dataset is collected from the snips personal voice assistant. For this dataset, there are a total of 14484 sentences. We use 13084 sentences to train, 700 sentences to verify, and about 700 sentences to test. There are 71 slot labels and 7 intent types.

4.2 Experimental Settings

In all experiments, we set the size of hidden vectors to 64. The dilated convolution layer contains 4 large Dilated CNN blocks of the same structure put together, and each block is a three-layer Dilated convolutional layer with a dilation width of 1, 2, 4. The heads of the multi-head attention layer is 8. The dropout of the model is 0.5. Our experiments mainly use torch framework, with NVIDIA 1060 graphics card and 8 G memory.

4.3 Baseline Methods

Overall Comparison. The experimental results on the dataset ATIS are shown in Table 3, and on the dataset snips are shown in Table 4. The best results are aggravated. All models are run on our preprocessed datasets. In this paper, we adopt Intent classification accuracy, slot filling F1, and sentence-level semantic frame accuracy indicators to evaluate our model.

As can been seen From Table 3, our model significantly outperforms the baseline models. On the dataset ATIS,our model achieves intent classification accuracy of 95.2% (from 94.1%), slot filling F1 of 96.1% (from 95.2%), and sentence-level semantic frame accuracy of 84.5% (from 82.6%). Our model can achieve good results, probably due to the multi-head attention mechanism, which may have improved the learning ability of the model.

Compared with the dataset ATIS, Snips is more complicated due to the various Intentions and numerous grammatical structures. This table shows that for the more complex Snips dataset, our model achieves intent classification accuracy of 97.2% (from

Table 3. Comparison to the baseline methods. Joint training model results on **ATIS**

Models	Intent	Slot	Sentence
	(Acc)	(F1)	(Acc)
RNN-LSTM	92.6	94.3	80.7
Attention-Based BiRNN	91.1	94.2	78.9
Slot-Gated RNN	94.1	**95.2**	**82.6**
Multi-Attention-Based IDCNN	**95.2**	**96.1**	**84.5**

Table 4. Comparison to the baseline methods. Joint training model results on **Snips**

Models	Intent	Slot	Sentence
	(Acc)	(F1)	(Acc)
RNN-LSTM	96.9	87.3	73.2
Attention-Based BiRNN	96.7	87.8	74.1
Slot-Gated RNN	97.0	**88.8**	75.5
Multi-Attention-Based IDCNN	**97.2**	87.2	**75.7**

97.0%) and sentence-level semantic frame accuracy of 75.7% (from 75.5%). However, in terms of slot filling, our model still does not surpass the existing algorithm. Considering different complexity of these datasets, the dataset could require other information to help learn the model.

4.4 Multi-head Attention

In this paper, the multi-head attention mechanism is applied to compute the Semantic information of the input words. Table 5 shows that our model achieves intent classification accuracy of 94.1% (from 92.4%) and slot filling F1 of 95.2% (from 95.1%). The computational for multi-head attention mechanism is very small compared to the rest of the other model. At the same time, compared to the attention mechanism, the multi-head attention mechanism performs h calculations, which allows the model to learn relevant information in different representation subspaces.

Table 5. Multi-head attention on different models

Models	Intent	Slot
	(Acc)	(F1)
IDCNN	91.2	93.1
Attention-Based IDCNN	92.4	95.1
Multi-Attention-Based IDCNN	**94.1**	**95.2**

4.5 Generation Speed

We evaluate the speed of our proposed model on the dataset ATIS. As is shown in Table 6. On the same GPU, our model has reached the fastest speed. Iterated dilated convolution can expand the receptive field arbitrarily without introducing additional parameters, but if the resolution is increased, the overall calculation amount of the algorithm will definitely increase.

Table 6. Training speed of different models on dataset ATIS

Models	Speed
Attention-Based RNN	$1\times$
Attention-Based CNN	$2.41\times$
Slot-Gated RNN	$1.32\times$
Multi-Attention-Based IDCNN	**2.45$\times$**

5 Conclusion

For the task of joint intent classification and slot filling, this paper proposed an iterated dilated convolution neural network model is combined with multi-head attention mechanism. By calculating the weight of the input words through the multi-head attention mechanism and combining with the training of the iterated dilated Convolutions, the weight of the keywords will be important, which can effectively obtain more semantic information, which can speed up model training. In the next work, we will explore how to join the BERT [28] model for joint intent classification and slot filling, so that our model can improve the accuracy of the joint model. Meanwhile, we can model the bidirectional connection between two tasks [29], and gradually strengthen each other through mutual characteristics to improve accuracy.

Acknowledgment. This work is supported by the Science & Technology project (41008114, 41011215, and 41014117).

References

1. Tur, G., De Mori, R.: Spoken Language Understanding: Systems for Extracting Semantic Information From Speech. John Wiley & Sons, 2011 (2011)
2. Mesnil, G., Dauphin, Y., Yao, K., et al.: Using recurrent neural networks for slot filling in spoken language understanding. IEEE/ACM Trans. Audio, Speech, Lang. Proc. **23**(3), 530–539 (2014)
3. Yao, K., Peng, B., Zhang, Y., et al.: Spoken language understanding using long short-term memory neural networks. In: 2014 IEEE Spoken Language Technology Workshop (SLT). IEEE, pp. 189–194 (2014)
4. Liu, B., Lane, I.: Attention-based recurrent neural network models for joint intent detection and slot filling. arXiv preprint arXiv:1609.01454 (2016)
5. Zhang, X., Zhao, J., LeCun, Y.: Character-level convolutional networks for text classification. Adv. Neural. Inf. Process. Syst. **2015**(28), 649–657 (2015)
6. Haffner, P., Tur, G., Wright, J.H.: Optimizing SVMs for complex call classification. In: 2003 IEEE International Conference on Acoustics, Speech, and Signal Processing, 2003. Proceedings (ICASSP 2003). IEEE, 1, pp. I–I (2003)
7. Kurata, G., Xiang, B., Zhou, B., et al.: Leveraging sentence-level information with encoder lstm for semantic slot filling. arXiv preprint arXiv:1601.01530 (2016)
8. Thang, V.N.: Sequential convolutional neural networks for slot filling in spoken language understanding. arXiv e-prints, 2016: arXiv: 1606.07783 (2016)
9. Raymond, C., Riccardi, G.: Generative and discriminative algorithms for spoken language understanding. In: Interspeech 2007–8th Annual Conference of the International Speech Communication Association (2007)
10. Peng, B., Yao, K., Jing, L., et al.: Recurrent neural networks with external memory for spoken language understanding. In: Natural Language Processing and Chinese Computing. Springer, Cham, pp. 25–35 (2015). https://doi.org/10.1007/978-3-319-73618-1
11. Cho, K., Van Merriënboer, B., Gulcehre, C., et al.: Learning phrase representations using RNN encoder-decoder for statistical machine translation. arXiv preprint arXiv:1406.1078 (2014)
12. Goo, C.-W., et al.: Slot-gated modeling for joint slot filling and intent prediction. In: NAACL-HLT, New Orleans, Louisiana, USA, June 1–6, 2018, Vol. 2 (Short Papers), pp, 753–757 (2018)
13. Louvan, S., Magnini, B.: Recent neural methods on slot filling and intent classification for task-oriented dialogue systems: A survey. arXiv preprint arXiv:2011.00564 (2020)
14. Xiaodong, Z., Houfeng, W.: A joint model of intent determination and slot filling for spoken language understanding. IJCAI (2016)
15. Kim, Y.-B., Lee, S., Stratos, K.: Joint Domain, Intent, Slot Prediction for Spoken Language Understanding (2017)
16. Liyun, W., Xiaojie, W., Zhenjiang, D., Hong, C.: Jointly Modeling Intent Identification and Slot Filling With Contextual and Hierarchical Information (2017)
17. Wang, Y., Shen, Y., Jin, H.: A bi-Model Based RNN Semantic Frame Parsing Model for Intent Detection and Slot Filling (2018)
18. Liu, B., Lane, I.: Attention-Based Recurrent Neural Network Models for Joint Intent Detection and Slot Filling (2016)
19. Hakkani-Tür, D., Tür, G., Celikyilmaz, A., et al.: Multi-domain joint semantic frame parsing using bi-directional RNN-LSTM. In: Interspeech, pp. 715–719 (2016)
20. Goo, C.W., Gao, G., Hsu, Y.K., et al.: Slot-gated modeling for joint slot filling and intent prediction. In: Proceedings of the 2018 Conference of the North American Chapter of the Association for Computational Linguistics: Human Language Technologies, vol. 2 (Short Papers), pp. 753–757 (2018)

21. Chen, Q., Zhuo, Z., Wang, W.: Bert for joint intent classification and slot filling. arXiv preprint arXiv:1902.10909 (2019)
22. Vaswani, A., Shazeer, N., Parmar, N., et al.: Attention is all you need. In: Advances in Neural Information Processing Systems, pp. 5998–6008 (2017)
23. Mikolov, T., Chen, K., Corrado, G., et al.: Efficient estimation of word representations in vector space. arXiv preprint arXiv:1301.3781 (2013)
24. Shaw, P., Uszkoreit, J., Vaswani, A.: Self-attention with relative position representations. arXiv preprint arXiv:1803.02155 (2018)
25. Strubell, E., Verga, P., Belanger, D., et al.: Fast and accurate entity recognition with iterated dilated convolutions. arXiv preprint arXiv:1702.02098 (2017)
26. Tur, G., Hakkanitur, D., Heck, L.: What's left to be understood in ATIS? In: Inproceedings (2015)
27. Coucke, A., Saade, A., Ball, A., et al.: Snips voice platform: an embedded spoken language understanding system for private-by-design voice interfaces. arXiv preprint arXiv:1805.10190 (2018)
28. Chen, Q., Zhu, Z., Wen W.: Bert for joint intent classification and slot filling. arXiv preprint arXiv:1902.10909 (2019)
29. Qin, L., et al.: A co-interactive transformer for joint slot filling and intent detection. In: ICASSP 2021–2021 IEEE International Conference on Acoustics, Speech and Signal Processing (ICASSP), IEEE (2021)

Big Data Intelligent Algorithms

Local Pyramid Attention and Spatial Semantic Modulation for Automatic Image Colorization

Jiawu Dai, Bin Jiang$^{(\boxtimes)}$, Chao Yang, Lin Sun, and Bolin Zhang

College of Computer Science and Electronic Engineering, Hunan University,
Changsha 410082, China
{jiawudai,jiangbin}@hnu.edu.cn

Abstract. Automatic image colorization is struggling due to its inherent multi-modal nature. Although many learning-based approaches have recently made tremendous progress in this area, they still suffer two limitations i) context confusion and ii) unfaithful color assignment. To cope with such issues, we propose a novel LPA-SSM-Net, which is based on encoder-decoder architecture and mainly consists of two components: the Local Pyramid Attention (LPA) module and the Spatial Semantic Modulation (SSM) module. The LPA strives to enhance the modeling of long-range dependency, leading to less context confusion and color bleeding. In addition, the SSM embeds semantic prior into the original image features via learnable affine transformations to encourage more plausible coloring output. Extensive experiments on benchmark datasets demonstrate the effectiveness of our method, and the results stand for comparable performance to existing methods in terms of quality metrics and qualitative evaluation.

Keywords: Image colorization · Local pyramid attention · Spatial semantic modulation

1 Introduction

Creating a vibrant color image from its grayscale counterpart, namely image colorization, is an interesting research topic in computer vision and image processing. This technology has been widely used in artistic creation (such as outline or manga colorization) and image compression. However, like most image-to-image translation tasks, image colorization is struggling for its immanent multi-modal property, which means there may be multiple colored images are coincide with a specific grayscale one.

Traditional image colorization methods based on references [8,10,12,21,22] or scribbles [1,9,15,27] have been proved to be capable of producing satisfactory color results with user interaction. But these methods are limited by some

---

J. Dai—Graduate student.

© Springer Nature Singapore Pte Ltd. 2022
X. Liao et al. (Eds.): BigData 2021, CCIS 1496, pp. 165–181, 2022.
https://doi.org/10.1007/978-981-16-9709-8_12

| Grayscale | Zhang et al. [35] | Zhang et al. [36] | Ours |

Fig. 1. The phenomenons of context confusion and implausible color assignment in previous automatic colorization methods. Left to right: grayscale input, Zhang et al. [35,36] and our method. As the top raw shows, the wool of sheep polluted by the green glass in [35] and grassland was clearly assigned in two colors for different parts in [36], which named context confusion. Meanwhile, the improper colors for girl skin and vehicle body could be observed in the middle two clowns of bottom raw. Our results outperform previous methods in both situations.

intractable issues, such as the difficulty to find a suitable reference image and the need for a mass of strokes from users. With the rapid development of deep neural networks, many automatic colorization methods [4,7,17,19,35] are proposed to alleviate the obstacles aforementioned. End-to-end automatic colorization aims to learn a parametric mapping from grayscale to color image based on large-scale datasets.

Unfortunately, most extant automatic colorization methods are plagued by two main limitations. Firstly, many encoder-decoder-based or GAN-based colorization models typically stack tons of convolutional layers to constitute the missing color channels from grayscale. Due to the limited receptive field, it is hard for colorization models to capture long-range dependency between different regions within a single image, leading to context confusion during color reconstruction. As a consequence, the colorization results always contain some unexpected color bleeding or artifacts. Secondly, most colorization methods establish the one-to-one mapping between grayscale and color images. As a result, these models tend to take the average of all the possible colors for a specific grayscale location, which causes implausible colorization results. We attribute this to a lack of semantic understanding. To depict the two limitations intuitively, we provide some examples from previous works [35,36] and our method for comparison in Fig. 1.

In this paper, we propose a novel attention module, named local pyramid attention (LPA), to reinforce the modeling of long-range dependency, which helps to relieve context confusion and encourage more rational color assignment. Meanwhile, to avoid unsaturated coloring results, we introduce a learned spatial transformation based on the semantic map of grayscale images in the procedure of color reconstruction, which is named Spatial Semantic Modulation (SSM). Compared to simply concatenate semantic maps with input or intermediate image features, SSM allows for more accurate semantic embedding in a spatially adaptive manner. We construct our backbone network with residual convolutional blocks [11] based on encoder-decoder architecture [28].

The main contributions of this paper can be summarized as follows:

- We propose a novel encoder-decoder-based method with semantic prior guidance for automatic image colorization.
- Two effective modules are proposed to mitigate the main limitations for image colorization. The local pyramid attention strengthens long-range dependency modeling by constructing local multi-scale features to alleviate the context confusion. And the spatial semantic modulation leads to more plausible colorization results by accurate semantic prior embedding with the collaboration of learned spatially adaptive transformation.
- Extensive experiments on two benchmarks stand for the effectiveness and comparable performance of our method compared to the state-of-the-art colorization models.

2 Related Works

In this section, we make a brief review on image colorization and attention mechanism.

Stroke-Based Colorization. Early attempts to image colorization heavily rely on high-level hints or strokes provided by users. Huang et al. [15] propose to transfer local color hints to another region based on low-level similarity, then the follow-up approaches strive to facilitate color propagations by introducing more efficient texture similarity [27] or using long-range connection. More recently, Endo et al. [1] try to model the pixel-by-pixel similarity automatically by neural networks. These stroke-based methods typically require numerous local hints to achieve vibrant colorization results. Therefore, Zhang et al. [36] combine the local color hints and a multi-branches neural network to partially reduce user efforts for manual editing.

Example-Based Colorization. Example-based colorization means transfer color statistics from a reference image to a grayscale one [10,22]. These methods calculate the correspondences between the reference and grayscale input based on different levels of similarity metrics. When the reference image and the grayscale share similar content and semantic, they could generate remarkable colorization results. However, finding an aligned reference image can be challenging and time-consuming even with the support of retrieval system [8]. Consequently, recent work [12] slightly addresses this issue and enables diverse colorization outputs by learning the mapping from a large-scale dataset. The system comprises two main components: similarity network and colorization network. The former sub-network aligns the target and reference via deep image analogy [21], while the latter is in charge of color reconstruction.

Learning-Based Colorization. Thanks to the tremendous advances in deep learning neural networks for different vision tasks, fully automatic learning-based colorization methods have received increasing attention for the past few years. Cheng et al. [7] introduce multiple linear layers to make chrominance prediction for each grayscale pixel-based on three levels image feature. However, this method results in potential artifacts in the low-texture region due to inefficient features fusion. Iizuka et al. [17] build a multi-branches fully convolutional network to fuse the local and global image features, achieving more plausible results compared to previous methods. To deal with the inherent multi-modality, Zhang et al. [35] treat colorization as a regression problem by modeling the color distribution for each pixel in grayscale. Meanwhile, as a typical image-to-image translation task, some approaches based on conditional generative adversarial networks (cGAN) [23] were proposed to translate grayscales to color ones automatically. Isola et al. [19] formulate a universal conditional GAN-based architecture named Pixel2Pixel for cross-domain image translation, and Cao et al. [4] extend this method with multiple layer noise input to ease mode collapse.

More recently, some works pay attention to embedding semantic prior to guide color modeling [13,37]. These approaches are driven by the intuition of human coloring experience, where humans have a clear knowledge about the category and the most possible color for a specific object in the scene. Zhao et al. [37] enforce pixel-level semantic prior embedding during colorization, and Man et al. [13] employ a sub-branch to inject semantic prior, whose weights are shared with encoder in the main branch. Xia et al. [34] propose a multiscale progressive colorization model with edge guidance to handle different scales in natural images. However, none of these methods is sufficient to make accurate semantic guidance for colorization. Based on this, we propose an efficient spatial semantic modulation for better semantic prior embedding.

Attention Mechanism. It is well-known that attention is crucial to human visual perception, and recent advances in many visual tasks attribute to the efficient attention mechanism, which makes clear guidance for models to focus on "what" and "where" in an image. The typical light-weight visual attention is CBAM [33], which is composed of a cascaded channel attention module and a spatial attention module. The channel attention component is similar to another plug-and-play module named Squeeze-and-Excitation block proposed in [14].

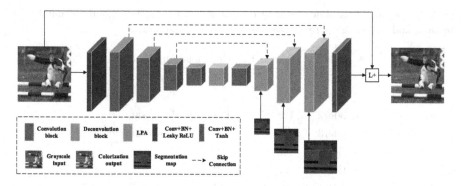

Fig. 2. The architecture of proposed method, which converts luminance input to chrominance output. Combining chrominance prediction with luminance, we can get a plausible color counterpart. In our method, LPA is embedded into the bottleneck. The segmentation maps produced by an off-the-shelf pretrained segmentation model are used in SSM during color reconstruction, which will be detailed in Sect. 3.3.

These two attention mechanisms benefit a mass of visual tasks, but neither of them has the capacity to model long-range dependency, which is significant to image colorization. Wang et al. [31] propose Non-local attention aims to capture the correspondences between distant pixels. Whereas, the non-local operation is extremely computationally cost and thus unfriendly for intensive prediction visual tasks such as image colorization. Based on these facts, we propose a novel local pyramid attention module for image colorization to better trade-off efficiency and complexity. The proposed module will be detailed in Sect. 3.

3   Method

Given a grayscale image as input, the proposed method could generate a faithful color counterpart. In Sect. 3.1, we make a brief description about the objective and overall framework of our approach. The local pyramid attention and spatial semantic modulation will be detailed in Sect. 3.2 and Sect. 3.3 respectively.

3.1   Objective and Framework

The overall architecture of our method is illustrated in Fig. 2. Like most existing colorization methods, we employ CIE Lab color space to make the restoration of grayscale. Assuming the colorization model as ϕ, grayscale input as I_L, and color ground truth as I_{ab}, the objective of colorization method could be formulated as follow:

$$L = \arg \min_{\theta} E \left\| \phi\left(I_L; \theta\right) - I_{ab} \right\| \tag{1}$$

where E stands for the expected value over all elements, and $\|x - y\|$ means Huber Loss [16], which was used to avoid the average problem during color

Table 1. Details of baseline architecture. Input feature spatial resolution, number of channels and sampling operations are listed for each module.

Module	Resolution	Channels	Operation
first Conv	256	3	/
encoder1	256	64	Dowmsample
encoder2	128	128	Downsample
encoder3	64	256	Downsample
bottleneck1	32	512	/
bottleneck2	32	512	/
decoder1	32	512	Upsample
decoder2	64	256	Upsample
decoder3	128	128	Upsample
final Conv	256	64	/

prediction in the previous automatic colorization method [36]. The definition of Huber Loss is:

$$\ell_\delta(x, y) = \frac{1}{2}(x - y)^2 \mathbb{1}_{\{|x-y|<\delta\}} + \delta \left(|x - y| - \frac{1}{2}\delta \right) \mathbb{1}_{\{|x-y|\geq\delta\}} \tag{2}$$

where θ is a hyper parameter, and we set $\theta = 1$ empirically.

As illustrated in Fig. 2, our backbone is a typical encoder-decoder architecture with skip connections [28] between symmetric layers. The convolution (deconvolution) block consists of two cascade convolution layers and a residual connection as [11], which has been proved beneficial to the convergence of deep neural networks. All downsample and upsample operations are achieved by stride convolutions and transposed convolutions respectively. Corresponding single convolution or deconvolution operation is used in the residual branch to match the dimension of feature maps. Each convolution layer is followed by batch normalization [18] and leaky ReLU activation layers except those in decoder blocks, where the batch normalization is replaced by proposed SSM to embed semantic prior during color reconstruction. And the proposed LPA is plugged into the bottleneck to refine the extracted feature maps.

In this paper, we build our baseline model by abandoning the proposed LPA and SSM modules. The details of our backbone are listed in Table 1. It's worth noting that the kernel size of each convolution layer is 3, whereas 4 for deconvolution layers. There is no batch normalization for the final convolution layer, and we utilize the activation function Tanh to make a constraint for the chrominance prediction in the range of $[-1.0, 1.0]$.

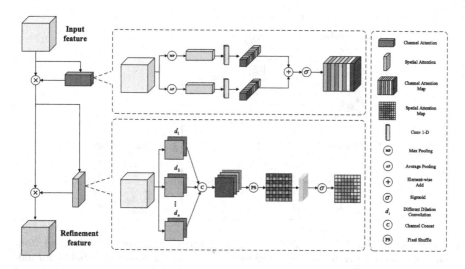

Fig. 3. Local Pyramid Attention. Similar to CBAM [33], the proposed LPA is composed of a channel attention module and spatial attention module in series. In the channel attention part, the input features pass through two branches pooling operations followed by 1-D convolution, then the element-wise add and sigmoid function are used to obtain channel attention map. While the spatial attention module employs dilation convolutions and PixelShuffle operation to build local pyramid represents for spatial attention map.

3.2   Local Pyramid Attention Module

Considering the lacking of ability to capture long-range dependency, we introduce a novel local pyramid attention module to strengthen context understanding, which helps to ease context confusion problem in image colorization. The LPA module is illustrated in Fig. 3.

3.2.1   Channel Attention of LPA

We utilize different pooling operations to build two branches of the channel attention module. This design choice has proven to be beneficial to the feature refinement in [33]. Inspired by [26], we replace the two fully connected layers with a 1-D convolution. There are two This approach has two advantages in this manner. Firstly, compared to the original two-layer FC with channel compression, a single 1-D convolution allows direct correspondence between channels. Secondly, it's more computation efficient due to significantly fewer parameters. The kernel size of 1-D convolution is proportional to channel dimension [26], which could be formulated as:

$$C = 2^{(\alpha * k + \beta)} \tag{3}$$

where C means channel dimension, k means kernel size of 1-D convolution, α and β are linear hyper-parameters for k. Therefore, k could be calculated by Eq. 4.

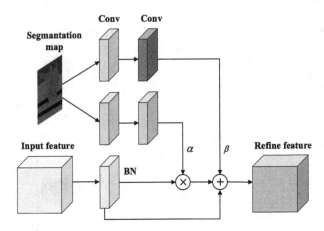

Fig. 4. Spatial Semantic Modulation. A paired learnable parameters obtained from separated stacked convolution layers are used to modulate the output of batch normalization layer. In addition, there is a residual connection between BN output and final output.

$$k = \left| \frac{\log_2^C}{\alpha} + \frac{\beta}{\alpha} \right|_{odd} \tag{4}$$

and $|t|_{odd}$ means the nearest odd number of t. In this paper, we set the hyper parameters $\alpha = 2$ and $\beta = 1$ by default.

3.2.2   Spatial Attention of LPA

In CBAM [33], the spatial attention map is obtained from channel pooing and the followed convolution transformation. However, the stacked convolution layers result in a local effect in feature refinement. There are many explorations about non-local dependency modeling, such as non-local [31] and self-attention [29], but the common problems of these approaches are complex and computation-consuming. In addition, Cao et al. [3] argue that the pixel-wise dependency modeling is redundant for some intensive prediction visual tasks. Intuitively, we can model the long-range dependency by transforming the features with different receptive fields into local ones, and then establishing correspondence between different regions in the local area. Based on this, we introduce LPA to get the best of both worlds, which means non-local effect and low computation cost.

Inspired by [6], we concatenate the representations from dilation convolution layers with different dilation rate firstly. Unlike [6], our proposed LPA does not maintain feature dimension by aggressive zero paddings, which introduces too much invalid information and results in large computation costs. As Fig. 3 shows, we well-design the paddings and strides for the n kinds of dilation convolution to promise the output feature with the same dimension. Assuming the input dimension for spatial attention module is $[H, W, C]$, we make the output for each dilation convolution layer with dimension of $\left[\frac{H}{\sqrt{n}}, \frac{W}{\sqrt{n}}, 1 \right]$, which could be concatenated to $\left[\frac{H}{\sqrt{n}}, \frac{W}{\sqrt{n}}, n\right]$. And then the PixelShuffle operation [30] is used to upsample the feature map by $\sqrt{n}$ times, results in a representation with dimension of $[H, W, 1]$, which follow the design philosophy of CBAM [33]. Finally, we use a convolution layer followed by sigmoid function to obtain a spatial attention map.

In our LPA, channel attention map and spatial attention map are firstly broadcast to match the dimension of the input feature map for each sub-modules, and then we execute tensor multiplication to perform feature refinement. Since the input and output maintain the same dimension, our LPA could be easily plugged into any architecture for any visual task, which guarantees the generalization of our proposed.

3.3 Spatial Semantic Modulation Module

Previous advances in image colorization [13,37] have emphasized the importance of semantic prior. Intuitively, we know that the sky is usually blue, and it's impossible for a puppy with green color. However, concatenating semantic maps into input or middle feature maps normally leads to imprecise semantic embedding. In other visual tasks, Wang et al. [32] proposed a spatial transformation layer to enhance the feature for the texture recovery in image super-resolution, which is achieved by a paired spatial transformation parameters to modulate the middle representation using semantic probability maps. Park et al. [25] argued the semantic information tends to be erased by the normalization layers in deep neural networks. This phenomenon should be attributed to the lack of spatial location-aware for most conditional normalization methods. Inspired by these, we introduce spatial semantic modulation to make accurate semantic embedding for image colorization, which encourages the model to assign more plausible colors for specific objects.

The proposed SSM module is illustrated in Fig. 4. Similar to [25], SSM allows the input feature to pass through a standard Batch Normalization layer [18] firstly, and then the features are modulated by a paired learnable transformation parameters α and β. The modulation parameters are obtained by two separate stacked convolution blocks with the same dimension as input features. ReLU is used to introduce nonlinearity after the first convolution layer within each block, and the number of hidden features is 128 in our setting. It's worth noting that we make a residual connection from BN output to the final output, which has been proved beneficial to preserve information from original features in [25].

Assume the input feature with dimension $[N, C, H, W]$, for a specific activation value at location $I_{n,c,h,w}$, where $(n \in N, c \in C, h \in H, w \in W)$, the output of spatial semantic modulation $O_{n,c,h,w}$ is:

$$O_{n,c,h,w} = (1 + \alpha_{c,h,w}) \frac{I_{n,c,h,w} - \mu_c}{\delta_c} + \beta_{c,h,w} \qquad (5)$$

where α and β with dimension $[C, H, W]$, μ and δ are the mean and standard deviation for input features along channel direction, whose definition as follow:

$$\mu_c = \frac{1}{NHW} \sum_{n,h,w} I_{n,c,h,w} \tag{6}$$

$$\delta_c = \sqrt{\frac{1}{NHW} \sum_{n,h,w} \left((I_{n,c,h,w})^2 - (\mu_c)^2 \right)} \tag{7}$$

Follow [25], we replace the BN with proposed SSM in the decoder part to refine the features during color reconstruction.

4 Experiments

In this section, we conduct extensive experiments on benchmark datasets to show the effectiveness of our proposed. We first state the experiment setting and evaluation metrics in Sect. 4.1, the quantitative and qualitative results for two datasets will be detailed in Sect. 4.2 and Sect. 4.3 respectively. Finally, we investigate the importance of proposed LPA and SSM modules by ablation study in Sect. 4.4.

4.1 Experiment Settings

Datasets. To evaluate the effectiveness and generation ability of our method, we experiment on two benchmark datasets: Pascal Context [24] and Coco Stuff [2]. Both datasets contain images from the natural scene and the corresponding segmentation annotation, which are used to finetune the pretrained Deeplabv2 [5] with luminance channel as input. Then we can use the off-the-shelf segmentation model to generate semantic maps for training and inferring end to end. The Pascal dataset contains 20 object classes and a background, whose training set consists of 10582 images, while 1449 images for testing. Compared to Pascal Context, the Coco Stuff dataset contains much more classes, including 182 object classes and a background on 8977 training images and 1000 test images. So it is more challenging to image colorization models.

Implement Details. We conduct all experiments on a single NVIDIA GeForce RTX 1080Ti 11 GB with the Pytorch toolbox. Considering the limitation of GPU memory, the batch size is set to 8. We choose Adam [20] as optimizer and the weight decay is 1e−6. To make sure convergence, we experiment with 300 epochs for each dataset, and the initial learning rate is 1e-4 with linear decay to zero. To avoid the overfitting issue, we conduct data augmentation for all experiments. We first resize the short side of images to 288 and then execute center crop to get samples with resolution 288 × 288. The random crop and horizontal flip are used to get final 256 × 256 resolution images for training.

Table 2. PSNR and SSIM comparison for different methods. Our method outperforms all baselines on two benchmark datasets. It should be noted that we do not add local color hints on the experiment of Zhang et al. [36], namely end-to-end training and inferring. (↑ means higher is better)

Method	Pascal context		Coco stuff	
	PSNR↑	SSIM↑	PSNR↑	SSIM↑
Zhang et al. [35]	21.15	0.9061	21.29	0.9058
Zhang et al. [36]	24.13	0.9258	24.14	0.9215
Man et al. [13]	27.70	0.9847	26.99	0.9791
Xia et al. [34]	28.03	**0.9889**	27.21	0.9841
Ours	**28.17**	0.9883	**27.40**	**0.9856**

Evaluation Metrics. To quantitatively evaluate the performance of different methods, we report SSIM and PSNR which are the commonly used metrics for image quality assessment and existing colorization methods.

4.2 Quantitative Comparison

We compare our method with the different state-of-the-art methods currently, including Zhang et al. [35,36] (without guided colors), Man et al. [13] (with semantic embedding) and Xia et al. [34]. To fairly compare the performance of the different approaches, we train all models from scratch based on the public source code provided by the authors. The evaluation results based on quantitative metrics are listed in Table 2, where we can see our method outperforms all baselines for both metrics with a considerable margin on two benchmark datasets.

The results on two datasets prove the effectiveness and generalization ability of our proposed. Compared to previous image colorization methods, the proposed local pyramid attention and spatial semantic modulation encourage more accurate feature refinement and semantic embedding, lead to colorization output with high quality and fidelity.

4.3 Qualitative Visual Results

Figure 5 shows a sample comparison of our method and baseline approaches on Pascal Context dataset. It is obvious to observe that the proposed method generates visually pleasing and high-quality colorization results. In detail, the grassland and airstrip are discriminative in the first row, and the colors of girl's skin and clothes are more saturated and natural in the 3rd and 4th rows. However, for previous methods, color bleeding in [35,36] and unsaturated color assignment in [13] result in implausible color prediction.

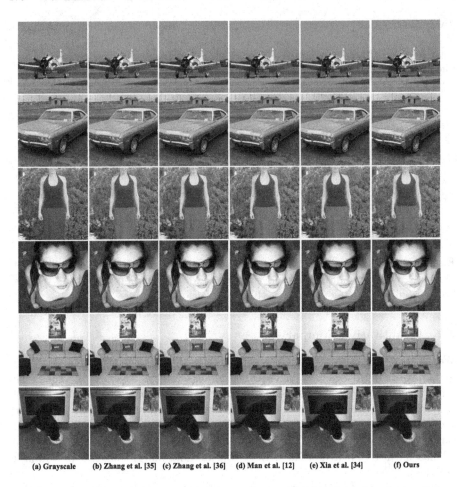

(a) Grayscale   (b) Zhang et al. [35]   (c) Zhang et al. [36]   (d) Man et al. [12]   (e) Xia et al. [34]   (f) Ours

Fig. 5. Quantitative comparison between proposed method and previous state-of-the-art models on Pascal Context dataset. Column (a) is the grayscale input, while column (b)–(f) are output from different models. Compared to previous approaches, our method generates more plausible results with less color bleeding.

To evaluate the performance of our method in more complex scenario, we conduct comparative experiments on the Coco Stuff datasets. The sample results comparison is shown in Fig. 6, where our method yields more faithful coloring results.

4.4 Ablation Study

To validate the importance and effectiveness of the proposed LPA and SSM modules, we conduct a comprehensive ablation study. As mentioned earlier, we establish an end-to-end baseline by discarding LPA and SSM modules. Table 3 shows the performance of different variants of baseline on the Pascal Context

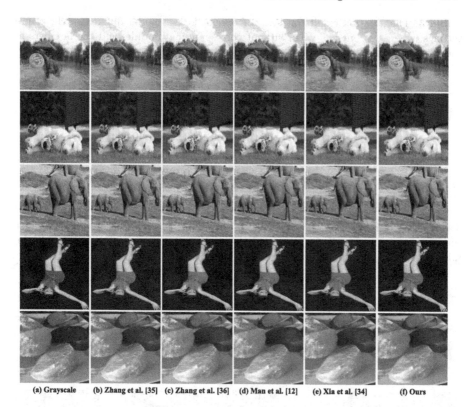

(a) Grayscale   (b) Zhang et al. [35]   (c) Zhang et al. [36]   (d) Man et al. [12]   (e) Xia et al. [34]   (f) Ours

Fig. 6. Sample results from different methods on Coco Stuff datasets. Our method generates more faithful colorization results. For example, the background in the 2nd row, the girl's shirt and skin color in the 4th row and the appearance of orange in the last row.

dataset [24]. It's worth noting that both the proposed LPA and SSM benefit baseline model with different margins, while the full model outperforms all the variants, which indicates the LPA and SSM module can obtain benefits from each other. For visual comparison, Fig. 7 illustrates colorization results under different ablation settings. We can observe more plausible color assignment (blue box) and less color bleeding (red box) in our full model. Consequently, the proposed method with LPA and SSM not only facilitates the long-range dependency modeling, but also encourages more accurate semantic embedding for image colorization.

In order to fairly compare the proposed LPA and existing attention modules, including CBAM [33] and Non-Local [31], we replace the LPA with the two efficient attention modules aforementioned under the same settings. And then all variants are evaluated on the Pascal Context Dataset [24]. The quantitative comparison on evaluation metrics and the number of parameters has been shown in Table 4. The experimental results prove that LPA is superior to CBAM, and its performance is close to Non-Local but with fewer parameters, which should be attributed to the efficient and lightweight design of LPA.

Table 3. The ablation results on Pascal Context dataset under different architecture settings, where $\sqrt{}$/– means with/without corresponding module, and the numbers in the brackets represent improvement compared to baseline.

Module			Metrics	
Baseline	LPA	SSM	PSNR	SSIM
$\sqrt{}$	–	–	27.16	0.9862
$\sqrt{}$	$\sqrt{}$	–	27.64 (+0.48)	0.9866 (+0.0004)
$\sqrt{}$	–	$\sqrt{}$	27.87 (+0.71)	0.9878 (+0.0016)
$\sqrt{}$	$\sqrt{}$	$\sqrt{}$	**28.17 (+1.1)**	**0.9883 (+0.0021)**

Table 4. Quantitative comparison between LPA and existing attention modules under the same experiment settings. It is worth noting that the number of parameters in the table represents only the parameters of the module, not the whole model.

	PSNR	SSIM	Params (M)
CBAM [33]	27.71	0.9881	0.033
Non-Local [31]	**28.17**	**0.9887**	0.526
LPA	**28.17**	0.9883	**0.019**

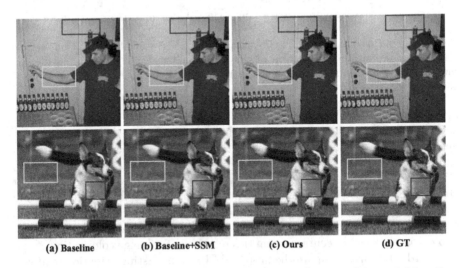

    (a) Baseline   (b) Baseline+SSM   (c) Ours   (d) GT

Fig. 7. Visual comparison for ablation study. (a)–(d) stands for baseline model, baseline with SSM, our full model and corresponding ground truth respectively. (Color figure online)

5 Conclusion

In this paper, we propose a novel automatic image colorization model with two efficient modules named local pyramid attention and spatial semantic modulation. The local pyramid attention is achieved by dilation convolution and PixelShuffle operation, it strengthens the long-range dependency modeling to migrate context confusion. While the spatial semantic modulation encourages accurate semantic prior embedding by spatial-ware affine transformation with learnable parameters to enable plausible color assignment. Extensive experiments and ablation studies on two benchmark datasets indicate the effectiveness of our method. Compared to existing methods, our proposed obtains coherent improvements in image fidelity and color saturation.

Acknowledgement. This work was supported in part by the National Natural Science Foundation of China under grant 62072169 and Changsha Science and Technology Research Plan under Grant KQ2004005.

References

1. An, X., Pellacini, F.: AppProp: all-pairs appearance-space edit propagation. In: ACM SIGGRAPH 2008 papers, pp. 1–9 (2008)
2. Caesar, H., Uijlings, J., Ferrari, V.: COCO-stuff: thing and stuff classes in context. In: Proceedings of the IEEE Conference on Computer Vision and Pattern Recognition, pp. 1209–1218 (2018)
3. Cao, Y., Xu, J., Lin, S., Wei, F., Hu, H.: GCNet: non-local networks meet squeeze-excitation networks and beyond. In: Proceedings of the IEEE/CVF International Conference on Computer Vision Workshops, pp. 1971–1980 (2019)
4. Cao, Y., Zhou, Z., Zhang, W., Yu, Y.: Unsupervised diverse colorization via generative adversarial networks. In: Ceci, M., Hollmén, J., Todorovski, L., Vens, C., Džeroski, S. (eds.) ECML PKDD 2017. LNCS (LNAI), vol. 10534, pp. 151–166. Springer, Cham (2017). https://doi.org/10.1007/978-3-319-71249-9_10
5. Chen, L.C., Papandreou, G., Kokkinos, I., Murphy, K., Yuille, A.L.: DeepLab: semantic image segmentation with deep convolutional nets, atrous convolution, and fully connected CRFs. IEEE Trans. Pattern Anal. Mach. Intell. **40**(4), 834–848 (2017)
6. Chen, LC., Papandreou, G., Schroff, F., Adam, H.: Rethinking atrous convolution for semantic image segmentation. arXiv preprint arXiv:1706.05587 (2017)
7. Cheng, Z., Yang, Q., Sheng, B.: Deep colorization. In: Proceedings of the IEEE International Conference on Computer Vision, pp. 415–423 (2015)
8. Chia, A.Y.S., et al.: Semantic colorization with internet images. ACM Trans. Graph. (TOG) **30**(6), 1–8 (2011)
9. Endo, Y., Iizuka, S., Kanamori, Y., Mitani, J.: DeepProp: extracting deep features from a single image for edit propagation. In: Computer Graphics Forum, vol. 35, pp. 189–201. Wiley (2016)
10. Gupta, R.K., Chia, A.Y.S., Rajan, D., Ng, E.S., Zhiyong, H.: Image colorization using similar images. In: Proceedings of the 20th ACM International Conference on Multimedia, pp. 369–378 (2012)

11. He, K., Zhang, X., Ren, S., Sun, J.: Deep residual learning for image recognition. In: Proceedings of the IEEE Conference on Computer Vision and Pattern Recognition, pp. 770–778 (2016)
12. He, M., Chen, D., Liao, J., Sander, P.V., Yuan, L.: Deep exemplar-based colorization. ACM Trans. Graph. (TOG) **37**(4), 1–16 (2018)
13. Ho, M.M., Zhang, L., Raake, A., Zhou, J.: Semantic-driven colorization. arXiv preprint arXiv:2006.07587 (2020)
14. Hu, J., Shen, L., Sun, G.: Squeeze-and-excitation networks. In: Proceedings of the IEEE Conference on Computer Vision and Pattern Recognition, pp. 7132–7141 (2018)
15. Huang, Y.C., Tung, Y.S., Chen, J.C., Wang, S.W., Wu, J.L.: An adaptive edge detection based colorization algorithm and its applications. In: Proceedings of the 13th Annual ACM International Conference on Multimedia, pp. 351–354 (2005)
16. Huber, P.J.: Robust estimation of a location parameter. In: Breakthroughs in Statistics, pp. 492–518. Springer, New York (1992). https://doi.org/10.1007/978-1-4612-4380-9_35
17. Iizuka, S., Simo-Serra, E., Ishikawa, H.: Let there be color! Joint end-to-end learning of global and local image priors for automatic image colorization with simultaneous classification. ACM Trans. Graph. (ToG) **35**(4), 1–11 (2016)
18. Ioffe, S., Szegedy, C.: Batch normalization: accelerating deep network training by reducing internal covariate shift. In: International Conference on Machine Learning, pp. 448–456. PMLR (2015)
19. Isola, P., Zhu, J.Y., Zhou, T., Efros, A.A.: Image-to-image translation with conditional adversarial networks. In: Proceedings of the IEEE Conference on Computer Vision and Pattern Recognition, pp. 1125–1134 (2017)
20. Kingma, D.P., Ba, J.: Adam: a method for stochastic optimization. arXiv preprint arXiv:1412.6980 (2014)
21. Liao, J., Yao, Y., Yuan, L., Hua, G., Kang, S.B.: Visual attribute transfer through deep image analogy. arXiv preprint arXiv:1705.01088 (2017)
22. Liu, X., et al.: Intrinsic colorization. In: ACM SIGGRAPH Asia 2008 papers, pp. 1–9 (2008)
23. Mirza, M., Osindero, S.: Conditional generative adversarial nets. arXiv preprint arXiv:1411.1784 (2014)
24. Mottaghi, R., et al.: The role of context for object detection and semantic segmentation in the wild. In: Proceedings of the IEEE Conference on Computer Vision and Pattern Recognition, pp. 891–898 (2014)
25. Park, T., Liu, M.Y., Wang, T.C., Zhu, J.Y.: Semantic image synthesis with spatially-adaptive normalization. In: Proceedings of the IEEE/CVF Conference on Computer Vision and Pattern Recognition, pp. 2337–2346 (2019)
26. Wang, Q., Wu, B., Zhu, P., Li, P., Zuo, W., Hu, Q.: ECA-Net: efficient channel attention for deep convolutional neural networks (2020)
27. Yingge, Q., Wong, T.-T., Heng, P.-A.: Manga colorization. ACM Trans. Graph. (TOG) **25**(3), 1214–1220 (2006)
28. Ronneberger, O., Fischer, P., Brox, T.: U-Net: convolutional networks for biomedical image segmentation. In: Navab, N., Hornegger, J., Wells, W.M., Frangi, A.F. (eds.) MICCAI 2015. LNCS, vol. 9351, pp. 234–241. Springer, Cham (2015). https://doi.org/10.1007/978-3-319-24574-4_28
29. Shaw, P., Uszkoreit, J., Vaswani, A.: Self-attention with relative position representations. arXiv preprint arXiv:1803.02155 (2018)

30. Shi, W., et al.: Real-time single image and video super-resolution using an efficient sub-pixel convolutional neural network. In: Proceedings of the IEEE Conference on Computer Vision and Pattern Recognition, pp. 1874–1883 (2016)
31. Wang, X., Girshick, R., Gupta, A., He, K.: Non-local neural networks. In: Proceedings of the IEEE Conference on Computer Vision and Pattern Recognition, pp. 7794–7803 (2018)
32. Wang, X., Yu, K., Dong, C., Loy, C.C.: Recovering realistic texture in image super-resolution by deep spatial feature transform. In: Proceedings of the IEEE Conference on Computer Vision and Pattern Recognition, pp. 606–615 (2018)
33. Woo, S., Park, J., Lee, J.Y., Kweon, I.S.: CBAM: convolutional block attention module. In: Proceedings of the European Conference on Computer Vision (ECCV), pp. 3–19 (2018)
34. Xia, J., Tan, G., Xiao, Y., Xu, F., Leung, C.S.: Edge-aware multi-scale progressive colorization. In: ICASSP 2021–2021 IEEE International Conference on Acoustics, Speech and Signal Processing (ICASSP), pp. 1655–1659. IEEE (2021)
35. Zhang, R., Isola, P., Efros, A.A.: Colorful image colorization. In: Leibe, B., Matas, J., Sebe, N., Welling, M. (eds.) ECCV 2016. LNCS, vol. 9907, pp. 649–666. Springer, Cham (2016). https://doi.org/10.1007/978-3-319-46487-9_40
36. Zhang, R., et al.: Real-time user-guided image colorization with learned deep priors. arXiv preprint arXiv:1705.02999 (2017)
37. Zhao, J., Han, J., Shao, L., Snoek, C.G.M.: Pixelated semantic colorization. Int. J. Comput. Vis. **128**(4), 818–834 (2019). https://doi.org/10.1007/s11263-019-01271-4

Quality-Sensitive Feature Extraction for End Product Quality Prediction in Injection Molding Processes

Fangyang Liu, Yalin Wang, and Kai Wang[✉]

School of Automation, Central South University, Changsha 410083, China
kaiwang@csu.edu.cn

Abstract. The injection molding process is a typical batch process. Injection molding production often has the characteristics of low volume and high quality. Product testing in the injection molding is usually carried out in a laboratory, which presents a severe delay issue and is of considerable cost. Moreover, it is often difficult for such products to install equipment for online real-time measuring. Process data and empirical knowledge plays a critical role in the prediction of end-product quality. The use of data in the injection molding process for quality prediction ordinarily associates with exists a series of challenges, such as nonlinearities, multiphase, three-way data, long sequence data and unequal lengths between batches. In response to these problems, this paper proposes a novel neural network structure, which consists of phase feature extraction layer, key time node extraction layer and sensitive phase extraction layer. The feature extraction layer is to overcome the non-linear problem in the injection molding process, the three-way data and the unequal length issue are addressed by the long short-term memory network. The key time node extraction layer extracts crucial points with attention mechanism. The sensitive phase extraction layer uses backpropagation on a single-layer fully-connected network to learn the contribution of each phase to the quality variables. The proposed model is verified in the experiment of the injection molding process and the positive result testifies the effectiveness of the proposed method.

Keywords: Injection molding process · Recurrent Neural Network · Attention mechanism · LSTM

1 Introduction

Batch processes are characterized by the repetitive production with limited durations. The injection molding process is a typical batch process, of which the production is various, such as glasses, medical equipment and other materials.

This is a student paper. Research supported by the National Natural Science Foundation of China (Grant No. U1911401) and the Young Scientists Fund of the National Natural Science Foundation of China (Grant No. 62003373).

© Springer Nature Singapore Pte Ltd. 2022
X. Liao et al. (Eds.): BigData 2021, CCIS 1496, pp. 182–193, 2022.
https://doi.org/10.1007/978-981-16-9709-8_13

In the injection molding process, with the installed sensors and data acquisition equipment, data of a large number of process variables could be collected, forming a situation of the industrial big data. What the operators concern mostly is the end product quality, which is still tested offline in labs or by sampling several products for evaluating the qualification rate. Rapid quality assessment is quite attractive and necessary for high efficient producing. In this paper, we will focus on how to use the data for effective end-quality prediction in the injection molding process.

The injection molding process is a typical multiphase production process, including the key phases of mold clamping, injection, pressure holding, cooling, and demolding. However, the influence of each phase on the final effect of injection molding is inconsistent. In the injection molding process, the collected sensor data are often repeated time series between batches, behaving as recurring curves. In this regard, many scholars have made relevant analysis. Ke et al. focuses on the injection pressure in the injection molding process, and extracted some key indicators from the injection pressure curve as the input of the multilayer perceptron (MLP) for predicting the size of the final product [7]. Nagorny et al. used Long Short-Term Memory (LSTM) and Convolutional Neural Network (CNN) to compare the impact on product size based on sensor data and thermal image data in the film and found that LSTM can achieve a good size prediction result using time series data. With thermal infrared images, CNN can also achieve a good size prediction [12]. Jung et al. used the injection state data to compare a series of machine learning methods to determine which has the advantage of feature extraction in the injection molding process and concluded that the autoencoder (AE) framework could predict the quality best [6]. Wang et al. combine LSTM and stacked autoencoders (SAE) to extract multi-stage features and nonlinear deep features of intermittent processes [15].

In the aforementioned researches, it can be found that the data generated by the process variables in the injection molding process in a batch time can be used to obtain the best feature learning effect through the LSTM network. In addition, the methods of SAE and MLP have also emerged as a powerfull settlement for some variable data that characterizes the state of the injection molding process. Therefore, inspired by these previous investigation, the LSTM and the SAE can be integrated and combined to form a new feature learning network to further strengthen the quality prediction performance of the injection molding process. The main work in this paper is as following: (1) Extract the features of the LSTM in segments during each operation phase of the injection molding process. (2) For some key time points that were previously focused empirically in the injection molding process, the attention mechanism is embedded for automatically assigning weights for these key time points. (3) All phases cannot be treated equally. For the features extracted by LSTM, we call them hidden variables, which reflect the state of a phase, but the impact of each phase on the end quality is different, and the relationship between the hidden variables and the end quality is not simply described, so the utilization of fully connected layer structure is a well-established and necessary approach in extraction.

2   Related Work

2.1   Injection Molding Process

The injection molding process is a typical discrete manufacturing process and characterized by small batches and high-valued products. Plastic injection molding production accounts for one-third of plastic production, and most of them are products with complex structures. The producing process of the injection molding need to meet specific physical and chemical requirements, relying on the target product. For predicting the end quality, a model for representing the injection molding is necessary. In the field of control, we usually describe the process by a transfer function [8]. In fact, there are different kinds of mathematical models attempting to establish the relationship between the process variables and the end quality in the injection molding process. Lwko et al. used mathematical functions to describe the pairwise relationship of key variables in the injection molding process [5]. Lindert et al. adopted a fluid dynamics model to describe the pressure change over time in the packing phase [9]. Due to the strong physical mechanism which is hard to discover, the description of these mathematical models is often simple and is limited by many assumptions, which cannot meet the practical application requirements for high precision prediction. Besides, the parameters selection in the injection molding process is also crucial. Chen et al. took injection pressure, ejection stroke, injection speed and other parameters as the inputs of the neural network, combined with self-organizing map for a good predictive effect on product quality [2]. Alvarado et al. used a three-layer RNN to predict warpage defects, in which melt temperature, molding temperature, holding pressure, holding time, and cooling time were selected as the network input, which has a certain predictive effect [1]. These studies provide certain guidance in terms of variable selection and model description.

With the continuous in-depth study of the injection molding process, a series of studies on the multiphase problems of the injection molding process have also been carried out [14,16,17]. E.g., Zhao improved the quality prediction effect of the injection molding process from phase division [18]. After phase division, Lu et al. proposed the use of multiphase partial least squares method for quality prediction in the injection molding process [11]. These works are the main direction for the further research.

2.2   Recurrent Neural Network

Recurrent Neural Network (RNN) is a type of recursive neural network for modeling process dynamics. RNN is recursive in the evolution direction of the sequence and its all nodes are connected in a fashion of chain [4]. RNN has memory, parameter sharing and turing completeness, therefore it has certain advantages when learning the nonlinear characteristics of the sequence. There are some applications in the injection molding process with RNN. Demarchi et al. compare the classification performance of the RNN using the camera vibration book with the CNN using the camera vibration image to determine whether the injection machine is in an overpressure state [3]. Diagonal Recurrent Neural Networks, the improved structure of RNN, is used in the predictive control to synchronize dynamic behaviors, so as to improve the precision and synchronization of predictive control of multizone melt temperature [13]. RNN is used in the non-linear predictive control of the injection molding process due to its strong ability to learn dynamic performance [10]. Hence, the RNN can be applied into the quality prediction in the injection molding process. LSTM is a special structure of RNN, which demonstrates growing memory performance for lon-term sequences.

3 Proposed Method

In this section, we will elaborate the proposed model structure for quality prediction. The model structure is divided into three parts: (1) Phase feature extraction; (2) Key time node extraction layer; (3) Sensitive phase extraction layer.

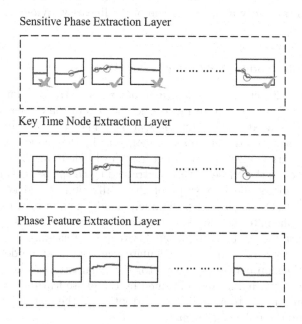

Fig. 1. The framework of the proposed model.

As shown in Fig. 1, the nonlinear and dynamic phase features are extracted firstly in each phase. Then, the key time node extraction layer captures the information at the key moments in the phase, and the sensitive phase extraction layer judges each phase whether there is an effective quality-related phase feature, which can filter a lot of insignificant features for the end quality.

3.1   Phase Feature Extraction Layer

The phases include the characteristics of nonlinearity, unequal length and dynamics. To deal with nonlinear problems, kernel methods or deep learning networks are commonly used. For unequal length problems, methods such as truncation (All batches are shortened to the same length as the shortest), dynamic time warping, and sliding time windows can be used. However, they will lose some information which may be very important for predicting the quality. Regarding the dynamic correlation, time series models make sense for representing the autocorrelation. In this paper, the RNN is used for phase feature extraction. Due to the inherent structure of the RNN, it can reflect the autocorrelation within the phase. To prevent the problems of gradient disappearance and gradient explosion, the LSTM network as a special RNN is used. At the same time, the LSTM can extract longer-term temporal correlations than the short-term phases. The RNN also possesses a good learning ability for nonlinear knowledge due to its framework. Moreover, because the RNN adopts the recurrent structure, it has no demand for the same length for all batches. Therefore, RNN is able to simultaneously adapt the issue of nonlinearity, dynamics and uneven length.

3.2   Key Time Node Extraction Layer

The LSTM can extract sequence features, but when extracting longer sequence features, there will be no way to retain the features of the earlier time. At this time, a method is needed to retain the features. The attention mechanism can analyze and weigh the quality-related moments in the sequence. The reason is that the attention mechanism integrates the hidden variables representing quality features and the phase features extracted by the phase feature extraction layer. Figure 2 shows the four steps of the realization of the key time point extraction layer: (1) calculate the alignment model results e, (2) calculate the weights α, (3) calculate the phased feature after integration c, (4) carry out the model representation of the correlations between the phases.

Specifically, the first step is to calculate the alignment model result e by using the relationship between the s vector that characterizes the quality and a series of features $(h_1, h_2, \dots, h_T)$ obtained by the phase feature extraction layer at each time in a phase to give different attention to the features at each time. e is obtained by the following formula.

$$e = \tanh(\mathbf{w}_{se}^T \mathbf{s} + \mathbf{w}_{he}^T \mathbf{h} + b_e) \tag{1}$$

where e is the alignment model result, s is the feature characterizing the quality, h is the phase feature extracted by the LSTM. The number of the phase features is the same as the length of the phase. Then the weight vector α is calculated by imposing the softmax function to the e obtained in the first step. The sum of all weights is 1. It is used for the subsequent merging of a series of vectors obtained by the feature extraction layer. The α is calculated by:

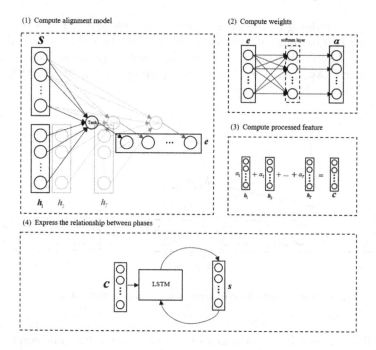

Fig. 2. The architecture of the key time node extraction layer.

$$\alpha = softmax(\mathbf{e}) \tag{2}$$

The third step is to use the weight vector α to perform a weighted summation of all the features from the first instance to the end of phase T to obtain a new phase feature representation $\mathbf{c}$. This feature includes the extraction of key time points. The $\mathbf{c}$ is calculated by:

$$\mathbf{c} = \alpha^T \mathbf{H} \tag{3}$$

$$\mathbf{H} = \begin{bmatrix} \mathbf{h}_1 & \mathbf{h}_2 & \cdots & \mathbf{h}_T \end{bmatrix} \tag{4}$$

where T is the length of the phase, $\mathbf{H}$ is the whole phase features of the phase. The dimension of the α is T, and each phase feature has a weight α. Finally, the feature $\mathbf{c}$ is input into the LSTM network to obtain a new vector characterizing the quality $\mathbf{s}$, and steps 1–4 are repeated to obtain a new feature representation $\mathbf{c}$ including the extraction of key time points in the next phase.

3.3 Sensitive Phase Extraction Layer

Even though we have extracted the comprehensive phase features, one fact worthy to be noticed is that different phases have unbalanced contributions to the end quality, i.e. judging whether it is a quality-sensitive phase. The batch process can be divided into many phases, but each phase of the batch process does not have the same effect on quality. Choosing the sensitive phase on the end quality can better improve the accuracy of quality prediction. The architecture of the model is shown as Fig. 3.

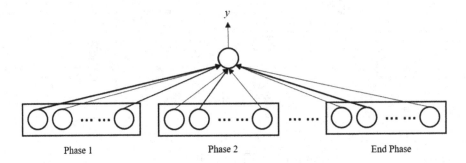

Fig. 3. The architecture of the sensitive phase extraction layer.

The Fig. 3 shows that the features extracted from the key time point extraction layer are combined into a perceptron input to learn the weight of each feature point on the quality. The purpose of this design is that different phases have different effects on the end quality. At the same time, the influence of each feature point on the end quality in different phases is different. The phase feature s is set as the phase representation because of its high relevance with both the quality and the phase.

4 Experiment

We apply the proposed method on plastic injection molding process, the data of which contains 22 process and more than 16597 batches. The whole process can be divided into 11 phases according to the operation phases. The length of each phase ranges from 50 to 400 sampling points. Due to the confidentiality principle, injection molding products are hidden in this paper. Our goal is predicting the size of the product through process variables which are partly listed in Table 1.

On a multi-GPU device, we completed the training of the proposed network through distributed training. On a multi-GPU device, we divided the dataset into training set with 11618 batches and test set with 4979 batches. We set the learning rate and batch size to 0.001 and 64 respectively, using the Adam optimizer to train the network on 4 GPUs in this process. The prediction performance index are mean square error (MSE) and R-Squared value which can be calculated as follows:

Table 1. The process variables that can be measured.

Name	Location
Internal mold pressure	In-mould
Internal mold temperature	In-mould
The flow rate of the water in	
The mold temperature controller	In-mould
The temperature of the chill water	Mold temperature controller
Injection pressure	Nozzle
Ejector stroke	Nozzle
The temperature of the recycled water	Mold temperature contoller

$$MSE = \frac{\sum_{i=1}^{M}(y_{(i)} - \hat{y_{(i)}})^2}{M} \tag{5}$$

$$R^2 = 1 - \frac{\sum_{i=1}^{M}(y_{(i)} - \hat{y_{(i)}})^2}{\sum_{i=1}^{M}(y_{(i)} - \bar{y})^2} \tag{6}$$

where M is the number of the batches, $y_{(i)}$ is the ith quality value, $\hat{y_{(i)}}$ is the ith predicted quality value, and $\bar{y}$ is the average of the quality values of all the batches.

Table 2. Comparative experimental results.

Method	MSE	R^2
MLP	0.30	0.70
LSTM-SAE	0.34	0.66
Proposed Model	0.24	0.76

The parameters of the proposed network are set as follows. The first parameters is the dimension of the hidden layer in the first-level LSTM. By changing the dimension from the candidate set $\{10, 20, 30, 40\}$, the prediction MSE and R-Squared on the test set is obtained after model training. Detailed results are given in Table 3. As can be seen from Table 3, the model achieves the best performance using the test set when the hidden state is 30. Thus, the hidden state in the first-level LSTM is set to be 30. Similarly, the number of neurons is selected as 15 shown in Table 4. Compared with MLP and the network structure of integrated LSTM and stacked autoencoder (LSTM-SAE), the proposed model has better prediction performance, the comparation result of these models can be shown in Table 2, Fig. 4 and Fig. 5.

MLP is a four-layer fully-connected network. The activation functions of all layers are hyperbolic tangent functions while the activation function of output

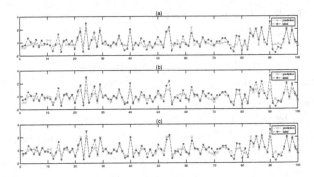

Fig. 4. Comparison results of the first 100 data in the test set. (a) MLP. (b) LSTM-SAE. (c) the Proposed Model.

Table 3. The impact of different hidden state numbers of the first level LSTM on proposed model.

Hidden state	MSE	R^2
10	0.31	0.69
20	0.26	0.74
30	0.24	0.76
40	0.27	0.73

Table 4. The impact of different hidden state numbers of the second level LSTM on proposed model

Hidden state	MSE	R^2
5	0.29	0.71
10	0.28	0.72
15	0.24	0.76
20	0.26	0.75

layer is the linear activation function. The first layer and the input layer inputs are 8 variables with a correlation coefficient greater than 0.5 from all 79 state variables. The dimension of the second layer, the third layer and the output layer is set to 10,5,1 respectively. In the LSTM-SAE, the LSTM cell is set to be 20 hidden variables. Only mold clamping, injection, pressure holding, and cooling in the injection molding process are selected for learning based on prior knowledge. The last hidden layer state of the cell is characterized as the feature extraction result of the current phase, and then merged into the input of the encoder. The output layer of the first layer encoder is 50 and the output layer of the second layer encoder is 5. Finally, the last fully-connected layer obtained predicted quality indicators.

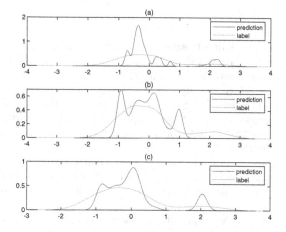

Fig. 5. The distributed learning effect of the model on the test set data. (a) MLP. (b) LSTM-SAE. (c) the Proposed Model.

Table 2 and Fig. 4 show the proposed model has better prediction effect on all data points than other models. It can be seen from the first 20 that our model has a higher quality prediction accuracy than the MLP. And for some quality data that is far from the center of the product size, that is, non-standard size, our model also performs as well as the MLP, while the LSTM-SAE model without the attention mechanism is inferior (data points between 20–30 and 80–100).

Figure 5 shows the proposed model has a better learning effect on the distribution of test set data than other models. This picture is a supplement to the description of the above picture. The data learned by MLP has the same two centers as the real quality data, but the data of normal size cannot obey the approximate distribution, indicating that the understanding of normal size data is weak. However, LSTM-SAE has no part of learning abnormal data at all. Finally, our model can strike a balance between the two.

5 Conclusions

Quality prediction is challenging in batch processes due to the complexity of batch process data. Deep learning has provided flexible models for complex data modeling and prediction. Based on the characteristics of nonlinearity, dynamics, multiphase and uneven length, we take the LSTM as the basic meta-model to build a specific network with three-layer feature extraction, which can discover the most sensitive features for quality prediction. Especially, the attention mechanism and the sensitive phase selection play crucial roles in extracting quality-sensitive features. Through comparative analysis, the result on a real dataset validates the superiority of the proposed method to other state-of-the-art approaches.

References

1. Alvarado-Iniesta, A., Valles-Rosales, D., García-Alcaraz, J., Maldonado-Macias, A.: A recurrent neural network for warpage prediction in injection molding. J. Appl. Res. Technol. **10**(6), 912–919 (2012)

2. Chen, W.C., Tai, P.H., Wang, M.W., Deng, W.J., Chen, C.T.: A neural network-based approach for dynamic quality prediction in a plastic injection molding process. Expert Syst. Appl. **35**(3), 843–849 (2008). https://doi.org/10.1016/j.eswa.2007.07.037. https://www.sciencedirect.com/science/article/pii/S0957417407002977

3. Demarchi, D.L., et al.: Convolutional and recurrent neural networks in time-series applied to injection molding processes. Master's thesis, Federal University of Santa Catarina Centro de Blumenau Department of Control Engineering and Automation and Computing (2019)

4. Goodfellow, I., Bengio, Y., Courville, A.: Deep Learning, vol. 1. MIT Press (2016)

5. Iwko, J., Steller, R., Wróblewski, R.: Experimentally verified mathematical model of polymer plasticization process in injection molding. Polymers **10**(9) (2018). https://doi.org/10.3390/polym10090968. https://www.mdpi.com/2073-4360/10/9/968

6. Jung, H., Jeon, J., Choi, D., Park, J.Y.: Application of machine learning techniques in injection molding quality prediction: implications on sustainable manufacturing industry. Sustainability **13**(8) (2021). https://doi.org/10.3390/su13084120. https://www.mdpi.com/2071-1050/13/8/4120

7. Ke, K.C., Huang, M.S.: Quality prediction for injection molding by using a multilayer perceptron neural network. Polymers **12**(8) (2020). https://doi.org/10.3390/polym12081812. https://www.mdpi.com/2073-4360/12/8/1812

8. Khomenko, M., Veligorskyi, O., Chakirov, R., Vagapov, Y.: An ANN-based temperature controller for a plastic injection moulding system. Electronics **8**(11) (2019). https://doi.org/10.3390/electronics8111272. https://www.mdpi.com/2079-9292/8/11/1272

9. Lindert, S.O., Reindl, G., Schlacher, K.: Identification and control of an injection moulding machine. IFAC Proc. Vol. **47**(3), 5878–5883 (2014). https://doi.org/10.3182/20140824-6-ZA-1003.01488. https://www.sciencedirect.com/science/article/pii/S1474667016425310. 19th IFAC World Congress

10. Lu, C.H., Tsai, C.C., Liu, C.M., Charng, Y.H.: Predictive control based on recurrent neural network and application to plastic injection molding processes. In: IECON 2007–33rd Annual Conference of the IEEE Industrial Electronics Society, pp. 792–797 (2007). https://doi.org/10.1109/IECON.2007.4460121

11. Lu, N., Gao, F.: Stage-based process analysis and quality prediction for batch processes. Ind. Eng. Chem. Res. **44**(10), 3547–3555 (2005). https://doi.org/10.1021/ie0488521

12. Nagorny, P., et al.: Quality prediction in injection molding. In: 2017 IEEE International Conference on Computational Intelligence and Virtual Environments for Measurement Systems and Applications (CIVEMSA), pp. 141–146 (2017). https://doi.org/10.1109/CIVEMSA.2017.7995316

13. Peng, Y., Wei, W., Wang, J.: Model predictive synchronous control of barrel temperature for injection molding machine based on diagonal recurrent neural networks. Mater. Manuf. Processes **28**(1), 24–30 (2012). https://doi.org/10.1080/10426914.2012.718476

14. Shi, H., Li, P., Su, C.: Robust predictive fault-tolerant control for multi-phase batch processes with interval time-varying delay. IEEE Access **7**, 131148–131162 (2019). https://doi.org/10.1109/ACCESS.2019.2940275

15. Wang, K., Gopaluni, R.B., Chen, J., Song, Z.: Deep learning of complex batch process data and its application on quality prediction. IEEE Trans. Industr. Inf. **16**(12), 7233–7242 (2020). https://doi.org/10.1109/TII.2018.2880968

16. Wang, L., Shen, Y., Li, B., Yu, J., Zhang, R., Gao, F.: Hybrid iterative learning fault-tolerant guaranteed cost control design for multi-phase batch processes. Can. J. Chem. Eng. **96**(2), 521–530 (2018)

17. Yao, Y., Dong, W., Zhao, L., Gao, F.: Multivariate statistical monitoring of multiphase batch processes with between-phase transitions and uneven operation durations. Can. J. Chem. Eng. **90**(6), 1383–1392 (2012)

18. Zhao, C.: A quality-relevant sequential phase partition approach for regression modeling and quality prediction analysis in manufacturing processes. IEEE Trans. Autom. Sci. Eng. **11**(4), 983–991 (2014). https://doi.org/10.1109/TASE.2013.2287347

Traffic Knowledge Graph Based Trajectory Destination Prediction

Zhuang Zhuang[1], Lu Wang[1], Zhenliang Hao[3], Heng Qi[1(✉)], Yanming Shen[1], and Baocai Yin[1,2]

[1] Dalian University of Technology, Dalian, China
zhuang97@mail.dlut.edu.cn, wanglu@dce.com.cn,
{hengqi,shen,ybc}@dlut.edu.cn
[2] Peng Cheng Laboratory, Shenzhen, China
[3] Information Technology Center of Tianjin Aviation Electromechanical Co. Ltd, Tianjin, China
13388023072@189.cn

Abstract. The issue of final destination prediction has recently attracted extensive attentions from academia and industry. However, the road segments in the traffic network are affected by the surrounding points of interest(POI) and functional regions, resulting in the low accuracy of destination prediction. Furthermore, the sparsity of the trajectory data also affects the accuracy. Therefore, it is a big challenge to predict the destination more accurately. In order to address this issue, we propose a traffic knowledge graph based destination prediction model. In this model, a three-layer knowledge graph consisting of road network layer, trajectory layer and function layer is constructed to model the spatial correlations of road segments, POI and functional regions. Then, we exploit relative spatial information by the Traffic Graph-bert algorithm which learns the features of nodes in the subgraph and the whole graph through Transformer. Finally, the model applies self-attention mechanism to incorporating the time information and functional region of starting point to improve the prediction accuracy. The extensive data-driven experiments based on the Didi dataset are conducted to prove the effectiveness of the proposed model.

Keywords: Destination prediction · Traffic knowledge graph · Self-attention · Deep learning · Taxi trajectory

1 Introduction

Destination prediction has gradually attracted wide attentions from academia and industry. The destination prediction refers to the prediction of the destination that has not yet arrived based on the generated trajectory and some other auxiliary information during the travel of the vehicle. It is of great significance whether it is promoted in commercial advertising, social public security management or traffic dispatch [1,2]. At present, there are a large number of destination prediction methods in the transportation field and the computer field. Most of the algorithms in

© Springer Nature Singapore Pte Ltd. 2022
X. Liao et al. (Eds.): BigData 2021, CCIS 1496, pp. 194–215, 2022.
https://doi.org/10.1007/978-981-16-9709-8_14

the transportation field are calculated based on the structure of the road network and theory in the transportation field. However, the problem of such approaches is external factors such as weather and time cannot be taken into account, and the excessive dependence on domain knowledge will also make the model not flexible enough. The algorithms in the computer field can learn the influence of different external factors on the prediction results from the past trajectory and the external information. However, data-driven algorithms will face the problem of data sparseness. For those trajectories that have never appeared before, when the data-driven algorithm is used, the efficiency of the algorithm will be greatly reduced [3]. Therefore, this paper proposes a model based on multi-layer knowledge graph to solve the above issues. We realize that based on the data-driven algorithm, the traffic system was modeled in the dataset with sparse trajectory. The model can learn the traffic information contained in a variety of trajectory data, as well as other factors such as time and functional region.

The main contributions of this paper include 3 aspects:

- We propose a destination prediction model based on a multi-layer knowledge graph, which consists of the road network layer, trajectory layer and function layer. To the best of our knowledge, this paper is the first destination prediction model based on the knowledge graph.
- We build a spatial index while using a depth-first search algorithm and road segment classification, thereby improving the speeds of finding neighbouring road segments and trajectories matching in the construction of the traffic knowledge graph.
- The proposed model was validated using the Chengdu taxi trajectory dataset published by Didi. The results show that our model is better than the SOTA modles. We also verified the robustness of the model in dealing with sparse trajectories by changing the data distribution.

2 Related Work

For current destination prediction algorithms, they are usually roughly divided into three categories. The first destination prediction algorithm is based on machine learning. Their use scenarios are usually for specific users. The prediction takes into account the personal preferences of the current vehicle driver when driving, learning the user's preferences and personal habits from the past trajectory and profiling the user, and because of this feature, this destination prediction algorithm usually has a high accuracy rate. BD Ziebart et al. [4] proposed the PROCAB algorithm based on Bayesian statistics. It models the contextual information in the trajectory and the underlying reasons for the different actions taken by the user, and extends the model, merging the contextual information to make it more generalisable. However, due to the characteristics of the Bayesian statistical algorithm, when faced with problems such as trajectory sparsity, it may not be able to accurately predict. As a classic probability prediction model, Markov model usually regards the region in the road network as the state of the Markov chain so as to realize the prediction of the destination.

Among them, as the most classic algorithm for destination prediction based on the Markov model, Xu [5] divides the regions in the map into grids, converts the trajectory sequence into a grid sequence, and uses each grid as a state in a Markov chain to predict the probability of reaching different regions. Xue [6] proposed a new sub-trajectory synthesis method to solve the problem caused by sparse trajectories. By decomposing historical data and then synthesizing them into new sub-trajectories, it effectively expanded the dataset of historical trajectories. This type of destination prediction algorithm based on low-order Markov chain usually has two main problems. The first problem is that the low-order Markov algorithm is unable to capture long-term dependencies in the sequence because it only merges the latest timestamps, future states depend only on the current state and not on past states. The second problem is that because of the sparsity of the trajectory data in the road network, the accuracy of prediction is likely to be affected for trajectories that never appear in the dataset.

Another common type of destination prediction is the deep learning algorithm based on time series. This type of algorithm regards the trajectory sequence as a GPS time sequence, and learns the time sequence information and node attributes in the sequence through the recurrent neural network (RNN) [7–10] and other time series models, and predicts the final destination. As a model for processing time series, RNN can model the time sequence information in the trajectory well. In 2015, Kaggle proposed a destination prediction task challenge. In this competition, the algorithm that finally won the first place used a neural network-based algorithm for destination prediction. Yuki Endo [11] proposed a method of destination prediction based on RNN, by representing the trajectory data as discrete features in grid space, and inputting it into the RNN model to estimate the transition probability of the next time stamp. However, although RNN can model the time series well, it cannot model the information contained in the space. Therefore, Qiang Liu et al. [12] extended the RNN model and proposed a spatio-temporal recurrent neural network method (ST-RNN), ST-RNN can construct time transition matrix and space transition matrix and model the context information of time and trajectory space respectively. Experiments show significant improvement of ST-RNN over RNN in destination prediction tasks.

The third type of destination prediction method is the algorithm based on graph convolutional neural network [13–16]. Compared with time series, this kind of method considers the information in the space more. Usually the trajectory is projected onto the map as a picture, and then the graph convolutional neural network (GCN) is used to learn the features in the graph. Lv et al. [17] proposed a destination prediction algorithm based on graph convolutional neural network. By modeling the trajectory as a two-dimensional image, inputting it into CNN, and extracting multi-scale patterns for accurate destination prediction and extracting correlations between local regions and predicting results through an attention mechanism. In order to solve the problems of noise and sparsity when modeling the trajectory as a two-dimensional image, Zhang et al. [18] uses the fast Fourier transform method to convert the image to the frequency domain to reduce the noise, and then uses CNN to learn the depth features in the noise-reduced trajectory images, and finally uses RNN to learn the dependencies of the data and predict the destination. Converting the trajectory data into a two-dimensional image can learn the spatial information in the trajectory, but since CNN has spatial invariance, the features and information learned by the CNN remain the same after the trajectory is translated in the road network, this idea is obviously not valid in the destination prediction task, for trajectories in different regions but with the same pattern they are likely to reach different destinations.

Therefore, in order to better solve the task of destination prediction, this paper proposes an algorithm that can solve the problem of trajectory sparsity and accurately capture the user's travel intentions while learning the local and global spatial information of road segments in the road network as well as the node and temporal information in the trajectory sequence.

3 Multi-layer Knowledge Graph Construction and Pre-training

Our proposed multi-layer knowledge graph consists of: 1) **the road network layer** that learns the road segments and POI as entities, and the relationships represent about the road segments and POI; 2) **the trajectory layer** are used to represent the upstream and downstream relationships between road segment nodes; 3) **the functional layer** that uses trajectory data as the medium to divide the entire map, with each region representing a functional region in the real world.

3.1 Road Network Layer Construction

The road network layer, as the first layer of the multi-layer knowledge graph, represents the association between road segment entities and POI entities and carries the basic attributes of the entities, such as road width, shopping region of interest, and so on. The road network layer constitutes the most basic road network structure. The main task in constructing the network layer is to capture the relationship between road segment and road segment, road segment and POI in order to accurately propagate the node characteristics. For the obtained data, the road segment data is expressed in the form of a GPS sequence, which is expressed as follows:

$$\zeta_i = (\delta_{i1}, \delta_{i2}, \cdots, \delta_{im}) \tag{1}$$

where ζ_i represents the i-th road segment, and δ_{im} represents the GPS coordinates of the m-th point in the i-th road segment. Similarly, a road segment is represented as a road segment entity E_i^R in the knowledge graph. For two road segment entities, if there is an adjacent or intersecting relationship between them, then there must be two GPS points in their trajectory sequence that are close to each other, they can be regarded as two overlapping points if certain errors are ignored. Therefore, we calculate the distance between two GPS coordinates in two road segment, and determines whether the distance is less than the distance threshold of the adjacent road segment, when the distance is less than the threshold, then the two road segment are judged to have an adjacent relationship. The formula is as follows:

$$R_1 = \{<E_i^R, E_j^R>, <E_i^R, E_u^P>|d(\delta_{im}, \delta_{jn}) \leq \gamma, d(\delta_{im}, \delta_u) \leq \gamma\} \qquad (2)$$

where R_1 represents the set of edges in the road network layer, E_i^R and E_j^R represents the i-th and the j-th entity in the knowledge graph respectively, and the entity type is road segment, E_u^P represents the u-th entity in the knowledge graph, and the entity type is the point of interest. $<E_i^R, E_j^P>$ represents the edge formed by the i-th link entity and the j-th link entity in the knowledge graph, and $<E_i^R, E_u^P>$ represents the edge formed by the i-th link entity and the u-th point of interest entity in the knowledge graph. d is the formula for calculating the Euclidean distance, and γ is the distance threshold. Points in the map that are smaller than the threshold can be considered as approximately overlapping. The formula for calculating the Euclidean distance is as follows:

$$d(X, Y) = \sqrt{\sum_{i=1}^{n} (x_i - y_j)^2} \qquad (3)$$

where X and Y are equivalent to δ mentioned above, which represent GPS coordinate points. When calculating the distance between GPS points, n = 2. In GPS coordinates, $\delta = (\Phi_1, \Phi_2)$, Φ_1 represents longitude and Φ_2 represents latitude, corresponding to x_1 and x_2 in the formula respectively.

In order to reduce the time complexity of the calculation, the algorithm is optimised to improve the efficiency of the calculation. For a road segment, the road segment with its adjacency is usually in the same or adjacent region as the road segment. Therefore, we use this idea to optimise the neighbouring segment search algorithm. To simplify the calculation, the map is first partitioned uniformly in the form of a drawn grid in order to partition the map. The steps of the optimised neighbouring segment search algorithm are, firstly, to calculate the region to which the segment belongs for all segments, there may be cases where a long segment crosses multiple regions at the same time. Secondly, we choose a depth-first search-based method to traverse each region of the map to search for adjacent road segments, starting from the region to which the road segment belongs, iteratively traverse the adjacent regions above, below, left and right of the region, while traversing the traversed region with marker bits, and calculate whether there is a target section in the region that is adjacent to the segment. If the target segment is adjacent to the segment, the segment is also added to the set of adjacent segments of the target segment; if the target segment is not adjacent to the segment, the target segment is added to the set that has been calculated but does not have an adjacent relationship; when the region is traversed and also contains the target segment, the target segment is not repeatedly calculated. If there are no adjacent segments in the current region, the search in that direction is stopped. When the search in all directions is completed, it is necessary to check whether the region to which the road segment belongs has been searched, and if there is still a remaining region that has not been searched, then it is traversed from the remaining region to its surrounding region by the same method, and when all the regions in which the road segment is located and its surrounding region have been traversed, then the search for the road segment adjacent to the road segment is completed. By drawing a grid on the map and using the depth-first search algorithm, the speed of searching for adjacent segments can be greatly improved.

3.2   Trajectory Layer Construction

As a representation of the basic structure of the road network, the road network layer only contains static information. In a real traffic network, the choice of road segment by drivers may affect the degree of association between road segment. And, the trajectory data not only contains the structural information of the road network, but also contains some customary preferences in the society. Through the road network layer, the multi-layer knowledge graph can capture the association of road segments in geographic space, but cannot capture the association between different road segment in the same trajectory during the driving process of the road segment. We matches the trajectory data with the road segment entities in the multi-layer knowledge graph, and the GPS in the trajectory data. The sequence is converted into the road segment entity sequence in the knowledge graph, and the trajectory is corresponding to the road segments. The formula for trajectory matching is as follows:

$$\zeta' = \{E_1^R, E_2^R, \cdots, E_k^R | (\delta_1, \delta_2, \cdots, \delta_{n_1}) \in E_1^R, \cdots, (\delta_{n_{k-1}+1}, \delta_{n_{k-1}+2}, \cdots, \delta_{n_k}) \in E_k^R\} \quad (4)$$

where ζ' represents the trajectory data after the matching, which E_k^R is composed of a sequence of road segment entities, and δ_{n_k} represents the GPS coordinate points in the trajectory sequence before the matching.

It can be seen from the formula that the matching of the trajectory and the road segment is mainly to determine the road segment to which a GPS coordinate point belongs, so as to convert the GPS coordinate point to the road segment entity where it is located. The time complexity of this algorithm is $O(mnk)$, where m represents the number of road segment entities in the road network layer, n represents the number of GPS coordinate points contained in the trajectory, and k represents the number of GPS coordinate points contained in the road segment. It can be seen from the algorithm that since the road segment and trajectories contain a large number of GPS coordinate points, calculating the distance between the GPS coordinate points in pairs will cause this algorithm to have a higher time complexity. Therefore, we improve the algorithm by introducing adjacent road segment in the road network layer and setting the priority of road segment entities to improve the execution speed of the algorithm. The algorithm is based on the following steps: First, a variable is used to store the road segment entity to which the previous coordinate point in the trajectory belongs, and the value of this variable is null at the starting point. Secondly, the road segment entities in the road network layer are divided into three priority levels, the first of which is the road segment entity of the previous coordinate point saved in the variable. This is because, for two adjacent coordinate points in the trajectory, in most cases these two coordinate points belong to the same road segment, so we save the road segment entity belonging to the previous coordinate point and compares with it first, if it hits then it does not need to compare with the remaining road segment entities. If it does not hit, then the point may fall within its downstream segment, so this paper uses the neighbouring segment as the second priority segment entity. When the first priority level is not achieved, the adjacent road segments are compared with those in the set of adjacent road segments in the variable that holds the road segment entities. If the second priority fails, the remaining road entities are compared to the remaining road entities, which are more numerous as the third priority, so if the first and second levels are not hit, it may take more time to calculate the third level, but in most cases, the road matching can be hit in the first and second levels, so it can save most of the matching time.

After matching, the GPS coordinate sequence of the trajectory is converted into a sequence of roadway nodes, and the roadway entities in the trajectory sequence are sorted in chronological order. Then, a directional relationship is established between the corresponding road segment nodes, and the direction of the relationship is from the upstream road segment to the downstream road segment, indicating the accessibility of the two road segments in that direction. As the same road segment will appear in different trajectories several times, in order to reflect the frequency of choosing different downstream road segments, this paper calculates the weights of different edges in the trajectory layer based on the trajectory data. The specific calculation method is, for any road segment entity in the trajectory data, it is considered as the upstream road segment in the relationship, the downstream road segment of the road segment in the statistics set and the corresponding number of times the downstream road segment and the road segment appear together in the dataset. Based on the number of occurrences of the downstream segment and the current segment together and the total number of occurrences of the upstream segment in the trajectory data, the number of occurrences of the downstream segment and the current segment together can be normalised to obtain the weight of the relationship between the current segment and the downstream segment, which represents the probability of traffic flowing from the current segment to the downstream segment. The following equation is constructed:

$$R_2 = \{<E_i^R, E_j^R>|(E_i^R, E_j^R \in \zeta') \cup (E_j^R \in N_{E_i^R})\} \tag{5}$$

$$P_{<E_i^R, E_j^R>} = \frac{t_{<E_i^R, E_j^R>}}{\sum\limits_{k \in N_{E_i^R}} t_{<E_i^R, E_k^R>}} \tag{6}$$

where R_2 represents the set of edges in the trajectory layer, E_i^R, E_j^R represents the road segment entity in the knowledge graph, ζ' represents the converted GPS sequence, $N_{E_i^R}$ represents the adjacent downstream road segment entities of all the road segment entities E_i^R in the trajectory ζ', and the edges in the trajectory layer have directions from the first link entity to the second link entity. Formula 6 is the calculation formula for the weight of the edge in the trajectory layer, which $P_{<E_i^R,E_j^R>}$ represents the weight of the edge pointed by E_i^R, expressed in the form of probability. $t_{<E_i^R,E_j^R>}$ represents the number of occurrences of downstream forms above E_i^R, E_j^R in the trajectory dataset, and $\sum_{k\in N_{E_i^R}} t_{<E_i^R,E_k^R>}$ represents the number of occurrences of the upstream road segment entity E_i^R in the trajectory data. Formula 6 can calculate the probability of each link entity going to each downstream link entity, and because of normalization, for each link entity, the weights of all edges starting from it add up to 1.

3.3   Functional Layer Construction

For the functional layer, it is necessary to cluster the start point and end point projected into the road network to obtain the functional region in the road network. We choose to use the Mean-Shift algorithm that is not easily affected by the uneven distribution of data density, to cluster the data in the clustering process of the start and end points of the trajectory.

The specific steps of the Mean-Shift algorithm are as follows. First, randomly select a point in the space and specify the radius of the region to divide a circular region in the space. The size of the circular region can determine the number of clusters, and the larger the radius, the fewer classification results will eventually be obtained. After obtaining the circular region, calculate the Mean-Shift vector of the center of the circle based on all the points contained in the circular region. The calculated vector indicates the direction and distance of the movement of the center of the circle. The center of the circular region will move towards the densest data. The calculation formula of the Mean-Shift vector is as follows:

$$M_h(x) = \frac{1}{\ell} * \sum_{X^i \in S_h} (X^i - X) \tag{7}$$

where h is the radius of the circular region, ℓ is the number of sample points falling into the region, and $X^i - X$ is the vector formed by a sample point in the circular region and the center of the circle. The meaning of this formula is that adding all the vectors formed by all points as well as the center of the region and taking the average is the direction in which the center of the circle moves. After clustering the points in the graph by Mean-Shift, the output of the algorithm is the category to which each point in the graph belongs, and the boundaries of each region after clustering are irregular. In order to identify the functional regions of the first two layers of the knowledge graph, this paper adds POI entity and the end point of the road segment entity to the data participating in the clustering. The final clustering result of the entity is used as the label of the functional region to which the entity belongs.

3.4   Representation Learning of Traffic Knowledge Graph

For the multi-layer traffic knowledge graph constructed in this paper, the purpose of pre-training is to obtain the representation of the road segments in the knowledge graph to reflect the location of the road segments in the road network, the attributes of the road segment entity itself, and the road segment functions played in trajectory data and upstream and downstream information of road segments. This paper decides to embed the knowledge graph by using the embedding algorithm based on Graph-Bert [19]. However, because the Graph-Bert algorithm is only suitable for single-layer graph networks, this paper improves Graph-Bert and proposes the Traffic Graph-Bert algorithm to adapt to the multi-layer traffic knowledge graph constructed in this paper. In order to sample the knowledge graph to obtain unbounded subgraphs, the first two layers in the knowledge graph are calculated based on the PageRank algorithm [20] to calculate the degree of correlation between nodes. The first layer is an undirected graph, using the adjacency matrix to represent the structure of the graph. The second layer is a directed probability graph. Unlike the adjacency matrix of the first layer, the graph in the second layer is represented by a weight matrix, where the i-th row and j-th column of the matrix represent the probability of travelling from the i-th road entity to the j-th road entity. The main idea behind PageRank is to spread the weight carried by the node itself to other nodes in the graph through random walk, which is similar to the feature propagation of road segments in a traffic network. The formula for calculating the final convergence value after random walk is as follows:

$$S_i = \alpha(I - (1 - \alpha)M)^{-1} \tag{8}$$

where S_i represents the node relevance of each layer of the graph, i = 1 or 2, represents the number of graph layers; $\alpha \in [0, 1]$ represents the probability of the node randomly jumping during a random walk; I is the unit diagonal matrix. In the first layer of the knowledge graph undirected graph, the directed graph $M = AD^{-1}$ is the normalization of the column vector of the graph's adjacency matrix A. And, D is the degree matrix of the graph's adjacency matrix; in the second-level knowledge graph directed probability graph, M is the input probability graph.

For the first two layers of the multi-layer knowledge graph, the first layer contains entities for road segments and POI, while the second layer contains only some road segment entities because it is a graph constructed from trajectory data. For the road segment entities, those that appear in the first layer but not in the second layer indicate that these road segments are hardly selected by drivers in actual traffic movements, and therefore these unselected road segments have a low degree of correlation with other road segments. In addition, for the POI entities, although they only exist in the first layer of the knowledge graph, the POI entities usually have a greater influence on the road segment entities. Therefore, in order to balance the association of road segment entities with other entities and the association with points of interest between the two layers, this paper decides to calculate the final convergence value by multiplying the association degree of the two layers by a certain weight to obtain the final association degree for road segment entities, and select the remaining k road segment entities with the highest association degree for the current road segment entities. At the same time, in order to consider the influence of the POI entities on the road section, this paper also selects the p POI entities with the highest association degree with the current road section entity. The k road entities and the p POI entities are stitched together to form an unbounded subgraph with the current road entity as the core. In this paper, the association degree of the two layers of road entities is calculated as follows:

$$S = \beta S_1 + (1 - \beta)S_2 \tag{9}$$

where S is the finally obtained correlation matrix between nodes, S_1 is the correlation matrix between road segment calculated based on the knowledge graph road network layer, S_2 is the correlation degree matrix between road segment calculated based on the knowledge graph trajectory layer, and β represents the weight of the node association degree in the road network layer. For each entity in the road network layer, a corresponding unbounded subgraph can be obtained, but the nodes in the subgraph are not in order at this time. Therefore, they are sorted by obtaining the final degree of relevance score, and the nodes with a greater degree of relevance are placed first.

Through the above method, the knowledge graph can be sampled to obtain an unbounded subgraph centered on each road segment entity, and the unbounded subgraph is embodied in the form of serialization of nodes. After obtaining multiple subgraphs, before inputting the subgraphs into $Transformer$ to learn sequence information, it is necessary to learn the embedding information carried by each node itself. In the $Traffic\ Graph - Bert$ algorithm, the node embedding considers the information carried by each node itself, the global information of the node and the local information in the unbounded subgraph, and in order to balance the global and local features of the node, the node is in the global graph. The distance is embedded as follows:

$$Embed^{formal}(E_j) = f(x_j) \tag{10}$$

For global information, the $Traffic\ Graph - Bert$ algorithm is based on the Weisfeiler-Lehman algorithm [21] to calculate the absolute position of the node in the entire graph structure. The Weisfeiler-Lehman algorithm is usually used to determine whether two graphs are isomorphic. Its core idea is to iteratively aggregate the information of neighbor nodes and update the feature vector of the central node until convergence. For irregular graph structures, most of the nodes in the graph have unique structures. Therefore, the unique representation of the central node in the whole world can be calculated by this algorithm. Since the nodes in the unbounded subgraph are sorted according to the degree of association with the central node, in order to embed the order information of the nodes in the subgraph into the feature vector space, after obtaining the global representation vector of each node in the subgraph, the position information of each node in the subgraph is captured by the position embedding based on the sine and cosine function, and the formula is expressed as:

$$Embed^{global}(E_j) = Position(WeisfeilerLehman(x_j)) \tag{11}$$

$$Position(x) = [\sin(\frac{x}{10000^{\frac{2l}{d_h}}}), \cos(\frac{x}{10000^{\frac{2l+1}{d_h}}})]_{l=0}^{\lfloor \frac{d_h}{2} \rfloor} \tag{12}$$

where d_h represents the dimensionality of the node embedded in the low-dimensional vector space.

For the local position information of the node in the edgeless subgraph, use a position scoring function P to score each node in the subgraph. For the first node in the edgeless subgraph, it is the center node. For the other nodes in the edgeless subgraph. The higher the degree of relevance is, the lower the score of the node is. Since the scoring function only scores based on the local information of the node, for the same node, it may exist in different unbounded subgraphs, and different unbounded subgraphs have different scores according to their different positions. Similarly, after obtaining the scores of all nodes in the subgraph, the position embedding algorithm is used to embed the position information into the representation vector. The formula is expressed as:

$$Embed^{local}(E_j) = Position(P(x_j)) \tag{13}$$

In order to associate the local information of the node with the global information and balance the two parts of information, *Traffic Graph – Bert* calculates the distance embedding of each node in the subgraph. The distance is to calculate the distance between other nodes in the subgraph and the center node in the unbounded subgraph in the whole graph, and use the position embedding algorithm to embed the position information into the final representation vector. Expressed by the formula as:

$$Embed^{distance}(E_j) = Position(H(x_j, x_i)) \tag{14}$$

Through the above four parts, for each node in the edgeless subgraph, four related representation vectors can be obtained, and the final representation vector of each node in the subgraph can be obtained by adding the four representation vectors. For each unbounded subgraph, the representation vectors of each node can be arranged to form a matrix. In order to encode the information contained in the unbounded subgraph sequence, *Traffic Graph – Bert* inputs the unbounded subgraph matrix into the N-layer *Transformer encoder*, encodes it, and updates the representation vector of the node. Expressed by the formula as:

$$H^{(n)} = softmax(\frac{QK^T}{\sqrt{d_h}})V + G - Res(H^{(n-1)}, X_i) \tag{15}$$

where $H^{(n)}$ is the representation vector when the node in the graph is in the n-th layer of the *Transformer*, and Q, K, and V are respectively obtained by multiplying $H^{(n-1)}$ and three different weight matrices (Fig. 1).

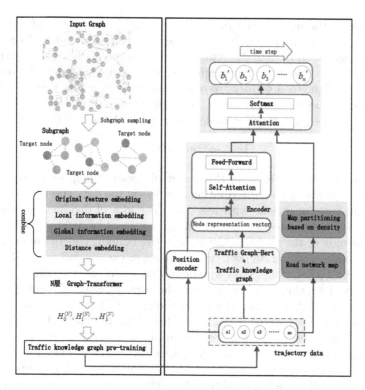

Fig. 1. Model architecture.

4 Destination Prediction Model Based on Self-attention Mechanism

4.1 Problem Definition

Destination prediction refers to the prediction of the GPS coordinates of the destination that the vehicle may eventually reach based on the historical trajectory data. The formula can be expressed as: Given part of the trajectory $\zeta = \{\delta_0, \delta_1, \cdots, \delta_k\}$, and predict the final destination $des = \{\delta\}$. Where δ_i represents the GPS coordinates of the i-th point in the trajectory sequence.

For the destination prediction module, its main task is to learn the information contained in the nodes in the trajectory sequence and the time sequence information carried to obtain the representation vector of the current vector, and realize the prediction of the final destination GPS coordinates of the current trajectory by classifying the trajectory vector.

4.2 Destination Prediction Module

Through the position embedding and self-attention mechanism, the node vector in the trajectory is the updated node vector, which contains the spatial information of the node in the road network and the temporal information in the trajectory. In order to finally obtain the representation vector of the trajectory, this paper will obtain the representation vector of the road segments in the trajectory and multiply the weight vector, so as to aggregate the representation vector of the road segment to obtain the final trajectory vector. After the aggregation of the trajectory vector, through the *softmax* layer to obtain the probability of the trajectory reaching each region. The formula is as follows:

$$Y = softmax(W^T X) \tag{16}$$

For each region in the map, this paper divides the map based on density. This is to avoid the uneven distribution of labels in the data and the inability to learn the features of regions with less data. The idea of dividing the map data is to divide the map into two parts with equal amount of data according to the median latitude of the nodes in the map as the boundary of the map division, and then continue to iterate over the two parts of the divided space, if the last division of latitude is done, then when iterating again, the median longitude of the nodes in the region is calculated and the current region is divided again. If latitude was divided last time, the median longitude of the nodes in the region is calculated and the current region is divided again. Similarly, if the graph was divided by longitude in the previous iteration, it is divided by the median of the latitudes in the next iteration. This paper also uses a combination of binary search trees and small top stacks to divide the road network region evenly. This is achieved by building a binomial tree in which the median longitude or latitude of the region is stored at each node of the tree. At the same time, in order to obtain the median of each division quickly, and because of the large amount of data, this paper chooses to use the construction of a big top heap and a small top heap to obtain the median, the object stored in the heap is the GPS coordinate point type.

After dividing the map, multiply the probability of trajectory reaching each region with the GPS coordinates of the center of each divided region. Since the probability obtained in this paper has been normalized, it is multiplied by the coordinates After that, the final predicted coordinates can be obtained. The formula is as follows:

$$\delta'_{t\,arg\,et} = \sum_{\alpha_i \in Y} \alpha_i \delta_i \tag{17}$$

Among them, δ_i is the GPS coordinates of the center of the i-th region, which α_i represents the predicted probability of reaching the i-th region.

5   Experiments and Results

In this segment, we use the destination prediction model proposed in this paper based on the multi-layer knowledge graph and self-attention mechanism, and conduct experiments on the Chengdu taxi trajectory dataset disclosed by Didi Company to verify the effectiveness of our method (Fig. 2).

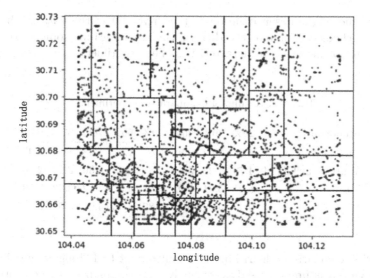

Fig. 2. Divide the map based on destination density.

5.1 Dataset

In order to verify the prediction effect of the model, this paper chooses to conduct experiments in the Chengdu taxi trajectory dataset disclosed by Didi Company. In the algorithm of destination prediction in the past, experiments are usually carried out on the public Bordeaux taxi trajectory dataset. But in the experiment of this paper, due to the need to construct the corresponding traffic knowledge graph according to the corresponding road network structure. In order to obtain the road segment data of the corresponding region of the trajectory data, this paper chooses to obtain the information of road segments and points of interest through the crawler from the open interface of GaoDe Maps, and for the dataset published by Gaode Map and Didi, because both use the same GPS coordinate system, so the data can be matched without converting the GPS coordinate system in the dataset.

Didi public trajectory Chengdu taxi trajectory data covers part of the Chengdu Second Ring Road, and its range is [30.727818, 104.043333], [30.726490, 104.129076], [30.655191, 104.129591], [30.652828, 104.042102]. The sample set contains 50G data. In this paper, 120,000 pieces of data are randomly selected to train the model. Taking into account the scale of the dataset in this paper, this paper divides the data set into 80%, 10%, and 10% as the training set, test set and validation set respectively.

5.2 Experiments and Results

In order to prove the effectiveness of the model proposed in this paper, this paper chooses to compare with several common algorithms in the field of destination prediction. The dataset used is also the taxi trajectory data disclosed by Didi.

However, due to the desensitization of the driver ID in the data set by Didi, this paper chooses to ignore the driver's characteristics for some of the algorithms that use the driver's characteristics. The experimental results are shown in Table 1.

Table 1. Results of Comparative experiments.

Proportion	20%	30%	40%	50%	60%	70%	80%	90%
Our method	4.34	3.62	2.94	2.37	1.87	1.65	1.54	1.47
Multi input LSTM	4.73	4.22	3.42	2.81	2.43	2.36	2.21	2.18
MLP	6.01	5.61	5.07	4.63	4.31	3.82	3.43	2.73
Markov	6.43	5.89	5.35	4.82	4.45	4.02	3.65	3.25

The first comparison algorithm is the multi-input LSTM algorithm [22]. The trajectory data is preprocessed accordingly, and the map is divided into multiple regions according to the density, and each region is embedded with its spatial information. The GPS coordinates in the trajectory sequence are converted into the divided space sequence, and the information contained in the trajectory sequence is learned through LSTM, and finally the GPS coordinate points reached are predicted.

The second comparison algorithm is the classic MLP algorithm. This algorithm [23] only considers the first k points and the last k points of the trajectory to avoid the influence of the variable length of the trajectory. Some meta-information such as date and time is input into the fully connected neural network for training, and the destination is clustered into multiple clusters to predict the probability of the final trajectory reaching each cluster.

The third comparison algorithm is a Markov-based destination prediction algorithm. This type of algorithm [24] also divides the region in the map into grids, converts the trajectory sequence into a grid sequence, and treats each grid as the state in the Markov chain, when predicting the next state, refer to each transition of the current state in the dataset to predict the probability of reaching a different region.

It can be seen from the experimental results that the algorithm proposed in this paper has achieved the best results in the Didi dataset, and the results of the multi-input LSTM algorithm are the closest to the model proposed in this paper. This is also because the two models are both based on the neural network prediction model, by dividing the road network map, the coordinate point sequence of the trajectory is converted into the divided region sequence. Due to the Markov-based destination prediction algorithm's characteristics, the information before the current position cannot be considered when predicting, and the problem of trajectory sparsity cannot be solved because it is obtained the worst result in all methods. While the MLP algorithm cannot learn the position information of the nodes in the trajectory in the space during learning, so it also achieves poor results (Fig. 3).

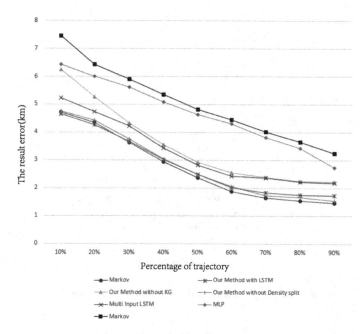

Fig. 3. Experimental result curve.

About the functional regions, this paper projects the starting point and the ending point in the trajectory data into the road network map. The projected result is shown in Fig. 4. The nodes after the projection are clustered into multiple regions using a clustering algorithm. This paper clusters the start point and the end point based on the Mean-Shift algorithm, and the final clustering result is shown in Fig. 5.

5.3 Data Processing Optimization Comparison Experiment

In this section, this paper will mainly analyze the computational performance of the algorithm after the optimization of the algorithm when constructing the multi-layer knowledge graph road network layer and trajectory layer.

First of all, the core idea of the algorithm for calculating the neighbouring segments of a node in the construction of a road network layer is to calculate the distance between two GPS coordinates in two trajectories. Therefore, the computational performance depends on both the size of the set of candidate trajectories and the number of GPS coordinates in the trajectories. The main idea of the proposed optimisation method is to reduce the size of the set of ticked trajectories, so in order to reduce the impact of the number of GPS coordinates on

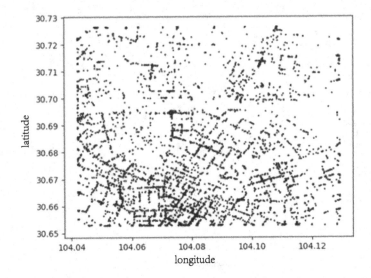

Fig. 4. Projection of start and end of trajectory.

the computational performance, the matching of trajectory segments is carried out in the dataset using the before and after optimisation algorithm, and the computational time spent is shown in Table 2. As can be seen from the table, the indexing of trajectories by grid division and the depth-first search of the divided grid can improve the matching rate very effectively. Secondly, for the construction of the trajectory layer, the GPS coordinate sequence of the trajectory is converted into a sequence of roadway entities, we select 1000 and 2000 data randomly from the trajectory data for the node matching experiment. The results are shown in Table 3. It can be seen from the experimental results that the matching algorithm before optimization consumes a lot of time for repeated matching work, while the efficiency of the optimized algorithm has been significantly improved, because the optimized algorithm uses the first obtained in the previous work. Therefore, there is no need for additional matching.

Table 2. Road network layer time overhead

Algorithm	Cost time
Before optimization	17 h 47 min
After optimization	3 h 24 min

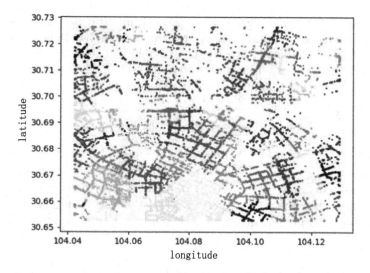

Fig. 5. Clustering result of trajectory starting point and ending point.

Table 3. Trajectory layer time overhead

Algorithm	1000	2000
Before optimization	22 h 18 min	47 h 32 min
After optimization	2 h 48 min	4 h 12 min

5.4 Ablation Experiment

In order to prove the effectiveness of each module in this model, this paper conducts ablation experiments by replacing or canceling each module in the model, and compares it with the complete model. In addition, since the main purpose of destination prediction is to predict the final destination through known partial trajectories, for different proportions of known trajectories, the final prediction of the model will have different accuracy. Therefore, this paper also tested the prediction accuracy of each model for the final destination under the condition of known trajectories in different proportions.

In the ablation experiment, in order to test the effectiveness of the self-attention mechanism module, we replace the self-attention mechanism module responsible for learning trajectory sequence information with LSTM; in order to test the effectiveness of the multi-layer knowledge graph, this paper removes the traffic knowledge graph, and uses grids to divide the road network uniformly, establish the association between the grids with adjacency, and obtain the representation vector of each grid through the random walk algorithm. The difference from the original method is that in the follow-up purpose In the ground prediction task, the trajectory sequence is converted into a divided grid sequence to learn the representation vector of the final trajectory; in order to test the effectiveness of the density-based road network map division algorithm, this paper only performs the map when the road network is partitioned at the end. Divide uniformly, and finally predict the probability of reaching each grid. The results of the ablation experiment are shown in Table 4. The unit of the error of the experiment results is kilometers.

Table 4. Results of Comparative experiments.

Proportion	10%	20%	30%	40%	50%	60%	70%	80%	90%
Our method	4.72	4.34	3.62	2.94	2.37	1.87	1.65	1.54	1.47
Our method with LSTM	4.66	4.27	3.66	3.01	2.49	2.02	1.82	1.75	1.72
Our method without KG	6.24	5.27	4.32	3.54	2.92	2.54	2.39	2.24	2.21
Our method without density split	4.76	4.42	3.76	3.03	2.49	2.06	1.73	1.66	1.54

From the experimental results, it can be seen that the proposed method achieves the best results in the range of 30% to 90% of the trajectories, reflecting the effectiveness of each module but in the range of 10%–20%, the model replacing the self-attention mechanism with the LSTM achieves the best results. For the multi-layer knowledge graph, it has contributed to the improvement of prediction accuracy. This is probably due to the fact that with the introduction of the knowledge graph, the nodes can perceive information about the surrounding regions and most importantly, the functional layer in the knowledge graph can provide information about the functional region where the trajectory starts. Although the advantage of using multi-layer knowledge graph is obvious when the trajectory information is small, when the proportion of trajectories increases, the final accuracy of the model using knowledge graph does not improve much compared with the beginning, which may be because the road sections used in the knowledge graph constructed in this paper are obtained from crawlers, and the road network is irregularly divided. For the density-based graph division method, the experimental results also show that this module can effectively improve the accuracy of destination prediction by reducing the sparsity of trajectories. Among the three modules, the multi-layer knowledge graph module has the highest contribution compared to the other two modules, while the density-based segmentation module has the lowest contribution compared to the other two modules. This also indicates that the information about the region of the origin and the role of the road segment entities in the network is more important for the destination prediction task than the uneven distribution of destination labels in this paper.

5.5   Model Robustness Experiment

In order to prove the robustness of the model in dealing with trajectory sparsity, this paper conducts experiments on several methods in the comparative experiment. The method of the experiment is to observe the change of the model's prediction accuracy after removing part of the trajectory data in the data set. If the data to be removed is selected randomly, the distribution of the data will not be changed. Therefore, this paper first divides the map evenly, and removes the data from only one region each time the data is removed. In this way, the distribution of trajectory data itself in the road network can be destroyed, thereby exacerbating the problem of trajectory sparsity. The experimental results are shown in Fig. 6.

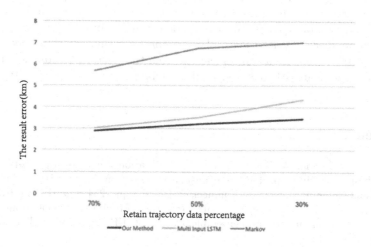

Fig. 6. Model robustness experiment results.

The abscissa in Fig. 6 is the percentage of the retained trajectory data in the total number of data sets, and the ordinate is the prediction error. It can be seen from the experimental results that for all methods, as more and more data are removed, the accuracy of the model prediction is decreasing. For the multi-input LSTM algorithm and the model proposed in this paper, these two models are more robust than the Markov-based prediction model when the trajectory sparsity increases. This may be because the Markov-based forecasting model relies too much on past data when forecasting and cannot deal with the problem of data sparseness. When 70% of the data is retained, it can be seen that the prediction accuracy of the model in this paper and the multi-input LSTM model are still relatively similar, but with the increase of removed data, the decline in the prediction accuracy of the model proposed in this paper is relatively stable. The forecast accuracy of the multi-input LSTM algorithm is decreasing. It shows that when a small part of the data is removed, these two models have good robustness. However, when too much data is removed, because the road entity is pre-trained before learning the trajectory sequence in this paper, The information of the road segment and its surrounding region is pre-embedded, so when the amount of trajectory data decreases, this information can be used as an additional supplement to avoid the impact of trajectory sparsity.

6   Conclusion

In this work, a new multi-layer traffic knowledge graph model is proposed for the first time to predict trajectory destinations. The multi-layer traffic knowledge graph which learn the explicit spatio correlations within the trajectory using Traffic Graph-Bert algorithm, is composed of road network layer, trajectory layer and functional layer. In order to pre-train the constructed multi-layer traffic knowledge graph, we propose the Traffic Graph-Bert algorithm based on the characteristics of the multi-layer knowledge graph, and calculates the nodes in each layer separately based on the random walk algorithm. We also use the self-attention mechanism to learn the temporal information contained in the trajectory sequence, which can be learned from the trajectory sequence. Experimental comparison with baseline models demonstrates the superiority of our model.

References

1. Xue, A.Y., Zhang, R., Zheng, Y., et al.: Destination prediction by sub-trajectory synthesis and privacy protection against such prediction. In: 2013 IEEE 29th International Conference on Data Engineering (ICDE), pp. 254–265. IEEE (2013)
2. Zhang, X., Zhao, Z., Zheng, Y., et al.: Prediction of taxi destinations using a novel data embedding method and ensemble learning. IEEE Trans. Intell. Transp. Syst. **21**(1), 68–78 (2019)
3. Wang, L., Wang, M., Ku, T., et al.: A hybrid model towards moving route prediction under data sparsity. In: 2017 20th International Conference on Information Fusion (Fusion), pp. 1–8. IEEE (2017)
4. Endo, Y., Nishida, K., Toda, H., Sawada, H.: Predicting destinations from partial trajectories using recurrent neural network. In: Kim, J., Shim, K., Cao, L., Lee, J.-G., Lin, X., Moon, Y.-S. (eds.) PAKDD 2017. LNCS (LNAI), vol. 10234, pp. 160–172. Springer, Cham (2017). https://doi.org/10.1007/978-3-319-57454-7_13
5. Xu, M., Wang, D., Li, J.: DESTPRE: a data-driven approach to destination prediction for taxi rides. In: Proceedings of the ACM International Joint Conference on Pervasive and Ubiquitous Computing, vol. 2016, pp. 729–739 (2016)
6. Xue, A.Y., Qi, J., Xie, X., et al.: Solving the data sparsity problem in destination prediction. VLDB J. **24**(2), 219–243 (2015)
7. Yang, D., Fankhauser, B., Rosso, P., et al.: Location prediction over sparse user mobility traces using RNNs: flashback in hidden states! In: Proceedings of the Twenty-Ninth International Joint Conference on Artificial Intelligence, pp. 2184–2190 (2020)
8. Zhao, K., Zhang, Y., Yin, H., et al.: Discovering subsequence patterns for next POI recommendation. In: IJCAI, pp. 3216–3222 (2020)
9. Wang, Q., Yin, H., Chen, T., et al.: Next point-of-interest recommendation on resource-constrained mobile devices. In: Proceedings of the Web Conference 2020, pp. 906–916 (2020)
10. Sun, K., Qian, T., Chen, T., et al.: Where to go next: modeling long-and short-term user preferences for point-of-interest recommendation. In: Proceedings of the AAAI Conference on Artificial Intelligence, vol. 34, no. 01, pp. 214–221 (2020)

11. Liu, Q., Wu, S., Wang, L., et al.: Predicting the next location: a recurrent model with spatial and temporal contexts. In: Thirtieth AAAI Conference on Artificial Intelligence (2016)
12. Rossi, A., Barlacchi, G., Bianchini, M., et al.: Modelling taxi drivers' behaviour for the next destination prediction. IEEE Trans. Intell. Transp. Syst. **21**(7), 2980–2989 (2019)
13. Xie, M., Yin, H., Wang, H., et al.: Learning graph-based poi embedding for location-based recommendation. In: Proceedings of the 25th ACM International on Conference on Information and Knowledge Management, pp. 15–24 (2016)
14. Christoforidis, G., Kefalas, P., Papadopoulos, A., et al.: Recommendation of points-of-interest using graph embeddings. In: 2018 IEEE 5th International Conference on Data Science and Advanced Analytics (DSAA), pp. 31–40. IEEE (2018)
15. Zhang, L., Sun, Z., Zhang, J., et al.: Modeling hierarchical category transition for next POI recommendation with uncertain check-ins. Inf. Sci. **515**, 169–190 (2020)
16. Liu, B., Qian, T., Liu, B., et al.: Learning spatiotemporal-aware representation for POI recommendation. arXiv preprint arXiv:1704.08853 (2017)
17. Zhang, L., Zhang, G., Liang, Z., et al.: Multi-features taxi destination prediction with frequency domain processing. PLoS ONE **13**(3), e0194629 (2018)
18. Tang, J., Zhang, J., Yao, L., et al.: ArnetMiner: extraction and mining of academic social networks. In: Proceedings of the 14th ACM SIGKDD International Conference on Knowledge Discovery and Data Mining, pp. 990–998 (2008)
19. Zhang, J., Zhang, H., Xia, C., et al.: Graph-BERT: only attention is needed for learning graph representations. arXiv preprint arXiv:2001.05140 (2020)
20. Page, L., Brin, S., Motwani, R., et al.: The PageRank citation ranking: bringing order to the web. Stanford InfoLab (1999)
21. Shervashidze, N., Schweitzer, P., Van Leeuwen, E.J., et al.: Weisfeiler-Lehman graph kernels. J. Mach. Learn. Res. **12**(9), 2539–2561 (2011)
22. Ebel, P., Göl, I.E., Lingenfelder, C., et al.: Destination prediction based on partial trajectory data. In: 2020 IEEE Intelligent Vehicles Symposium (IV), pp. 1149–1155. IEEE (2020)
23. De Brébisson, A., Simon, É., Auvolat, A., et al.: Artificial neural networks applied to taxi destination prediction. arXiv preprint arXiv:1508.00021 (2015)
24. Alvarez-Garcia, J.A., Ortega, J.A., Gonzalez-Abril, L., et al.: Trip destination prediction based on past GPS log using a Hidden Markov Model. Expert Syst. Appl. **37**(12), 8166–8171 (2010)

Aligning Networks by Maximizing Topological Consistency Between Neighborhoods

Boshen Shi[1,2(✉)], Yongqing Wang[1], Huawei Shen[1], and Xueqi Cheng[1]

[1] Data Intelligence System Research Center, Institute of Computing Technology, Chinese Academy of Sciences, Beijing, China
shiboshen19s@ict.ac.cn
[2] University of Chinese Academy of Sciences, Beijing, China

Abstract. Network is widely used to model interactions and relationships between entities from various domains. Aligning networks refers to finding node correspondence across different networks, and could be applied to many researches including anchor link prediction on social networks, inter-network connectivity of molecular networks and information diffusion across networks. Traditionally, network alignment techniques utilize topology information, especially topological consistency to guide alignment process. In this paper, we first propose a graph structure which is the minimum unit to directly represent topological consistency and integrate topological consistency from multiple networks. We then propose a model integrating such structure on a single Kronecker product graph. In addition, our model utilizes the positive correlation between number of quadrilaterals and alignment probability which is rarely used before. We also do experiments on multiple kinds of real world datasets and baselines to prove potentials of our method.

Keywords: Network alignment · Topological consistency · Kronecker product

1 Introduction

Network is a universal tool to model interactions and relationships between entities in various fields, such as social networks, protein-to-protein (PPI) networks, traffic networks and financial networks. Network alignment refers to finding node correspondence across different networks, and it's always the first step of network analysis between multiple networks. For example, aligning users which belong to the same individual person from different social networks could be applied to cross-network recommendation or link prediction, and aligning proteins from two or more PPI networks is crucial to understand biological processes.

Y. Wang, H. Shen, X. Cheng—These authors contributed equally to this work.
B. Shi—Master student from University of Chinese Academy of Sciences.

© Springer Nature Singapore Pte Ltd. 2022
X. Liao et al. (Eds.): BigData 2021, CCIS 1496, pp. 216–232, 2022.
https://doi.org/10.1007/978-981-16-9709-8_15

Traditionally, network alignment techniques could be organized into two categories [1]: 1) topology based, such as IsoRank [2] and FINAL [3], and 2) representation learning based, such as PALE [4] and IONE [5]. All these methods leverage topological consistency to guide alignment process. Topological consistency claims that nodes in one network tend to transfer their close neighbors to another network in order to preserve consistency between neighborhoods, which reflects network homophily. IsoRank computes nodes alignment score under the consumption that two nodes from two networks are similar if their neighborhoods are similar as well. FINAL claims that two cross-network node pairs are structurally similar if nodes from the same graph are close to each other. PALE and IONE map nodes from two networks to the same embedding space which satisfies two principles: 1) neighbors in original graphs are close to each other 2) nodes in aligned node pairs are close to each other. Thus, they simultaneously preserve both structural similarity of original networks and topological consistency.

Although all methods take topological consistency into consideration, they only model consistency into objective functions, but fail to take full advantage of it. **However, topological consistency is scattered in multiple graphs. Thus, we propose a graph structure, quadrilateral, to integrate topological consistency on a single graph.** Quadrilateral is the minimum unit to directly represent topological consistency. For example, in the left part of Fig. 1, cross-network node pairs (u,v) and (k,w) are aligned, and (u,k), (v,w) are edges from original network G, H, then (u,v,w,k) forms a quadrilateral. The original quadrilateral (u,v,w,k) is mapped to two connected nodes (uv, wk) with positive labels on Kronecker product graph $G \otimes H$. Thus, topological consistency is integrated on Kronecker product graph in the form of quadrilateral.

We made detailed statistics to explore quadrilateral related features in real world datasets. According to Table 1, one pair of aligned nodes tend to co-occur with many other aligned node pairs in its one-hop neighborhood. Thus, one aligned node pair may join in multiple quadrilaterals. Most traditional methods model such feature as an application of topological consistency. However, another view of topological consistency is that nodes in a cross-network node pair which is surrounded by multiple quadrilaterals are more likely to be aligned. Such phenomenon is rarely utilized by traditional methods, and our method models the positive correlation between number of quadrilaterals in one-hop neighborhood and probability of cross network node pairs being aligned.

We maximize topological consistency between neighborhoods of node pairs by maximizing the number of quadrilaterals on the product graph. In addition to positive labels, negative labels also exist, for we make the assumption that the number of aligned nodes for a node should not be greater than one. For example, on Fig. 1 node kj is negative because k is aligned with w. As aligned pairs tend to join in multiple quadrilaterals, positive nodes also prefer to connect with many other positive nodes and form multiple quadrilateral structures on product graph. Thus, if a node has more positive neighbors and less negative neighbors, its corresponding cross network node pair should be aligned with high probability. We use a simplified relation method [6] to model the positive correlation between number of quadrilaterals and alignment probability and compute probabilities of any cross-network node pairs being aligned in order to maximize quadrilaterals.

To summarize, the contributions of this paper are as follows:

- We propose a graph structure, quadrilateral, to integrate and reflect topological consistency on a single graph.
- We discover the positive correlation between number of quadrilaterals and probability of cross network node pairs being aligned.
- We propose a model which both integrates topological consistency in Kronecker product graph and models positive correlation between number of quadrilaterals and alignment probability. We also optimize time and space complexity of the proposed model.
- We do detailed experiments to show the great potentials of our proposed model.

Table 1. Quadrilateral statistics. First column: datasets we explored. Second column: quadrilateral numbers. Third column: average number of quadrilaterals that one aligned pair joins. Fourth column: the percentage of aligned pais that join in quadrilateral.

Dataset	#	# per aligned pair	% aligned pairs
Twitter-Foursquare [7]	13432	4.75	87%
Douban Online-Offline [8]	3022	2.7	100%
DBP15K ZH-EN [9]	67731	12.4	94.6%
Citation-network V1[a] [10]	707	0.7	43%

[a]Citation-network V1 from https://www.aminer.org/citation

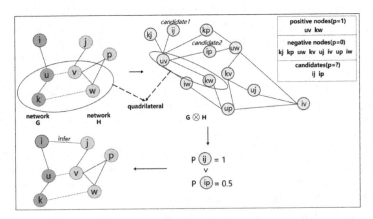

Fig. 1. Upper left part shows the two original graphs: G and H. Node pairs (u,v) and (k,w) are known aligned pairs, (i,j) is true aligned pair but remains to be inferred. (i,p) is another possible aligned pair. Upper right part shows the product graph, $G \otimes H$. The probabilities of candidate nodes ij, ip being positive needs to be inferred. Our model predicts (i,j) aligned with 1 and (i,p) aligned with 0.5, so (i,j) is inferred to be aligned.

2   Related Works

2.1   Network Alignment

Network alignment, the task of recognizing the corresponding nodes between two or multiple networks, is crucial to many cross network applications in various domains. Basically network alignment techniques could be organized to topology based methods and representation learning based methods. All these methods leverage topological consistency to guide alignment process.

Among topology based methods, NetAlign [11] utilizes max-product belief propagation on network topology. IsoRank computes nodes alignment score using PageRank on product matrix under the consumption that two nodes from two networks are similar if their neighborhoods are similar as well. BigAlign and UniAlign [12] aim to infer the soft alignment based on the assumption that the adjacency matrix of one network is a noisy permutation of another network. FINAL combines topological consistency, node similarity and edge similarity to compute alignment score between nodes.

Representation learning method first learns a embedding function to embed each node into embedding space, then they learn a mapping function to map embedding matrices from one graph to the other. Alignment score is computed by the similarity of two node embeddings. PALE learns mapping functions which satisfy two principles: 1) neighbors in original graphs are close to each other 2) nodes in aligned node pairs are close to each other, and it uses a simple Multi-layer Perceptron (MLP) based mapping function. IONE uses the same mapping function as PALE, but it learns a more complicated embedding function as edge directions and two-hop neighbors are also modeled.

2.2   Kronecker Product

Given two graphs G and H and their corresponding adjacency matrices $A(G)$, $A(H)$, the product graph is defined on Kronecker product matrix $A(G) \otimes A(H)$ [13]. Other names for the Kronecker product include tensor product, categorical product, cardinal product and others. Kronecker product is widely used in graph generation and network simulation [14,15]. Many network alignment techniques utilize Kronecker product to combine two networks as one. In product graph, two original cross network nodes are mapped to one node, and two edges from two networks are mapped to one edge. For example, IsoRank and iNEAT [16] use Kronecker product to combine graph topology, and FINAL combines edge similarities by product graph. GCN-ALP [17] learns graph convolutional networks on the product graph constructed by sampled subgraphs with node information.

3   Problem Formulation

There are a source network $G^s = (V^s, E^s, A^s)$ and a target network $G^t = (V^t, E^t, A^t)$, where V^s, V^t represent node sets and E^s, E^t represent edge sets in G^s, G^t. A^s and A^t are adjacency matrices for G^s, G^t. Both two networks are undirected and weighted, with edges weighted by floats between $[0,1]$. Additionally, neither of them have self-loops. The two networks share a set of aligned nodes which join in both networks. We use $Anchors=\{(u,v) \mid u \in G^s, v \in G^t \}$ to mark aligned nodes.

Given the above graph adjacency matrices A^s and A^t of sizes $n^s \times n^s$ and $n^t \times n^t$ respectively, the Kronecker product matrix A^{st} of dimensions $(n^s \cdot n^t) \times (n^t \cdot n^t)$ is given by:

$$A^{st} = A^s \otimes A^t = \begin{pmatrix} a^s_{1,1}A^t & a^s_{1,2}A^t & \cdots & a^s_{1,n^s}A^t \\ a^s_{2,1}A^t & a^s_{2,2}A^t & \cdots & a^s_{2,n^s}A^t \\ \vdots & \vdots & \ddots & \vdots \\ a^s_{n^s,1}A^t & a^s_{n^s,2}A^t & \cdots & a^s_{n^s,n^s}A^t \end{pmatrix} \tag{1}$$

The product graph G^{st} is derived from Kronecker product matrix A^{st}, so we use $G^{st} = G^s \otimes G^t$ to represent the construction of G^{st}. G^{st} has $|V^s| \times |V^t|$ nodes and $2 \times |E^s| \times |E^t|$ edges. As G^{st} is constructed by nodes and edges from both G^s and G^t, nodes and edges in G^{st} are marked as hyper nodes and hyper edges.

Definition 1. (Hyper Node). *Given $a \in V^s$ and $b \in V^t$, the product graph G^{st} has a hyper node ab, $ab \in V^{st}$, $|V^{st}| = |V^s| \times |V^t|$. Suppose the neighbors of a and b are $N(a)$ and $N(b)$ respectively, then the neighbors of ab are $\{a'b' \mid a' \in N(a), b' \in N(b)\}$.*

Definition 2. (Hyper Edge). *Given $a_1a_2 \in E^s$ with weight $w(a_1a_2)$ and $b_1b_2 \in E^t$ with weight $w(b_1b_2)$, the product graph G^{st} has a hyper edge (a_1b_1, a_2b_2) with weight $w(a_1b_1, a_2b_2) = w(a_1a_2) \times w(b_1b_2)$.*

$$A^{st}_{a_1b_1,a_2b_2} = \begin{cases} w(a_1a_2) \times w(b_1b_2) & a_1a_2 \in E^s, b_1b_2 \in E^t \\ 0 & otherwise \end{cases} \tag{2}$$

$(a_1a_2, b_1b_2) \in E^{st}$, and $|E^{st}| = 2 \times |E^s| \times |E^t|$.

Definition 3. (Positive and Negative Labels). *Each pair of aligned nodes $(u, v) \in Anchors$ is related with a hyper node uv, which is labeled as positive sample. As we only consider one-to-one alignment, which means one node from G^s could be aligned to at most one node in G^t, a group of hyper nodes: $\{uv' \mid v' \in G^t, v' \neq v\}$ and $\{u'v \mid u \in G^s, u' \neq u\}$ are labeled as negative samples. Overall, one aligned pair is mapped to one positive hyper node and several negative hyper nodes on product graph. For example, in Fig. 1 two aligned pairs are mapped to two positive hyper nodes and eight negative hyper nodes.*

Similar with IsoRank, the alignment probability for each cross network node pair is computed as the probability of corresponding hyper node being positive. Formally, the network alignment problem is defined as follows:

Given source network $G^s = (V^s, E^s, A^s)$ and target network $G^t = (V^t, E^t, A^t)$ with $n1$ and $n2$ nodes respectively, the product graph G^{st} is constructed by $G^s \otimes G^t$ and probabilities of hyper nodes being positive are computed. Such probabilities are transformed into alignment score matrix S of $n1 \times n2$ where $S(x, y)$ represents the probability of cross network node pair (x, y) being aligned.

4 Methodology

The basic idea of proposed method is maximizing the number of quadrilateral structures on product graph, for a possible aligned node pair tend to join in multiple quadrilaterals. If a hyper node has more positive neighbors, its corresponding node pair has high alignment score and it's likely to form new quadrilaterals with its positive neighbors. Thus, the number of quadrilateral increases. For example, in Fig. 2, the number of quadrilaterals increase from one to three if hyper node Q is finally inferred as positive. The complete algorithm is shown at Algorithm 1. Basically the algorithm is divided into two sequential steps: sorted mini-batch sampling and maximizing the number of quadrilaterals. By repeatedly executing the above two steps on known aligned nodes, the algorithm sequentially process small product graphs, one at a time, and finally gives the optimized alignment score matrix. The complete algorithm is illustrated in Fig. 3.

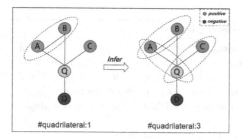

Fig. 2. On the product graph the number of quadrilateral increases if hyper node Q is finally inferred positive. Quadrilaterals are marked with dotted ellipse.

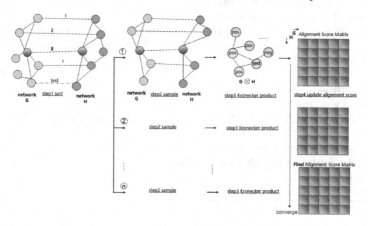

Fig. 3. Complete algorithm

4.1 Preprocess

The most common type of obtained graphs are unweighted. Edge weight is defined afterwards to measure similarity between nodes. For example, two nodes

$u \in G^s$ and $u' \in G^s$ have feature vectors x_u and $x_{u'}$ respectively, then edge (u, u') has weight $w(u, u') = similarity(x_u, x_{u'})$.

However, node information is not easy to obtain in all type of networks. Furthermore, extracting feature vectors from node information varies from graph to graph. Thus, we apply graphlets as a universal method to extract node features. A graphlet is a small, connected and induced subgraph of a larger network [18]. Within each graphlet, some nodes are topologically identical to each other; such identical nodes are said to belong to the same automorphism orbit. Overall in 5-node graphlets there are 73 different automorphism for one node. Graphlet vectors preserve its local structural information, so edge weight computed from graphlet vectors could reveal structural similarity between nodes, which is useful in both sampling and label propagation. Sampling strategy uses structural similarity to preserve neighbors, and label propagation uses weights on hyper edge computed from edge weights in original graphs to enhance performance.

Algorithm 1. Proposed Method

Require: Source network $G^s = (V^s, E^s, A^s)$(unweighted) and target network $G^t = (V^t, E^t, A^t)$(unweighted) with $n1$ and $n2$ nodes respectively; Train aligned nodes Train=$\{(u, v)|u \in G^s, v \in G^t\}$; Test nodes Test=$\{u', v'|u \in G^s, v \in G^t\}$; Parameters=$\{$subgraph maximum size δ, propagation rounds $\lambda\}$.

Ensure: Alignment score matrix PROB; TopN inferred aligned pairs(here N=1).

1: // training
2: **add** edge weight to G^s and G^t // preprocess
3: **sort** Train by the number of quadrilaterals each aligned pair joins in descending order
4: **set** PROB ← Zero-Matrix of ($n1$, $n2$)
5: **for** aligned pair (u,v) **in** Train **do**
6:      G_{st}^{uv}, POS, NEG = Sampling(G^s, G^t, Train, Test, δ) // see Algorithm 2
7:      PROB ← Quadrilateral_Propagation(G_{st}^{uv}, POS, NEG, λ) // see Algorithm 3
8: **end for**
9: // inferring
10: infer_result ← {}
11: **for** node x in Test **do**
12:      $PROB_x$ ← all nodes in the other network which have probabilities of being aligned with x
13:      x_anchor ← $max(PROB_x)$
14:      **update** infer_result **with** (x, x_anchor)
15: **end for**
16: Return PROB infer_result

4.2 Sampling Strategy

Unlike PPI networks which only consist of up to hundreds of nodes, many networks are at least ten times larger, which result in high space and time complexity in computing product graph. We made experiments on Twitter-Foursquare dataset and found that even sparse methods which try to build the complete product graph took over 100G memory, and they were fairly slow. Therefore, sampling strategy is necessary to reduce both space and time complexity. Sampling strategy is shown as Algorithm 2.

Before sampling, train and test aligned nodes are split from known aligned pairs. Both sampling and label propagation are proceeded on training set. For test aligned nodes, we only know nodes themselves, while the alignment remains unknown. For an aligned pair $(u, v) \in Train, u \in G^s, v \in G^t$, sampling strategy treats u v as central node and samples one-hop neighbors as sub-graph G_u^s and G_v^t. However, not all one-hop neighbors are sampled. The strategy sets a maximum sub-graph size δ, and it will first sample neighbors in training and test sets. If the size of sub-graph is still smaller than δ, neighbors which have higher edge weights with central node are more preferred to be sampled. After G_u^s and G_v^t are sampled, the mini-batch product graph G_{uv}^{st} is computed by: $G_{uv}^{st} = G_u^s \otimes G_v^t$.

To utilize quadrilateral structures in network alignment problem, train aligned pairs must be preferentially preserved in the product graph. According to Sect. 1, one train aligned pair is mapped to one positive hyper node and several negative hyper nodes on product graph. If the central aligned pair join more quadrilaterals, there are more positive samples on the product graph, which leads to better calculation. Thus, we first sort the aligned pairs in training set by the number of quadrilaterals they join in descending order, then sampling neighbors for each pair. Neighbors in test sets are preserved because they must be inferred at last.

Sampling would break local structure to a certain degree. In order to preserve local structure as much as possible, neighbors having higher edge weight with central node are sampled. Edge weight measures structural similarity between central node and its neighbors.

Algorithm 2. Sampling Strategy

Require: Source and target social graph G^s G^t; Train anchor nodes Train=$\{(u,v)|u \in G^S, v \in G^t\}$; Test nodes Test=$\{u', v'|u' \in G^S, v' \in G^t\}$; A central aligned pair $(u, v) \in Train$; Subgraph maximum size δ.

Ensure: Mini-Batch product graph G_{uv}^{st} with positive samples POS and negative samples NEG.

1: set POS← {}
2: set NEG← {}
3: set U_{nodes} ← {u}
4: set V_{nodes} ← {v}
5: // make sure train and test nodes are sampled For u
6: **for** node **in** u.neighbors **do**
7:     **if** node **in** Train **then**
8:         anchor_node← Train[node]
9:         **if** anchor_node **in** v.neighbors **then**
10:             **add** node **to** U_{nodes}
11:             **add** anchor_node **to** V_{nodes}
12:         **end if**
        elsif node **in** Test
13:         **add** node **to** U_{nodes} else
14:         **continue**

15:     **end if**
16: **end for**
17: // if subgraph's size is still not enough
18: **if** U_{nodes}.length< δ **then**
19:     **Sort** u.neighbors by edge weight in descending order.
20:     **for** node **in** u.neighbors **do**
21:         **if** U_{nodes}.length< δ **then**
22:             **add** node to U_{nodes}
23:         **end if**
24:     **end for**
25: **end if**
26: Similarly do step 5-25 For v to further expand U_{nodes} and V_{nodes}
27: $G_u^s \leftarrow$ Sample subgraph from G^s using U_{nodes}
28: $G_v^t \leftarrow$ Sample subgraph from G^t using V_{nodes}
29: $G_{uv}^{st} \leftarrow G_u^s \otimes G_v^t$
30: //Map each pair of train anchor pairs to positive and negative hyper nodes
31: **for** n **in** U_{nodes} **do**
32:     **if** n **in** Train **then**
33:         m $\leftarrow$ Train[node]
34:         nm$\leftarrow$Compute hyper node index nm on G_{uv}^{st}
35:         **add** nm to POS
36:         **for** p **in** G_v^t **do**
37:             **if** p **not in** Train **then**
38:                 np $\leftarrow$Compute hyper node index np on G_{uv}^{st}
39:                 **add** np to NEG
40:             **end if**
41:         **end for**
42:         **for** q **in** G_u^s **do**
43:             **if** q **not in** Train **then**
44:                 qm$\leftarrow$Compute hyper node index np on G_{uv}^{st}
45:                 **add** qm to NEG
46:             **end if**
47:         **end for**
48:     **end if**
49: **end for**
50: Similarly do step 32-50 For V_{nodes} to further expand POS and NEG.
51: Return G_{uv}^{st} POS NEG

4.3   Maximizing the Number of Quadrilateral

Maximizing the number of quadrilateral refers to computing possible quadrilateral structures on product graph to maximize the number of quadrilaterals. If a hyper node has more positive neighbors and less negative neighbors, it's more easier to be positive and form new quadrilaterals with its positive neighbors. The basic model is a simplified version of probabilistic relational classifier [6]. A hyper node's label is the weighted average-sum of its neighbors' labels on product graph. The whole process is listed as Algorithm 3. $nbr(pq)$ represents hyper node pq's neighbors.

$$P(pq \in l) = \sum_{xy \in nbr(pq)} P(pq|xy)P(xy \in l)$$

$$= \frac{\sum_{xy \in nbr(pq)} w(xy, pq)P(xy \in l)}{\sum_{xy \in nbr(pq)} w(xy, pq)} \quad l \in [0, 1] \qquad (3)$$

Each hyper nodes should be initially labeled with 0, 1, 0.5 or other floats between [0,1] reflecting its probability of being positive at the very beginning. For hyper nodes in positive or negative sets, their labels are 1 and 0 respectively. For a pair of nodes: $(p, q), p \in G^s, q \in G^t$ and their corresponding hyper node pq in G_{uv}^{st}, if $P(pq \in 1)$ is already obtained in the previous steps, it's used as initial value in the following propagation. Otherwise, $P(pq \in 1)$ is set to 0.5.

During computation, we compute the probability of hyper node being positive one after another on product graph. After one propagation, all hyper nodes have updated its probability once. The propagation is repeated λ times. Details of choosing λ is given in experiment section. However, one should be aware that convergence of propagation is not guaranteed.

After the process is repeated λ times, all hyper nodes should upload its latest probability into the alignment score matrix $PROB$ for the next use as initial value. For instance, hyper node pq with probability $P(pq \in 1)$ is stored as $PROB(p,q) = P(pq \in 1)$.

Relation Classifier vs. PageRank. Here we discuss the benefit of using simplified version of relational classifier instead of PageRank [19] to compute alignment score. IsoRank and IsoRankN [20] used personalized PageRank [21] on complete product graph G^{st} of two PPI networks to compute local consistency score R_{ij} For nodes $i \in G^s, j \in G^t$. However, these two methods are unsupervised, and their product graphs are complete. As we have some positive and negative samples as supervised signal, and for better use of quadrilateral structures on mini-batch product graph, relational classifier is a better choice than PageRank. In addition, product graph constructed by subgraph sampling introduces plenty of noise into PageRank as the complete structure is missing.

4.4 Complexity Analysis

In this section we analyze time and space complexity of the proposed model. For space efficiency, we could use sparse methods when we load the original two graphs and the Kronecker product graph(one at a time) into memory. Thus, the total space complexity is $O(nnz(A^s) + nnz(A^t) + \delta^2)$ where nnz implies number of non-zero elements in adjacency matrix and δ is subgraph maximum size which is usually small.

Following the steps shown in Fig. 4, we first compute time complexity in each step and finally add all results up. The sorting step is $O(mlogm)$ as we used time-sort algorithm, and m implies number of training aligned pairs. Each sampling step is $O(\delta)$ as sampling on two graphs could be done in parallel. Building a Kronecker product graph could consume up to $O(\delta^3)$ but could also be processed in parallel. The final step, computing alignment probability for candidates, could consume up to $O(\delta^3)$ at each iteration, and sparse methods could accelerate operations in it. To summarize, total time complexity could be $O(m(logm + \lambda\delta^7))$, but all steps could be optimized by sparse methods or parallel processing.

In addition to sparse methods and parallel processing, sorting largely helps our model to converge. As we first sort training aligned pairs by the number of quadrilaterals they joins in descending order, relational classifier is proceeded on product graphs where the number of positive labels also decreases in sequential manner. Node pairs could have better initial alignment probabilities, and will reach global optimal faster. Another idea is computing probabilities of aligned pairs on product graphs in parallel, and the overall probability for one node pair averages all its probabilities from previous processes. This method performs faster but poorer than serial method, for it does not take advantage of the product graphs with more positive labels. Our experiments also proved this point.

Algorithm 3. Maximizing the Number of Quadrilaterals

Require: mini-batch product graph G_{uv}^{st}; Positive and negative hyper nodes POS and
    NEG; Alignment score matrix PROB, which stores the probability of any node pair
    being aligned; Propagation rounds λ.
Ensure: Alignment score matrix PROB(updated).
 1: EPOCH=0
 2: $TEMP_{PROB} \leftarrow \{\}$
 3: **while** $EPOCH < \lambda$ **do**
 4:    **for** Hyper Node pq **in** G_{uv}^{st} **do**
 5:       $w = 0$
 6:       $r = 0$
 7:       **for** Hyper Node mn **in** pq.neighbors **do**
 8:          $w+ = weight(mn, pq)$
 9:          **if** mn **in** POS **then**
10:             $r+ = weight(mn, pq)$ elsif (m,n) **in** PROB
11:             $r+ = PROB(m,n) * weight(mn, pq)$
12:          **else**
13:             $r+ = 0.5 * weight(mn, pq)$
14:          **end if**
15:       **end for**
16:       $TEMP_{PROB}[(p,q)] = \frac{r}{w}$
17:    **end for**
18:    $EPOCH+ = 1$
19: **end while**
20: **for** Node pair (m,n) **in** $TEMP_{PROB}$ **do**
21:    $PROB(m,n) = TEMP_{PROB}[(m,n)]$
22: **end for**
23: Return PROB

---

5 Experiments

For performance comparison, we employ three networks: Twitter-Foursquare dataset Douban Online-Offline dataset and a knowledge graph dataset DM-AI we built from DBLP. We conduct experiments to evaluate the effectiveness of our model on the above datasets and compare to some state-of-art network alignment models which only utilize topology information. We also test the sensitivity of our model to its parameters claimed in Algorithm 1 and compare different model architectures including sampling strategy and quadrilateral number maximization.

5.1 Experiment Settings

In this section we introduce the datasets, baseline methods and other settings in our experiments.

5.1.1 Datasets

- **Twitter-Foursquare**: Twitter network has 5120 nodes and 130575 edges, while Foursquare network has 5313 nodes and 54233 edges. We select about 87% aligned node pairs from original aligned pairs which join in at least one quadrilateral. Thus, the number of aligned pairs is 3142.
- **Douban Online-Offline**: This Douban dataset was collected in 2010. All the nodes in offline network is contained in online network. The online network has 3906 nodes and 8164 edges, while offline network has 1118 nodes and 1511 edges. Thus, there are 1118 aligned node pairs in all and they each join at least one quadrilateral.
- **DBLP DM-AI**: We select Citation-network V1 from Aminer [10] website and construct source and target networks by co-author relationship from two domains respectively: Data Mining and Artificial Intelligence. For each domain, we choose ten topics, journals or conferences related with it and build co-author network. The DM network has 14377 nodes and 20359 edges, while AI network has 15310 nodes and 24386 edges. We only pick up aligned pairs which join in at least one quadrilateral, and the number of aligned pairs is 452.

5.1.2 Comparison Methods

- **MNA**: MNA [22] extracts pairwise network features and heterogeneous features to train a classifier, and infer the aligned pairs by solving "table marriage problem" to find the global matching of aligned nodes.
- **IONE**: IONE [5] learns a network embedding with the followership/followeeship of each user explicitly modeled as input/output context vector representations so as to preserve the proximity of users with "similar" followers/followees in the embedded space. Then a mapping function is learned to map aligned node pairs.
- **C-RWR**: C-RWR is the second step of CLF [7] and can propagate information of both anchor and social links across networks.

5.1.3   Evaluation Metrics

We use Precision@N score to measure the performance of our model, given as:

$$Precision@N = \frac{|CorrUser@N|^S + |CorrUser@N|^T}{2 \times |UnAlignedPairs|} \qquad (4)$$

where $|CorrUser@N|$ is the number of test aligned nodes with their corresponding nodes found among candidates in the top-N highest alignment scores. $|UnAlignedPairs|$ is the number of aligned nodes in test set which need to be inferred.

5.1.4   Implementation Settings

When we compare all methods on Twitter-Foursquare dataset, we randomly sample aligned pairs by 70%, 40% and 10% for training and the rest for testing. For parameters, we hold propagation rounds $\lambda = 20$ and subgraph maximum size $\delta = 30$ for better performance in all settings except for parameter sensitivity study. For graphlet vectors, we use ORCA [23] to compute for each dataset.

5.2   Experimental Results

Table 2 shows the comparison results on Twitter-Foursquare dataset where the training ratio decreases from 70% to 10%. Basically, all methods become worse as training ratio decreases. Firstly, our model beats other baseline methods when the training ratio is above 0.4. There are more quadrilaterals exist in the dataset when training ratio is higher, so our method which directly uses quadrilateral structure is more efficient in utilizing topological consistency. However, being sensitive to the number of quadrilaterals makes our model perform slightly worse than IONE when train ratio reaches 0.1, as there are not enough quadrilaterals to support a good quadrilateral propagation. MNA hardly gives correct prediction when training ratio reaches 0.1, because it does not have enough samples to train a good classifier. Besides, it only extract pairwise structure features, lacking full use of topology information. Both IONE and our model take network topology into consideration.

To further explore how our model is sensitive to the number of quadrilaterals, we compare experiment results on three datasets with the same implementation settings. The results are depicted in Fig. 4. Our model performs the best on Douban dataset because all nodes in offline network are aligned and all nodes join in at least one quadrilateral. The overall performance drops with quadrilateral decreasing. However, as we have pointed out in Sect. 1, quadrilaterals widely exist in various types of networks, and it's a direct reflection of topological consistency. Thus, our model is still competitive in many cases.

As we have sorted the training aligned pairs by the number of quadrilaterals they join in descending order, we noticed that the performance may become worse at the end of the algorithm. The reason is there are some cross network pairs which are not aligned having big local topological consistency. Most methods which only take network topology into account suffer from such phenomenon, and integrating node attribute may alleviate this problem. As a temporary solution, we introduced early-stopping into our algorithm, which terminates the training process once the performance keeps getting worse.

5.3 Ablation Study

In this section we explore the effectiveness of different parameter settings and model architecture.

5.3.1 Sampling Strategy

We do experiments to prove the benefit of using sorted mini-batch sampling instead of normal mini-batch sampling which does not firstly sort all aligned pairs. Results shows that model using sorted mini-batch sampling could reach higher precision score at the very beginning. For example, on Twitter-Foursquare it could predict 10% test aligned pairs correctly after three epochs, while model using normal sampling strategy only predicts about 4%. Besides, the final precision of model using sorted mini-batch sampling is about 10% higher. The result proves that after propagating on product graphs with more positive samples, node pairs get good initial probabilities and the number of quadrilaterals will be maximized finally.

5.3.2 Quadrilateral Number Maximization

As we mentioned in Sect. 4.2, the algorithm runs in serial, but it could also have another parallel version, which computes probabilities of aligned pairs on product graphs in parallel and averages all probabilities from previous processes for one pair to obtain overall probability. Parallel version reaches about 0.4 on precision@30, which is 17% lower than serial version. Besides, serial version achieves good inferred results faster for the use of sorted mini-batch sampling.

5.3.3 Propagation Rounds λ

We hope propagation rounds to be as bigger as possible, for a clear convergence guarantee does not exist for quadrilateral propagation. Our experiments find that model performs better with the increase of λ before λ reaches 20. When λ increases beyond 20, there is no significant improvement, and the training becomes much slower. Figure 5 depicts such phenomenon for λ in $[5, 10, 15, 20, 25, 30]$ on Twitter-Foursquare. Thus, we choose $\lambda = 20$ as a trade-off between performance and time complexity.

Table 2. Comparison results on Twitter-Foursquare dataset.

Training ratio	0.7	0.4	0.1
Methods	Precision@30		
MNA	0.561	0.358	0.020
IONE	0.512	0.343	**0.144**
C-RWR	0.12	0.11	0.12
Ours	**0.570**	**0.361**	0.136

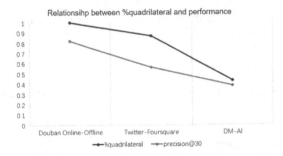

Fig. 4. Sensitivity to #quadrilateral. Blue line shows the percentage of aligned pairs that join at least one quadrilateral, and orange line shows model performance. (Color figure online)

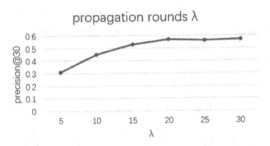

Fig. 5. How performance changes with λ on Twitter-Foursquare.

5.3.4   Subgraph Maximum Size δ

As we have mentioned in Algorithm 2, the sampled subgraph for a pair of nodes must contain all nodes in training set and test set. Thus, increasing subgraph size introduces more candidates into product graph but makes propagation process noisier. However, if the sampling size is not enough, there will be node pairs which will never be sampled and computed alignment score. So we choose $\delta = 30$ as a trade-off between better propagation and more sampled candidates.

6   Conclusion

In this paper, we propose a graph structure *quadrilateral* as a minimum unit to represent local topological consistency, and we also reach a conclusion that aligned node pairs tend to join in multiple quadrilaterals through observation and statistics. We then utilize Kronecker product to combine two graphs as product graph and propagate quadrilaterals in order to maximize the number of quadrilaterals on product graph. We also evaluate our model on three real-world datasets and three baseline models. In the future, we will improve our propagation algorithm and explore other structures which preserve topological consistency.

References

1. Trung, H.T., et al.: A comparative study on network alignment techniques. Expert Syst. Appl. **140**, 112883 (2020)
2. Singh, R., Xu, J., Berger, B.: Pairwise global alignment of protein interaction networks by matching neighborhood topology. In: Speed, T., Huang, H. (eds.) RECOMB 2007. LNCS, vol. 4453, pp. 16–31. Springer, Heidelberg (2007). https://doi.org/10.1007/978-3-540-71681-5_2
3. Zhang, S., Tong, H.: Final: fast attributed network alignment. In: Proceedings of the 22nd ACM SIGKDD International Conference on Knowledge Discovery and Data Mining, pp. 1345–1354 (2016)
4. Man, T., Shen, H., Liu, S., Jin, X., Cheng, X.: Predict anchor links across social networks via an embedding approach. In: IJCAI, vol. 16, pp. 1823–1829 (2016)
5. Liu, L., Cheung, W.K., Li, X., Liao, L.: Aligning users across social networks using network embedding. In: IJCAI, pp. 1774–1780 (2016)
6. Taskar, B., Segal, E., Koller, D.: Probabilistic classification and clustering in relational data. In: International Joint Conference on Artificial Intelligence, vol. 17, pp. 870–878 (2001). Lawrence Erlbaum Associates LTD
7. Zhang, J., Philip, S.Y.: Integrated anchor and social link predictions across social networks. In: Twenty-fourth International Joint Conference on Artificial Intelligence (2015)
8. Zhong, E., Fan, W., Wang, J., Xiao, L., Li, Y.: ComSoc: adaptive transfer of user behaviors over composite social network. In: Proceedings of the 18th ACM SIGKDD International Conference on Knowledge Discovery and Data Mining, pp. 696–704 (2012)
9. Sun, Z., Hu, W., Li, C.: Cross-lingual entity alignment via joint attribute-preserving embedding. In: d'Amato, C., et al. (eds.) ISWC 2017. LNCS, vol. 10587, pp. 628–644. Springer, Cham (2017). https://doi.org/10.1007/978-3-319-68288-4_37
10. Tang, J., Zhang, J., Yao, L., Li, J., Zhang, L., Su, Z.: Arnetminer: extraction and mining of academic social networks. In: KDD 2008, pp. 990–998 (2008)
11. Liang, Z., Xu, M., Teng, M., Niu, L.: Netalign: a web-based tool for comparison of protein interaction networks. Bioinformatics **22**(17), 2175–2177 (2006)
12. Koutra, D., Tong, H., Lubensky, D.: Big-align: fast bipartite graph alignment. In: 2013 IEEE 13th International Conference on Data Mining, pp. 389–398 (2013)
13. Weichsel, P.M.: The Kronecker product of graphs. Proc. Am. Math. Soc. **13**(1), 47–52 (1962)
14. Leskovec, J., Chakrabarti, D., Kleinberg, J., Faloutsos, C., Ghahramani, Z.: Kronecker graphs: an approach to modeling networks. J. Mach. Learn. Res. **11**(2), 985–1042 (2010)
15. Mahdian, M., Xu, Y.: Stochastic Kronecker graphs. In: Bonato, A., Chung, F.R.K. (eds.) WAW 2007. LNCS, vol. 4863, pp. 179–186. Springer, Heidelberg (2007). https://doi.org/10.1007/978-3-540-77004-6_14
16. Zhang, S., Tong, H., Tang, J., Xu, J., Fan, W.: iNEAT: incomplete network alignment. In: 2017 IEEE International Conference on Data Mining (ICDM), pp. 1189–1194 (2017)
17. Gao, H., Wang, Y., Lyu, S., Shen, H., Cheng, X.: GCN-ALP: addressing matching collisions in anchor link prediction. In: 2020 IEEE International Conference on Knowledge Graph (ICKG), pp. 412–419 (2020)
18. Prˇzulj, N., Corneil, D.G., Jurisica, I.: Modeling interactome: scale-free or geometric? Bioinformatics **20**(18), 3508–3515 (2004)

19. Page, L., Brin, S., Motwani, R., Winograd, T.: The pagerank citation ranking: bringing order to the web. Technical report, Stanford InfoLab (1999)
20. Liao, C.-S., Lu, K., Baym, M., Singh, R., Berger, B.: IsoRankN: spectral methods for global alignment of multiple protein networks. Bioinformatics **25**(12), 253–258 (2009)
21. Bahmani, B., Chowdhury, A., Goel, A.: Fast incremental and personalized pagerank. arXiv preprint arXiv:1006.2880 (2010)
22. Kong, X., Zhang, J., Yu, P.S.: Inferring anchor links across multiple heterogeneous social networks. In: Proceedings of the 22nd ACM International Conference on Information & Knowledge Management, pp. 179–188 (2013)
23. Hočevar, T., emšar, J.: A combinatorial approach to graphlet counting. Bioinformatics **30**(4), 559–565 (2014)

OVAE: Out-of-Distribution Detection with Multi-label-enhanced Variational Autoencoders

Zhenyu Yan[✉] and Qinliang Su[✉]

Sun Yat-sen University, Guangzhou, China
`yanzhy9@mail2.sysu.edu.cn`, `suqliang@sysu.edu.cn`

Abstract. Existing out-of-distribution (OOD) detection methods are mainly established on the use of output probability of softmax classifiers. However, the classifier-based approach only leverages the relationship between the input data and their associated labels, without making use of the information hidden in the abundant input data at all. Moreover, the inherent normalization characteristic in the softmax function is prone to make the output prediction probability large even for an OOD input. To address these issues, a generative-model-based approach is proposed. Specifically, to make full use of the input data and associated label, we propose to employ variational auto-encoder (VAE) to model the input data and their associated labels simultaneously. Moreover, to alleviate the issue of false large output probability, we transform the one-hot label into multi-label forms and propose to model the label with a multi-label branch in the VAE. Through experimental comparisons, it is verified that the model can effectively improve the OOD detection performance.

Keywords: Out-of-distribution detection · Variational auto-encoder · Sigmoid multi-label classification

1 Introduction

In recent years, deep models have been widely used in image recognition thanks to its excellent nonlinear modeling ability. However, its powerful expressiveness sometimes also result in some detrimental effects, *e.g.*, producing over-confident predictions for unknown objects. When deep models are applied to recognize the category of images, they will always judge the test image as one of the known categories with a fairly high probability, even if the category of the input image is not seen before. For an instance, the two-layer convolution and one-layer fully connected classifier have achieved very good results in the ordinary in-distribution sample classification problem. However, when the random Gaussian noise is input into the classifier trained on MNIST, the model always recognizes the input noise as a digit with a very high probability.

In many practical applications, to avoid serious consequences caused by misjudgment, the classifier needs to have the ability of detecting testing samples

© Springer Nature Singapore Pte Ltd. 2022
X. Liao et al. (Eds.): BigData 2021, CCIS 1496, pp. 233–247, 2022.
https://doi.org/10.1007/978-981-16-9709-8_16

that are far away from the ones used during the training. Existing OOD detection methods mostly follow the procedures of first training a classifier on in-distribution data, and then using the classifier to recognize the OOD samples according to the absolute value of prediction probability. The prediction probability will generally be high for in-distribution samples, while relatively small for OOD ones. But there are two main problems with the this widely-adopted approach. 1) Inadequate use of data information: During the training, the model only leverage the relationship between the input data and its associated labels, while ignoring the abundant information hidden in the input data. 2) Over-confidence prediction given by softmax function: Due to the normalization characteristic of softmax function, the softmax classifiers are often prone to give confident predictions, even for OOD inputs. The contributions of this paper include: To make full use of the input data and their associated labels, we propose to employ variational auto-encoder (VAE) to model the input data and their associated labels simultaneously. Comparing to traditional VAE, the latent features are able to retain the label information and enhance the model's ability to describe the data distribution. To alleviate the issue of false large output probability in softmax classifier, we transform the one-hot label into multi-label forms and propose to model the label with a multi-label branch in the VAE.

2   Related Work

Many efforts have been devoted to the field of out-of-distribution sample detection, and most of the methods are based on the use of classifiers. These methods detect OOD samples by training classifiers on in-distribution data and then comparing the output probabilities with a threshold value. According to the comparison between the classification probability and the threshold value, the samples larger than the threshold value are divided into the in-distribution samples, and the samples smaller than the threshold value are out-of-distribution samples.

A basline OOD detection method is first proposed in [2] by using the maximum softmax probabilities as the prediction confidence, while the in-distribution examples tends to get higher scores than OOD ones. In 2017, Shiyu Liang et al. [7] proposed the ODIN model based on pre-trained neural network. By adding temperature scaling in the input, further expanded gap between normal and abnormal samples. But the detection performance of the model still depends on the effect of pre-trained classifier. In 2018, Kimin Lee et al. [5] proposed an improved classifier method of combining training classifier and generative adversarial network. The paper [1] added a branch to calculate estimated value of confidence score based on classifier. The paper [13] improves the representation of labels on the basis of classifiers, and uses several different word vectors as semantic label training classification models. Kimin Lee et al. [6] proposed a generating classifier based on Mahalanobis distance. When the pre-trained features can be well fitted by gaussian distribution. Mahalanobis distance is used to define the confidence score closest to the conditional distribution. This method is more robust when there are noise labels and the number of samples is small. Pramuditha Perera et al. [12] used the convolution kernel obtained by different classes as the negative filter of other categories, and the global negative filter had a certain effect on reducing the probability value of non-samples. The article [15] put forward using autoencoder to train directly on confounding data. The autoencoder can still learn the normal data distribution by using the confounding data training directly. In paper [14], a semi-supervised model of an encoder and two decoders is proposed. The decoders are used to reconstruct normal data and abnormal data respectively. In the article [9], the steps of adding reverse training anomaly data on the basis of autoencoder are proposed, which increases the reconstruction error of abnormal data.

3   The Proposed Method

3.1   Preliminaries

Autoencoder. (AE) [3] is an unsupervised deep learning model, which consists of an encoder and decoder. Specifically, $z = f_\phi(x)$ represents the encoding process and $\hat{x} = g_\theta(z)$ denotes the decoding process, both of which are nonlinear transformation functions. z and $\hat{x}$ represent the latent representation obtained in the encoding process and the reconstructed data obtained in the decoding process, respectively.

Variational Autoencoder. (VAE) [4] is a generative model with similar structure to AE. However, the training goal of AE is to improve the quality of reconstructed data, while the goal of VAE is to learn the overall probability distribution of training data. To model the distribution of training data $p(x)$, a latent representation z is introduced. We define the joint distribution of latent representation z and data x as follows

$$p_\theta(x) = \int p_\theta(x|z)p_\theta(z)dz. \tag{1}$$

We assume that z follows a Gaussian distribution. The VAE first calculates the distribution of the latent variable z through the encoding process $q_\phi(z|x)$, with the z sampled from this distribution. The decoding process $p_\theta(x|z)$ is used to calculate the distribution of data x. We assume that $p(x|z)$ maintains a form of Gaussian distribution with unit variance, and the mean obtained from the decoding process $p(x|z)$ is viewed as the reconstructed data $\hat{x}$. To increase the modeling ability, the mean in the conditional Gaussian probability $p(x|z)$ is related to the input z through a neural network. The model is trained by maximizing the evidence lower bound (ELBO)

$$L(\theta, \phi) = E_z\left[\log p_\theta(x^{(i)}|z)\right] - D_{KL}(q_\phi(z|x^{(i)})||p_\theta(z)). \tag{2}$$

In formula (2), Maximizing the lower bound $L(q)$ is to maximize corresponding $p(x|z)$, so the data can be reconstructed as much as possible. At the same time, the KL divergence of the second approximate posterior distribution and the prior distribution is reduced to make z conform to the expected Gaussian distribution.

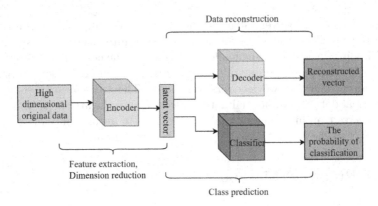

Fig. 1. The overall structure of OVAE

3.2   The Proposed OVAE Model

OVAE not only models data x, but also employ a multi-label head to model the associated labels. Therefore, the model can more accurately describe the data distribution, and extract more representative features of the samples, thereby boosting the model's ability to detect OOD samples. As shown in Fig. 1, the OVAE model include the label information during the training, with the goal of learning the joint distribution of data and labels $p_\theta(x, y)$, which is defined to have the following form

$$p_\theta(x, y, z) = p_\theta(x, y|z)p_\theta(z)$$
$$= p_\theta(x|z)p_\theta(y|z)p_\theta(z). \qquad (3)$$

Here, we introduce a latent variable z, and variables x and y are conditionally independent given z. We assume that z obeys a Gaussian distribution, that is, $p_\theta(z) = N(0, 1)$. We use the decoder to model the distribution $p_\theta(x|z)$, and the classifier to model the distribution $p_\theta(y|z)$.

Data Generation. Assume $p_\theta(x|z)$ obeys the Gaussian distribution $p_\theta(x|z) = N(x; \mu(z), \sigma^2)$ with unit variance. So we just need the mean to determine the distribution. The decoder uses latent variable z as input, and uses the output as the distribution mean $\mu(z)$, which can determine the distribution of $p_\theta(x|z)$. According to the different complexity of training data, we can adopt different neural networks to build the decoder.

Label Generation. We can regard the process of generating label y from the latent variable z as a classification process. The classifier usually uses softmax to predict the probabilities of belonging to different categories. Assuming $p_\theta(y|z)$ follows the categorical distribution, it can be represented as

$$p_\theta(y|z) = \prod_{c=1}^{K} \mu_c^{y_c}, \qquad (4)$$

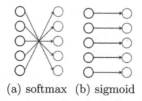

(a) softmax   (b) sigmoid

Fig. 2. The different relationship between the result and input in the softmax activation function and the sigmoid activation function

where $y = [y_1, ..., y_K]$ with $y_i \in \{0, 1\}$ and $\sum_{k=1}^{K} \mu_k = 1$. We can utilize the $\mu(z)$ to determine the distribution. The probability of μ_k is modeled by the output of a classifier

$$\mu(z) = softmax(f_y(z)) \tag{5}$$

The output is used as the mean parameter of the distribution.

In the existing classifier-based OOD detection methods, the prediction probability of in-distribution samples is encouraged to be as high as possible, while the maximum probability of OOD samples is encouraged to be as low as possible, so that the two types of samples can be distinguished easily. However, many work [10,11] has pointed out that the softmax function always tends to output confident prediction, even for OOD samples, due to its normalization characteristic. Therefore, we transform the multi-classification problem into multiple two-classification problem and use the sigmoid function instead, which can eliminate the detrimental normalization impact from the softmax function (Fig. 2).

After transforming the original one-hot classification problem into a multi-label classification problem, the distribution $p_\theta(y|z)$ now need to follow a multi-dimensional Bernoulli distribution as

$$p_\theta(y|z) = \prod_{c=1}^{K} \mu_c^{y_c} (1 - \mu_c)^{1-y_c}. \tag{6}$$

It can be seen that the labels on different dimensions y_c are independent and it is possible to output probabilities that are close to 0 on all categories. Thus, a testing sample is allowed not belonging any categories. The characteristic of sigmoid function makes it possible to use the maximum probability to distinguish and detect OOD samples. The mean vector $\mu = [\mu_1, \cdots, \mu_c, \cdots, \mu_K]$ is now obtained as

$$\mu(z) = sigmoid(f_y(z)). \tag{7}$$

The main difference between the sigmoid function and the softmax function is that sigmoid function does not require the normalization as in the softmax function. In this way, it allows novel samples to produce the prediction probability values that are close to 0 in all categories. In the OOD detection task, the OOD samples do not belong to any known category. Ideally, the prediction probability of OOD samples for any category should be close to 0, which, obviously, is compatible with the sigmoid-based multi-label generative model.

3.3 Model Training

The whole training process can be summarized as Algorithm 1.

Algorithm 1: Parameter optimization process of OVAE

Input: Normal training samples with label

1 **foreach** *training sample x* **do**
2 | /*The encoding process*/
3 | The training sample is input to the encoder to obtain the distribution of the latent variable z

$$\mu(x), \sigma^2(x) = q_\phi(z|x)$$

| /*Reparameterization*/
4 | Sample ϵ from the Gaussian distribution $N(\epsilon; 0, I)$, to obtain the corresponding sampling result of the latent variable z

$$z = \mu(x) + \sigma(x) * \epsilon$$

| /*The decoding process*/
5 | Use the latent variable z to decode, and generate the reconstructed data $\hat{x}$ and predicted category results $\hat{y}$

$$\hat{x}, \hat{y} = p_\sigma(x, y|z)$$

| /*Parameter update*/
6 | Use gradient back propagation to maximize the lower bound

$$L(\theta, \phi) = -KL[q_\phi(z|x)||p_\theta(z)] + E_{q_\phi(z|x)}[log p_\theta(x|z)] + E_{q_\phi(z|x)}[log p_\theta(y|z)]$$

7 The error convergence

Variational Inference. The purpose of the model is to maximize joint distribution $p_\theta(x, y) = \int p_\theta(x, y|z)dz$, but since we can't integrate z directly, we're going to maximize its lower bound ELBO

$$L(x^{(i)}, \theta, \phi) = -KL[q_\phi(z|x^{(i)})||p_\theta(z)] + E_{q_\phi(z|x^{(i)})}[\log p_\theta(x^{(i)}, y^{(i)}|z)]. \tag{8}$$

To use the ELBO, we need to introduce a variational posterior $q_\phi(z|x, y)$ to approximate the true $p_\theta(z|x, y)$. For simplicity, it is assumed that $q_\phi(z|x, y)$ maintain a Gaussian form, that is, $q_\phi(z|x) = N(z; \mu(x), \sigma^2(x))$. The encoder gives the mean and variance of the distribution $q_\phi(z|x)$, so we easily get the approximate posterior distribution $q_\theta(z|x, y)$. The goal of model optimization is to maximize the lower bound $L(x^{(i)}, \theta, \phi)$. The KL divergence term drives the variational distribution $q_\phi(z|x^{(i)})$ to move toward the prior distribution of $p_\theta(z)$. At the same time, $L(x^{(i)}, \theta, \phi)$ includes the reconstruction error of generated data $\hat{x}$ and input sample x, and the error of label prediction classification result $\hat{y}$ and true label y. Because x and y are conditional independent, the optimization objective can be decomposed into two parts .

$$E_{q_\phi(z|x)}[\log p_\theta(x,y|z)] = E_{q_\phi(z|x)}[\log p_\theta(x|z)] + E_{q_\phi(z|x)}[\log p_\theta(y|z)] \quad (9)$$

Since $p(x|z)$ follows the Gaussian distribution, the reconstruction term on x, i.e., $E_{q_\phi(z|x)}[\log p_\theta(\bar{x}|z)]$, can be written as

$$E_{q_\phi(z|x)}[\log p_\theta(\bar{x}|z)] = \frac{1}{N}\sum_{i=1}^{N}(x^{(i)} - \hat{x}^{(i)})^2. \quad (10)$$

Similarly, since $p(y|z)$ follows the binomial distribution, the reconstruction term of y, i.e., $E_{q_\phi(z|x)}[\log p_\theta(y|z)]$, can be written as

$$E_{q_\phi(z|x)}[\log p_\theta(y|z)] = \sum_{c=1}^{M}[y_c \log \hat{y}_c + (1 - \hat{y}_c)\log(1 - \hat{y}_c)]. \quad (11)$$

Reparameterization. When gradient descent is used to optimize the lower bound, the sampling of the variational distribution is not differentiable and can not propagate back. So it is difficult to obtain the gradient. The reparameterization method is used to solve the problem. For the latent variable z that follows the Gaussian distribution, we sample a ϵ from the Gaussian distribution $N(\epsilon; 0, 1)$. After passing it through the encoder, we get the mean $\mu(x)$ and the variance $\sigma^2(x)$ of the variational distribution. Thus, with the reparameterization method, we can easily get $z_i = \mu_i(x) + \sigma_i * \epsilon, \epsilon \sim N(0, I)$ and the ELBO can be approximately estimated as

$$L(x^{(i)}, \theta, \phi) = -KL[q_\phi(z|x^{(i)})||p_\theta(z)] + \frac{1}{L}\sum_{j=1}^{L}\log p_\theta(x^{(i)}, y^{(i)}|z^{(i,j)}), \quad (12)$$

where

$$z^{(i,j)} = \mu^{(i)}(x) + \sigma^{(i)} * \epsilon^{(j)}, \epsilon^{(j)} \sim N(0, I) \quad (13)$$

4 Experiments

4.1 Datasets

The training data sets are MNIST, CIFAR10, CIFAR100 and SVHN. MNIST, a handwritten digital data set, has ten categories of black and white images, containing 60,000 training images and 10,000 test images; CIFAR10 has ten categories of color images, including 50,000 training images and 10,000 test images; CIFAR100 has 100 categories of color images, including 50000 training images and 10000 test images; The house number dataset SVHN has ten categories of color images, including 50,000 training images and 10,000 test images. The test data set includes the training set, and the classification accuracy within the distribution is calculated for the normal samples. In order to test the detection effect of the out-of-distribution samples, different test sets are used as the

Table 1. Data set settings

In-distribution data set	Out-of-distribution data set
MNIST	GAUSSIAN
	UNIFORM
	CIFAR10
	CIFAR100
SVHN	CIFAR10
	LSUN
	ImageNet
CIFAR10	GAUSSIAN
	SVHN
	LSUN
	ImageNet
CIFAR100	GAUSSIAN
	SVHN
	LSUN
	ImageNet

out-of-distribution data according to different training sets. We adopt CIFAR10 CIFAR100, SVHH, ImageNet, LSUN and random Gaussian noise, Uniform on the whole model test. There are 10,000 normal data samples in the test set, so we set the number of out-of-distribution samples as 10,000, as shown in Table 1. For the in-distribution samples, both the training set and the test set are included, and the out-of-distribution samples are only used in the test set.

4.2   Evaluation Metrics

We use the following two metrics to measure the effectiveness of the OVAE model on the OOD detection task.

1) **AUROC** is the area under the Receiver operating characteristic curve (ROC), which is depicted by horizontal axis $FPR = \frac{FP}{FP+TN}$ and vertical axis $TPR = \frac{TP}{TP+FN}$. The false positive rate (FPR) represents the probability of being predicted as a positive sample in a negative sample, while the true rate (TPR) represents the probability of being predicted as a positive sample in an actual positive sample. AUROC represents the probability that the model gives a higher score for positive samples than for negative samples under the given situation of positive and negative samples.

2) **AUPR** represents the area under the PR curve. The precision-recall curve (PR) was described by the horizontal axis $recall = \frac{TP}{TP+FN}$ and vertical axis $precision = \frac{TP}{TP+FP}$. Recall refers to the probability that an actually positive sample is predicted to be a positive sample, and precision refers

Table 2. AUROC(%) results of OVAE model, baseline model, ODIN model

In-distribution samples	Out-of-distribution samples	Baseline [2]	ODIN [8]	OVAE
CIFAR10(ResNet)	SVHN	89.9	96.7	**98.1**
	ImageNet	91	94	**96.2**
	LSUN	91	94.1	**95.6**
CIFAR10(DenseNet)	SVHN	89.9	95.5	**98.2**
	ImageNet	94.1	98.5	**98.8**
	LSUN	95.4	**99.2**	**99.2**
CIFAR100(ResNet)	SVHN	79.5	93.9	**95.3**
	ImageNet	77.2	87.6	**90.2**
	LSUN	75.8	85.6	**87.6**
CIFAR100(DenseNet)	SVHN	82.7	93.8	**97.1**
	ImageNet	71.7	85.2	**89.5**
	LSUN	70.8	85.5	**88.0**
SVHN(ResNet)	CIFAR10	92.9	92.1	**97.2**
	ImageNet	93.5	92	**98.5**
	LSUN	91.6	89.4	**99.4**
SVHN(DenseNet)	CIFAR10	91.9	91.4	**97.2**
	ImageNet	94.8	95.1	**98.3**
	LSUN	94.1	94.5	**99.2**
Average		87.1	92.5	**95.6**

to the probability that a positively predicted sample is actually a positive sample. When the distribution of positive and negative samples is uneven, PR can better reflect the effect of the classification model than ROC.

4.3 Training Setups

According to the complexity of different datasets, fully connected MLP, ResNet and DenseNet are used in the encoder, fully connected and deconvolution networks are used in the decoder, and one-layer full join is used for classifier. For CIFAR10, CIFAR100, SVHN data sets, the network structure of encoder and classifier includes ResNet and DenseNet; For the MNIST dataset, the network structure is the MLP network structure.

4.4 Experimental Results

The experimental results are shown in Table 2. We compare our OVAE model with the naive baseline model [2] and ODIN model [8], which are mature models designed for the OOD task. According to the experimental results, the OVAE model is better than the baseline model and ODIN model on all experimental

Table 3. Effects of label on detection performance of out-of-distribution samples

In-distribution samples	Out-of-distribution samples	AUROC(%)	
		No labels	Using labels
CIFAR10	GAUSSIAN	20.6	**99.6**
	SVHN	19.7	**98.2**
	ImageNet	81.8	**98.9**
	LSUN	87.2	**99.2**
CIFAR100	GAUSSIAN	88.6	**97.2**
	SVHN	19	**97**
	ImageNet	68.7	**89.5**
	LSUN	71.1	**88.1**
SVHN	CIFAR10	94.6	**97.2**
	ImageNet	94.3	**98.3**
	LSUN	93.3	**99.1**
MNIST	GAUSSIAN	95.1	**100**
	UNIFORM	94.7	**100**
	CIFAR10	88.1	**100**
	CIFAR100	88.3	**100**
Average		73.7	**97.5**

data sets. On average, the average AUROC of our model is 8.6% higher than that of the baseline model, and 3.2% higher than that of ODIN model, indicating that the improved model has better detection performance.

4.5 Ablation Study

Through the ablation experiment, we demonstrate the influences of data reconstruction, label reconstruction, softmax classification and sigmoid classification on the overall detection performance of the model. The following table shows the results of the OVAE models with different components for the OOD samples. It can be seen that including the label reconstruction component lead to an increase of 23% in AUROC and 19.8% in AUPR on average. The average AUROC and AUPR increases by 5.4% and 3.9% respectively. Sigmoid brings an 1% increase in AUROC and 1.1% increase in AUPR over softmax on average.

Effects of Label Information. In order to assess the influence of the label reconstruction part on the OOD detection performance, we set the weight this term to 0. That is, only the reconstruction error of data x is used in the training of the model. As shown in Table 3, for all datasets, the overall performance of the model for OOD detection decreases significantly after the label reconstruction term is removed. AUROC is decreased by 23%. It can be seen that the label part plays a key role in the model detection performance. Among them, when CIFAR is used as an in-distribution sample, the reconstruction effect of SVHN is better,

Table 4. Effect of reconstructed data on out-of-distribution sample detection performance

In-distribution samples	Out-of-distribution samples	AUROC(%)	AUPR(%)
		Without/with data reconstruction	
CIFAR10 (ResNet)	GAUSSIAN	96.2/**98.7**	98.6/**99.2**
	SVHN	90.7/**98.1**	92.5/**98.7**
	ImageNet	91.4/**96.2**	93.2/**97.6**
	LSUN	91.2/**95.8**	94.6/**97.0**
CIFAR10 (DenseNet)	GAUSSIAN	99.2/**99.6**	99.4/**99.8**
	SVHN	93.4/**98.2**	95.0/**98.9**
	ImageNet	94.3/**98.9**	96.5/**99.2**
	LSUN	95.5/**99.2**	97.4/**99.5**
CIFAR100 (ResNet)	GAUSSIAN	88.6/**94.7**	92.1/**98.1**
	SVHN	81.6/**95.3**	85.1/**98.3**
	ImageNet	80.3/**90.4**	84.0/**92.3**
	LSUN	75.9/**87.6**	78.8/**86.5**
CIFAR100 (DenseNet)	GAUSSIAN	92.5/**97.2**	95.5/**96.3**
	SVHN	85.7/**97.0**	87.5/**97.2**
	ImageNet	76.4/**89.5**	78.8/**93.6**
	LSUN	77.6/**88.1**	81.0/**87.0**
SVHN (ResNet)	CIFAR10	96.2/**97.1**	98.7/**98.9**
	ImageNet	96.4/**98.7**	98.7/**99.5**
	LSUN	96.1/**99.4**	98.6/**99.8**
SVHN (DenseNet)	CIFAR10	96.0/**97.2**	98.6/**98.9**
	ImageNet	96.2/**98.3**	98.7/**99.4**
	LSUN	95.9/**99.1**	98.5/**99.6**
MNIST (MLP)	GAUSSIAN	99.4/**100**	99.6/**100**
	UNIFORM	98.4/**100**	98.9/**100**
	CIFAR10	94.5/**100**	96.0/**100**
	CIFAR100	94.8/**100**	96.7/**100**
Average		91.3/**96.7**	93.6/**97.5**

so the detection performance was worse than that of other groups, indicating the necessity of introducing labels for training.

Effects of Data Reconstruction. As shown in Table 4, the AUROC and AUPR of the proposed model without the data reconstruction part reduced by 5.4% and by 3.9% on average, respectively. Obviously, the data generation component improves the detection performance significantly. Not only for a certain part of the datasets, but even if the reconstruction effect between the datasets has a certain gap, the data generation can improve the settings of each data set to a certain extent. By adding data reconstruction part, the information of original data can be preserved to the maximum extent in the latent representation z. Hence, the

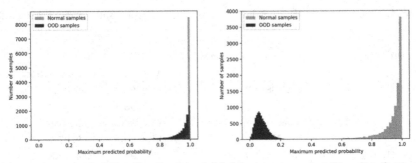

(a) Maximum probability distribution of softmax classification
(b) Maximum probability distribution of sigmoid classification

Fig. 3. The maximum probability distribution of test data

model's performance of detecting OOD samples can be improved to a considerable extent.

Effects of Sigmoid Multi-label Classification. Because the detection performance is adversarially affected by the over-confidence of softmax function, we propose to use sigmoid classification to model the associated label information. Figure 3 shows the distribution of the maximum predicted probability of the in-distribution and OOD samples. It can be seen that with the continuous training of the model, the maximum probability of OOD and in-distribution samples are very close. In this case, it is very difficult to find the boundaries to separate the samples inside and outside the distribution. In the OVAE model that adopts sigmoid for classification, the maximum probability values of the OOD samples mainly concentrate between 0 and 0.2, while the normal data mainly concentrate between 0.8 and 1.0, which is significantly different. The maximum probability distribution results of the test data under the two classifiers shown in Fig. 3 clearly demonstrate that the sigmoid multi-label classification method can solve the detection failure problem caused by the over-confidence of softmax function, and to a large extent promote the distinction between the samples inside and outside the distribution.

We conduct extensive experiments on multiple datasets and settings, and analyze the improvement of sigmoid multi-label classification for OOD detection performance through a comprehensive comparison. In order to verify the generalization of sigmoid multi-label classification, at the same time, we compared the difference of detection performance of the two classification methods in OVAE model, and divide the OVAE model into OVAE (sigmoid) and OVAE (softmax) models according to the different label generation modes. It can be seen from the data in the Table 5 that the result of sigmoid classifier is better than that of softmax classifier in all settings. Compared with the results of softmax classifier, the results of Sigmoid classifier respectively improve the AUROC by 2% and AUPR by 1.6% on average. At the same time, the results of OVAE (sigmoid) model

Table 5. Influence of softmax classification and sigmoid multi-label classification on out-of-distribution sample detection performance

In-distribution	Out-of-distribution	AUROC(%)	AUPR(%)
		Softmax classifier/Sigmoid classifier	
		OVAE (softmax)/OVAE (sigmoid)	
CIFAR10 (ResNet)	GAUSSIAN	94.5/96.2/97.6/**98.7**	98.0/98.6/98.5/**99.2**
	SVHN	87.3/90.7/96.9/**98.1**	90.4/92.5/97.8/**98.7**
	ImageNet	89.2/91.2/94.3/**96.2**	92.5/93.2/96.5/**97.6**
	LSUN	89.0/91.2/94.1/**95.8**	91.4/94.6/96.3/**97.0**
CIFAR10 (DenseNet)	GAUSSIAN	98.8/99.2/99.6/**99.6**	99.1/99.4/99.7/**99.8**
	SVHN	91.8/93.4/97.1/**98.2**	93.9/95.0/97.6/**98.9**
	ImageNet	92.4/94.3/97.4/**98.9**	94.4/96.5/98.2/**99.2**
	LSUN	92.7/95.5/98.1/**99.2**	94.7/97.4/98.6/**99.5**
CIFAR100 (ResNet)	GAUSSIAN	87.7/88.6/91.6/**94.7**	91.2/92.1/92.4/**98.1**
	SVHN	79.3/81.6/94.4/**95.3**	82.3/85.1/96.0/**98.3**
	ImageNet	77.4/80.3/88.5/**90.4**	77.2/84.0/90.0/**92.3**
	LSUN	73.5/75.9/86.6/**87.6**	79.7/78.8/85.6/**86.5**
CIFAR100 (DenseNet)	GAUSSIAN	88.4/92.5/96.0/**97.2**	90.9/95.5/**97.7**/96.3
	SVHN	80.8/85.7/96.9/**97.0**	84.6/87.5/**97.2**/97.2
	ImageNet	72.8/76.4/87.2/**89.5**	77.5/78.8/90.5/**93.6**
	LSUN	75.1/77.6/86.6/**88.1**	79.6/81.0/85.8/**87.0**
SVHN (ResNet)	CIFAR10	96.2/96.2/96.7/**97.1**	98.6/98.7/98.8/**98.9**
	ImageNet	96.2/96.4/98.6/**98.7**	98.8/98.7/**99.5**/99.5
	LSUN	95.8/96.1/99.3/**99.4**	98.5/98.6/99.7/**99.8**
SVHN (DenseNet)	CIFAR10	95.8/96.0/96.9/**97.2**	98.5/87.6/98.7/**98.9**
	ImageNet	95.8/96.2/98.2/**98.3**	98.4/98.7/99.3/**99.4**
	LSUN	95.2/95.9/99.0/**99.1**	98.3/98.5/**99.6**/99.6
MNIST (MLP)	GAUSSIAN	96.7/99.4/**100**/100	98.0/99.6/**100**/100
	UNIFORM	95.8/98.4/**100**/100	97.6/98.9/**100**/100
	CIFAR10	92.3/94.5/98.1/**100**	94.0/96.0/97.0/**100**
	CIFAR100	92.1/94.8/97.3/**100**	93.5/96.7/94.8/**100**
Average		89.3/91.3/95.7/**96.7**	92.0/93.6/96.4/**97.5**

are better than those of OVAE (softmax) model in most data settings. Sigmoid improves 1% AUROC and 1.1% AUPR on OVAE model on average compared with softmax, which fully indicates that sigmoid has a certain improvement in the detection capability of the out-of-distribution sample detection model, and the method has good generalization. Based on the observations above, we can see that label information improves the model's detection ability greatly, while the contribution of reconstruction error is only one quarter of it. Thus, we may adjust the weights of the two parts for OOD detection to obtain better results.

5   Conclusions

To address the issues of insufficient data utilization and high confidence of softmax in existing OOD detection methods, this paper proposes the solutions: 1) For inadequate data utilization, we introduce the combination of label information and data reconstruction, which not only utilizes the image itself information but also its label information; 2) For the over-confidence problem associated with softmax-classifier, we use sigmoid to replace softmax, and transform the multi-classification problem into multi-label classification problem. Finally, the effectiveness of the model is tested on multiple data sets and the experimental results demonstrate the superior performance of the proposed model comparing with baselines.

References

1. DeVries, T., Taylor, G.W.: Learning confidence for out-of-distribution detection in neural networks. CoRR, abs/1802.04865 (2018)
2. Hendrycks, D., Gimpel, K.: A baseline for detecting misclassified and out-of-distribution examples in neural networks. arXiv preprint arXiv:1610.02136 (2016)
3. Salakhutdinov, R.R., Hinton, G.E.: Reducing the dimensionality of data with neural networks. Sci. Am. Assoc. Adv. Sci. **313**, 504–507 (2006)
4. Kingma, D.P., Welling, M.: Auto-encoding variational Bayes. In: 2nd International Conference on Learning Representations, ICLR (2014)
5. Lee, K., Lee, H., Lee, K., Shin, J.: Training confidence-calibrated classifiers for detecting out-of-distribution samples. In: 6th International Conference on Learning Representations (ICLR) (2018)
6. Lee, K., Lee, K., Lee, H., Shin, J.: A simple unified framework for detecting out-of-distribution samples and adversarial attacks. In: Advances in Neural Information Processing Systems, vol. 31: Annual Conference on Neural Information Processing Systems 2018 (NeurIPS), pp. 7167–7177 (2018)
7. Liang, S., Li, Y., Srikant, R.: Principled detection of out-of-distribution examples in neural networks. arXiv preprint arXiv:1706.02690 (2017)
8. Liang, S., Li, Y., Srikant, R.: Enhancing the reliability of out-of-distribution image detection in neural networks. In: 6th International Conference on Learning Representations (ICLR) (2018)
9. Munawar, A., Vinayavekhin, P., De Magistris, G.: Limiting the reconstruction capability of generative neural network using negative learning. In: 27th IEEE International Workshop on Machine Learning for Signal Processing (MLSP), pp. 1–6 (2017)
10. Nguyen, A.M., Yosinski, J., Clune, J.: Deep neural networks are easily fooled: High confidence predictions for unrecognizable images. In: IEEE Conference on Computer Vision and Pattern Recognition, CVPR, pp. 427–436 (2015)
11. Nguyen, K., O'Connor, B.: Posterior calibration and exploratory analysis for natural language processing models. In: Proceedings of the 2015 Conference on Empirical Methods in Natural Language Processing, EMNLP, pp. 1587–1598 (2015)
12. Perera, P., Patel, V.M.: Deep transfer learning for multiple class novelty detection. In: IEEE Conference on Computer Vision and Pattern Recognition (CVPR), pp. 11544–11552 (2019)

13. Shalev, G., Adi, Y., Keshet, J.: Out-of-distribution detection using multiple semantic label representations. CoRR, abs/1808.06664 (2018)

14. Tian, K., Zhou, S., Fan, J., Guan, J.: Learning competitive and discriminative reconstructions for anomaly detection. In: The Thirty-Third AAAI Conference on Artificial Intelligence (AAAI), pp. 5167–5174 (2019)

15. Xia, Y., Cao, X., Wen, F., Hua, G., Sun, J.: Learning discriminative reconstructions for unsupervised outlier removal. In: 2015 IEEE International Conference on Computer Vision (ICCV), pp. 1511–1519 (2015)

Big Data Privacy and Security

Anomalous Crowd Detection with Mobile Sensing and Suspicious Scoring

Lili Jiang[1], Lifeng Sun[1(✉)], and Kai Hwang[2]

[1] Tsinghua University, Beijing 10084, China
jll13@mails.tsinghua.edu.cn, sunlf@tsinghua.edu.cn
[2] The Chinese University of Hong Kong, Shenzhen 518172, Guangdong, China
hwangkai@cuhk.edu.cn

Abstract. In this paper, we present a new mobile sensing scheme to extract spatiotemporal information from citizens' Wi-Fi CL (Connection Log) data, and provide a unified suspicious scoring algorithm to score and detect anomalous Crowd aggregation in heavily populated metropolitan areas. Smart phones could be city's sensors to generate these CL data when their owners having access to Wi-Fi hotspot, meanwhile, wireless network transfer them in real-time back to the datacenter server. Totally, CL dataset includes 900 million sessions over 27 million users connecting to 28 million Wi-Fi hotspots within one month. We formulated Crowd detection problem and we carried out extensive experiments on CL dataset collected from four big cities in China, namely Beijing, Shanghai, Guangzhou, and Shenzhen. The suspicious score algorithm could reflect the density of Crowd, lasting period, and area coverage even with the same density of people. The experiments results are reported based on their suspicious scores. As the most crowded places, airports always get the highest marks, and shopping malls and tourist locations follow them. We believe these results are very useful for smart city safety maintenance or preventing tragedy events, etc.

Keywords: Data mining · Anomaly detection · Mobile sensing

1 Introduction

Mobile sensing [17] enables smart city management solutions [18] across many areas such as urban dynamics mining, public safety, traffic planning, and hazard avoidance. On 2015 New Year's Eve in Shanghai, the light show attracted a large number of people jammed in a small area, which causes 36 people died and 42 injured because Crowd density was underestimated. Thus, we attempt to deploy mobile sensing scheme and alert Crowd aggregation situations like this tragedy in metropolises in this paper.

It is a highly urgent issue to detect Crowd aggregation and evaluate their suspicious level on time, because anomalous people gathering in some specific area might mean some serious events behind [9]. Today, in many developed cities, smart phones with digital positioning devices have been widely used in people' daily life. Because of this,

---

The primary author of this work is a registered student.

X. Liao et al. (Eds.): BigData 2021, CCIS 1496, pp. 251–266, 2022.
https://doi.org/10.1007/978-981-16-9709-8_17

users do not need report their geographical locations on their own initiative, and their cellphone could do this automatically. With these geolocational information [19], we could measure Crowd density and prevent serious events such as riot, traffic accident or natural disaster in large cities.

Many advances in Crowd detection begin from image understanding or scene analysis [3]. However, image and video detection are computationally expensive [4] and hardly to achieve real-time responses. While, depending on Wi-Fi scanner or sniffers [5, 6], mobile phone's connection records can be easily obtained to estimate Crowd density or Crowd flow in a given area. However, RF (Radio-Frequency) technology requires extra infrastructure assisted, and people must carry RF based device, such as mobile phone or RFID tag. The major challenge in social media [7] and web data mining [8] is how to extract the usable information from voluminous data and how to verify the veracity of the information. Because the valuable information is relatively sparse when it comes to measure Crowd density from them in city scale.

Since smartphone could remember the time of connection with some Wi-Fi AP (Access Point), we collect Wi-Fi CL dataset and transmit them back to the server in the real-time if one app could be installed in users' cellphones. This is the mobile sensing scheme (Fig. 1) we explored in this paper for the large scale of data collection.

Besides privacy, transparency, scalability, and ease of deployment [2], there are some other aspects the mobile sensing system need to consider. The user's app and back-side server involved in mobile sensing system should run steadily all the time. And real-time data transmission requires simple data format and low delay network to guarantee. For encouraging more users' participation, discovering and measuring nearby Wi-Fi hotspots could be the incentive aiding users to identify AP with better usage performance such as better download speed or better signal strength. Moreover, algorithm efficiency and accuracy should be considered either.

In this paper, our contributions are as follows:

- We present a unified model to detect Crowd aggregation on Wi-Fi CL dataset, and use suspicious score function [16] to label Crowd. With the help of POI (Point of Interest) dataset, the locations in CL dataset involve both geographical and semantic information.
- It is more practical and realistic to transmit and analyze Wi-Fi data analytics than image, scene, and social media. Meanwhile, collecting data from smart phone is more widely applied and easy employed than installing Wi-Fi scanner or sniffers in advance.
- Besides Wi-Fi source, our Crowd detection model could be applied upon other sensing sources such as GPS (Global Positioning System) [9, 10], CDR (Call Detail Record) [14], SC (Smart Card)[11, 12], GTSM (Geo-Tagged Social Network) [1], and BSS (Bicycle Sharing System) [13] etc.

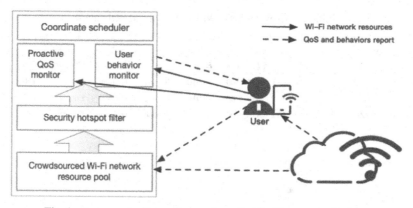

Fig. 1. Framework of crowdsourced app installed in users' cellphone

2 Interpretation of Wi-Fi CL Dataset

The Wi-Fi data are collected from one crowdsourced app (Fig. 1) and it has been downloaded over 360 million times. Totally, this CL dataset includes 900 million sessions of CL over 27 million users connecting to 28 million Wi-Fi hotspots within one month from four big cities of China: Beijing, Shanghai, Guangzhou and Shenzhen. Each Wi-Fi CL record has four features to represent one connection log. Individuals are anonymous with unique guid in our dataset. Date means the time when this guid starts connecting to some AP, and this AP's mac address is denoted as bssid.

Meanwhile, POI dataset offers accurate and detailed geolocation information to each AP, but only one third of APs in CL data have their corresponding POI information. POI could make each AP and users' location explicit, easily understood and located. In detail, POI dataset provides geographic locations (Longitude, Latitude), administrative location in different scales (City, District) and semantic location (POI, Category). Table 1 gives one example to depict user A connecting to AP named THU at 10:00 am, and then user A stays in Holiday Inn at 8:00 pm.

3 Bipartite Graph Representation of Crowd Information

We consider users' visits to some places as bipartite graph with two types of nodes: user and location (Fig. 2). Recent researches such as customer buying goods, viewers grading movies and tweeters posting tweets could be described with bipartite graph. Whereas, CL data make some differences, and different geographical locations have the relationship of geographic distance. Sometimes we need consider several nearby locations as a whole when computing Crowd density. And sometimes we must consider the number of people visited here together with the former time bin, because from our suspicious scoring algorithm, the longer lasting time, the higher suspicious score the Crowd could be labeled.

Table 1. An example for Wi-Fi CL data and POI data.

Wi-Fi CL Data					POI Data				
Date	guid	ssid	bssid	Longitude	Latitude	City	District	Category	POI
10:00	A	THU	11.11.11.11	116.3100	39.9106	Beijing	Haidian	Hotel	THU
20:00	A	Holiday Inn	12.12.12.12	116.3200	39.9107	Beijing	Haidian	Education	Holiday Inn
01:00	B	SZU	22.22.22.22	113.3700	29.91.8	Shezhen	Nanshan	Education	SZU

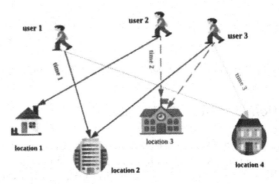

Fig. 2. Different users visit different locations

The edges in Fig. 2 represent visit relationship from user to location. In reality, the number of users is bigger than the number of locations, because different users could visit the same location at the same time. However, as Fig. 2 shows, within one time period $\Delta t = $ time3 - time1, the degree of each user could be bigger than one.

Suspicious score function [16] is based on an assumption of bipartite graph in which someone's visits are randomly distributed across each location. Binary value corresponds to a ERP model [20], where the visits of each location follow Possion distribution $d(l) \sim \Pr(\rho)$. The visits on some location within this time slice can be depicted like the last one in Fig. 3 and ρ can be computed by $\rho = 4/7$. The denser visits on some places, the larger suspicious score will be obtained from our suspicious score algorithm.

4 Mobile Crowd Detection Methods

For proactive response, we aim to deploy mobile Crowd sensing scheme to detect Crowd aggregation situation in real time. When more people appear on the same place, the connections to this place's AP will increase, and the size of Crowd could be estimated by our suspicious score algorithm from density, lasting time and occupation areas in city wide.

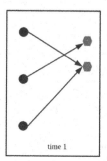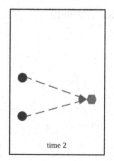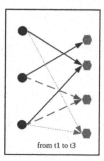

Fig. 3. Interpretate users' visits into bipartite graph

4.1 Symbols and Definitions

For imitating the real-world scene, our anomaly detection method performs once a time on the arriving input data for each time bin. The symbols and definitions about this model are given in Table 2.

Crowd detection method follows two steps for each time bin: 1) Identify the users with unbalanced visits on each location to filter out the initial locations l where Crowds might appear most likely. The location can be one AP, one POI or one grid of geographic coordinates, and these locations can be input for the latter scoring algorithms. 2) Score Crowd at each time slice t. In fact, for each time slice, we only need compute the score from the former time slice to this time slice. If we can obtain the larger score after combining two time slices, we update the score for this location for this time slice.

Time Slice t: Time is partitioned into the continuous time slice t, and our model computes all input once a time slice. Because the time stamp in CL dataset is discrete, the time when each connection started could fit into different time bin.

Time Period Δt: Several continuous time slices are described together as $\Delta t = tj - ti, j > i, i = 1 \ldots n, j = 1 \ldots n$ and Crowd aggregation is considered not only from one time slice, but from the continuous several time slices.

Location l_m: The place where the user visits, and it is the minimal unit in our approach. It could be one AP (m = 1), one POI (m = 2) according to its semantic information or one grid (m = 3) partitioned by the geographical coordinates.

Set A of locations including location l: In each time slice, we aim to find as larger areas as possible with the higher Crowd density, and the locations near to each other should be considered as a whole according to suspicious score function. Set A means theses APs or these grids and |A| = the number of APs or grids.

Crowd: Crowd means a huge amount of people who aggregate on some location l_m with higher density ρ at time slice t, lasting the longer time Δt, and scaling on the larger areas A.

Table 2. Symbols and definitions.

Symbol	Definition
t	*One time slice*
Δt	$\Delta t = tj - ti, j > i, i = 1 \ldots n, j = 1 \ldots n$
l_m	*One location spot (AP: m = 1, POI: m = 2 and grid: m = 3)*
N^t	*Total number of locations at time slice t*
C^t	*Total number of users in time slice t on all locations*
n^t	*Number of units (set A)*
c^t	*Number of users within n^t*
$\overline{\rho}$	*The average density of C^t/N^t*
ρ	*The specific density of c^t/n^t*
A	*Set of locations in Areas of POI or Grid*

4.2 Suspicious Score Function

In this paper, the suspicious score function [16] was explored on Wi-Fi CL dataset to measure the suspiciousness of metropolitan Crowd gathering. These measurements are implemented on each time slice sequentially and continuously.

When mobile sensing scheme collects Wi-Fi CL data from user side, scoring and detecting algorithms in server side consists of three steps for the newly data input at each time slice: 1) Select the most probably locations as initial input for suspicious score function. 2) Update the suspicious score by Time Extension algorithm with the former time slice on each location, and the locations consists of APs, POIs and Grids. 3) Explore Area Scaling algorithm on these Grids to obtain the converged suspicious score with the largest areas. We illustrate these steps in next Sect. 4.3.

Density: density should be computed for each time slice t, because the total number of users C^t changes hourly and daily, the criteria should change as well with density in different time slice. Time period Δt equals to 1 for one time slice, and the overall number of N^t means all locations appeared in our CL dataset within time slice t. We define density function $\overline{\rho} = C^t/N^t$ to describe the average density, and $\rho = c^t/n^t$ to describe Crowd on one specific location l. So

$$\overline{\rho} = C^t/N^t \tag{1}$$

$$\rho = c^t/n^t \tag{2}$$

for each area, $n^t = |A|$.

Suspicious Score Function: For estimating anomalous Crowd, suspicious score function is defined to describe Crowd aggregation on Wi-Fi CL data mathematically, and it is based on Kullback-Leibler divergence as (3) shows:

$$f\left(n^t, c^t, N^t, C^t\right) \approx c^t\left(\log\frac{c^t}{C^t} - 1\right) + C^t\frac{n^t}{N^t} - c^t\log\frac{n^t}{N^t} = n^t\left(\overline{\rho} - \rho + \rho\log\frac{\rho}{\overline{\rho}}\right)$$
$$= n^t D_{kl}(\rho||\overline{\rho})$$
(3)

Time Extension: When each time slice CL data is newly arriving at the server, newer suspicious scores should be calculated with the former time slice together so as to confirm whether this new Crowd could get the larger mark upon the longer time period. Consequently, maximal value is updated and kept for this Crowd of time slice t on this location l.

Area Scaling: When studying Crowd gathering on some area, we should compute the place not only solely, but also the areas around location l. Crowd can be measured on several locations with total visits to obtain the larger suspicious score from (3).

Crowd Scoring and Anomaly Detecting: Our final optimal objective is to implement Time Extension algorithm to update the score for each AP, POI and grid at each time slice, and then to implement Area Scaling algorithm to locate maximum area with highest suspicious score. For each time slice, suspicious Crowds is scored by the function of (3). Meanwhile, if we combine the continuous time slices to score one Crowd, the score increases, which means the Crowd is more suspicious. If we consider the conjoined grids together, getting the higher score expresses Crowd is more suspicious.

Our anomalous Crowd definition follows the criteria of definition of suspicious score function: Density, Size and Contrast [16]. Density in our Crowd detection algorithm means More Users (Fig. 4a) appeared on the same range of areas at time $t2$ but with the higher density compared with time $t1$. The Crowd density keeps the same, but on other locations Less users (Fig. 4b) appeared, which means this Crowd is more suspicious than the former time.

Metropolitan Wi-Fi CL dataset has particular advantage to explore Contrast rule, because we could study the Crowd from all citizens in the whole city to compute average density $\overline{\rho}$. If the density of users maintains the same, but spread on the larger area (Fig. 4c) at the time $t2$ or lasting the longer time (Fig. 4d), it is more suspicious at the time $t2$ compared with time $t1$.

4.3 Location Selection Algorithm

This scheme performs the scoring and detecting process once when the input data is arriving at each time slice, and evaluate whether it is suspicious that c^t people visit n^t locations for Δt time period. Profiling users' visit frequencies on different spots is the fast way to decide where anomalous Crowd emerges most likely.

In Algorithms 1, the first step is to select the location l where anomalous Crowds emerge most likely at time slice t by measuring users with unbalanced visits on each location. Imagine that one sport match or entertainment activities attract many audiences to watch, but some of them may not hear of or enter these spots so often in their early daily life. Thus, we could filter these users with serious unequally visit frequencies and

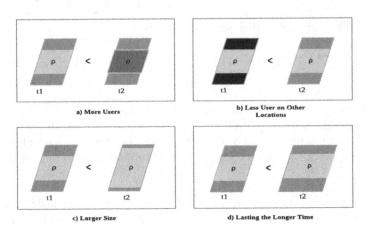

Fig. 4. User's density variation in the Crowd aggregation process

rank these locations visited. These locations will be the initial inputs for the latter Crowd detection calculation.

Algorithm 1: Location Selecting lm m = 1, 2, 3

1: **INPUT:** CL U^t at time slice t on location l_m, σ, ε, $\Gamma_{u(t-1)}$

2: **OUTPUT:** The unbalanced tuples $< u, t, l_1 >$ at time t

3: Construct user trajectories for each user $\Gamma_{u(t-1)}$

4: **for** each connection log U^t **do:**

5:     Extract feature frequency vector for each user

6:         **if** l_1 in $\Gamma_{u(t-1)}$ **then:**

7:             Frequency Vm+= 1 m=1,...,n

8:         **else:**

9:             Frequency Vm = 1

10:     Count Z-score Z^t_{vm} for this tuple (u, t, l_1)

11:     Update user trajectories $\Gamma_{ut} \leftarrow \cup U^t$

12: **end for**

13: **if** $|Z^t_{vm}|$ >1 **then:**

14:     filter out tuple (u, t, l_1) with unbalanced visits

15: Aggregating and ranking the number of users on each l_1

16: **return** Locations lm with t, number of users

We assume individuals appearing in the different places with the frequencies follow Gaussian distribution, and they visit some places more frequently, but visit the new places relatively rare. We use thresholds $\varepsilon = \sigma$ and $\varepsilon = 2\sigma$ to measure and filter these users with unequal frequency seriously [15] and the tuple $<$ user, time, geolocation $>$ will be the input for next detection process, while, paper [16] starts algorithm from random seed, resulting in the longer computation time.

$$Z - score = \frac{(x - \mu)}{\varepsilon} \tag{4}$$

The more suspicious locations will be found to start next detection algorithm, if we set the lower value threshold ε, which costs the longer running time but with the higher accuracy. If your application needs quick response results for suspicious Crowd detection, the higher threshold set can satisfy it.

4.4 Suspicious Scoring Algorithm

At each time slice t, we count total number of citizens C^t and the number of locations N^t. Then we consider the previous time together to measure Crowd over the recent two time slices. That means, we only need consider current time slice with the former time slice, the mark is ensured to maximal value at each time slice.

The score S_m^t is computed by relative entropy in (3), which uses relative density within this location compared with the density over the general location tensor. When exploring Time Extension and Area Scaling algorithm, n^t means the time expansion this Crowd lasted or the number of grids this Crowd covered. Meanwhile, these locations should be next to each other, no matter time or location.

Algorithm 2: Suspicious Scoring (l_m, t)   m = 1, 2, 3

1: **INPUT:** CL at time slice t, Score list S_m^{t-1} of time slice $t - 1$

2: **OUTPUT:** Score list S_m^t with highest f aggregated by this time t

3: Read score list S_m^{t-1} of time slice $t - 1$

4: Read CL data and check whether some visits appeared

5: **if location l_m is visited by users then**

6:      $N^t = \cup\ l_m^t$

7:      $C^t =$ total users in this time slice

8:      $\bar{p}^t = C^t / N^t$

9:      $S_m^t \leftarrow f(n^t + n^{t-1}, c^t + c^{t-1}, N^t + N^{t-1}, C^t + C^{t-1})$,

10: **for each location l_m in S_m^t do**

11:      **Compute** $\tilde{f}(n^t + n^{t-1}, c^t + c^{t-1}, N^t + N^{t-1}, C^t + C^{t-1})$,

12:      **if** $\tilde{f}(n^t + n^{t-1}, c^t + c^{t-1}, N^t + N^{t-1}, C^t + C^{t-1}) > f(n^t + n^{t-1}, c^t + c^{t-1}, N^t + N^{t-1}, C^t + C^{t-1})$,

13:      **then**

14:           Update S_m^t

15:      $S_m^t \leftarrow$ all locations at current time t with the highest $f(n^t, c^t)$

16: **end for**

17: **return** S_m^t

For each location l_m, we compute the suspicious score at time t, then implement Time Extension Algorithm 2 with the former time slice to test whether we could get a higher score. The Crowd with the same density but lasting longer period has the higher suspicious score. In fact, at each time slice, we only compute two successive suspicious scores. If we can obtain the larger score after combining them, we update the score for this time slice t and calculate the average density for the locations within these two time slices.

We apply Time Extension algorithm on AP, POI and grid, but apply Area Scaling algorithm only on grid. If citizens only concern the Crowd on POI, they can get the information they want by this step. If the administrative sectors need to know the precise geographical range, they could calculate the final suspicious score on grid. From each suspicious grid l_3, the nearby grids should be considered together to converge to the maximal value.

5   Experiments and Results

Because we could only obtain users' cellphone connection to some AP when having access to it, CL data is inconsecutive and incomplete. The number of users who appeared every day (continuous 30 days) is 461094, and the total users in our CL dataset is 27425217. The total number of POIs is 4144950, which accounts for one third of APs of CL dataset.

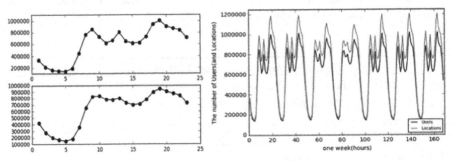

Fig. 5. Users' CL distribution by hour over one weekday in four metropolises

For imitating real-world detection process, we aggregate the number of users in each hour of one day and depict a line chart over one week (the right one in Fig. 5). The results imply the peak visiting time for each day period and periodical pattern on weekday and weekend. The third and fourth series of crests and troughs are corresponding to the weekend.

The left drawing of Fig. 5 shows the difference of number of users appeared between weekday and weekend. The peak value of weekend is lower than weekday and the troughs in weekend is higher than the weekday. Maybe most of citizens do not go to work on weekend, but they enjoy staying outside so that the peak number is declining on weekend. The higher troughs in weekend mean the relatively more people connecting to APs because they choose staying at home not office. The number of visits is higher than the number of locations after we aggregate users' visits into one hour, and this ensures overall density (2) for each time slice always is lower than one.

5.1 Dataset Measurement

Before detection process starts, we discretize time of day into time bins to imitate the real-time input. Time slice should be with reasonable length period to fit dataset well, and we set one hour for our Wi-Fi CL dataset and differentiate weekday from weekend. If time slice is set too short, the data in bipartite graph is too sparse, and if time bin is too long, users' transition among different locations will be vague and Crowd aggregation process will not be obvious.

In this paper, the first 10 days data was profiled for initial locations selection as Algorithm 1. When someone appeared in some historical place with the small frequency or visit a new place, that place was thought as unbalanced visits. We use Z-score to filter out the users with unequal frequency seriously and then to aggregate citizens' visits on each location. These locations are the most suspicious and will be the start point for latter Crowd detection process, because mining all locations in one time execution is not realistic.

5.2 Experiments Setting and Results

We compared the results on AP, POI and grid for the one following week, and we found the detection process on POI can always get highest suspicious score, which shows semantic description is most effective way for Crowd scoring problem.

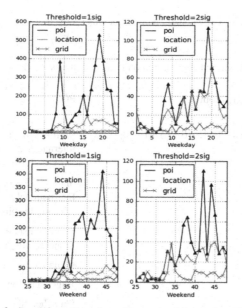

Fig. 6. Suspicious Crowd scoring on weekday and weekend

As shown in Fig. 6, POI always receives the highest suspicious score, however, the Crowd on AP or the grid have the relative lower score. For higher score of POI, maybe because several nearby APs belong to one same POI. As a result, more users on one

POI will get larger density value from (2). The lower score on grid maybe because we compute the density from (2) with more locations involved as denominator. Besides, the initial setting with different threshold seriously affects the results for both weekday and weekend. Since threshold $= 2\sigma$ might be too strict to choose enough guide user to start detection process, the smaller threshold could be set if the application is not urgent.

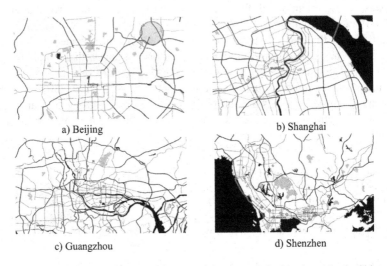

a) Beijing   b) Shanghai

c) Guangzhou   d) Shenzhen

Fig. 7. Anomalous Crowd spots with suspicious scores in 4 major cities in China

Table 3. Crowd aggregation on POIs and their suspicious scores.

Week	Time of day (hours)	POI	Suspicious score
Weekday	8,9,10,12,13,14,15,16,17,18,19,20,21,22	Beijing Capital International Airport, Terminal 3	530.245336
Weekday	18,19,20	Shanghai Pudong International Airport, Terminal 2	117.492629
Weekday	16	Lingang Estate Manufacture Park	90.961426
Weekday	19,20	Fuqiao Mansion	76.769077
Weekday	20,21	Jingu Mansion	73.495338
Weekday	20	Shenzhen Shahe Hospital	73.495338

(*continued*)

Table 3. (*continued*)

Week	Time of day (hours)	POI	Suspicious score
Weekday	18	NanJingHaoTing Residence Community	69.77546
Weekday	19	Qianhai Hotel	69.565149
Weekday	20	Renrenhao Department Store	67.042633
Weekday	13	Shenzhen Wuzhou Integrated traditional Chinese and Western Medicine Hospital	66.365717
Weekday	18	Guanshanyue Zone 2 Residence Community	60.294093
Weekday	19	Shenzhen Renai Hospital	60.104992
Weekend	32,34,37,38,39,40,41,42,43,45,46,47,48	Beijing Capital International Airport, Terminal 3	411.480108
Weekend	45	Guohuikang Shopping Mall	118.064844
Weekend	45,47	Jingu Mansion	63.783428
Weekend	44	Dongsanqi Hotel	63.599303
Weekend	45	Fuli Bitaowan Residence Community	60.644001
Weekend	42,43,44,45,47	Shanghai Pudong International Airport,Terminal 2	60.466508
Weekend	47,48	Wanminle Department Store(Chanzhen Road)	49.690590
Weekend	47	Shenzhen Fenghuang Hostpital	45.997430

(*continued*)

Table 3. (*continued*)

Week	Time of day (hours)	POI	Suspicious score
Weekend	46	NanJingHaoTing Residence Community	45.717967
Weekend	43	Yundu Fashion Trade City	42.277047

We carried out extensive experiments on Wi-Fi dataset collected from four big cities in China, namely Beijing, Shanghai, Guangzhou, and Shenzhen. The red circles in Fig. 7 are detection results of anomalous Crowds, and their sizes are drawn based on their suspicious scores.

We listed most suspicious Crowds appeared in Table 3 with highest suspicious scores with respect to POIs and it is obvious that airports always are the most crowded places, and shopping malls and tourist locations follow them. It is worth mentioning why Shanghai's the oriental pearl TV tower and Guangzhou cannon tower are so crowded from our results. Maybe it is related to the characteristics of Wi-Fi infrastructure. They are both indoor tourist places and guests are likely to stay inside for a long period time for relaxation, which contributes to Wi-Fi CLs generated more.

Table 4. Activities list for anomalous Crowd aggregation.

Activity name	Time (2015)	Location of activity	Metropolis
NPC & CPPCC	March 5–15, March 3–13		Beijing
Spring Festival travel rush	February 4 to March 15	Railway station Airport	Beijing, Shanghai, Guangzhou, Shenzhen
Entertainment activities	March 25 March 28	Shenzhen Bay Sport Center (19551)	Shenzhen
Sport activities	CHINA LEAGUE	Shenzhen Gymnasium	Shenzhen
Weather impact	March 15–20 Damp season		Shenzhen
Festival accidents	April 4–6 Qingming Festival		Beijing, Shanghai, Guangzhou, Shenzhen

Besides, the marks on weekdays are larger than on weekends, even for the same spot for example, Beijing Capital International Airport, Terminal 3, which means, the relatively density on other locations are lower on weekday from the formular (3).

5.3 Validation of Results

Some activities have been collected from news website and Table 4 will be validated for the results of our experiments.

Especially, we expect that our results can validate the entertainment activities on Shenzhen Bay Sport Center on March 25, whereas, this location exists in our detecting results but with the small suspicious score. In our opinion, maybe because the audiences are so concentrating on the wonderful entertainment party that they have no interests on connecting to Wi-Fi.

6 Conclusion

In summary, we present an anomalous Crowd detection scheme to discover potential social hazards with excessive people jammed in small areas. We considered data collection work from mobile users and data mining in back server. Both mobile sensing and suspicious scoring methods are proven effective in building the safe, hazard-free and people friendly smart cities.

Since Wi-Fi infrastructure has much stronger signals inside the building, the suspicious scoring approach on Wi-Fi CL dataset become the effective way in detecting indoor anomalous Crowds Aggregation. For wide range of outdoor areas, the connected Cloud is required to build the more appropriate protection scheme and they are still open problems for further research.

References

1. Yuan, Q., Cong, G., Sun, A.: Graph-based point-of-interest recommendation with geographical and temporal influences. In: Proceedings of the 23rd ACM International Conference on Information and Knowledge Management, pp. 659–668 (2014)
2. Draghici, A., Van Steen, M.: A survey of techniques for automatically sensing the behavior of a crowd. ACM Comput. Surv. **51**(1), 1–40 (2018)
3. Sharma, D., Bhondekar, A.P., Shukla, A.K., Ghanshyam, C.: A review on technological advancements in crowd management. J. Ambient. Intell. Humaniz. Comput. **9**(3), 485–495 (2016). https://doi.org/10.1007/s12652-016-0432-x
4. Li, T., Chang, H., Wang, M., Ni, B., Hong, R., Yan, S.: Crowded scene analysis: a survey. IEEE Trans. Circuits Syst. Video Technol. **25**(3), 367–386 (2015)
5. Chilipirea, C., Petre, A.C., Dobre, C., Van Steen, M.: Presumably simple: monitoring crowds using WiFi. In: Proceedings of the IEEE International Conference on Mobile Data Management, vol. 1, pp. 220–225 (2016)
6. Basalamah, A.: Crowd mobility analysis using WiFi sniffers. Int. J. Adv. Comput. Sci. Appl. **7**(12), 374–378 (2016)
7. Sakaki, T., Okazaki, M., Matsuo, Y.: Earthquake shakes Twitter users: real-time event detection by social sensors. In: International World Wide Web Conference Committee, pp. 851–860 (2010)

8. Konishi, T., Maruyama, M., Tsubouchi, K., Shimosaka, M.: CityProphet: city-scale irregularity prediction using transit app logs. In: Proceedings of the 2016 ACM International Joint Conference on Pervasive and Ubiquitous Computing, pp. 752–757 (2016)

9. Fan, Z., Song, X., Shibasaki, R., Adachi, R.: CityMomentum: an online approach for crowd behavior prediction at a citywide level. In: Proceedings of the 2015 ACM International Joint Conference on Pervasive and Ubiquitous Computing, pp. 559–569 (2015)

10. Witayangkurn, A., Horanont, T., Sekimoto, Y., Shibasaki, R.: Anomalous event detection on large-scale GPS data from mobile phones using hidden Markov model and cloud platform. In: Proceedings of the 2013 ACM International Joint Conference on Pervasive and Ubiquitous Computing, pp. 1219–1228 (2013)

11. Huang, Z., Wang, P., Zhang, F., Gao, J., Schich, M.: A mobility network approach to identify and anticipate large crowd gatherings. Transp. Res. B Methodol. **114**, 147–170 (2018)

12. El Mahrsi, M.K., Come, E., Oukhellou, L., Verleysen, M.: Clustering smart card data for urban mobility analysis. IEEE Trans. Intell. Transp. Syst. **18**(3), 712–728 (2017)

13. Zhang, J., Pan, X., Li, M., Yu, P.S.: Bicycle-sharing system analysis and trip prediction. In: Proceedings of the IEEE International Conference on Mobile Data Management, pp. 174–179 (2016)

14. Ma, Y., Lin, T., Cao, Z., Li, C., Wang, F., Chen, W.: Mobility viewer: an Eulerian approach for studying urban crowd flow. IEEE Trans. Intell. Transp. Syst. **17**(9), 2627–2636 (2016)

15. Le, V.D., Scholten, H., Paul, H.: FLEAD: online frequency likelihood estimation anomaly detection for mobile sensing. In: ACM International Joint Conference on Pervasive and Ubiquitous Computing, pp. 1159–1166 (2013)

16. Jiang, M., Beutel, A., Cui, P., Hooi, B., Yang, S., Faloutsos, C.: Spotting suspicious behaviors in multimodal data: a general metric and algorithms. IEEE Trans. Knowl. Data Eng. **28**(8), 2187–2200 (2016)

17. Lane, N., Miluzzo, E., Hong, L., Peebles, D., Choudhury, T., Campbell, A.: A survey of mobile phone sensing. IEEE Commun. Magaz. **48**(9), 140–150 (2010)

18. Aggarwal, A., Toshniwal, D.: Data mining techniques for smart mobility—a survey. In: Sa, P.K., Bakshi, S., Hatzilygeroudis, I.K., Sahoo, M.N. (eds.) Recent Findings in Intelligent Computing Techniques. AISC, vol. 709, pp. 239–249. Springer, Singapore (2018). https://doi.org/10.1007/978-981-10-8633-5_25

19. Xu, G., Gao, S., Daneshmand, M., Wang, C., Liu, Y.: A survey for mobility big data analytics for geolocation prediction. IEEE Wirel. Commun. **24**(1), 111–119 (2017)

20. Newman, M.E.J., Watts, D.J., Strogatz, S.H.: Random graph models of social networks. Self-Organ. Complex. Phys. Biol. Soc. Sci. **99**, 2566–2572 (2002)

Research on User Identity Authentication Based on Online Behavior Similarity

Yong Li, Zhongying Zhang[✉], Jingpeng Wu, and Qiang Zhang

College of Computer Science and Engineering, Northwest Normal University, Lanzhou, China

Abstract. Network security is not only related to social stability, but also an important guarantee for the digital intelligent society. However, in recent years, problems such as user account theft and information leakage have occurred frequently, which has greatly affected the security of users' personal information and the public interest. Based on the massive user click behavior data and graph embedding technology, this paper proposes the Graph2Usersim (Gp2-US) to analyze the similarity between the user's historical behavior characteristics and online behavior characteristics to accurately identify the user's identity, and then distinguish the user's abnormal online behavior. To be specific, firstly, based on the empirical click-stream data, the user's historical behavior and online behavior are modeled as two attention flow networks respectively. Secondly, based on the Graph2vec method and drawing on the theory of molecular fingerprinting, the nodes of the attention flow network are characterized as atoms, and edges are characterized as chemical bonds, and the network is simplified using the structural features of compounds to generate feature vectors that can identify users' historical and online behaviors. Finally, the behavior similarity algorithm Gp2-US proposed in this paper is used to accurately identify users. A large number of experiments show that the accuracy of the algorithm Gp2-US is much higher than that of the traditional algorithm. Based on 10 days of historical user behavior data, it can accurately identify its identity characteristics and accurately determine abnormal account behavior. The research conclusions of this paper have important theoretical value and practical significance in inferring abnormal user behaviors and monitoring public opinion.

Keywords: Attention flow network · Graph embedding · Similarity measurement · Feature vector · Identity authentication

1 Introduction

With the rapid development of the mobile Internet and the popularization of social networking technologies such as Weibo and WeChat, virtual space has become a brand-new living space for human beings. According to the 47th Statistical Report on Internet Development in China, as of December 2020, 38.3% of Internet users have encountered network security problems in the past six months, among which personal information leakage and account password theft accounted for more than 30%. Timely monitoring of abnormal online behaviors of users has become an important means to protect public

© Springer Nature Singapore Pte Ltd. 2022
X. Liao et al. (Eds.): BigData 2021, CCIS 1496, pp. 267–280, 2022.
https://doi.org/10.1007/978-981-16-9709-8_18

information security. Studying online behaviors of users can effectively identify account abnormalities, thereby reducing network security risks caused by anonymous use, and can also provide effective means for public opinion monitoring [1].

The online click behavior of users in the virtual space will leave a corresponding digital footprint. By analyzing the similarity between user's historical behavior and online behavior, it can accurately identify whether the user account is stolen. The traditional similarity calculation method focuses on the overall difference between users. This article knows that there are few studies on the behavioral similarity of individual users [2]. Inspired by the concept of molecular fingerprints and the similarity of compounds, based on the concept of molecular fingerprints [3], this paper constructs user historical behavior and online behavior into two attention flow networks, abstracts the network as feature vectors, and analyzes the similarity of feature vectors so as to accurately identify the user's identity.

As an important branch of network science, attention flow network has important theoretical significance and application value to study and analyze network structure characteristics. Based on the modeling method of network science, based on the Graph2vec model and molecular fingerprint theory, this paper characterizes the attention flow network as a compound structure, abstractly extracts the user's online behavior characteristics, and proposes the user behavior similarity algorithm Gp2-US, which analyzes the user's behavior characteristics to distinguish the similarities and differences of their interests, and at the same time fix the problem of inconsistent metrics that may exist among users. Therefore, the similarity measurement Gp2-US algorithm proposed in this paper can more effectively and standardly measure the similarity of individual users' online behaviors, and achieve precise identification of user identities. The contributions of this article are as follows:

- Based on the empirical data of users' online behavior, extract the click stream sequence and construct the attention stream network scientifically.
- Drawing on the concept of molecular fingerprints, abstracting the attention flow network structure to extract user behavior characteristics, and presenting the Gp2-US algorithm to measure the online behavior similarity of individual users.
- Experiments show that the Gp2-US algorithm proposed in this paper verifies that the online behavior similarity of individual users is as high as 95%, and there are differences between different individuals. The algorithm in this paper can be used to identify user identities and provide a method that can be used as effective means of public opinion monitoring and account abnormality detection. The objectives of the work and provide an adequate background, avoiding a detailed literature survey or a summary of the results.

2   Related Work

2.1   Attention Flow Network

Attention flow network is an emerging branch of network science. Attention flow refers to the sequence of attention behaviors generated when users click on a series of information sources. Attention flow network means that the user clicks and jumps between different sources of information. Directional weighted graph, where the information source is a node, and the user's attention degree jumps between different information sources form a directed edge. The weighted directed complex network is constructed based on the scientific method of the network. This network is produced by the collective cooperation of humans, and provides a powerful quantitative analysis and prediction tool for studying the interaction law of the ternary space of man, machine and object.

In 2012, Weng and others studied the distribution of human collective attention on different Internet resources based on social media data and found that different cultural genes (Meme) compete for limited human attention [4]. In 2015, Li regarded the influence of the site as metabolism, and the group attention flow of online users as the energy of the site. The attention flow network established based on empirical data studied the attention flow of group users between different sites. Distribution and flow [5]. In 2015, Shi and others studied the decentralized flow structure of the attention flow network. Based on the browsing behavior of large-scale network users, a flow network was formed, where nodes are websites and edges are formed by users jumping between sites. The influence of site i is represented by Ci. It is found that Ci is linearly related to the traffic Ai of site i, and there is a relationship between $Ci \sim Ai\gamma$ ($\gamma < 1$) between the two [6]. In 2017, Li used collective users as the research object in the research of attention flow network, and found a number of important universal laws, such as allometric scaling law and dissipation law [7].

2.2 User Behavior Similarity

Previous studies have shown that users' daily online behavior has certain regularity, and users' daily online behavior can be studied through similarity. In 2015, Tang proposed an individual user behavior model with user similarity based on microblog data and combined with multi-task learning, and predicted individual forwarding behavior, and studied the relationship between users by considering social similarity [8]. In 2018, Andrea Esuni introduced embedding into the similarity of user movement behavior and proposed the TRAJ2User model to learn user embedding, which could better capture user similarity [9]. In 2019, Zhong measured user similarity through the check-in data of users' mobile devices, and proposed a multicenter clustering algorithm, which used location and time context to measure user similarity [10]. In 2020, M. S. Bhuvaneswari identified the browsing behavior of the user by calculating the similarity between the page sets belonging to the user. A new index for measuring user similarity is proposed [11]. In 2020, Qian using online consumer behavior data and based on the optimized definition of online consumer behavior sequence, can effectively calculate the sequence similarity, so as to describe online consumer behavior more comprehensively [12].

However, most studies focus on user groups and need to consider the connections between users. Few studies analyze the daily online behavior of individuals from the perspective of individual users. Starting from individual users, this paper proposes a Graph2vec based user behavior similarity Gp2-US algorithm that can be used for account anomaly detection. Existing studies have proposed methods for individual research in network security. For example, in 2019, Zhuo analyzed the network access behavior of users by analyzing the DNS logs of campus networks, and established a behavior fingerprint model for each user. The fingerprints of different users at different times or even the same user can be used to determine whether the user's access is abnormal or safe, and whether it is infected with malicious code [13]. The research of early scholars provides a theoretical basis for this article.

3 Model Construction

3.1 Building an Attention Flow Network

In this paper, a directed weighted graph is used to represent users' online click behaviors, Gs = {$G_{U1}, G_{U2}, ..., G_{Un}$} so as to construct an attention flow network of n users. The attention flow network of the individual user U1 is represented as $G_{Ui} = (V_{Ui}, E_{Ui}, T_{Ui}, F_{Ui})$, which V_{Ui} represents the collection of the click processes of the user U1, E_{Ui} represents the dynamic changes of the user U1 between the click processes, and T_{Ui} represents the residence time of the user U1 on each click process. F_{Ui} indicates the weight of the edge E_{Ui}, that is, the click jump frequency of the user U1 between the two processes. The attention flow network of user U1 is shown in Fig. 1:

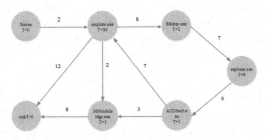

Fig. 1. Schematic diagram of user U1 attention flow network

3.2 Molecular Fingerprint

In the study of compound similarity, the characteristics of atoms and bonds are extracted from the molecular structure diagram based on the graph convolution method. The bonds between atoms and atoms form the nodes and edges of the graph respectively, and the distribution of the graph is used to characterize the molecular structure, thereby Instead of fingerprint descriptors in traditional machine learning [14, 15]. Because the molecular structure is very complicated, it is difficult to analyze the similarity between compounds based on the graph model. Molecular fingerprinting is the most common method for abstracting and simplifying the molecular structure. The core idea is to encode the molecule as a series of bit strings [16]. In this paper, molecular fingerprints are introduced into the attention flow network, and the constructed individual user attention flow network structure is abstracted into a compound structure for simplification. The nodes in the network are represented by atoms, and the connections between nodes in the network are represented by chemical bonds. Abstractly generate feature vectors of individual users to characterize the online behavior of individual users. During the user's activity on his computing device, his online behavior similarity can be used to identify the user and detect account abnormalities in time.

3.3 Graph Embedding

Graph embedding [17] aims to represent graphs as low-dimensional vectors while preserving graph structure. It combines graph analysis [18] and graph representation learning [19], and focuses on low-dimensional representation learning of graphs. Set up a graph G = (V, E), where nodes are represented v ∈ V and edges are represented e ∈ E.G correlation with node type mapping function $f_v : V \rightarrow T^v$ and edge type mapping function $f_e : E \rightarrow T^e$. T^v and T^e respectively represent the set of node type and edge type. Each node $v_i \in V$ belongs to a specific type, $ie(v_i) \in T^v$. Similarly, for $e_{ij} \in E, f_e(e_{ij}) \in T^e$. Based on the above definition of graph, graph embedding is a mapping $f : v_i \rightarrow y_i \in Rd\forall i \in [n]$ so that $d|V|$ [20, 21]. Specifically, graph embedding transforms the graph into a low-dimensional space that retains the graph information. By expressing the graph as a low-dimensional vector (or a set of), it can be calculated efficiently.

3.4 Online Behavior Similarity Model of Individual Users

The online behavior similarity model of individual users constructs a click stream sequence based on the original data source, and then performs segmentation processing on this sequence, constructs an attention stream network in the form of daily divided data, and analyzes the attention stream network based on the concept of molecular fingerprints combined with graph embedding technology simplify and abstract, generate feature vectors, and compare the cosine similarity to finally obtain the similarity curve of individual users' daily online behaviors. The overall framework of the model is shown in Fig. 2:

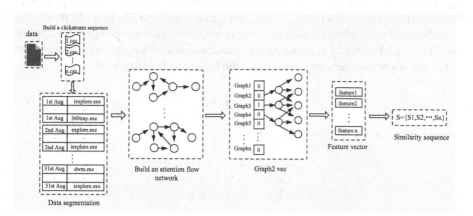

Fig. 2. Framework diagram of the overall idea of the online behavior similarity model of individual users

Based on the user online behavior data provided by CNNIC, this paper firstly preprocessed the data, extracted the timestamp and the corresponding click information source, and generated the click stream sequence. Secondly, an individual user attention flow network is constructed based on network scientific modeling. A single information source is represented as a node, and the jump between information sources is represented as an edge. The residence time of each information source is the weight of nodes, and the jump frequency between information sources is the weight of the edge. The modeling algorithm of attention flow network is as follows:

Algorithm 1: Attention flow network modeling algorithm

input: User online click behavior txt file T={T1,T2,...,Tn }

output: User attention flow network Gs={G1,G2,...,Gn }

---

1. Initialization Gs=list
2. Compose the Tn file of each user's online behavior G = digraph
3.   Tn←(raw of C1)
4.   G←(source,sink,C1,edge)
5.   Tn←(raw of C2)
6.   If Residence time difference>=30min:
7.   G←(sink,edge)
8.   else is G.hasNode
9.   update weight←same
10.   otherwise，G←(edge) and update weight
11. repeat 5-10，Add G to Gs
12. Return Gs

In this paper, feature extraction is based on Graph2vec model, and the substructure in the compound is used as the basic embedded unit to obtain the final cembedded form of the molecule. The Graph2vec [23] model is similar to Doc2vec [24], [25]. Given a set of documents $D = \{d_1, d_2, ..., d_n\}$ and a sequence of words $d_i \in D$ sampled from the documents $(d_i) = \{w_1, w_2, ..., w_{li}\}$, skip-gram learns the file $d_i \in D$ sum is the δ-dimensional embedding of each word w_j sampled from the sample $c(d_i)$, namely the sum. The model works by considering the occurrence of words $w_j \in c(d_i)$ in the context of the document and attempts to maximize the following log likelihood:

$$\sum_{j=1}^{l_i} \log Pr\left(w_j|d_i\right) \tag{1}$$

Among them, the probability is defined as,

$$\frac{exp\left(\vec{d} \cdot \vec{w_j}\right)}{\sum_{w \in V} exp\left(\vec{d} \cdot \vec{w}\right)} \tag{2}$$

Where V is the set of all words in all documents in D. Similarly, in Graph2vec, a graph is similar to a document composed of root subgraphs, and the document embedding model is extended to learn graph embedding. The maximum probability that a subgraph appears in the graph is

$$J(\Phi) = -\log Pr\left(sg_n^{(d)}|\Phi(G)\right) \tag{3}$$

By comparing the probability of the appearance of subgraphs, using skip-gram to learn vertex embedding, the graph is transformed into a low-dimensional matrix feature representation. Based on the obtained feature vector, the similarity measurement of the online behavior of individual users is carried out. The cosine of the angle in geometry can be used to measure the difference between two vectors in direction. Machine learning borrows this concept to measure the difference between sample vectors. Cosine similarity uses the cosine value of the angle between two vectors in a low-dimensional space to measure the difference between two individuals. The closer the cosine value is to 1, the closer the angle is to 0 °, that is, the more similar the two vectors are. The formula for calculating the similarity of n-dimensional variables is as follows:

$$\cos \theta = \frac{\sum_{i=1}^{n}(A_i \times B_i)}{\sqrt{\sum_{i=1}^{n}(A_i)^2} \times \sqrt{\sum_{i=1}^{n}(B_i)^2}} = \frac{A \cdot B}{|A| \times |B|} \tag{4}$$

The Gp2-US algorithm of online behavior similarity of individual users is as follows:

Algorithm 2: Gp2-US algorithm of online behavior similarity of individual users

input: User's personal attention flow network G={G1,G2,...,Gn }, each figure represents Gi=(Vi,Ei,Ti,Fi), user eigenvector matrixΦ

output: User's personal online behavior similarity sequence S={S1,S2,...,Sn }

1. $\Phi = \emptyset$
2. SHUFFLE all graph nodes in G mean φ
3.   for n in Ni do
4.   for d=0 to D do:
5. $sgn^{(d)} := GETWLSUBGRAPH(n, G_i, d)$
6. $J(\Phi) = -\log Pr\left(sg_n^{(d)}|\Phi(G)\right)$
7. update Φ with stochastic gradient descent
8. S=list[]
9. i=0
10. while i+1<n:
11.   add the value of Cosine Similarity of Φ[i] and Φ[i+1] to S
12.   i=i+1
13. return S

---

4 Experimental Evaluation

4.1 Experimental Data

The experimental data set is online user behavior log data provided by China Internet Network Information Center (CNNIC). The data elements extracted in the data set include the information source clicked by each user and the click time corresponding to each information source, and the click time is recorded in a standard time format. For the convenience of analysis, about 150 million data records were randomly selected from 1000 sample users in one month based on the average distribution of 6 social attributes (gender, age, education, region, income, and occupation).

Using the data of 1,000 users for one month (31 days) as the basic data of the experiment, it is divided according to the click time corresponding to each information source to generate daily click stream data. The generated single-day clickstream data is sequentially superimposed, and the data is divided into the previous 1 day, the previous 2 days the previous 30 days, and the previous 31 days, in the form of an arithmetic series. The data processing process is shown in Fig. 3.

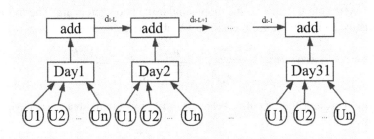

Fig. 3. Data processing diagram

Among them, add represents the function of superimposing single-day clickstream data, and d_{t-1} represents the output of the previous function add. Specifically, the single-day click stream data division and the superimposed day click stream data division of a user are shown in Table 1 and Table 2, respectively:

Table 1. A user's single-day clickstream data partition table.

Time	Source	Time	Source	...	Time	Source
8/1 12:06	['iexplore.exe']	8/2 4:31	['explorer.exe']	...	8/31 4:28	['dwm.exe']
...	...	...	...	...	...	...
8/1 12:55	['360tray.exe']	8/2 7:22	['iexplore.exe']	...	8/31 5:49	['iexplore.exe']

Table 2. A user superimposed daily click stream data partition table.

Time	Source	Time	Source	...	Time	Source
8/1 12:06	['iexplore.exe']	8/1 12:06	['iexplore.exe']	...	8/1 12:06	['iexplore.exe']
...	...	...	...	...	...	...
8/1 12:55	['360tray.exe']	8/2 7:22	['iexplore.exe']	...	8/31 5:49	['iexplore.exe']

4.2   Experiment Analysis

Similarity Analysis of Individual Users' Online Behaviors

For individual users, the attention flow network is constructed in the form of data division in Table 2, and abstracted to obtain 31 feature vectors. The similarity of the feature vectors corresponding to the historical behaviors and online behaviors of the users was compared one by one. In order to facilitate the observation of the curve changes of the results, 6 users were randomly selected. The online behavior similarity of individual users is shown in Fig. 4, for users of different orders of magnitude. The average similarity of online behavior is shown in Fig. 5.

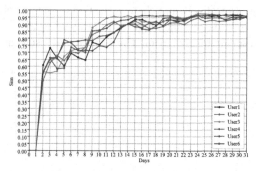

Fig. 4. Comparison of the similarity between individual user's historical behavior and online behavior

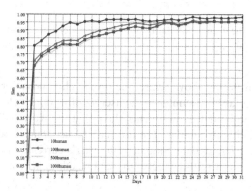

Fig. 5. Comparison of the average similarity between historical behaviors and online behaviors of users of different magnitudes

As can be seen from the above figure, the online behavior similarity trend for different individual users is the same. As the number of days is superimposed, for the Gp2-US algorithm proposed in this paper, the online click behavior similarity of individual users gradually increases until it shows a stable trend. The similarity is as high as 95%. When a user's behavior fluctuates abnormally, it can be judged by the user's online behavior similarity curve. In addition, for users of different orders of magnitude, the average similarity curve of user online behavior has no large-scale fluctuations and the growth trend is roughly the same.

Analysis of Online Behavior Similarity of Individual Users in Different Time Periods

According to the experimental results in Fig. 5, the online clicking behavior of an individual user in the first 24 days can accurately describe the user's online clicking behavior in that month. Therefore, this paper continues to investigate whether users can be identified with less historical user behavior data. Data also using the form in Table 2, the history of n days before the user behavior and online behavior separate build attention flow network and data abstraction, will simplify the representation of historical behavior characteristic vectors respectively and characterization of online behavior feature vector (online behavior of 31 days of the month) similarity comparison, average similarity calculation of 1000 users online behavior, The comparison results are shown in Fig. 6.

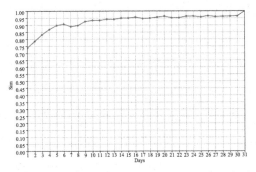

Fig. 6. Comparison of the average similarity of user online behavior between the superimposed day and the current month

As can be seen from the above figure, the online click behavior of the user in the first 10 days is as high as 90% similar to the user's online click behavior in the current month, and it tends to be flat. Experiments show that the daily online click behavior of individual users is highly similar. The user can be accurately located by using the user's 10-day online behavior data. Similarly, the user's current online behavior can be identified by using the user's 10-day behavior data whether the behavior is abnormal.

Comparative Analysis of Online Behavior Similarity of Different Users

In order to verify the accuracy of the above inference, this paper selects the user's historical behavior data and the current month's online behavior data at two time points in the previous 10 days and the previous 31 days to conduct experiments. For the convenience of analysis, we extract 6 users and 180 other users the online click behavior data (including the user itself) is compared vertically, and the results are shown in Fig. 7 and Fig. 8. The similarity comparison of a user's online behavior with other users at 5 time points is shown in Fig. 9.

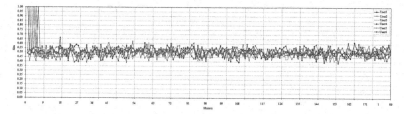

Fig. 7. Comparison of similarity of different users in the first 10 days

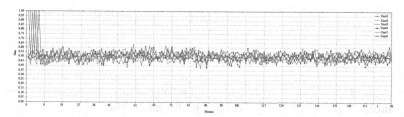

Fig. 8. Comparison of similarity of different users in the first 31 days

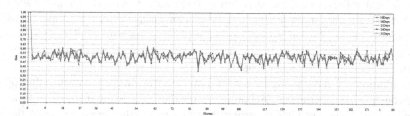

Fig. 9. Comparison of similarity between a user at 5 time points and different users

From the above figure, it can be seen that the similarity of online click behaviors of different users in the two time periods is relatively poor, stable between 40–60%, indicating that there are differences between the online click behaviors of different users, and the same user every day the online click behavior of is highly similar. In addition, for the same individual user, the similarity curve trends of the above five time nodes are also roughly the same. From this we can infer that the online click behavior of individual users is more unique than that of individuals, and there are differences in online click behaviors between different individuals. This reflects the diversity of human behavior. Even when clicking on the same information source, what everyone stops at the time and the order of clicks are also different.

Comparative Analysis of Different Models

According to the characteristic properties of the network structure, comparative experimental analysis is carried out with the Node2vec algorithm. Node2vec preserves the higher-order proximity between nodes by maximizing the probability of subsequent nodes appearing in a fixed-length random walk. The comparison of the average similarity of users of different models is shown in Fig. 10.

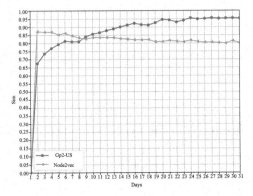

Fig. 10. Comparison chart of average similarity of model users

For the Node2vec algorithm, the average similarity of individual user online behaviors gradually becomes flat after reaching a peak, and the similarity is stable at about 80%. For the Gp2-US algorithm proposed in this paper, the average similarity of individual users' online behavior is stable at about 95%, which is more advantageous. This paper finds that the average user similarity curve is completely flat within the accuracy value of ±0.001 when it reaches 24 days. When comparing the user's historical behavior and online behavior, the corresponding similarity curve fluctuates, and it can be inferred that the account is abnormal. When the user's 10-day historical behavior data is provided, the user's identity can be authenticated.

In addition, for the running rates of the two models, this paper verifies the following through some experiments. According to the data processing methods of historical behavior and online behavior constructed in this paper, the running time of the two models is compared, as shown in Fig. 11.

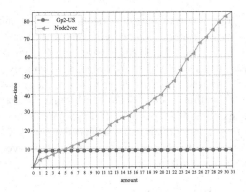

Fig. 11. Model running rate comparison chart

As can be seen from the above figure, the running time of the Gp2-US algorithm in this paper is less affected by the scale of the data, and the server running time is not significantly improved compared with the stand-alone running time. The running time of the Node2vec algorithm is greatly affected by the scale of the data, which shows a linear growth trend. The algorithm in this paper runs faster than the Node2vec algorithm, and is more universal and superior.

5 Conclusion

Based on the online behavior data provided by China Internet Network Information Center (CNNIC), starting from the similarity and independence of individual user behavior in virtual space, we study the similarity of individual user online behavior and the method of identifying their identity. We use clickstream data for network modeling, uses graph embedding technology to convert the attention network into a vector form with graph feature attributes, and proposes the Gp2-US algorithm to analyze the similarity curve of users' online behaviors, which can identify the user's identity and whether the account exists abnormal behavior. In this paper, we find that the daily online behaviors of individual users are highly similar, which can be identified by user 10-day online behavior data, and the behaviors of different individuals have a greater degree of discrimination. In future work, we can conduct group commonality research through feature recognition, and continue to introduce concepts in biology, chemistry and other fields into the attention flow network.

Acknowledgements. This research was partially supported by the grants from the Natural Science Foundation of China (No. 71764025, 61863032); major scientific research projects of Northwest Normal University (NWNU-LKZD2021-06); the Research Project on Association of Fundamental Computing Education in Chinese Universities (Grant No. 2020-AFCEC-355); the Research Project on Educational Science Planning of Gansu, China (Grant No. GS [2018] GHBBKZ021). Author contributions: Yong Li and Zhongying Zhang are co-first authors who jointly designed the research.

References

1. Guo, J.Y., Li, R.H., Zhang, Y., Wang, G.R.: Graph neural network based anomaly detection in dynamic networks. J. Softw. **31**(3), 748–762 (2020)
2. Echihabi, K.: High-dimensional vector similarity search: from time series to deep network embeddings. In: Proceedings of the 2020 ACM SIGMOD International Conference on Management of Data, pp. 2829–2832 (2020)
3. Kearnes, S., McCloskey, K., Berndl, M., Pande, V., Riley, P.: Molecular graph convolutions: moving beyond fingerprints. J. Comput. Aided Mol. Des. **30**(8), 595–608 (2016)
4. Weng, L., Flammini, A., Vespignani, A., Menczer, F.: Competition among memes in a world with limited attention. Sci. Rep. **2**(1), 335 (2012)
5. Li, Y., Zhang, J., Meng, X.-F., Wang, C.-Q.: Quantifying the influence of websites based on online collective attention flow. J. Comput. Sci. Technol. **30**(6), 1175–1187 (2015)
6. Shi, P., Huang, X., Wang, J., Jiang, Z., Wu, Y.: A geometric representation of collective attention flows. PLOS ONE **10**(9), e0136243 (2015)
7. Li, Y., Meng, X.F., Zhang, Q., Zhang, J., Wang, C.Q.: Common patterns of online collective attention flow. Sci. China Inf. Sci. **60**(5), 059102 (2017)
8. Tang, X., Miao, Q.G., Quan, Y.N., Tang, J., Deng, K.: Predicting individual retweet behavior by user similarity: a multi-task learning approach. Knowl.-Based Syst. **8**, 681–688 (2015)

9. Esuli, A., Petry, L.M., Renso, C., Bogomy, V.: Traj2User: exploiting embeddings for comput-ing similarity of users mobile behavior (2018). https://arxiv.org/abs/1808.00554. Accessed 10 Oct 2021

10. Zhong, H.D., Lyu, H.B., Zhang, S.D., Ping, L., Justin, Z., Li, X.: Measuring user similarity using check-ins from LBSN: a mobile recommendation approach for e-commerce and security services. Enterp. Inf. Syst. **14**(1), 1–20 (2019). https://doi.org/10.1080/17517575.2019.168 6655

11. Bhuvaneswari, M.S., Muneeswaran, K.: User community detection from web server log using between user similarity metric. Int. J. Comput. Intell. Syst. **14**(1), 266 (2020)

12. Qian, X.D., Li, M.: E-commerce user type recognition based on access sequence similarity. J. Organ. Comput. Electron. Commer. **30**(3), 209–223 (2020)

13. Jia, Z.S., Han, Z.: Research and analysis of user behavior fingerprint on security situational awareness based on DNS Log. In: 6th International Conference on Behavioral, Economic and Socio-Cultural Computing, pp. 1–4 (2019). https://doi.org/10.1109/BESC48373.2019. 8963120

14. Duvenaud, D., et al.: Convolutional networks on graphs for learning molecular fingerprints. In: Proceedings of the 28th International Conference on Neural Information Processing Systems, pp. 2224–2232 (2015)

15. Wu, Z., et al.: MoleculeNet: a benchmark for molecular machine learning. Chem. Sci. **9**(2), 513–530 (2018)

16. Cereto-Massagué, A., Montes, M., Valls, C., Mulero, M., Garcia-Vallve, S., Pujadas, G.: Molecular fingerprint similarity search in virtual screening. Methods **71**, 58–63 (2015)

17. Cai, H., Zheng, V.W., Chang, C.C.: A comprehensive survey of graph embedding: problems, techniques and applications. IEEE Trans. Knowl. Data Eng. **30**(9), 1616–1637 (2017)

18. Satish, N., et al.: Navigating the maze of graph analytics frameworks using massive graph datasets. In: Proceedings of the 2014 ACM SIGMOD International Conference on Management of Data, pp. 979–990 (2014)

19. Bengio, Y., Courville, A., Vincent, P.: Representation learning: a review and new perspectives. IEEE Trans. Pattern Anal. Mach. Intell. **35**(8), 1798–1828 (2013)

20. Wang, D.X., Cui, P., Zhu, W.W.: Structural deep network embedding. In: Proceedings of the 22nd ACM SIGKDD International Conference on Knowledge Discovery and Data Mining, pp. 1225–1234 (2016)

21. Goyal, P., Ferrara, E.: Graph embedding techniques, applications, and performance: a survey. Knowl.-Based Syst. **151**, 78–94 (2017)

22. Narayanan, A., Chandramohan, M., Venkatesan, R., Chen, L.H, Liu, Y., Jaiswal, S.: graph2vec: Learning Distributed Representations of Graphs (2017). https://arxiv.org/abs/ 1707.05005. Accessed 10 Oct 2021

23. Le, Q., Mikolov, T.: Distributed representations of sentences and documents. In: Proceedings of the 31st International Conference on Machine Learning, pp. 1188–1196 (2014)

24. Grohe, M.: word2vec, node2vec, graph2vec, X2vec: towards a theory of vector embeddings of structured data. In: Proceedings of the 39th ACM SIGMOD-SIGACT-SIGAI Symposium on Principles of Database Systems, pp. 1–20 (2020)

Image and Natural Language Big Data

Video Based Fall Detection Using Human Poses

Ziwei Chen[1,2], Yiye Wang[1,2], and Wankou Yang[1,2(✉)]

[1] School of Automation, Southeast University, Nanjing 210096, China
wkyang@seu.edu.cn
[2] Key Lab of Measurement and Control of Complex Systems of Engineering,
Ministry of Education, Southeast University, Nanjing 210096, China

Abstract. Video based fall detection accuracy has been largely improved due to the recent progress on deep convolutional neural networks. However, there still exist some challenges, such as lighting variation, complex background, which degrade the accuracy and generalization ability of these approaches. Meanwhile, large computation cost limits the application of existing fall detection approaches. To alleviate these problems, a video based fall detection approach using human poses is proposed in this paper. First, a lightweight pose estimator extracts 2D poses from video sequences, and then 2D poses are lifted to 3D poses. Second, we introduce a robust fall detection network to recognize fall events using estimated 3D poses, which increases respective field and maintains low computation cost by dilated convolutions. The experimental results show that the proposed fall detection approach achieves a high accuracy of 99.83% on large benchmark action recognition dataset NTU RGB+D and real-time performance of 18 FPS on a non-GPU platform, 63 FPS on a GPU platform.

Keywords: Fall detection · Human pose estimation · Convolutional neural network

1 Introduction

Nowadays, the ageing of the population has become a global phenomena. There were 727 million persons aged 65 or over in 2020 and the number of the elderly worldwide will be projected to more than double over the next three decades, sharing around 16.0 per cent of the population in 2050 [8]. According to the World Health Organization (WHO) [37], adults older than 60 years suffer the greatest number of fatal falls, which could cause serious injuries or even death. Therefore, intelligent fall detection has drawn increasing attention from both academia and industry, becoming an urgent need for vulnerable people, especially the elderly.

The existing fall detection methods can be roughly divided into two categories, which are wearable sensor based methods and vision based methods

© Springer Nature Singapore Pte Ltd. 2022
X. Liao et al. (Eds.): BigData 2021, CCIS 1496, pp. 283–296, 2022.
https://doi.org/10.1007/978-981-16-9709-8_19

[9]. Wearable sensors, including accelerometer, gyroscopes, pressure sensor and microphone, can detect the location change or acceleration change of human body for fall detection. However, inconvenience is still the main problem. A large number of the elderly are unwilling to wear sensors all day. Besides, wearable sensors may be affected by noise and some daily activities like lying or sitting on the sofa quickly may also lead to false alarm. Recently, with the rapid development of computer vision and deep learning techniques in recent years, the number of proposed vision based methods has increased a lot [40]. Compared with wearable sensor based methods, vision based methods are free from the inconvenience of wearing the device. While the detection accuracy of vision based methods has increased a lot in recent years, false detection may still occur as a result of lighting variation or complex background. Furthermore, vision based methods, especially deep learning based methods, have a large computation cost which makes it hard to achieve real-time performance. To conclude, how to maintain a high detection accuracy while lower the computation cost is a valuable research topic.

Human pose estimation, aiming to localize human keypoints in a image or 3D space, is a fundamental task in computer vision. Human pose estimation has many applications, including human action recognition, human-computer interaction, animation, etc. Nowadays, 2D human pose estimation [4,38,41] has achieved convincing performance on some large public datasets [2,18] and the performance of 3D human pose [14,22,34] estimator has been improved greatly. Using human poses can alleviate the problem of lighting variation or complex background in fall detection task, so as to effectively improve the accuracy and generalization ability of fall detection methods.

Although existing vision based methods have brought fall detection accuracy to such a high level, they rely on a large computation [20,23] and features extracted for classification are not robust for some challenging conditions. Meanwhile, the period of falling differs among people [36]. The fall of the elderly lasts longer than other groups and some daily activities such as lying to bed differ from fall. Thus, more video frames should be taken as the input. However, previous works [12,15,32] only take a short video sequence as the input which may lead to the false detection.

To address the above problems, we propose a video based fall detection approach using human poses in this paper. Our fall detection approach consists of two steps: (1) estimating 3D poses in video sequences (2) recognize fall events from estimated 3D poses. The first step is compatible with any state-of-the-art pose estimator. We formulate 3D pose estimation as 2D pose estimation followed by 2D-to-3D pose lifting. A lightweight 2D pose estimator and a lifting network are adopt to lower the computation cost. At the second step, we present a fall detection network taking 3D poses of each frame as input. In order to achieve a convincing accuracy while maintaining the low computation cost for long video sequences, one-dimensional dilated temporal convolution [11] is adopt.

In summary, this paper has three contributions:

- We propose a fall detection model, which includes a 3D pose estimator and a fall detection network based on human poses.
- We explore the effects of factors which could contribute to the performance of fall detection including input joints and loss function.
- Our approach achieves a high accuracy at 99.83% on NTU RGB+D dataset and real-time performance on non-GPU platform when processing video sequences.

2 Related Work

The related work on vision based fall detection are first reviewed. The difference between them and our work are also discussed. Then we review some work on human pose estimation.

2.1 Vision Based Fall Detection

Many approaches have been proposed for vision based fall detection [3,17,19,39]. These approaches differ in terms of the used sensors and classify algorithms.

Sensors for most vision based approaches are RGB cameras, depth cameras, infrared cameras and Kinect. In [19], Lu et al. propose to detect fall on RGB videos using 3D CNN combined with LSTM to address the problem of insufficient fall data. Shojarei et al. [29] obtain 3D coordinates of human keypoints using depth camera and then do fall detection based on these poses. Zhong et al. [43] propose an end to end solution within a multi-occupancy living environment by thermal sensors. Nowadays, the use of Kinect for fall detection [13,17] has greatly increased a lot as 3D information can be obtained. However, depth camera in Kinect has a restricted distance which makes it unsuitable for a large space.

Decision trees, SVM and threshold are used to classify fall action categories [24,27]. Compared with these algorithms, deep neural network can achieve higher classification accuracy and avoiding feature engineering task. Adhikari et al. [1] propose a fall detection system using CNN to recognize Activities of Daily Life (ADL) and fall events. A 3D CNN is developed in [26] to improve fall detection accuracy by exploring spatial and temporal information. In [44], Variational Auto-encoder (VAE) with 3D convolutional residual block and a region extraction technique for enhancing accuracy are used to detect fall actions.

Our approach is similar to Tsai et al. [32], thus more detailed comparison are provided. Tsai et al. [32] propose a traditional algorithm to transform depth information into 3D poses and use 1D CNN to detect fall events. In [32], depth camera is used while our human pose estimator can obtain 3D poses directly from RGB images which makes it free from limited measurement distance. Though 1D CNN is used in both works, only 30 frames are taken as input in their approach while our model can take 300 frames as input at most. Some actions last longer and the elderly fall slower than the young so it is necessary to recognize fall events using long video sequences.

2.2   Human Pose Estimation

Human Pose Estimation is to localize human keypoints, which can be categorized as 2D and 3D human pose estimation according to the output.

Deep learning has become a promising technique in 2D human pose estimation in recent years. Firstly, CNN is introduced to solve 2D pose estimation problem by directly regressing the joint coordinates in DeepPose [31]. Then joint heatmaps [30] have been widely adopt as training signals in 2D human pose estimation for great performance. Newell et al. [25] propose an U-shape network by stacking up several hourglass modules to refine prediction. The work by Cao et al. [4] detects all human keypoints first and then assembles them to different person by part affinity fields (PAFs), which achieves real-time performance in multi person pose estimation task. HRNet [35] adapts the top-down pipeline and generates convincing performance via maintaining the high resolution of feature maps and multi-scale fusion.

3D human pose estimation is to localize the position of human keypoints in 3D space from images or videos. The early 3D human pose estimation methods directly predict the 3D joint coordinates via deep neural networks [16]. While a set of features suitable for the task can be spontaneously learned, these models usually have large computation cost and high complexity. Due to the development of 2D human pose estimation, methods based on 2D poses [5,21,33] have become the main stream. 2D poses are concatenated as the input to predict the depth information of each keypoint, greatly reducing the complexity of the model. In order to overcome the problem of insufficient data in 3D human pose estimation, wandt et al. [33] apply weak supervised learning to 3D human pose estimation by using reprojection method to train 3D mapping model. Cheng et al. [7] explore video information to further modify the human poses to avoid incorrect pose estimation. He et al. [10] use multi view images to overcome the occlusion problem based on epipolar geometry and achieve great performance.

3   Video Based Fall Detection

The goal of this work is to establish a video based fall detection approach using human poses. The general framework of the proposed approach is shown in Fig. 1. Firstly, human pose estimator is applied to each video frame to generate a set of human poses. Then fall detection network works to recognize whether there is a fall event based on human poses.

3.1   Human Pose Estimator

Our fall detection approach do not rely on any specific pose estimator. When obtaining 3D poses, we follow the widely-used pipeline in 3D human pose estimation [21], which predicts 2D human poses in the first step and lifts 2D poses to 3D poses. For 2D human pose estimation, we adapt off-the-shelf Lightweight Pose Network (LPN) [42] considering its low complexity and adequate accuracy.

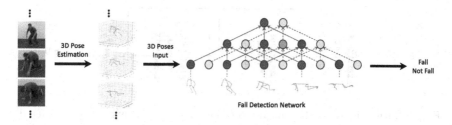

Fig. 1. Overall structure of our fall detection approach. Video sequences are first sent into pose estimator to get 3D poses, then fall detection network takes 3D poses to classify action class.

LPN is pretrained on MS COCO [18] dataset and fine tuned on NTU RGB+D dataset [28] for our task.

Lifting network takes 2D human poses $x \in \mathbb{R}^{2J}$ as input and lifts them to 3D poses $y \in \mathbb{R}^{3J}$, here J stands for the number of joints. The goal is to find a function $f^* : \mathbb{R}^{2J} \to \mathbb{R}^{3J}$ which can minimize the prediction error of N poses over a dataset:

$$f^* = \min_f \frac{1}{N} \sum_{i=1}^{N} \mathcal{L}(f(x_i) - y_i) \qquad (1)$$

Figure 2 shows the structure of our lifting network which consists of two residual blocks. 2D coordinates of joints are concatenated so one-dimensional convolution can be adopt to reduce parameters and complexity. The core idea of our lifting network is to predict depth information of keypoints effectively and efficiently. Note that what we care is not the absolute location of keypoints in 3D space but the relative location between them. So before a 2D pose is lifted to 3D, it is normalized by centering to its root joint and scaled by dividing it by its Frobenius norm. We define the prediction error as the squared difference between the prediction and the ground-truth pose:

$$\mathcal{L}(\hat{y}_i, y_i) = ||\hat{y}_i - y_i||_2^2 \qquad (2)$$

where y_i and y_i are estimated and the ground-truth relative position of the i-th pose.

3.2 Fall Detection Network

Our fall detection network is a fully convolutional architecture with residual connections. The nerwork takes a sequence of 3D poses $X \in \mathbb{R}^{T \times 3J}$ as input and predicts whether there is a fall behavior, where T is the number of frames. In convolutional networks, the path of gradient between output and input has a fixed length, which mitigates vanishing and exploding gradients. It is important for our task as T was set to 300 to recognize falls in such a long video sequence.

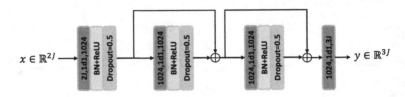

Fig. 2. Lifting network. "$2J$" means 2D coordinates of J joints are concatenated.

Moreover, dilated convolutions are applied in our network to model long-term dependencies while maintaining efficiency.

When 3D poses are obtained by pose estimator, we also do the centering and scaling. Besides, 3D poses are firstly rotated by paralleling the bone between hip and spine to the z axis. Then by paralleling the bone between left shoulder and right shoulder to the x axis, normalized 3D poses can be obtained.

Figure 3 shows our fall detection network. 3D coordinates (x, y, z) of J joints for each frame are concatenated as the network input and a convolution with kernel size 3 and C output channels is applied. This is followed by N residual blocks. Each block includes two one-dimensional convolutions, the first one is dilated and dilation factor is $W = 3^N$, followed by another 1D convolution with kernel size 1. Batch normalization, rectified linear units and dropout are used after every convolution except the last one. With dilation factor, each block increases the receptive field to exploit temporal information without too much computation increasement. We use unpadded convolutions so the output size of each block is different. Details can be seen in Table 1. Average pool is used to fuse features and change the dimension for the final convolution. The length of video sequence is 300 and we set $N = 4$ to increase the receptive filed. For convolutions, we set $C = 512$ output channels to maintain a balance between accuracy and complicity and the dropout rate $p = 0.25$.

4   Experiments

4.1   Dataset

The proposed fall detection model was trained and evaluated on NTU RGB+D Action Recognition Dataset [28] made available by the ROSE Lab at the Nanyang Technological University, Singapore. This dataset contains 60 action classes and 56,880 video samples including falling. The videos are captured by three synchronous Microsoft Kinect v2 cameras installed at the same height with three different horizontal angles: $-45°, 0°, +45°$. The dataset contains RGB videos, depth map sequences, 3D skeletal data, and infrared (IR) videos for each sample. The resolution of RGB frames are 1920×1080 and the speed are 30 FPS. 3D skeletal data are composed of 3D coordinates of 25 joints. To best of our knowledge, this is the largest action recognition dataset available which contains 3D skeletal data and falling samples. Some of the video samples have

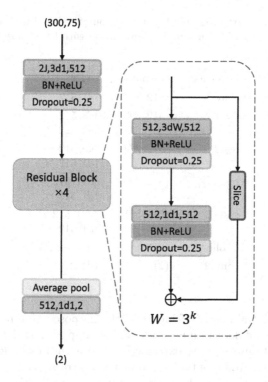

Fig. 3. Fall detection network.

missing frames, poses or involve more than one person, we removed these samples. Consequently, the total amount of samples we used was 44372, in which 890 samples were falling samples. Following previous action recognition work [6], we trained on data coming from camera 0° and +45°, tested on data from camera −45°.

4.2 Training Details

We trained our fall detection model step by step. Firstly, for human pose estimation, we adopt off-the-shelf LPN to predict 2D poses from each video frame. LPN was pretrained on COCO dataset and fine-tuned on NTU RGB+D dataset. When fine-tuning LPN on NTU RGB+D dataset, joint heatmaps were generated according to annotations as the output target which could avoid directly learning the mapping from images to coordinates. Then by calculating the center of mass of heatmaps, 2D joint coordinates could be obtained.

Before lifting 2D poses to 3D poses, 2D poses were normalized by centering to its root joint and then scaled by dividing its Frobenius norm. Adam optimizer was used to train the lifting network combined with MSE loss for 60 epochs with an initial learning rete of 0.0001 and exponential decay at $20th$ and $40th$ epoch.

Table 1. This table shows the architecture and output size of each block for our fall detection network. "3d3, 512" means 1D convolution with kernel size 3, dilation factor 3 and 512 channels.

Layer name	Output size	Layer
conv_1	(512, 298)	3d1, 512
res_1	(512, 292)	3d3, 512 1d1, 512
res_2	(512, 274)	3d9, 512 1d1, 512
res_3	(512, 220)	3d27, 512 1d1, 512
res_4	(512, 58)	3d81, 512 1d1, 512
pooling	(512)	*Average pool*
conv_2	(2)	1d1, 2

Similar to the training of lifting network, 3D poses were normalized before being sent to the fall detection network. Video samples from dataset have different frames, so all samples were expanded to 300 frames by padding null frames with previous ones. Adam optimizer and Cross Entropy Loss were used to train fall detection network. We set initial learning rate to 0.0001 with exponential decay. We train the network on one Nvidia GTX 1660 GPU for 20 epochs.

4.3 Results

Human Pose Estimation. Most previous skeleton based action recognition works directly use 3D annotations on NTU RGB+D dataset. Here we use predicted 3D poses for fall detection to test feasibility of our approach. Human pose estimation accuracy is measured by Joint Detection Rate (JDR). JDR represents the percentage of successfully detected joints. A joint is regarded as successfully detected if the distance between the estimation and ground-truth is smaller than a threshold. Here we set the threshold to be half of the distance between neck and head.

Table 2. This table shows pose estimation accuracy on NTU RGB+D dataset. JDR (%) of nine joints are showed due to limited space. "B spi" means base spine and "L wri" means left wrist.

B spi	Head	L elb	L wri	R elb	R wri	R ank	Neck	L thumb
99.69	98.02	98.45	97.91	94.22	90.82	71.06	93.18	64.34

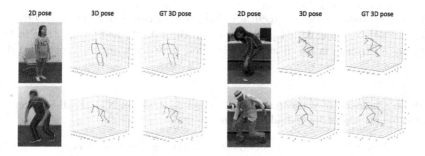

Fig. 4. Qualitative results of some example images. Initial image, 2D poses, 3D poses and GT 3D poses are presented. Blue poses are estimated 3D poses and green ones are GT 3D poses.

Table 3. This table shows mean JDR (%) of three aggregations of joints.

Joints	mJDR
25 joints	86.02
16 joints	94.07
8 joints	94.52

Table 2 shows pose estimation results of our method on NTU RGB+D dataset. JDR of some joints are presented. For some joints including head, elbow and shoulder, JDRs achieve larger than 90% and the prediction of these joints is accurate. However, JDR of ankle and thumb are not high as a result of frequent occlusion and inaccurate 2D pose. Table 3 shows mean JDR of three aggregations of joints. Details of three aggregations of joints are showed in Fig. 5 The evaluation of our proposed fall detection method using different number of joints as inputs will later be reported. Some qualitative results are shown in Fig. 4

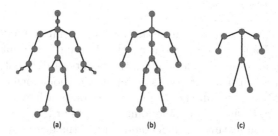

Fig. 5. Skeleton information of different inputs. (a) All 25 joints. (b) Selected 16 joints. (c) Selected 8 joints.

Fall Detection. Table 4 shows the result of our proposed method and other fall detection methods. It can be seen that our proposed method achieves a quite high performance of 99.83% accuracy and outperforms other methods. Our fall detection network has 4.2 M parameters which is 0.7 M lower than that in [32] and only 30 frames is taken as input in their network while our network takes 300 frames.

Table 4. Comparison of different fall detection methods on NTU RGB+D dataset. Params are calculated for the fall detection network.

Methods	Input	Feature	Network	Params	Accuracy
Xu et al. [39]	RGB	Pose	2D conv	–	91.70%
Anahita et al. [29]	Depth	Pose	LSTM	–	96.12%
Han et al. [32]	Depth	Pose	1D conv	4.9 M	99.20%
Ours	RGB	Pose	1D conv	4.2 M	**99.83%**

Table 5. Fall detection results of different methods on NTU RGB+D dataset. The naming convention of the methods follows the rule of "A-B" where "A" indicates how many joints are used in fall detection. "B" denotes the loss. "CEL" means Cross Entropy Loss and "WCEL" means weighted Cross Entropy Loss.

Method	Accuracy	Precision	Recall
8 joints-CEL	99.72%	97.15%	89.74%
8 joints-WCEL	99.29%	98.70%	74.32%
16 joints-CEL	**99.83%**	97.47%	**94.25%**
16 joints-WCEL	99.50%	**98.73%**	80.67%
25 joints-CEL	99.77%	97.79%	91.35%
25 joints-WCEL	99.66%	97.47%	87.11%

We also evaluate the influence of the number of input joints, as shown in Fig. 5, we select 8 and 16 joints from all the 25 joints as input and calculate the classification accuracy. Table 5 shows the results of different joint input. It can be seen that when using 16 joints as input, the model achieves the highest accuracy of 99.83%. Using all the 25 joints or 8 joints achieve a lower but still high accuracy. We consider that some joints like eyes or hands could disturb the model to learn action features, which could lead to the degradation of accuracy. Besides, few joints may not be able to model the variance of different actions.

Considering that the number of falling samples only takes a part of 1.67% of the whole dataset, it is necessary to test whether our model can truly classify fall from other actions rather than just classifying all the samples to not fall class. So Precision is also calculated to test whether our model can really recognize fall behaviour. Moreover, we use Weighted Cross Entropy Loss to train this fall detection network follow previous method and evaluate it on this dataset. For falling class, we set $\alpha = 59/60$ and $\beta = 1/60$ for other samples. Table 5 shows the evaluation results, it can be seen that our network truly learns how to classify a fall behavior and the precision achieves 1.26% improvement using Weighted Cross Entropy Loss while accuracy decreased by 0.83%. The variation of Recall is very large as the number of falling samples is much smaller than it of other actions.

Actual inference speed, defining whether our fall detection method can achieve real time performance, is what we also care about. We test number of parameters, FLOPs and inference speed of every part of our fall detection approach. The speed test is based on two platforms. One is a non-GPU platform with Intel Core i5-9400F CPU (2.9 GHZ × 6) and the other is one Nvidia GTX 1660 GPU. Table 6 shows the measurements and it can be found that our method has a speed of 18 FPS on a non-GPU platform and 63 FPS on one Nvidia GTX 1660 GPU. As reported in [32], the compared method achieves 15 FPS on NVIDIA Fetson TX2 (Pascal GUP). Moreover, the inference speed of lifting network and fall detection network is very fast which only takes a few milliseconds. The 2D pose estimator, LPN, is the one mainly limits the inference speed. It is worth mentioning that our fall detection method does not rely on any specific 2D human pose estimator, LPN can be changed to other pose estimator for more efficiency and robustness.

Table 6. Measurement of Params, FLOPs and Speed of each part of our proposed fall detection method on different platforms. "LN" means lifting network and "FDN" means fall detection network.

Part	Params	FLOPs	Non-GPU	GPU
LPN	2.7 M	1.0 G	20 FPS	74 FPS
LN	2.2 M	0.28 G	560 FPS	1450 FPS
FDN	4.2 M	0.9 G	260 FPS	590 FPS
Whole	9.1 M	2.18 G	18 FPS	63 FPS

5   Conclusion

In this paper, we propose an approach to recognize fall events from video sequences. More specifically, the proposed approach includes a 3D pose estimator based on lifting 2D poses to 3D poses and a fall detection network using dilated convolution. Our approach achieves a high accuracy of 99.83 on NTU RGB+D dataset and realtime performance of 18 FPS on a non-GPU platform, 63 FPS on a GPU platform.

Acknowledgments. This work was supported by the National Natural Science Foundation of China under Nos. 61773117 and 62006041.

References

1. Adhikari, K., Bouchachia, H., Nait-Charif, H.: Activity recognition for indoor fall detection using convolutional neural network. In: MVA, pp. 81–84 (2017). https://doi.org/10.23919/MVA.2017.7986795
2. Andriluka, M., Pishchulin, L., Gehler, P., Schiele, B.: 2D human pose estimation: new benchmark and state of the art analysis. In: CVPR, June 2014
3. Cameiro, S.A., da Silva, G.P., Leite, G.V., Moreno, R., Guimarães, S.J.F., Pedrini, H.: Multi-stream deep convolutional network using high-level features applied to fall detection in video sequences. In: IWSSIP, pp. 293–298 (2019). https://doi.org/10.1109/IWSSIP.2019.8787213
4. Cao, Z., Hidalgo, G., Simon, T., Wei, S.E., Sheikh, Y.: Openpose: realtime multi-person 2d pose estimation using part affinity fields. IEEE Trans. Pattern Anal. Mach. Intell. **43**(1), 172–186 (2021). https://doi.org/10.1109/TPAMI.2019.2929257
5. Chen, C.H., Ramanan, D.: 3D human pose estimation = 2d pose estimation + matching. In: CVPR, July 2017
6. Cheng, K., Zhang, Y., Cao, C., Shi, L., Cheng, J., Lu, H.: Decoupling gcn with dropgraph module for skeleton-based action recognition. In: European Conference on Computer Vision, pp. 536–553 (2020)
7. Cheng, Y., Yang, B., Wang, B., Tan, R.T.: 3D human pose estimation using spatio-temporal networks with explicit occlusion training. In: AAAI, vol. 34, pp. 10631–10638 (2020)
8. United Nations Department of Economic and Social Affairs: World Population Ageing 2020: Highlights. United Nations (2021)
9. Gutiérrez, J., Rodríguez, V., Martin, S.: Comprehensive review of vision-based fall detection systems. Sensors **21**(3), 947 (2021). https://doi.org/10.3390/s21030947
10. He, Y., Yan, R., Fragkiadaki, K., Yu, S.I.: Epipolar transformers. In: CVPR, June 2020
11. Holschneider, M., Kronland-Martinet, R., Morlet, J., Tchamitchian, P.: A real-time algorithm for signal analysis with the help of the wavelet transform. In: Combes, J.M., Grossmann, A., Tchamitchian, P. (eds.) Wavelets Inverse Problems and Theoretical Imaging, pp. 286–297. Springer, Heidelberg (1990). https://doi.org/10.1007/978-3-642-75988-8_28
12. Hwang, S., Ahn, D., Park, H., Park, T.: Poster abstract: maximizing accuracy of fall detection and alert systems based on 3d convolutional neural network. In: International Conference on Internet-of-Things Design and Implementation (IoTDI), pp. 343–344 (2017)
13. Kasturi, S., Filonenko, A., Jo, K.H.: Human fall recognition using the spatiotemporal 3d cnn. In: Proceedings IW-FCV, pp. 1–3 (2019)
14. Kocabas, M., Athanasiou, N., Black, M.J.: Vibe: Video inference for human body pose and shape estimation. In: CVPR, June 2020
15. Li, S., Xiong, H., Diao, X.: Pre-impact fall detection using 3d convolutional neural network. In: International Conference on Rehabilitation Robotics (ICORR), pp. 1173–1178 (2019). https://doi.org/10.1109/ICORR.2019.8779504
16. Li, S., Chan, A.B.: 3D human pose estimation from monocular images with deep convolutional neural network. In: Cremers, D., Reid, I., Saito, H., Yang, M.H. (eds.) ACCV 2014. LNCS, vol. 9004, pp. 332–347. Springer, Cham (2015). https://doi.org/10.1007/978-3-319-16808-1_23

17. Li, X., Pang, T., Liu, W., Wang, T.: Fall detection for elderly person care using convolutional neural networks. In: CISP-BMEI, pp. 1–6 (2017). https://doi.org/10.1109/CISP-BMEI.2017.8302004
18. Lin, T.Y., et al.: Microsoft coco: common objects in context. In: Fleet, D., Pajdla, T., Schiele, B., Tuytelaars, T. (eds.) ECCV 2014. LNCS, vol. 8693, pp. 740–755. Springer, Cham (2014). https://doi.org/10.1007/978-3-319-10602-1_48
19. Lu, N., Wu, Y., Feng, L., Song, J.: Deep learning for fall detection: three-dimensional CNN combined with LSTM on video kinematic data. IEEE J. Biomed. Health Inf. **23**(1), 314–323 (2019). https://doi.org/10.1109/JBHI.2018.2808281
20. Ma, C., Shimada, A., Uchiyama, H., Nagahara, H., Taniguchi, R.J.: Fall detection using optical level anonymous image sensing system. Opt. Laser Technol. **110**, 44–61 (2019)
21. Martinez, J., Hossain, R., Romero, J., Little, J.J.: A simple yet effective baseline for 3d human pose estimation. In: ICCV, October 2017
22. Mehta, D., et al.: Monocular 3d human pose estimation in the wild using improved CNN supervision. In: International Conference on 3D Vision (3DV), pp. 506–516 (2017). https://doi.org/10.1109/3DV.2017.00064
23. Menacho, C., Ordoñez, J.: Fall detection based on cnn models implemented on a mobile robot. In: International Conference on Ubiquitous Robots (UR), pp. 284–289 (2020). https://doi.org/10.1109/UR49135.2020.9144836
24. Min, W., Yao, L., Lin, Z., Liu, L.: Support vector machine approach to fall recognition based on simplified expression of human skeleton action and fast detection of start key frame using torso angle. IET Comput. Vis. **12**(8), 1133–1140 (2018)
25. Newell, A., Yang, K., Deng, J.: Stacked hourglass networks for human pose estimation. In: Leibe, B., Matas, J., Sebe, N., Welling, M. (eds.) ECCV 2016. LNCS, vol. 9912, pp. 483–499. Springer, Cham (2016). https://doi.org/10.1007/978-3-319-46484-8_29
26. Rahnemoonfar, M., Alkittawi, H.: Spatio-temporal convolutional neural network for elderly fall detection in depth video cameras. In: Big Data, pp. 2868–2873 (2018). https://doi.org/10.1109/BigData.2018.8622342
27. Senouci, B., Charfi, I., Heyrman, B., Dubois, J., Miteran, J.: Fast prototyping of a SOC-based smart-camera: a real-time fall detection case study. J. Real-Time Image Process. **12**(4), 649–662 (2016)
28. Shahroudy, A., Liu, J., Ng, T.T., Wang, G.: NTU RGB+D: a large scale dataset for 3d human activity analysis. In: CVPR, pp. 1010–1019 (2016)
29. Shojaei-Hashemi, A., Nasiopoulos, P., Little, J.J., Pourazad, M.T.: Video-based human fall detection in smart homes using deep learning. In: ISCAS, pp. 1–5 (2018). https://doi.org/10.1109/ISCAS.2018.8351648
30. Tompson, J.J., Jain, A., LeCun, Y., Bregler, C.: Joint training of a convolutional network and a graphical model for human pose estimation. Adv. Neural Inf. Process. Syst. **27**, 1799–1807 (2014)
31. Toshev, A., Szegedy, C.: Deeppose: human pose estimation via deep neural networks. In: CVPR, June 2014
32. Tsai, T.H., Hsu, C.W.: Implementation of fall detection system based on 3d skeleton for deep learning technique. IEEE Access **7**, 153049–153059 (2019). https://doi.org/10.1109/ACCESS.2019.2947518
33. Wandt, B., Rosenhahn, B.: Repnet: weakly supervised training of an adversarial reprojection network for 3d human pose estimation. In: CVPR, June 2019
34. Wandt, B., Rudolph, M., Zell, P., Rhodin, H., Rosenhahn, B.: Canonpose: self-supervised monocular 3d human pose estimation in the wild. In: CVPR, pp. 13294–13304, June 2021

35. Wang, J., et al.: Deep high-resolution representation learning for visual recognition. IEEE Trans. Pattern Anal. Mach. Intell. **43**, 3349–3364 (2020). https://doi.org/10.1109/TPAMI.2020.2983686
36. Wang, X., Ellul, J., Azzopardi, G.: Elderly fall detection systems: a literature survey. Front. Rob. AI **7**, 71 (2020). https://doi.org/10.3389/frobt.2020.00071
37. WHO: Fall. https://www.who.int/news-room/fact-sheets/detail/fall. Accessed 26 Apr 2021
38. Xiao, B., Wu, H., Wei, Y.: Simple baselines for human pose estimation and tracking. In: Ferrari, Vi., Hebert, M., Sminchisescu, C., Weiss, Y. (eds.) ECCV 2018. LNCS, vol. 11210, pp. 472–487. Springer, Cham (2018). https://doi.org/10.1007/978-3-030-01231-1_29
39. Xu, Q., Huang, G., Yu, M., Guo, Y.: Fall prediction based on key points of human bones. Phys. A Stat. Mech. Appl. **540**, 123205 (2020). https://doi.org/10.1016/j.physa.2019.123205
40. Xu, T., Zhou, Y., Zhu, J.: New advances and challenges of fall detection systems: a survey. Appl. Sci. **8**(3), 418 (2018). https://doi.org/10.3390/app8030418
41. Yang, S., Quan, Z., Nie, M., Yang, W.: Transpose: keypoint localization via transformer. In: ICCV (2021)
42. Zhang, Z., Tang, J., Wu, G.: Simple and lightweight human pose estimation. arXiv preprint arXiv:1911.10346 (2019)
43. Zhong, C., Ng, W.W.Y., Zhang, S., Nugent, C.D., Shewell, C., Medina-Quero, J.: Multi-occupancy fall detection using non-invasive thermal vision sensor. IEEE Sens. J. **21**(4), 5377–5388 (2021). https://doi.org/10.1109/JSEN.2020.3032728
44. Zhou, J., Komuro, T.: Recognizing fall actions from videos using reconstruction error of variational autoencoder. In: ICIP, pp. 3372–3376 (2019). https://doi.org/10.1109/ICIP.2019.8803671

Characterizing the Performance of Deep Learning Inference for Edge Video Analytics

Zhenxiao Luo[1,2], Xinglong Wang[1,2], Yuxiao Zhang[1,2], Zelong Wang[1,2], Miao Hu[1,2], and Di Wu[1,2(✉)]

[1] School of Computer Science and Engineering, Sun Yat-Sen University, Guangzhou 510006, China
wudi27@mail.sysu.edu.cn
[2] Guangdong Key Laboratory of Big Data Analysis and Processing, Guangzhou 510006, China

Abstract. Real-time video analytics is a killer application for edge computing, however, it has not been fully understood how much edge resource is required to support compute-intensive video analytics tasks at the edge. In this paper, we conduct an in-depth measurement study to unveil the resource requirement of deep learning (DL) inference for edge video analytics (EVA). We measure the DL inference time under various resource combinations, with different physical resources (e.g., processor types, core numbers, memory), video resolutions, and DL inference models. It is observed that the relationship between DL inference time and resource configuration is complicated, which cannot be captured by a simple model. Considering the coupling effects, we model the resource requirements of the DL inference by utilizing tensor factorization (TF) method. Our TF-based DL inference model can match well with the observations from field measurements. Different from previous models, our model is completely explainable and all the components have their physical meanings. Especially, it is possible to match the top three components extracted from the TF-based model with the practical DL functional layers, namely, convolutional layer, pooling layer, and fully-connected layer. The measurement results show that the top three components contribute approximately 50%, 25%, and 10% time for DL inference execution, which provides clear instruction on fine-grained DL task scheduling for edge video analytics applications.

Keywords: Deep learning inference · Modeling · Tensor factorization · Edge video analytics

1 Introduction

With the increase of camera installation, video analytics applications have attracted more and more attention in recent years. IHS Markit reported that

© Springer Nature Singapore Pte Ltd. 2022
X. Liao et al. (Eds.): BigData 2021, CCIS 1496, pp. 297–309, 2022.
https://doi.org/10.1007/978-981-16-9709-8_20

there is a camera installed for every 29 citizens, and the number of cameras will grow by 20% every year in the coming years [5]. With the increase of camera installation, video analytics applications have attracted more and more attention in recent years. As reported by Fortune Business Insights, the global video analytics market size is projected to reach USD dollars 12 billion by the end of 2026, exhibiting a Compound Annual Growth Rate (CAGR) of 22.67% during the forecast period [2].

Nowadays, video analytics tasks are generally based on deep-learning (DL) models, which bring tremendous computational pressure on both training and inference of the DL models [16,20,24]. As cameras are always constrained by computing resources, DL training is executed on the resource-abundant cloud servers, while DL inference takes the edge-assisted solutions [12,13]. The edge servers can be idle servers, smartphones, laptops, or other computation-powerful devices at the proximity of end users. Although edge-based video analytics can achieve a low response latency, edge servers are heterogeneous in nature, which have different DL inference patterns [7,14]. In this work, we focus on modeling and analysis of DL inference with heterogeneous edge computing resources and different DL models.

The relation between resource configurations and DL inference is obviously non-linear and coupling, and a few studies made some initial attempts. The works [6,22,23] discussed the performance of some models (e.g., ResNet and VGG) under different resource constraints, but they did not focus on modeling the relation between resource configurations and DL inference. Lane et al. [19] performed a measurement study on deep learning models, but they only discussed each factor separately, thus failing to explain the coupling relation between different configurations and the DL inference time. Jiang et al. [17] considered a combination of frame rate, image size, and object detection models as a configuration, and then balanced resource and accuracy by selecting a suitable inference configuration. However, they did not consider the influence of heterogeneous edge servers' computational resources.

Despite the above-mentioned research, quite a few challenges still remain: (1) *DL inference in the resource-constrained scenario.* The DL inference performance has been extensively studied in scenarios with sufficient resources. However, to the authors' best knowledge, there is very limited work on the measurement of DL inference in the resource-constrained edge computing scenario. (2) *DL inference modeling.* The performance of video analytics tasks is influenced by not only model configurations but also the provisioned resources. Most importantly, it is essential but not easy to learn the performance on edge servers before performing actual task execution. (3) *Physical explanation of the DL inference model.* A number of modeling methods can be used for DL inference modeling, however, it is essential but non-trivial to know the relations between the modeling process and the practical DL operations. Once knowing such mapping relations, it will be more efficient to conduct DL model optimization and scheduling algorithm design.

In this paper, we conduct an in-depth measurement study to obtain the DL inference time under different resource configurations. The measurement shows that the DL inference time will be affected by different kinds of resources in different ways, which makes it hard to be fit by a simple linear model. Since the DL inference time is affected by multiple coupling factors, we leverage the tensor factorization (TF) method to model the resource requirements of DL inference for edge video analytics. By applying the TF-based model on the measured data, we find that the DL inference time is mainly affected by three key components. The physical explanation of these components can help to classify and schedule DL tasks, however, it cannot be directly achieved by the TF method. We find that the DL inference model can also be decomposed into three kinds of functional layers. Compared to the extracted components, we match them to actual layers of the convolutional neural networks, i.e., the convolutional layer, pooling layer, and fully-connected layer. Finally, we track the inference programs to obtain the consumed time of each function, and build the relations between the TF model components and the actual DL functions.

In summary, our main contributions in this paper can be listed as follows:

- We conduct measurements on DL inference performance on heterogeneous edge servers to reveal the relation between resource configurations and inference performance. The measurement results point out that different kinds of resources will affect the DL inference time in different degrees, making it hard to be fit by a simple model.
- We leverage tensor factorization method to model the resource requirements of deep-learning inference for edge video analytics. We decompose the DL inference time and find that it can be mainly decomposed into three key components in all tested cases.
- To the authors' best knowledge, we are the first to map each of the three components from the TF-based model with the actual DL functions. Both theoretical and experimental results show the top three influential functions are the convolutional layer, the pooling layer, and the fully-connected layer.

The rest of this paper is organized as follows: Sect. 2 introduces a measurement study. Section 3 elaborates the tensor factorizations that we leverage for modeling the resource requirements of deep-learning inference for edge video analytics, while we interpret our model and verify the physical explanation in Sect. 4. Section 5 concludes this work and outlooks future research directions.

2   A Measurement Study on DL Inference Time

In this section, we discuss the relation between DL inference time and computational resource, including processor type (i.e., CPU/GPU), processor core numbers and memory size. The inference time is the time used for the computation of a video analytic task of one frame. We choose four DL models (i.e., *SSD_MobileNet*, *SSD_Inception*, *FasterRCNN_ResNet*, *FasterRCNN_Inception*), three video resolution (480p, 720p, 1080p) and four kinds of video contents

(Beach, Store, Párking, School) as the default experimental settings. We use the average value of the object detection task in different video contents as the final result. We measure the inference time on three general processor types, i.e., a GPU, a weak CPU and a more powerful CPU. The difference between a weak CPU and a powerful CPU is the CPU frequency, where the CPU frequency of a powerful processor is 3.7 GHz and the weak CPU is with frequency 2.6 GHz. The tested core numbers in the measurement are 2, 4 and 8, while the memory sizes are 1 GB, 2 GB and 4 GB. As for GPU, we adopt NVIDIA GTX 1080ti in our expriments. The measurements are conducted on Ubuntu 18.10.1, VMware 15.5.0 and implemented in Python 2.7, Tensorflow 1.14.0. The DL inference models can be found in [1], and pre-trained on the COCO dataset [15].

Table 1. Inference time (seconds) versus different DL models, video resolutions, and processor types.

	Resolution	*SSD_MobileNet*	*SSD_Inception*	*FasterRCNN_ResNet*	*FasterRCNN_Inception*
Weak CPU	480p	0.0455	0.0795	1.5365	0.4089
	720p	0.0465	0.0798	1.5674	0.4157
	1080p	0.0516	0.0856	1.5860	0.4203
Strong CPU	480p	0.0329	0.0433	0.7388	0.2032
	720p	0.0343	0.0500	0.7333	0.2019
	1080p	0.0389	0.0506	0.7326	0.2096
GPU	480p	0.0559	0.0531	0.0884	0.0743
	720p	0.0567	0.0573	0.0996	0.0714
	1080p	0.0587	0.0583	0.1051	0.0725

2.1   Inference Time v.s. DL Models

As shown in Table 1, the DL inference time differs with DL models. For example, by fixing other factors, *SSD_MobileNet* always takes less than 60 ms for DL inference, while *FasterRCNN_ResNet* needs more than 1.5 s. This might be due to the relationship between inference time and DL models discussed widely before, e.g., [17,19]. In summary, the DL inference time is proportional to the complexity of DL models.

2.2   Inference Time v.s. Video Resolutions

As indicated in Table 1, video resolution also affects the DL inference time, as different resolutions lead to different input sizes of DL models. However, video resolution affects the DL inference less than other factors. By fixing other factors, the inference time gap between 480p and 1080p videos is around 10 ms. Even so, 10 ms is still important for light-weight models such as *SSD_MobileNet*, because the total inference time of a light-weight model maybe only takes milliseconds. In conclusion, different video resolutions may still lead to a 20% gap of the total DL inference time, even if their effects on DL inference time are relatively less than that from other factors.

2.3   Inference Time v.s. Resource Configuration

Inference Time v.s. Processor Types. First, we attempt to understand the impact of processor types, i.e., GPU or CPU. As shown in Table 1, we can observe that a weak CPU takes longer time to run inference than a stronger one in all configurations, while GPU shows different patterns. For example, the weak CPU inference time is about 1.4x as long as that from the strong CPU on a 480p image with *SSD_MobileNet*. When it comes to *FasterRCNN_Inception*, it increases to 2x. Besides, the gap between the inference time of two CPUs is also diverse, depending on other configurations like resolutions and deep learning models. Surprisingly, GPU takes longer time than CPU using *SSD_MobileNet*, while GPUs can significantly improve the performance over 10x when using *FasterRCNN*.

Table 2. Inference time (seconds) versus different core numbers.

	Core number	*SSD_MobileNet*	*SSD_Inception*	*FasterRCNN_ResNet*	*FasterRCNN_Inception*
Weak CPU	2	0.0635	0.1367	3.4904	0.8549
	4	0.0684	0.1135	1.9730	0.4957
	8	0.0516	0.0856	1.5860	0.4203
Strong CPU	2	0.0549	0.0779	1.8825	0.4936
	4	0.0433	0.0559	0.9965	0.2746
	8	0.0389	0.0506	0.7326	0.2096

Inference Time v.s. Processor Core Numbers. For CPUs, we also compare the DL inference time versus different numbers of processor cores. With the growth of both virtualization and cloud, we may use a portion of cores to run inference instead of a total CPU. We conduct experiments on both weak and strong CPU with 2, 4 and 8 cores. As shown in Table 2, we find that the DL inference process can be accelerated by providing more processor cores. The degree of acceleration depends on models, core numbers and CPU processor. For a light-weight model like MobileNet [11], running with a strong CPU, or increasing cores will not bring a great improvement, while it will reduce a half time for a heavy-weight model running with a weak CPU. For example, running inference on a strong CPU with 2 cores and 8 cores takes about 55 ms and 39 ms, while a weak CPU with 2 cores and 8 cores takes 64 ms and 52 ms instead. The difference shows that the CPU core number is also an important factor for inference time. It is easy to find that the DL inference time will decrease with the increase of core number, but such a non-linear relation between inference time and core number is hard to model. The reason is that the non-linear relation is also affected by other factors like DL models.

Table 3. Inference time (seconds) versus memory size

	Memory	SSD_MobileNet	SSD_Inception	FasterRCNN_ResNet	FasterRCNN_Inception
CPU	1 GB	0.2857	killed	killed	killed
	2 GB	0.0405	0.0573	0.9425	0.2029
	4 GB	0.0389	0.0506	0.7326	0.2096

Inference Time v.s. Memory Size. Memory size also affects inference performance a lot, especially when the DL model is run with insufficient memory. It is always impossible when the server cannot provide enough memory, as a heavy-weight DL model needs huge memory. Table 3 shows the result of running inference separately on virtual machines with 1 GB, 2 GB and 4 GB memory. When the server provides 1 GB memory, only MobileNet can finish the inference while the others are all killed by the operating system due to insufficient memory. Even so, MobileNet takes much longer time than that with 2 GB or 4 GB. Note that the performance with 2 GB approaches to that with 4 GB. This infers that providing more memory will accelerate the inference when the memory is insufficient, and there is a threshold for memory needed for a specific model. If above the threshold, the inference will not be accelerated even if we provide more memory. The reason is that when the operating system cannot provide enough memory for inference, the processor needs to load part of models into the memory first and exchange the rest part needed in the next period instead of loading all the models at the beginning. Exchanging memory incurs extra latency.

Another observation is that DL models perform differently if with insufficient memory. As mentioned above, with 1 GB memory, the inference process using models other than MobileNet will be killed. In addition, the memory threshold of every model is also different, leading to different marginal benefits of memory.

To sum up, the measurement shows that it is difficult to form a simple model because different kinds of resources have effects on the DL inference time in different degrees. Considering the coupling effects, we aim to theoretically model the resource requirements of the DL inference.

3   DL Inference Modeling

For video analytics at the edge, the relation between DL inference time and resource configuration is important for many tasks such as scheduling. However, because the relation is affected by video content, it changes every frame when the video content varies. In order to reduce delays brought by obtaining the relation, we try to model the relation. As the influence of different factors on DL inference cannot be easily decomposed, we use one of the most popular tensor factorization models, called the CP model (Canonical Decomposition (CAN-DECOMP)/Parallel Factor Analysis (PARAFAC) [8,9]) to extract the coupling patterns. The CP model is used for tensor decomposition. An R-component CP model of a d-way array (d-order tensor) $\mathcal{X}$, whose size is $n_1 \times ... \times n_d$, can be formulated as:

$$\mathcal{X} \approx \sum_{r=1}^{R} A_r^{(1)} \otimes A_r^{(2)} \otimes ... \otimes A_r^{(d)}, \tag{1}$$

where $A_r^{(d)} \in \mathbb{R}^{n_d \times R}$ corresponds to factor matrices in dimension d, $\otimes$ indicates the *Kronecker product* [18]. For example, the estimated value of an element of tensor $\mathcal{X}$ in the location $(k_1, k_2, ..., k_r)$ is represented as:

$$\mathcal{X}_{k_1 k_2 ... k_r} \approx \sum_{r=1}^{R} a_{k_1 r}^{(1)} a_{k_2 r}^{(2)} ... a_{k_d r}^{(d)}. \tag{2}$$

In order to fit our data to an R-component CP model, we can define the objective function as the square of the residuals and formulate our problem as an optimization problem:

$$\min_{A_r^{(1)} A_r^{(2)} ... A_r^{(d)}} \frac{1}{2} \| \mathcal{X} - \sum_{r=1}^{R} A_r^{(1)} \otimes A_r^{(2)} \otimes ... \otimes A_r^{(d)} \|^2, \tag{3}$$

where $\|.\|$ indicates the Frobenius norm.

However, we cannot obtain the performance of all the configurations in reality because of our real-time requirements and high latency of video analytics tasks in some configurations. It means that we need to handle some missing data while fitting the CP model. Therefore, we use another CP model called CP-Weighted OPTimization (CP-WOPT) [3] to solve this problem. Define a non-negative weight tensor $\mathcal{W}$, whose size is the same as $\mathcal{X}$, such that

$$w_i = \begin{cases} 1 & \text{if } x_i \text{ is known,} \\ 0 & \text{otherwise.} \end{cases} \tag{4}$$

Then the objective function can be converted into:

$$\frac{1}{2} \| \mathcal{X} - \sum_{r=1}^{R} A_r^{(1)} \otimes A_r^{(2)} \otimes ... \otimes A_r^{(d)} \|_{\mathcal{W}}^2 = \frac{1}{2} \| \mathcal{Y} - \mathcal{Z} \|^2, \tag{5}$$

where $\mathcal{Z} = \mathcal{W} * (\sum_{r=1}^{R} A_r^{(1)} \otimes A_r^{(2)} \otimes ... \otimes A_r^{(d)})$ and $\mathcal{Y} = \mathcal{W} * \mathcal{X}$. The procedure of using CP-WOPT algorithm to compute a CP decomposition is given in [3]. Denoted by $\langle \mathcal{Y}, \mathcal{Z} \rangle$, the *inner product* of two tensors $\mathcal{Y}, \mathcal{Z}$ with the same size is the sum of the products of their entries. α is the learning rate of gradient descent. For $n = 1, 2, ..., d$, $A^{(-n)}$ is defined as:

$$A^{(-n)} = A^{(d)} \odot ... \odot A^{(n+1)} \odot A^{(n-1)} \odot ... \odot A^{(1)}, \tag{6}$$

where the symbol $\odot$ denotes the *Khatri-Rao product* [21].

4   Model Analysis

We first evaluate the performance of the TF-based model, and then decompose the model into several key components. To introduce the physical meanings of the CP model, we map the influence of the top three components with the practical functional layers of the DL inference model.

4.1   Model Fit of CP Model

The model fit result is shown in Table 4, where the model fit metric is used for performance evaluation [4], i.e.,

$$ModelFit = 1 - \frac{\|\mathcal{X} - \sum_{r=1}^{R} A_r^{(1)} \otimes \times \otimes A_r^{(d)}\|^2}{\|\mathcal{X}\|^2}.$$

We use a 6-component CP model to analyze the 5-dimensions tensors of DL inference time obtained from the experimental results. When the input data is relatively complete (missing data ratio less than 40%), the CP-WOPT algorithm can reconstruct the data almost perfectly for all R values except $R = 1$. The model fit keeps falling while the missing data ratio is increasing. Even so, the model fit of 90% missing data is still above 0.6 for most R values. In addition, the chosen R value will influence the model fit a lot, and the influence is related to the missing data ratio. When the missing data ratio is below 40%, the model fit increases monotonously with the increase of R. Instead, the model fit trend shows multiple peaks when the missing data ratio is above 40%. We can find the model fit peaks of 60%, 80% and 90% missing data ratio are under different R values. It means that we need to choose proper R value for every missing data ratio, in order to obtain the best model fit.

Table 4. Model Fit of CP Model (5-Way)

α [a]	Components (R value)							
	1	2	3	4	5	6	7	8
0	0.84	0.98	1.00	1.00	1.00	1.00	1.00	1.00
20%	0.83	0.99	0.98	0.99	1.00	1.00	1.00	1.00
40%	0.83	0.94	0.94	0.95	0.96	0.97	0.97	0.96
60%	0.71	0.83	0.84	0.95	0.91	0.89	0.94	0.86
80%	0.75	0.82	0.75	0.80	0.82	0.82	0.84	0.83
90%	0.63	0.76	0.54	0.71	0.55	0.72	0.63	0.61

[a]Missing Data Ratio

4.2   Component Decomposition

To explain the patterns of components in the DL inference modeling, we illustrate six components in Fig. 1.

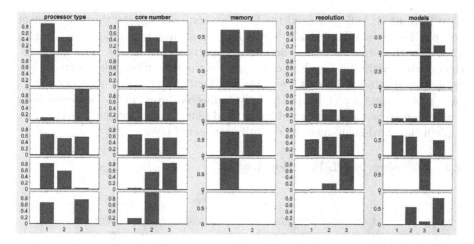

Fig. 1. CP model of 5-Way tensors with 6 Components. Each row represents a component and each column represents a factor, i.e., a resource configuration like memory (2 GB, 4 GB). The components are sorted by normalized load in a descending order, which reveal the contribution of different component to the DL inference.

Component 1: The first component takes the longest time in all the components (above 50%). It is strongly influenced by DL model and becomes lower with the increase of processors computational power and core numbers. Also, it remains unchanged when the memory size and video resolution changes. These characteristics inspire us to relate it to the convolutional layer. The convolutional layers are the core of a convolutional network that does most of the computational operations [10]. They transform the input to activation maps by some filters, and these processes will be repeated across the whole convolutional layer. Obviously, the processes are compute-intensive and require strong computational power, which is dependent on models, processors and core numbers. Therefore, we explain the first component as the convolutional layer.

Component 2: The second component accounts for about 25% of the total DL inference time. There are two factors with different patterns between the first and the second component, and other factors keep the same pattern. The first is the core number. When the core number reaches to the maximum, the second component's normalized load becomes extremely high. We conjecture that it is caused by the multi-cores' gathering operations. When the core number increases, the main process has to spend more time on gathering other cores' information. The second is the memory size. Obviously, the second component is memory-dependent and contributes much less running time with enough memory. We relate the second component to the pooling layer, because object detection needs to extract crops from the input tensor and resize them in the pooling layer. These operations require enough memory to finish, so the second component reveals this pattern in the memory plot. Therefore, we explain the second component as the pooling layer.

Component 3: Different from the first two components, the third component occupies less than 10%, which is hardly influenced by core numbers and memory size. It is the same as other components' patterns in models. The most distinct characteristics of the third component is the resolution plot's pattern. The resolution affects the input tensor size and further the tensor operations (e.g., cast, reshape and multiply) in the fully-connected layer. Fully-connected layer will compute the class scores and hence need tensor computation. Therefore, we explain the third component as the fully-connected layer.

4.3 Mapping to DL Function Layers

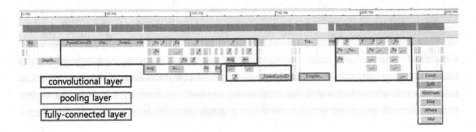

Fig. 2. DL inference timing diagram on the functional layers, including the convolutional layer, pooling layer, and fully-connected layer. (Color figure online)

To explain the physical meaning of the proposed TF-based model, we track the function calls through the DL inference tasks. We first record the consumed time of every function called by DL inference process. Then, we try to match them with the components extracted from the TF-based model.

Convolutional Layer. Figure 2 shows that many convolution functions (blue and green color functions in blue box) like $\_FusedConv2D$. For all the models in our experiment, the convolution functions occur most of consumed time, more than the sum of other functions like $MaxPool$. We can map the first component to the convolutional layer, which occupies more than half part of the total DL inference time. At first, the convolutional layer contributes most of computational time to a convolutional network, which matches the characteristic of the first component mentioned above. In addition, the convolution needs lots of computation to extract features from inputs, which means that its consumed time is directly related to computational power. The stronger computational power leads to less consumed time of the convolutional layer. At the same time, as shown in Fig. 1, we can find that the first component reveals this characteristic, too. With the processor's computational power being stronger and the increase of core numbers, the first component's contributing part of DL inference time becomes lower and lower. In summary, we map the first component to the convolutional layer, according to the computation requirements for the convolutional layer.

Pooling Layer. As we aim to verify whether the second component is related to the pooling layer and the most distinct characteristics is the DL inference time plot's pattern in memory factor, we print the recording inference time plots under different memory sizes. Figure 2 shows that the *CropandResize* function (brown color functions in green box) and *MaxPool* function (red color functions in green box) will cost less time in 4G memory, while they take longer time in 2G memory. For example, the *CropandResize* function takes about 18 ms in 4G memory, compared with 28 ms in 2G memory. These functions will be called in the pooling layer, so we further conclude that the memory size will influence the performance of pooling layer. According to the discussion before, it is reasonable to match the second component to the pooling layer. In addition, we find some pooling function like *AvgPool* (red color functions in green box) will be called when the convolution function is running.

The second component's normalized load becomes extremely high when the core number reaches the maximum in Fig. 1. This is unexpected as the normalized load will decrease with the computing power being stronger. To explain this phenomenon, we conjecture that the CP model separates a part of computation-consuming operations from the second component and merges them into the first component. As a result, the first component's contributions to the total increase a lot, while the second component loses some contributions and cannot reveal the characters of the pooling layer perfectly. In summary, the second component cannot perfectly match the pooling layer, but the difference between them is caused by divide-merge operations by CP model as we explain above.

Fully-Connected Layer. In DL models, the fully-connected layer runs in the final stage, so we can focus on the functions called in the final stage and observe their changes with video resolution changing. Similarly, we print the recording plots when running inference with different video resolutions. In the final stage, many tensor operations, such as *Mul*, *Cas*, and *Gather*, will run at the same time. Of course, the specific functions will be different while the model changes. What's more, we can find that these functions are scheduled to many threads and called at the same time, which reduces time cost of the fully-connected layer. Thus, the proportion of the fully-connected layer is not so large. Then, we want to know whether the fully-connected layer's time cost pattern is similar to the third component's pattern. According to the discussion above, if the fully-connected layer's time cost changes with the video resolution, we can verify whether our explanation is reasonable. The third component's proportion is not large, which can be mapped to the fully-connected layer.

In summary, we build our model based on the experiment data, interpret our CP model by analysing its components, and verify our interpretation by dissecting the function details of our experiment. As the majority of our model can be matched to existed convolutional network, the TF-based model is believed to be effective in reality.

5   Conclusion

This paper conducted a measurement study on the deep-learning inference performance with different combinations of various configurations and resources for edge video analytics. We find that not only the computational resources will affect the inference performance, but also the influence of resources is affected by other configurations. By utilizing a tensor factorization tool called CP model, we decomposed the inference time into six components and extracted the patterns between each component and each factor. According to the pattern characteristics of each component, we can match the first three components to convolutional layer, pooling layer and fully-connected layer by theoretical analytics and interpret our results reasonably. We provide the pattern characteristic of the relation between resource and deep-learning inference for edge video analytics, and prove the validity of our method. In the future, we plan to apply our findings to edge video analytics and improve the system performance.

Acknowledgements. This work was supported by the National Natural Science Foundation of China under Grants U1911201, U2001209, 62072486, 61802452, and Natural Science Foundation of Guangdong under Grants 2021A1515011369, 2018A030310079.

References

1. Tensorflow detection model zoo. https://github.com/tensorflow/models/blob/master/research/object_detection/g3doc/detection_model_zoo.md/
2. Video analytics market analysis. https://www.fortunebusinessinsights.com/industry-reports/video-analytics-market-101114
3. Acar, E., Kolda, T.G., Dunlavy, D.M., Morup, M.: Scalable tensor factorizations for incomplete data. Chemometr. Intell. Lab. Syst. **106**(1), 41–56 (2010)
4. Acar, E., Yener, B.: Unsupervised multiway data analysis: a literature survey. IEEE Trans. Knowl. Data Eng. **21**(1), 6–20 (2008)
5. Ananthanarayanan, G., et al.: Real-time video analytics: the killer app for edge computing. IEEE Comput. **50**(10), 58–67 (2017)
6. Cai, S., Chen, G., Ooi, B.C., Gao, J.: Model slicing for supporting complex analytics with elastic inference cost and resource constraints. PVLDB **13**(2), 86–99 (2019)
7. Cao, K., Li, L., Cui, Y., Wei, T., Hu, S.: Exploring placement of heterogeneous edge servers for response time minimization in mobile edge-cloud computing. IEEE Trans. Industr. Inf. **17**(1), 494–503 (2020)
8. Carroll, J.D., Chang, J.J.: Analysis of individual differences in multidimensional scaling via an n-way generalization of "eckart-young" decomposition. Psychometrika **35**(3), 283–319 (1970)
9. Harshman, R.A.: Foundations of the PARAFAC procedure: models and conditions for an "explanatory" multi-modal factor analysis (1970)
10. He, K., Sun, J.: Convolutional neural networks at constrained time cost. In: Proceedings of the IEEE Conference on Computer Vision and Pattern Recognition, pp. 5353–5360 (2015)
11. Howard, A., et al.: Searching for MobileNetV3. In: Proceedings of IEEE/CVF International Conference on Computer Vision (ICCV), Seoul, Korea (South), 27 October–2 November 2019, pp. 1314–1324 (2019)

12. Hu, M., Fu, Y., Wu, D.: Privacy-preserving edge video analytics. In: Chang, W., Wu, J. (eds.) Fog/Edge Computing For Security, Privacy, and Applications. AIS, vol. 83, pp. 171–190. Springer, Cham (2021). https://doi.org/10.1007/978-3-030-57328-7_7

13. Hu, M., Zhuang, L., Wu, D., Huang, Z., Hu, H.: Edge computing for real-time video stream analytics. In: Shen, X., Lin, X., Zhang, K. (eds.) Encyclopedia of Wireless Networks. Springer, Cham (2019). https://doi.org/10.1007/978-3-319-32903-1_275-1

14. Hu, M., Zhuang, L., Wu, D., Zhou, Y., Chen, X., Xiao, L.: Learning driven computation offloading for asymmetrically informed edge computing. IEEE Trans. Parallel Distrib. Syst. **30**(8), 1802–1815 (2019). https://doi.org/10.1109/TPDS.2019.2893925

15. Huang, J., et al.: Speed/accuracy trade-offs for modern convolutional object detectors. In: Proceedings of IEEE Conference on Computer Vision and Pattern Recognition (CVPR), Honolulu, HI, USA, 21–26 July 2017, pp. 3296–3297 (2017)

16. Ibrahim, N., Maurya, P., Jafari, O., Nagarkar, P.: A survey of performance optimization in neural network-based video analytics systems. arXiv preprint arXiv:2105.14195 (2021)

17. Jiang, J., Ananthanarayanan, G., Bodík, P., Sen, S., Stoica, I.: Chameleon: scalable adaptation of video analytics. In: Proceedings of the 2018 Conference of the ACM Special Interest Group on Data Communication (SIGCOMM), Budapest, Hungary, 20–25 August 2018, pp. 253–266 (2018)

18. Kolda, T., Bader, B.: Tensor decompositions and applications. SIAM Rev. **51**, 455–500 (2009)

19. Lane, N.D., Bhattacharya, S., Georgiev, P., Forlivesi, C., Kawsar, F.: An early resource characterization of deep learning on wearables, smartphones and internet-of-things devices. In: Proceedings of the 2015 International Workshop on Internet of Things towards Applications, IoT-App 2015, Seoul, South Korea, 1 November 2015, pp. 7–12 (2015)

20. Li, Y., Padmanabhan, A., Zhao, P., Wang, Y., Xu, G.H., Netravali, R.: Reducto: on-camera filtering for resource-efficient real-time video analytics. In: Proceedings of the Annual conference of the ACM Special Interest Group on Data Communication on the Applications, Technologies, Architectures, and Protocols for Computer Communication, pp. 359–376 (2020)

21. Liu, S., Trenkler, G., et al.: Hadamard, Khatri-Rao, Kronecker and other matrix products. Int. J. Inf. Syst. Sci. **4**(1), 160–177 (2008)

22. Molchanov, P., Tyree, S., Karras, T., Aila, T., Kautz, J.: Pruning convolutional neural networks for resource efficient inference. In: Proceedings of 5th International Conference on Learning Representations (ICLR), Toulon, France, 24–26 April 2017 (2017)

23. Motamedi, M., Fong, D., Ghiasi, S.: Machine intelligence on resource-constrained IoT devices: the case of thread granularity optimization for CNN inference. ACM Trans. Embedded Comput. Syst. **16**(5), 151:1–151:19 (2017)

24. Wang, C., Zhang, S., Chen, Y., Qian, Z., Wu, J., Xiao, M.: Joint configuration adaptation and bandwidth allocation for edge-based real-time video analytics. In: IEEE INFOCOM 2020-IEEE Conference on Computer Communications, pp. 257–266. IEEE (2020)

Deep Structured Clustering of Short Text

Junxian Wu, Xiaojun Chen$^{(\boxtimes)}$, Shaotian Cai, Yongqi Li, and Huzi Wu

College of Computer Science and Software Engineering, Shenzhen University,
Shenzhen 518000, China
xjchen@szu.edu.cn

Abstract. Short text clustering is beneficial in many applications such as articles recommendations, user clustering and event exploration. Recent works of short text clustering boost the clustering results by improving the representation of short text with deep neural networks, such as CNN and autoencoder. However, existing short text deep clustering methods ignore the structure information of short texts. In this paper, we present a GCN-based clustering method for short text clustering, named as Deep Structured Clustering (DSC) method, to explore the relationships among short texts for representation learning. We first construct a k-nn graph to capture the relationships among the short texts, and then jointly learn the short text representations and perform clustering with a dual self-supervised learning module. The experimental results demonstrate the superiority of our proposed method, and the ablation experimental results verify the effectiveness of the modules in our proposed method.

Keywords: Short text clustering · Structured clustering · Graph convolutional network · Sparse autoencoder

1 Introduction

Due to the rapid development of social media and online forums such as Sina Weibo, Zhihu, Stack Overflow, short texts containing only a few words have become prevalent. Text clustering, an important task on short texts, is to group semantically similar texts without manually assigned labels. In recent years, text clustering has been proven to be beneficial in many natural language processing applications, such as articles recommendations [1], user clustering [2] and event exploration [3].

In the long text clustering task, the long texts are usually represented as vectors and partitioned into homogeneous groups with clustering method such as K-means [4]. As for the short text clustering, the early methods usually represent text with hand-crafted features, such as bag-of-words and TF-IDF. However, short texts contain limited information because they usually contain only a small

---

The primary author of this work is a registered student at the time of submission.

© Springer Nature Singapore Pte Ltd. 2022
X. Liao et al. (Eds.): BigData 2021, CCIS 1496, pp. 310–323, 2022.
https://doi.org/10.1007/978-981-16-9709-8_21

number of words. Therefore, short text clustering suffers from the data sparsity problem that most of the words only occur once [5].

With the success of deep learning, many deep learning based short text clustering methods have been proposed [4,6–8]. In these methods, the short texts are represented by pre-trained word embedding and Universal Sentence Embedding [9]. However, the above methods ignore the relationships among short texts when learning the representation. For example, we can construct a weighted graph $G = (V, \mathbf{A})$ to capture the relationships among short texts, where the nodes in v associates the graph associate the set of short texts, and the affinity matrix $\mathbf{A}$ denotes the similarities among short texts. Such structure reveals the latent similarity among short texts, and therefore provides a valuable guide on learning the short text representation. Existing methods seldom take the (graph) structure information of short texts into account.

Recently, graph convolutional neural network (GCN) has attracted wide attention [10–12], since they can deal with the structural information underlying the data for representation learning. Although GCN-based methods have been used for text classification and other text processing tasks, few works about GCN-based clustering methods have been proposed for short text clustering.

In this work, we present a GCN-based clustering method for short text clustering, named as the Deep Structured Clustering (**DSC**) method, to explore the relationships among short texts for clustering. The main contributions of this work are summarized as follows:

- We have proposed to construct a k-nn graph to capture the relationships among the short texts.
- We have proposed to jointly learn the short text representations and perform clustering with a dual self-supervised learning module, which enables both sparse autoencoder and GCN for representation learning.

2   Related Work

2.1   Short Text Clustering

The key problem in short text clustering is how to effectively represent short texts. The early works [4–6] directly concat multiple word embeddings [13] to represent the short texts for clustering. The self-taught convolutional neural network (STCC) [4,5] feeds multiple word embeddings in a short text into the convolutional neural network to learn deep feature representations, and cluster them with k-means. Self-Train [6] uses the Smoothed Inverse Frequency (SIF) embedding [14] for representing the short texts, and performs clustering by jointly optimizing autoencoder and k-means in a self-training manner. Attentive representation learning (ARL) [8] applies adversarial training to short text clustering, by injecting perturbations into the cluster representations. However, the above methods ignore the relationships among short texts, which is important for representation learning.

2.2 GCN-based Clustering

Recently, some GCN-based clustering methods have been proposed to cope with the structural information underlying the data. For instance, Variational Graph Auto-encoder (VGAE) [15] applies GCN as an encoder to integrate graph structure information into nodes to learn node embeddings. Deep Attentional Embedded Graph Clustering (DAEGC) [16] applies an attention network to capture the importance of the neighboring nodes. Structural Deep Clustering Network (SDCN) [12] combines the strengths of both autoencoder and GCN with a novel delivery operator and a dual self-supervised module.

3 Methodology

In this paper, we propose a new short text clustering method, named as the deep structured clustering (DSC), which is able to capture the relationship among short texts for better clustering performance. The pipeline of our proposed method DSC is shown in Fig. 1. Given a set of short texts, we first apply Sentence-BERT [9] model to obtain the embeddings matrix $\mathbf{X} \in \mathbb{R}^{N \times d}$ of these short texts. x_i represents the i-th samples, and N is the number of short texts sample, while d is the dimension of vector representations. To capture the relationships among the short texts, we construct a weighted graph $G = (V, \mathbf{A})$. Then we propose to simultaneously learn the short text representations and perform clustering with a dual self-supervised learning module, which enables both sparse autoencoder and GCN to learn representations $\mathbf{H}^L$ and $\mathbf{Z}^L$ from both G and $\mathbf{X}$, and performs clustering on both $\mathbf{H}^L$ and $\mathbf{Z}^L$. The detailed descriptions of our proposed method are as follows.

3.1 Graph Construction

With the initial representations $\mathbf{X}$, we propose to construct a weighted graph $G = (V, \mathbf{A})$ to capture the relationships among short texts, where the nodes in V associate the set of short texts, and the affinity matrix $\mathbf{A}$ denotes the similarities among short texts. A simple method to compute the weight matrix $\mathbf{A}$ is to use Gaussian kernel $K_h(\mathbf{x}_i - \mathbf{x}_j)$ with a bandwidth h to compute the similarity between two short texts $\mathbf{x}_i$ and $\mathbf{x}_j$. Usually, we wish to obtain a normalized weight matrix $\mathbf{A}$. Moreover, exploring the local connectivity of data points is

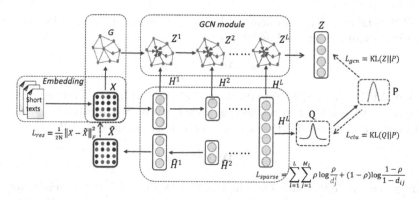

Fig. 1. The pipeline of the proposed method. $\mathbf{X}$ and $\hat{\mathbf{X}}$ are the representations of input data and the reconstructed representations. $\mathbf{H}^L$ is the representation of the l-th layer of the sparse autoencoder module and $\mathbf{Z}^l$ is the representation of the l-th layer of the GCN module. $\mathbf{Q}$ is the soft assigning distribution calculated by the learned representation $\mathbf{H}^L$, and the target distribution $\mathbf{P}$ is calculated by $\mathbf{Q}$.

indispensable. Therefore, we wish to construct a normalized k-nn weight matrix $\mathbf{A}$. To achieve this goal, we propose to obtain a_{ij} by solving the following problem

$$\min_{\sum_{j=1}^n a_{ij}=1, a_{ij} \geq 0,} \sum_{j=1}^n a_{ij}\|\mathbf{x}_i - \mathbf{x}_j\|_2^2 + \gamma \sum_{j=1}^n a_{ij}^2 \tag{1}$$

where $\{a_{i1}, \cdots, a_{in}\}$ contains only k positive elements.

According to the analysis in [17], the optimal solution a_{ij} to problem (1) is

$$a_{ij} = \begin{cases} \frac{d_{i,k+1} - \|\mathbf{x}_i - \mathbf{x}_j\|_2^2}{k d_{i,k+1} - \sum_{h=1}^k d_{i,h}} & \mathbf{x}_j \in \mathcal{N}_k(\mathbf{x}_i) \\ 0 & \text{otherwise} \end{cases} \tag{2}$$

where $d_{i,j}$ is the square of Euclidean distance between $\mathbf{x}_i$ and its j-th nearest neighbor, and $\mathcal{N}_k(\mathbf{x}_i)$ contains the k nearest neighbors of $\mathbf{x}_i$.

3.2   Deep Representation Learning Module

With the initial representation matrix $\mathbf{X}$ and constructed weighted graph G, the next step is to learn better representations for clustering. In this paper, we propose a dual self-supervised module, which unifies the sparse autoencoder and GCN modules for end-to-end clustering.

3.2.1   Sparse Autoencoder

In this paper, we employ the autoencoder to learn the representations of the raw data in order to accommodate for different kinds of data characteristics. We assume that both the autoencoder E and decoder D consist of L layers and H^l be the representation learned by the l-th layer. In the encoder part, $\mathbf{H}^l$ $(1 \leq l \leq L)$, can be obtained as follows:

$$\mathbf{H}^l = \sigma(\mathbf{W}_e^l \mathbf{H}^{l-1} + \mathbf{b}_e^l) \tag{3}$$

where $\sigma(.)$ is the Relu activation function, and $\mathbf{W}_e^l$ and $\mathbf{b}_e$ are the weight matrix and bias of the l-th layer in the encoder, respectively. Specifically, $\mathbf{H}^0 = \mathbf{X}$.

In the decoder part, $\hat{\mathbf{H}}^l$ $(1 \leq l \leq L - 1)$, can be obtained as follows:

$$\hat{\mathbf{H}}^l = \sigma(\mathbf{W}_d^l \hat{\mathbf{H}}^{l+1} + \mathbf{b}_d^l) \tag{4}$$

where $\sigma(.)$ is the Relu activation function, and $\mathbf{W}_d^l$ and $\mathbf{b}_d$ are the weight matrix and bias of the l-th layer in the decoder, respectively. Specifically, $\hat{\mathbf{H}}^0 = \hat{\mathbf{X}}$.

The reconstruction loss is the mean squared error of the input $\mathbf{X}$ and the reconstructed $\hat{\mathbf{X}}$, which is defined as follows:

$$\mathcal{L}_{res} = \frac{1}{2N} \left\| \mathbf{X} - \hat{\mathbf{X}} \right\|_F^2 = \frac{1}{2N} \sum_{i=1}^{N} \|x_i - \hat{x}_i\|_2^2 \tag{5}$$

where N is the number of short text samples. By limiting the number of hidden units, the encoder network is forced to learn a compressed representation of the input $\mathbf{X}$. It can discover some correlations of input $\mathbf{X}$.

Since the short texts in a downstream task usually contains a small number of words, we want to learn sparse representations in order to better characterize the sort texts. Sparse autoencoder imposes a sparsity constraint to achieve an information bottleneck. Sparse autoencoder can discover interesting structure of data, even if the dimension of hidden representations is large. We consider a neuron unit as being active when its output value is close to 1, or as being inactive when its output value is close to 0. In this paper, we impose a sparsity constraint on the hidden units [18]. Let d_j^l be the average activation of the j-th unit in l-th hidden layer:

$$d_j^l = \frac{1}{N} \sum_{i=1}^{N} h_{ij}^l = \frac{1}{N} \|\mathbf{h}_j^l\|_1 \tag{6}$$

where N is the number of short texts and h_{ij}^l is the j-th unit in l-th hidden representation of the i-th sample. The sparsity of h can be achieved by imposing a constraint such that d_j^l be closed to a small value ρ, due to the sparsity property of ℓ_1 norm. Then the KL divergence between d_j^l and ρ is introduced to achieve the sparsity as

$$\mathcal{L}_{sparse} = \sum_{l=1}^{L} \sum_{j=1}^{M_l} \rho \log \frac{\rho}{d_j^l} + (1 - \rho) \log \frac{1 - \rho}{1 - d_j^l} \tag{7}$$

where M_l is the number of hidden units in the l-th layer of the encoder, and ρ is a sparsity parameter with a small value close to zero such as $\rho = 0.02$. To satisfy this constraint, the neuron unit must be inactive in most of samples.

3.2.2 GCN Module

The GCN module is proposed to propagate the hidden representations learned by the sparse autoencoder, such that we can learn the deep representations from both data itself and the relationships between short texts. Specifically, GCN learns the hidden representations $\mathbf{Z}^l$ from the relationship between short texts. The representation of the l-th layer $\mathbf{Z}^l$ can be obtained by the following convolutional operation:

$$\mathbf{Z}^l = \eta\sigma(\tilde{\mathbf{D}}^{-\frac{1}{2}}\tilde{\mathbf{A}}\tilde{\mathbf{D}}^{-\frac{1}{2}}\mathbf{Z}^{l-1}\mathbf{W}_g^{l-1}) + (1 - \eta)\mathbf{H}^l \tag{8}$$

where $\mathbf{W}_g^l$ is the weight matrix of the l-th layer in GCN and $\mathbf{H}^l$ is the representation of the l-th layer in the sparse autoencoder. $\tilde{\mathbf{A}} = \mathbf{A} + \mathbf{I}$ is the adjacent matrix of the undirected graph G with added self-connections, where $\mathbf{I}$ is the identity diagonal matrix of the adjacent of the adjacent matrix $\mathbf{A}$ for the self-loop in each node. $\tilde{\mathbf{D}} = \sum_j \tilde{\mathbf{A}}_{ij}$. $\sigma(\cdot)$ denotes an activation function, and setting to RelU function for experiments. η is a balance coefficient.

Note that the output $\mathbf{Z}$ of the last layer in GCN can be treated as the probability distribution. The last layer is a multiple classification layer with a softmax function as the activation function:

$$\mathbf{Z} = \sigma(\tilde{\mathbf{D}}^{-\frac{1}{2}}\tilde{\mathbf{A}}\tilde{\mathbf{D}}^{-\frac{1}{2}}\mathbf{Z}^L\mathbf{W}_g^L) \tag{9}$$

where z_{il} indicates the probability of i-th short text sample to l-th cluster.

We use the target distribution $\mathbf{P}$ in Eq. 12 to guide training the GCN. By minimizing the KL divergence of the clustering assignment $\mathbf{Z}$ and the target representation $\mathbf{P}$, we can use $\mathbf{P}$ to supervise $\mathbf{Z}$ as follows:

$$\mathcal{L}_{gcn} = \mathrm{KL}(\mathbf{P}\|\mathbf{Z}) = \sum_{i=1}^N \sum_{l=1}^K p_{il} log \frac{p_{il}}{z_{il}} \tag{10}$$

where z_{il} is the representation of the l-th feature of the i-th short text and p_{il} is the pseudo label of the i-th short text on the l-th feature.

3.2.3 Structured Clustering

We use the Student's t-distribution to compute the probability matrix $\mathbf{Q}$, in which the probability of assigning i-th short text instance to the l-th cluster q_{il} is computed as follows:

$$q_{il} = \frac{(1 + \|h_i - \mu_l\|^2/\nu)^{-\frac{1+\nu}{2}}}{\sum_{l'=1}^{K}(1 + \|h_j - \mu_l'\|^2/\nu)^{-\frac{1+\nu}{2}}} \tag{11}$$

where h_i is the i-th row of $\mathbf{H}^L$, μ_l is the l-th cluster center vector and is initialized by k-means and K is the number of clusters. ν is the degrees of freedom. To simplify optimization problem, we set $\nu = 1$. The target distribution $\mathbf{P}$ is calculated from the distribution $\mathbf{Q}$ as follows:

$$p_{il} = \frac{q_{il}^2/f_l}{\sum_{l'} q_{il'}^2/f_{l'}} \tag{12}$$

where $f_l = \sum_{i=1}^{N} q_{il}, l = 1, ..., K$ can be considered as the soft cluster frequencies. The target distribution $\mathbf{P}$ has higher confidence compared to the soft cluster probability q_{il}, because the target distribution is sharpened by squaring q_{il} and normalized by the associated cluster frequency f_l. The clustering objective function is defined as follows:

$$\mathcal{L}_{clu} = \text{KL}(\mathbf{P}\|\mathbf{Q}) = \sum_{i=1}^{N}\sum_{l=1}^{K} p_{il} \log\frac{p_{il}}{q_{il}} \tag{13}$$

By minimizing the KL divergence loss of the target distribution $\mathbf{P}$ and distribution $\mathbf{Q}$, we are able to perform clustering in a self-supervised mechanism.

3.2.4   Loss Function

The final loss function, which consists of four loss functions in Eqs. 5, 7, 10 and 13, is shown as follows:

$$\mathcal{L} = \mathcal{L}_{res} + \alpha\mathcal{L}_{sparse} + \beta\mathcal{L}_{gcn} + \gamma\mathcal{L}_{clu} \tag{14}$$

where $\alpha > 0$ is a hyper-parameter that controls the sparsity of the representations, $\beta > 0$ is a hyper-parameter that controls the disturbance of GCN module to the embedding space and $\gamma > 0$ is a hyper-parameter that balances the clustering and representation learning. We use back-propagation to train the network using mini-batches and then apply gradient-based optimization to minimize the objective function $\mathcal{L}$. By minimizing the above loss function, we can jointly update representations $\mathbf{Z}$ and $\mathbf{H}$ and soft clustering assignments $\mathbf{Q}$ and $\mathbf{P}$. Therefore, we can jointly perform representations learning and clustering in a self-supervised manner.

Table 1. Main statistics of benchmark datasets: C is the number of categories, N is the number of samples, Len is the average length of short texts, V is the vocabulary size.

Dataset	C	N	Len	V
StackOverflow	20	20 k	8.3	23 k
SearchSnippets	8	12.3 k	17.9	31 k
Biomedical	20	20 k	12.9	19 k

4 Experimental Results and Analysis

4.1 Benchmark Datasets

We used three benchmark datasets to evaluate our proposed method. The main statistics of these datasets are shown in Table 1 and the detailed descriptions as follows:

(1) *StackOverflow* is a text collection of question posts from Stack Overflow, which is a question and answer site for professional and enthusiast programmers. This dataset contains 20 different categories and each selected question post is associated with only one tag [4].

(2) *SearchSnippets* is a text collection composed of Google search snippets on 8 different topics. The texts in the *SearchSnippets* dataset represent sets of keywords, rather than being coherent texts [19].

(3) *Biomedical* is a text subset of the PubMed data from BioASQ, with paper titles randomly selected from 20 categories [4].

4.2 Evaluation Metrics

We adopt two widely used performance metrics for text clustering, accuracy (ACC) and normalized mutual information (NMI) [5]. The accuracy (ACC) is defined as follow:

$$ACC = \frac{\sum_{i=1}^{N} \delta(y_i, map(c_i))}{N} \tag{15}$$

where $\delta(a, b)$ is an indicator function that equals 1 if $a = b$ and equals 0 otherwise, $map(\cdot)$ maps the clustering label c_i to group label by the Hungarian algorithm, and y_i is the ground truth label of x_i.

NMI measures the shared information between the cluster set A and the ground truth set B as follows

$$NMI = \frac{I(A, B)}{\sqrt{H(A)H(B)}} \tag{16}$$

where $I(A, B)$ is the mutual information between A and B. $H(\cdot)$ is the entropy. The denominator $\sqrt{H(A)H(B)}$ normalize the mutual information to be in the range of $[0, 1]$. Higher value of ACC or NMI indicate better clustering quality.

Table 2. Clustering results (ACC: accuracy, NMI: normalized mutual information).

	StackOverflow		SearchSnippets		Biomedical	
	ACC	NMI	ACC	NMI	ACC	NMI
K-means(TF)	13.5	7.8	24.7	9.0	14.3	9.2
K-means(TF-IDF)	20.3	15.6	33.8	21.4	28.3	23.2
K-means(Skip-Thought)	9.3	2.7	33.6	13.8	16.3	10.7
K-means(Sentence-BERT)	52.7	47.3	66.8	52.0	38.0	32.5
STCC	51.1	51.1	77.0	63.2	43.6	38.1
Self-Train	59.8	54.8	77.1	56.7	**54.8**	**47.1**
DSC	**79.2**	**69.4**	**80.1**	**64.5**	41.2	39.1

4.3 Baselines

To experimentally verify the effectiveness of our proposed method, we compare our proposed method with the following baselines:

- K-means(TF) represents short texts with term frequency (TF) and applies k-means to the TF features for clustering.
- K-means(TF-IDF) represents short texts with term frequency-inverse document frequency (TF-IDF) and applies k-means to the TF features for clustering.
- K-means(Skip-Thought) [20] learns the representations of short texts with autoencoder and applies k-means to the learned features for clustering.
- K-means(Sentence-BERT) [9] learns the representations of short texts with Sentence-BERT and applies k-means to the learned features for clustering.
- STCC [4,5] first pretrains word embeddings on in-domain corpus by Word2Vec method [13], and then uses the convolutional neural network to obtain the deep representations that are fed into K-means approach for clustering.
- Self-Train [6] uses weighted average embeddings of word embeddings by Smoothed Inverse Frequency (SIF) and then jointly fine-tune the representations by autoencoder and perform clustering.

4.4 Implementation Details

In this paper, we apply the frozen Sentence-BERT model [9] to represent short text data as embedding vectors with the size of 1×768. We set the sizes of hidden layers in sparse autoencoder and GCN to 768-500-500-2000-50 for all datasets. We pretrained the sparse autoencoder by using all short text samples and set the learning rate to 0.001. We implemented experiments, setting the balance coefficient $\eta = 0.5$ in Eq. 8. We set $\alpha = 0.01, \beta = 0.01, \gamma = 0.05$ in Eq. 14.

4.5 Results and Analysis

We computed the average results over five runs and report the clustering results in Table 2. Our method achieves highly competitive performance on short text

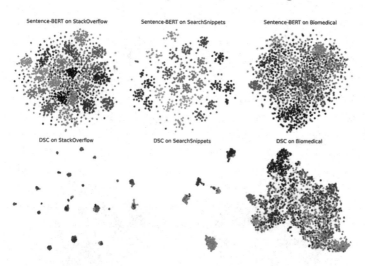

Fig. 2. t-SNE visualization of representations generated by the Sentence-BERT and our proposed method on three benchmark datasets. Each color indicates a ground truth category of short text samples.

clustering as shown in Table 2. From these results, we can observe that our proposed method DSC produces better results than all baselines on two datasets. To be specific, on the *StackOverflow* dataset, DSC achieves a nearly 33% improvement in terms of ACC compared with the second best method Self-Train, and a nearly 27% improvement in terms of NMI compared with the second best method Self-Train. On the *SearchSnippets* dataset, DSC achieves a nearly 4% improvement in terms of ACC compared with the second best method Self-Train, and an over 2% improvement in terms of NMI compared with the second best method STCC. But on the *Biomedical* dataset, our proposed method DSC produces comparable results as STCC and worse results than Self-Train. This may be because *Biomedical* is a dataset in bioinformatics and is much less related to the general domains used by our pre-train model, which was trained only on Wikipedia and NLI data. On the contrast, Self-Train [6] learns the word embeddings on the biomedical corpus to enrich the representations. Among the baselines, we can observe that the deep learning based methods outperform bag-of-words (BoW) based methods.

In the previous work, sentence representations such as Skip-Thought and Sentence-BERT have demonstrated to be beneficial for many other NLP tasks. To visually verify the superiority of our proposed method for representation learning, we use t-SNE [21] to visualize the representations generated by the Sentence-BERT and our proposed method on three benchmark datasets. The results are shown in Fig. 2. From these figures, we can observe that our proposed method produces better representations on the *StackOverflow* and *SearchSnippets* datasets, which again indicate the superiority of our proposed method for representation learning of short text by capturing the relationships among short texts.

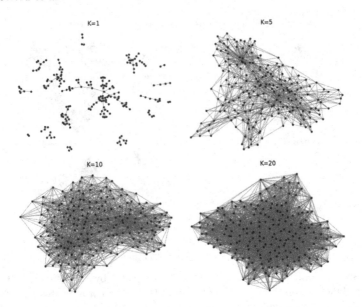

Fig. 3. Graphs with the nearest neighbors $k \in \{1, 5, 10, 20\}$ on the *StackOverflow* dataset.

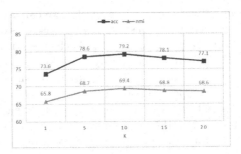

Fig. 4. Clustering performance of DSC versus the number nearest neighbors k on the *StackOverflow* dataset.

4.6   Hyperparameter Analysis

By varying the number of the nearest neighbors $k \in \{1, 5, 10, 20\}$ of the k-nn graph construction on the *StackOverflow* dataset, we show different k-nn graphs in Fig. 3. From these plots, we can observe that the k-nn graph contains poor structural information when k is too small, but indistinctive structural information when k is too large. Therefore, we should carefully set proper k in order to fed high quality structural information to the deep representation learning module. In this paper, we set $k = 10$ for our experiments.

We conduct experiments on the *StackOverflow* dataset to investigate how the two hyperparameters in our method, i.e., the number of nearest neighbors k and balance coefficient η, affect the clustering performance. Figure 4 shows

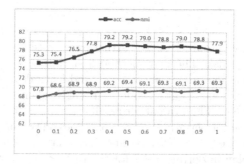

Fig. 5. Clustering performance of DSC versus η on the *StackOverflow* dataset.

Table 3. Ablation study results on the *StackOverflow* dataset.

	$\mathcal{L}_{res}$	$\mathcal{L}_{gcn}$	$\mathcal{L}_{sparse}$	$\mathcal{L}_{clu}$	ACC	NMI
DSC-w/g	✓	✗	✓	✓	69.7	55.6
DSC-w/s	✓	✓	✗	✓	75.2	66.1
DSC-w/c	✓	✓	✓	✗	37.8	38.1
DSC	✓	✓	✓	✓	**79.2**	**69.4**

the clustering results with $k \in \{1, 5, 10, 15, 20\}$, which indicates that our proposed method produces the best result when $k = 10$. The clustering performance drops significantly when k is too small or too large, which are caused by the low quality graphs shown in Fig. 3. Figure 5 shows the clustering results with $\eta \in \{0, 0.1, 0.2, 0.3, 0.4, 0.5, 0.6, 0.7, 0.8, 0.9, 1\}$, which indicates that our proposed method produces the best result when $\eta = 0.5$.

4.7 Ablation Study

To validate the effectiveness of the modules in our proposed method, we conduct the ablation study on the *StackOverflow* dataset. In this experiment, we define the following variants:

1. **DSC-w/g**: This variant is DSC without GCN, which is used to validate the advantages of GCN in learning structural information.
2. **DSC-w/s**: This variant is DSC without sparse constraint on the autoencoder, which is used to validate the advantages of sparse constraint in representation learning.
3. **DSC-w/c**: This variant is DSC without clustering module, which is used to validate the effectiveness of the clustering module.

The results are shown in Table 3, which indicates the effectiveness of the GCN, sparse autoencoder and clustering modules. Obviously, clustering module plays the most important role in the short text clustering task. Besides, both GCN and sparse autoencoder show their effectiveness in the short text clustering task.

5 Conclusion

In this paper, we have proposed a deep structured clustering (DSC) method for short text clustering task. The new method first construct a graph to capture the structure information among short texts, and learn deep representations of short texts with both sparse autoencoder and GCN, along with clustering in a self-supervised manner. The evaluation results demonstrate that our proposed method achieves superior performance over baselines on two benchmark datasets. Further, the ablation experimental results show that all three modules in our proposed method play important roles for the task.

In this paper, we compute the similarity of sentence embeddings to capture the structure information of short texts. In the future work, we will explore more ways to capture the structure information of short texts and develop new deep clustering method to cope with multiple graphs in the short text clustering task.

References

1. Bouras, C., Tsogkas, V.: Improving news articles recommendations via user clustering. Int. J. Mach. Learn. Cybern. **8**(1), 223–237 (2014). https://doi.org/10.1007/s13042-014-0316-3
2. Liang, S., Yilmaz, E., Kanoulas, E.: Collaboratively tracking interests for user clustering in streams of short texts. IEEE Trans. Knowl. Data Eng. **31**(2), 257–272 (2019)
3. Feng, W., et al.: Streamcube: hierarchical spatio-temporal hashtag clustering for event exploration over the twitter stream. In: 2015 IEEE 31st International Conference on Data Engineering, pp. 1561–1572 (2015)
4. Xu, J., et al.: Self-taught convolutional neural networks for short text clustering. Neural Netw. **88**, 22–31 (2017)
5. Xu, J., et al.: Short text clustering via convolutional neural networks. In: Proceedings of the 1st Workshop on Vector Space Modeling for Natural Language Processing, Denver, Colorado, pp. 62–69 (2015)
6. Hadifar, A., Sterckx, L., Demeester, T., Develder, C.: A self-training approach for short text clustering. In: Proceedings of the 4th Workshop on Representation Learning for NLP (RepL4NLP-2019), Florence, Italy, pp. 194–199 (2019)
7. Zhang, D., et al.: Supporting clustering with contrastive learning. In: Proceedings of the 2021 Conference of the North American Chapter of the Association for Computational Linguistics: Human Language Technologies, pp. 5419–5430 (2021)
8. Zhang, W., Dong, C., Yin, J., Wang, J.: Attentive representation learning with adversarial training for short text clustering. IEEE Trans. Knowl. Data Eng. (2021). https://doi.org/10.1109/TKDE.2021.3052244. Date of Publication: 18 January 2021
9. Reimers, N., Gurevych, I.: Sentence-BERT: sentence embeddings using siamese BERT-networks. In: Proceedings of the 2019 Conference on Empirical Methods in Natural Language Processing (2019)
10. Liu, X., Luo, Z., Huang, H.: Jointly multiple events extraction via attention-based graph information aggregation. In: Proceedings of the 2018 Conference on Empirical Methods in Natural Language Processing, Brussels, Belgium, pp. 1247–1256 (2018)

11. Yao, L., Mao, C., Luo, Y.: Graph convolutional networks for text classification. In: Proceedings of the AAAI Conference on Artificial Intelligence, vol. 33, pp. 7370–7377 (2019)
12. Bo, D., Wang, X., Shi, C., Zhu, M., Lu, E., Cui, P.: Structural deep clustering network. In: Proceedings of The Web Conference 2020. WWW 2020, pp. 1400–1410. Association for Computing Machinery, New York (2020)
13. Mikolov, T., Sutskever, I., Chen, K., Corrado, G.S., Dean, J.: Distributed representations of words and phrases and their compositionality. In: Advances in Neural Information Processing Systems, vol. 26 (2013)
14. Arora, S., Liang, Y., Ma, T.: A simple but tough-to-beat baseline for sentence embeddings. In: 5th International Conference on Learning Representations, ICLR 2017 (2017)
15. Kipf, T.N., Welling, M.: Variational graph auto-encoders. arXiv preprint arXiv:1611.07308 (2016)
16. Wang, C., Pan, S., Hu, R., Long, G., Jiang, J., Zhang, C.: Attributed graph clustering: a deep attentional embedding approach. In: Proceedings of the Twenty-Eighth International Joint Conference on Artificial Intelligence, IJCAI-19, pp. 3670–3676 (2019)
17. Nie, F., Wang, X., Jordan, M., Huang, H.: The constrained laplacian rank algorithm for graph-based clustering. In: Proceedings of the Thirtieth AAAI Conference on Artificial Intelligence, pp. 1969–1976 (2016)
18. Ng, A., et al.: Sparse autoencoder. CS294A Lect. Notes **72**(2011), 1–19 (2011)
19. Phan, X.-H., Nguyen, L.-M., Horiguchi, S.: Learning to classify short and sparse text & web with hidden topics from large-scale data collections. In: Proceedings of the 17th International Conference on World Wide Web, pp. 91–100 (2008)
20. Kiros, R., et al.: Skip-thought vectors. In: Advances in Neural Information Processing Systems, vol. 28 (2015)
21. Van der Maaten, L., Hinton, G.: Visualizing data using t-SNE. J. Mach. Learn. Res. **9**(11), 2579–2605 (2008)

Author Index

Printed in the United States
by Baker & Taylor Publisher Services